The English Cult of Literature

Victorian Literature and Culture Series

Jerome J. McGann and Herbert F. Tucker, Editors

THE ENGLISH CULT OF LITERATURE

Devoted Readers, 1774–1880

William R. McKelvy

University of Virginia Press   *Charlottesville and London*

University of Virginia Press
© 2007 by the Rector and Visitors of the University of Virginia
All rights reserved
Printed in the United States of America on acid-free paper
First published 2007

9 8 7 6 5 4 3 2 1

Library of Congress Cataloging-in-Publication Data

McKelvy, William R., 1967–
    The English cult of literature : devoted readers, 1774–1880 / William R. McKelvy.
      p.   cm. — (Victorian literature and culture series)
    Includes bibliographical references and index.
    ISBN-13: 978-0-8139-2571-4 (alk. paper)
    1. English literature—19th century—History and criticism. 2. Religion and literature—Great Britain—History—19th century. 3. Religion in literature. 4. Great Britain—Intellectual life—19th century. I. Title. II. Series.
PR468.R44M45   2007
820.9′382—dc22

                                              2006015952

Title page illustration from the title page of *The Sunday Book of Poetry,* selected and arranged by C. F. Alexander (London: Macmillan, 1887).

for PFM

Contents

List of Illustrations   viii
Acknowledgments   ix
List of Abbreviations   xi

Introduction   1
ONE   Orthodox Narratives of Literary Sacralization   9
TWO   Zealous Protestants in Literature: Lowth, Warton, and Percy   36
THREE   Entertaining Salvation: Scott's Jovial Priests   93
FOUR   Common Things Hallowed: Keble and Macaulay   127
FIVE   Primitive Traditions and Modern Readers: Gladstone's Homer   180
SIX   Clerical Fictions: Eliot's Scribal Authority   221
Conclusion: Sacred Anthologies in the Age of Paper   255

Notes   273
Works Cited   291
Index   315

Illustrations

1. "Dr. Syntax & Bookseller" 22
2. "Dr. Prosody Correcting His Proof in a Printing office 23
3. Robert Lowth 42
4. Thomas Percy 74
5. The Lady in Her Secret Bower 112
6. "Hursley Churchyard with Porch and Vicarage" 153
7. "The Lament of the Hebrew Minstrel" 177
8. "Critics" 182
9. "Two Girls from the Period" 235
10. "Caxton Showing the First Specimen of His Printing" 268
11. "A Wolf in Sheep's Clothing" 269

Acknowledgments

IN WRITING AN interdisciplinary literary history of extended chronological scope, I have said some things the are likely to be disputed. One thing I trust will not be challenged: my extraordinary indebtedness to others. Over the past few years, numerous people have read earlier versions or parts of what follows, and I have benefited in particular from both criticism and encouragement from Jim Adams, Guinn Batten, Miriam Bailin, David Damrosch, Richard Davis, Emily Doyle, Dillon Johnston, Joe Loewenstein, the late Colin Matthew, Steven Meyer, Thomas Pinney, Emily Richard, Lisa Rodensky, Christopher Stray, Frank Turner, and Steve Zwicker. The anonymous readers at the University of Virginia Press also deserve my thanks. As this project concluded, I was fortunate to be guided by Cathie Brettschneider, Humanities Editor at the Press. Mark Mones and Colleen R. Clark also provided exemplary assistance and advice.

The making of this book at Washington University has been a pleasure and a possibility thanks to three supportive departmental Chairs: Dan Shea, Miriam Bailin, and David Lawton. My ongoing education here has also depended much on students at all levels, particularly the following authors of completed dissertations (in both History and English): Misty Beck, Richard Floyd, Victoria Houseman, Jed Mayer, Kristina Hochwender, Debie Rudder, Michael Rutz, Susan Stiritz, and Cynthia Westerbeck. Two University librarians—Nada Vaughn and Erin Davis—have been especially helpful in key ways. Before coming to St. Louis, I laid the foundations for this narrative with research conducted at the Houghton and Andover-Harvard Theological libraries, the British Library, and St. Deniol's Library in Wales. My thanks go to the librarians at all of these places.

Some passages from "William Ewart Gladstone," my contribution to *Nineteenth-Century British Book Collectors,* DLB 184: 161–72, © 1997, are reprinted by permission of The Gale Group. For permission to reprint portions of this work that first appeared in "Primitive Ballads, Modern Criticism, Ancient Skepticism: Macaulay's *Lays of Ancient Rome*" (*Victorian Literature and Culture* 28.2 [Oct. 2000]: 287–309), I thank the editors of that journal and the Cambridge University Press. For permission to reprint material that appeared in "In the Valley of the Shadow of Books" (*Victorian Poetry* 41.4 [Winter 2003]: 544–52), I thank that journal's editor. And to the Anthem Press I owe thanks for permission to reprint material from my article "Ways of Reading 1825: Leisure, Curiosity, and Morbid Eagerness" from *John Keble in Context,* ed. Kirstie Blair, pp. 75–88, © 2004. Preliminary versions of parts of this book were also presented to routinely gracious audiences at conferences sponsored by the Victorians Institute, the Northeast Victorian Studies Association, the Midwest Victorian Studies Association, and the North American Victorian Studies Association. I am grateful to those that spent precious time making these events possible.

As a graduate student, I was lucky to be exposed to the faculty plying nineteenth-century British literature in the 1990s at the University of Virginia. Steve Arata, Alison Booth, Paul Cantor, and Karen Chase have all taught me essential things—and in many cases without knowing it. At the heart of this schooling of mine stand Jerome McGann and Herbert Tucker, two extraordinary scholars and educators. But my oldest intellectual debts are to my parents, Dana and Bill McKelvy. They long ago inspired my historical curiosity with what at times felt like forced marches through museums, ruins, and all manner of locales initially foreign to me. This study should make it clear I have forgiven them, as I know my children, Jane and Hugh, will one day forgive me and Patricia Flynn McKelvy, their mother. To her, my one and only, I dedicate this book.

Abbreviations

Add. MSS	The Gladstone Papers: Additional Manuscripts 44086–44835, British Library, London.
Apo.	Newman, John Henry. *Apologia Pro Vita Sua*. Ed. Martin J. Svaglic. Oxford: Clarendon, 1990.
CCR	*Correspondence on Church and Religion of William Ewart Gladstone*. Ed. D. C. Lathbury. 2 vols. New York: Macmillan, 1910.
CE	*The Works of Thomas Carlyle*. Ed. H. D. Traill. Centenary ed. 30 vols. New York: AMS, 1969.
CTW	*The Correspondence of Thomas Warton*. Ed. David Fairer. Athens: U of Georgia P, 1995.
CW	*The Collected Works of Samuel Taylor Coleridge*. 16 vols. (in 23 pts.). Bollingen Ser. 75. Princeton: Princeton UP, 1970–2002.
CPW	*The Complete Prose Works of Matthew Arnold*. Ed. R. H. Super. 11 vols. Ann Arbor: U of Michigan P, 1960–77.
GD	*The Gladstone Diaries*. Ed. M. R. D. Foot and H. C. G. Matthew. 14 vols. Oxford: Clarendon, 1968–94. (Dates, as in *GD*, are day/month/year.)
GEL	*The George Eliot Letters*. Ed. Gordon S. Haight. 9 vols. New Haven: Yale UP, 1954–78.
H	*Hansard's Parliamentary Debates*.
LD	*The Letters and Diaries of John Henry Newman*. Ed. Ian Ker, Thomas Gornall, and Gerard Tracey. Vols. 1–8. Oxford: Clarendon, 1978–99.
Letters	*The Letters of Sir Walter Scott*. Ed. H. J. C. Grierson. 12 vols. London: Constable, 1932–37.
LM	*The Letters of Thomas Babington Macaulay*. Ed. Thomas Pinney. 6 vols. Cambridge: Cambridge UP, 1974–81.

OPR	Keble, John. *Occasional Papers and Reviews*. Oxford: Parker, 1877.
PL	*The Percy Letters*. Gen. eds. David Nichol Smith and Cleanth Brooks (1944–61) and Cleanth Brooks and A. F. Falconer (1977–88). 9 vols. Baton Rouge: Louisiana State UP, 1944–57; New Haven: Yale UP, 1961–88.
PW	*The Poetical Works of Sir Walter Scott*. Ed. J. G. Lockhark. 12 vols. Edinburgh: Cadell, 1833–34.
W	*The Works of Walter Scott, Esq.* 5 vols. London and Edinburgh: Longman, Hurst, Rees, and Orme; Constable, 1806.
WLM	*The Works of Lord Macaulay, Complete*. Ed. Lady Trevelyan. 8 vols. London: Longmans, Green, 1866.

The English Cult of Literature

Introduction

THIS BOOK EXPLORES THE foundation and significance of a claim made repeatedly in nineteenth-century Britain: Literature was becoming modernity's functional religion, and the author, with the power to sanctify human experience and redeem national life, had assumed a sacred vocation.

We can, of course, find and reconstruct collusions and confrontations between the literary and the religious before the nineteenth century. There is a long-standing tradition that recognizes a congruence between prophetic and poetic vocations, for example, and literacy and heresy are topics deeply involved before the rise of modern print culture (Kugel; Biller and Hudson). But it was only in the nineteenth century that the putative religious function of literature became a self-defining subject for public debate. Our favorite derivative of the ancient word *cultus* became a modern concept mostly thanks to its utility in brooding over the fate and prospects of religious authority in the modern world; and our recognition of the 1860s as the time when our notion of culture was formulated and popularized is a token of a time when writers addressed readers fluent in comparing versions of literary and religious authority. When Matthew Arnold in 1879 asked readers to compare Shakespeare and the Thirty-Nine Articles (a com-parison of apples and oranges, one might say), he was relying on just such a fluency.[1] "Religion as men commonly conceive it," he said, "religion depending on the historicalness of certain supposed facts, on the authority of certain received traditions, on the validity of certain accredited dogmas—how much of this religion can be deemed unalterably secure? Not a dogma that does not threaten to dissolve, not a tradition which is not shaken, not a fact that has its historical character free from question. Compare the stability of Shakespeare with the stability of the Thirty-Nine Articles!" (*CPW* 9.63). As Arnold's intended audience well knew, England's most venerated literary figure and the Church of England's Articles of Religion had both come into the world in the 1560s, but they were aging with an unequal grace that had been starkly clarified in 1864. In that year, everyone—including prominent Anglican ecclesiastics—was eager to honor the tercentenary of Shakespeare's birth on an unprecedented scale. The authority of the Thirty-Nine Articles, on the other hand, was being hotly contested, and this debate issued in an explicit diminution of the public significance of the sixteenth-century creeds with the passage of the Clerical Subscription Act of 1865. Assent to the Articles during the 1860s and '70s—thanks to the 1865 Act, the Universities Tests Act of 1871, and other legislation—was on its way to becoming a private affair.[2]

"Shakespeare and the Thirty-Nine Articles" can operate as a cipher for a realignment of authority familiar to students of the nineteenth century, one in which a waning, institutionalized religious power finds compensatory expression in acts of cultural faith. Arnold, his age's most influential apostle of culture, certainly saw it this way, and since the 1860s he had been busy preaching two relevant ideas: the religious function of literary culture and the literary nature of Scripture. Outside Arnold's work, it is easy to find cases both notorious and unremarkable in which the idea of literature and the idea of Scripture, the vocation of the man of letters and the function of the clergy, speak to each other. By 1897, when Oscar Wilde, exhausted and incarcerated, wrote about his "lifelong cult of literature" (*Complete Letters* 779), this prodigal son of Arnold spoke for an age that had witnessed the rise and propagation of many literary sects. And we need not wait for the 1860s and later. To Thomas Carlyle—born in 1795, the same year as Arnold's father—the newly assumed power of a literary priesthood was plain to see in the 1820s, and he duly set about constructing his own literary authority on the related premises that "Literature was but a branch of religion" and that "Literary Men" made up "a perpetual priesthood" (*CE* 28.23, 26.58). Before Carlyle started to reach a wide audience with this message in the late 1830s, Samuel Taylor Coleridge, for a smaller number of readers, had helped to coordinate literary and religious vocations with his notion of the clerisy.

Many nineteenth-century literary sages—figures such as Carlyle, Arnold, George Eliot, and Walter Pater—actively accommodated the institution of this literary priesthood; and by the late 1860s, important dissenting traditions were recognizable as well. One centered on John Henry Newman, who identified the liberal religion that he hated as "a literary religion" (*Discussions* 293). An implacable enemy of the liberal cult of literature, Newman nevertheless was inducted into it, thereby illustrating the cult's power to canonize reluctant saints. Another dissenting literary sect was antinomian and satanic. Its manifesto came in Algernon Charles Swinburne's *William Blake* (1868). There Swinburne begged for a birching from mainstream liberals by condemning "the great moral heresy," the age's tendency to admire the corruption of Art by the base stain of Religion. "Let us hear no more," Swinburne wrote, "of the moral mission of earnest art; let us no longer be pestered with the frantic and flatulent assumptions of quasi-secular clericalism willing to think the best of all sides, and ready even, with consecrating hand, to lend meritorious art and poetry a timely pat or shove" (92–93). From a standpoint equally at odds with Newman's and Swinburne's, the fallen priest and rising man of letters Leslie Stephen produced a body of work critiquing the aestheticized religious sensibility that had allowed freethinkers and agnostics to maintain professional options in the church and the ancient universities.[3] And from yet another perspective, leaders of a self-consciously reformist scientific community derided culture's broader mission as reconstructed priestcraft. In his 1880 address "Science and Culture," T. H. Huxley characterized the literary educational ideal as the last enchantment of "Levites in charge of the ark of culture."[4]

What does all this talk about literature, religion, and their relation mean? That was to me initially the obvious question, and it is—I now believe—the wrong question, or at least a question that has been raised and answered many times before. The better question is rather when and how did the religious vocation of literature become a politically significant theme in British intellectual life. The answer the following chapters endorse is that this vocation had such an import from the 1770s to the 1880s, a period that saw the materialization of the nation's first mass reading public and the secularization of the state. Before 1770 political and social facts had the effect of regulating the relationship of literary and religious authority. Because the institutions and laws that then united church and state assumed that literature (signifying learning in general) was bound to serve religious truth, literary endeavors that challenged the interest of the established church became potentially heretical and political. After 1880 the state no longer had a substantial religious identity for literature to challenge; and to bestow a religious vocation on literature in this new political context was to claim to place it above and beyond politics. The foregoing narrative thus begins in the late eighteenth century, when the state had an important religious character and when the idea of the reading nation became a preoccupation for many writers. It ends at a moment when the reading nation had become a reality and when the polity had ceased to discriminate between devotees of any particular literary or religious cult. In between, many will recognize elements of a familiar history of modernity, the tale of culture's triumph over religion. But the full story is more subtle and sinuous, a bit perverse at times. For it turns out that the modern cult of literature was instituted with the theoretical and material resources of the religious authority it had allegedly displaced. And as the new vernacular literary culture occupied a frontier once policed by religious forces, so too did that upstart literary culture adopt a religious habit and evince a longing to participate in the most sacred rites—this at a time, moreover, when an embattled religious culture often saw its most promising future in literary terms. The long period of 1774–1880, therefore, is not held together by any single assertion about the relationship of religion and literature. Rather, I underscore the significance of their repeated collusion and confrontation. In doing so, I demonstrate that any reading of either the eighteenth or the nineteenth century is impoverished when we heed the claim that modern literary history begins at that point where consequential religious history expired.

The following six chapters illustrate my major thesis that literature assumes a religious vocation in modern Britain in concert with the creation of a reading nation during a period featuring an increasingly unencumbered freedom of religious confession. Chapter 1 appraises past interpretive approaches to the cult of literature, recounts my dissatisfaction with them, and explains my reasons for often focusing on ways in which authors figured priests and priests figured authorship or the authority of letters. Integrating debates about literary periodization with recent findings of book history and historiographies at odds with conventional secularization theory, I unfold the reasons for the chronological scope of this study and its close attention to the practice and representation of reading. While such attention to reading has been useful to scholars of many periods, my introduction emphasizes how the subject has particular interest in this setting of "the single century," as William St. Clair writes, when "Great Britain became a reading nation" (13).[5] The remaining chapters present a series of case studies challenging the assumption that modern literary authority rises with—and because of—religion's decline. Attending to episodes in which the ideas of both literary and religious authority play significant roles, each section takes its character from the extent to which these categories foster concordance or conflict, or, as is most often the case, a bit of both. Chapter 2 focuses on the careers of three clerical men of letters—Robert Lowth, Thomas Warton, and Thomas Percy—with particular emphasis on the making of Lowth's *Isaiah: A New Translation* (1778), Warton's *History of English Poetry* (1774–1781), and the third edition of Percy's *Reliques of Ancient English Poetry* (1775). These writers have been recognized as important agents in the rise of the late eighteenth century's new sense of literary tradition, but literary history has either ignored or apologized for their clerical dress. I emphasize how their contributions extended out of ecclesiastical careers that helped to endow the future's increasing dialogue between versions of biblical and bibliographic devotion. Many of the activities highlighted—lecturing in Latin, theorizing translation, preaching and publishing sermons, brawling in pamphlets, editing texts of all kinds (from ancient Hebrew songs to modern English ballads), and writing grammars, massive serial histories, or short handbooks—are distanced from Romantic concepts of literary creativity. But it is in this broader context, I argue, that our notion of English Literature developed. Chapter 3 takes up the first decade of the writing life of Walter Scott, whose *Minstrelsy of the Scottish Border* (1802) was modeled on Percy's *Reliques* and bore a title-page epigraph from Warton's hand. I show how Scott won fame by addressing the age's interest in negotiating varieties of literary and religious authority. Often reminding his audience that the modern author's duty was to entertain, Scott defined his relationship with readers in materialistic terms. But this overt context for the consumption of his writing was set against repeated references to the poet's sacred task.

The next two chapters highlight a clerically dominated debate about historical criticism that begins in the post-Peterloo Britain of the 1820s and draws to a close in the 1860s. Together, they constitute a critique of a myth of modern origins in which British intellectual life is suddenly transformed by the appearance of Darwin's *On the Origin of Species* (1859), closely followed by *Essays and Reviews* (1860). In this familiar narrative, one ironically creationist and catastrophic in tone, an unforeseen deluge, announced by the dual-thunderclap of "Genesis and Geology," suddenly reshapes the cultural landscape. But just as "the *Origin* was important in resolving a crisis, not creating one" (Secord 514), it is also important, I maintain, to see how consequential controversies about biblical hermeneutics unfolded in the four decades leading up to *Essays and Reviews*.[6] Conventional histories of this terrain have stressed the clash of clerical parties inspired by theological differences, with the Oxford Movement in particular taking center stage in a drama of conversion, apostasy, or professional martyrdom. In my account, these parties and these theological differences are prompted by a larger debate about the promise and peril of becoming a nation of independent readers. This debate, as I argue, subsumed arguments about national education, controversies about reading the literary remains of antiquity (increasingly defined in national terms), and contested readings of the literary tradition in English that had been reconceived in the late eighteenth century.

Chapter 4 shows how two of the century's best-selling volumes of verse—John Keble's *The Christian Year* (1828, 1st complete ed.) and Thomas

Babington Macaulay's *The Lays of Ancient Rome* (1842)—were central poetic gestures in extensive literary campaigns. Inspired by different aims, Keble and Macaulay nevertheless both composed pseudo-liturgical books that stand out as related attempts to model normative encounters between readers and texts of all kinds. Chapter 5 exploits the century's largest record of individual reading, the *Diaries* (1825–1896) of four-time prime minister William Ewart Gladstone, a figure who entered Parliament after considering the ministry and thereafter sought to reconstruct an ecclesiastical vocation in the context of an increasingly liberal political life. Using the diaries to wed conventional intellectual history to a cultural materialism that has the printed text as its primary artifact, I describe the commencement of Gladstone's career as a Homeric scholar in the 1840s, and I argue that his reading of ancient epics as religious texts was a representative legacy of the period when the state's claim to legitimacy came to rest on religiously plural foundations.

In the next chapter, I close with a new look at the pseudo-ecclesiastical career of George Eliot. I show how her final fictional hero in *Daniel Deronda* (1876) lives out Gladstone's vocational trials in reverse, as Deronda turns from a career in English politics to become an alien priest. The works that lead to the writing of *Deronda* reveal a growing skepticism about conventional literary authority, and Eliot's career, in my reading of it, culminates with a strange revival of priestcraft and scribal modes of literary production. A conclusion then argues that Deronda's sacerdotal initiation was characteristic of an age that had seen the proliferation of competing clerical types. Focusing on related episodes in publishing history in the late 1870s when an agenda for religious liberty was close to full achievement, I show how the politics of secularization were attended by a resilient agency of clerical figures in an array of creative and institutional modes. At the same time, I document the prevalence of a new variety of sacred anthologies that fulfilled the textual legacies of earlier figures such as Lowth, Warton, and Percy. Implicitly or explicitly disputing the essential definition of sacred textuality, these anthologies appear as relics of a common, underlying cult of print even as the first glimpses of new technologies pointed to the approaching end of what I call Britain's Age of Paper.

In all of this I construe a broad culture of letters that comprehends lyric and epic poetry, philosophical and historical writing, political and religious tracts, literary criticism and biblical hermeneutics, lectures, sermons and speeches, parodies and devotional texts, folklore and ecclesiology, novels, periodicals, newspapers, and private journals. I frame the discussion with reference to figures such as Coleridge, Carlyle, and Arnold, the triumvirate that has dominated past discussions of the topic. But I have also sought to feature in the narrative itself a cast of characters other than the usual suspects. This is not to say that my protagonists are historically marginal. The eight major figures featured in chapters 2 through 6 derived and exercised their power, with one exception, from elite professional or institutional vantages. Out of the eight, seven earned university degrees at a time when that distinction was an extraordinary demographic rarity. One (Scott) emerged from the legal profession cultivated at the University of Edinburgh. The other six passed through either Oxford or Cambridge. Four of the six (Lowth, Warton, Percy, and Keble) were, by different measures, distinguished Anglican clerics, and three of the four (Lowth, Warton, and Keble) held the Oxford Chair of Poetry. Even the glaring interloper (Eliot) would frame her writing career with fictional creations worthy of induction into the fraternity described above: in both "The Sad Fortunes of the Reverend Amos Barton" and *Daniel Deronda* our hero is a Cambridge man struggling to discover his authentic priestly vocation. But while products of Britain's semi-ecclesiastical universities and members of the established British churches dominate my story, this preeminence is not a dismissal of other kinds of religious experiences and traditions. My interest in orthodoxy is historically driven, a reckoning with a defined political context bordered at one extreme (1880) by the demise of its privileged status.

Here at the end of my beginning, I should also make it clear that this book is not intended as a history of religious belief that draws on so-called literary evidence. Nor is it, strictly speaking, a history of literary practice that draws on religious history. I am much indebted to both kinds of work, and I am happy to be writing at a time when others are paying more attention to religion in the nineteenth century.[7] But my primary goal is something more specific: to highlight a period when the conceptualization of religious truth assumed a particular public character in coordination with the transformation of reading in a culture of print that had its elliptic foci in London and Edinburgh. Some present readers might be put off by my nonproscriptive definition of religion and my willingness to suspend a general discrimination between the religious and the supernatural. I am not indifferent to the desire for tightly bound definitions of religion (which literally means "bound back" or "tied up"), and this book will at times showcase writers and readers trying to prevent confusion on this issue. In the end, though, I have decided that what is gained in my approach is at least equivalent to what gets lost when a scholar finds it convenient to pretend that human history has ever featured either a widely held definition of true religion or a widely held distinction between the supernatural and the religious. Along these same lines, I avoid trying to define in any theoretical terms what is properly religious or what is properly literary. My commitment to avoiding these tasks is pragmatically motivated by my view that historical attention to readers during the period reveals a sustained debate about the nature of literary and religious experience.

1

Orthodox Narratives of Literary Sacralization

SO FAR, MOST RESPONSES to the nineteenth-century cult of literature fall into two broad categories, declinist and constructionist accounts. Declinist accounts see in the modern cult of literature a reaction to the passing of God, who, after a long illness commencing in the Enlightenment, died during Victoria's reign. This account is most frequently repeated in Marxist versions in which a depoliticized aesthetic sphere becomes the favored post-theological mystification for bourgeois elites: while other classes dissipate their political consciousness with the stronger draughts of gin or old-time religion, the liberal intelligentsia prefers the more refined anodynes of poetry and painting. And thus, as David Riede concludes in his study *Oracles and Hierophants,* "The institutionalization of literary culture as a quasi religion during the nineteenth century could only take place in the space vacated, at least among many intellectuals, by an increasingly unconvincing religion" (240). Or as Terry Eagleton puts it (focusing on literature's pedagogical fate), "If one were asked to provide a single explanation for the growth of English studies in the later nineteenth century, one could do worse than reply: 'the failure of religion'" (20). The declinist account in its most potent form derives from materialist assumptions, but coordinating the rise of modern literary authority with the lurid fate of an embattled religious culture is hardly the privilege of Marxist critique. Thomas Carlyle's career illustrates how a good hater of materialism could announce the institution of literature's modern moment by invoking decrepit religion. As he would testify in one of his pioneering essays on the birth of the modern author, "The History of Literature, especially for the last two centuries, is our proper Church History; the other Church, during that time, having more and more decayed from its old functions and influence, and ceased to have a history" (*CE* 28.201–2). And Carlyle's major twentieth-century commentators have never strayed far from this account. In Chris Vanden Bossche's important study, Carlyle's search for literary authority develops in reaction to the dissolution of a "theocratic" authority that could not survive the empiricism and individualism of the eighteenth century (1–5).

The other main interpretive context for the cult of literature, the constructionist response, likewise finds opportunity in the notion of declining or embattled religion, but the emphasis is on an aesthetic-religious revival born out of this social and spiritual crisis, "the assimilation and reinterpretation of religious ideas," as M. H. Abrams put it (13). Northrop Frye, like Abrams born in 1912, was another influential figure to affiliate the literary and the religious in a productive way, though Frye was also careful to resist the temptation to level at large Scripture and literature. His religious vocation—he had been ordained (United Church of Canada) in 1936—seems to dominate his character as a critic when he says that the Bible "is as literary as it can well be without actually being literature" (62). Even with such hesitations, this approach stresses the compatibility of literary with religious experience and locates in the recognition of that compatibility the essential identity of Romantic aesthetics. Witness, for example, how *literature* rides to the Bible's rescue in David Jasper's *The Sacred and Secular Canon in Romanticism* (1999), a book written out of the tradition exemplified by the work of Abrams, Frye, and critics of a later generation such as Stephen Prickett.[1] Jasper maintains, in terms no less Arnoldian than Riede's, that Romanticism allowed the biblical canon "to be incorporated into a living literary tradition free from the dead hand of literalism" (8). In an English context this is Coleridgean literary history, and behind Samuel Taylor Coleridge, Immanuel Kant looms as the great architect of a philosophy that sets itself at odds with both theocratic and empiricist traditions.

In the declinist accounts, the erosion of sacred authority is the precondition for the cult of literature. In constructionist accounts, a new understanding of the literary character of Scripture redeems that authority, and in the process literature and the human imagination ascend to sacred heights. Influential and eloquent advocates have spoken for both, and this raises a dilemma for the literary historian. Was the rise of the nineteenth-century cult of literature a break with a sacred past, or was it the fulfillment of a religious development? Does the nineteenth century reveal "a transference of 'authority' from the Bible to the 'author,'" as Joss Marsh, following Michel Foucault, puts it (169)? Or did the rise of the modern author signal the dismantling and discarding of religious authority? Given the ready evidence that religion and literature were speaking to each other during the nineteenth century on an unprecedented scale, what larger narrative sponsors this dialogue? Did Matthew Arnold fulfill or betray his father's clerical vocation by leveling poetry and religion and pitting dogma against literature?

Did the extraordinary career of Charlotte Brontë (another major writer, like Jane Austen, Coleridge, Alfred Tennyson, and Arnold, sprung from priestly loins) signal literary culture's power to blaze a trail of liberation out of the repressive regions of religious patriarchy? Or did her fate—to die bearing the child of her father's curate—illustrate the enduring power of an unreformed parsonage? Such dilemmas can be resolved through ideological commitment, that is, by becoming either a Marxist or a Coleridgean humanist, but they will not depart so quickly for the scholar dedicated to the free exertion of research.

Take, for example, James Anthony Froude's novel *The Nemesis of Faith* (1849), an account of the life and death of an apostate Anglican priest, Markham Sutherland. By measure of its reviews, the *Nemesis* was one of the most talked-about books of the late 1840s, and the furor over its publication became linked with a later scandal about the Sterling Club, and eventually to Carlyle's 1851 *Life of Sterling,* a work that echoes the *Nemesis* by telling the story of a real-life doubting clergyman tempted by a life in letters. An even fuller story about the *Nemesis,* then, can extend to the 1880s when Froude would write the authorized nineteenth-century life of Carlyle (2 vols., 1882–84), a work featuring the same vocational drama: an intellectually ambitious young man has his religious faith compromised, is unable to pursue a career in the church, and takes to literature instead.[2] In these terms, the *Nemesis* demonstrates how literary authority depended on a discredited religious authority. And at the heart of this process was the total naturalization of Scripture, the understanding that the Bible was, as Froude described it in his preface, "the collective Hebrew literature . . . and shows no generic difference from other literature" (x). This literary Bible made both Froude (who had been ordained deacon in 1845) and his fictional hero renounce their clerical livings, and in deciding to tell this story, Froude initiated himself into a counterclerical profession of literature. In this scheme, literature is not only the vocational alternative to religious professions. Because a literary conception of the Bible is said to debar conventional religious faith, literature is also the primary solvent of orthodox religious authority.

The *Nemesis,* in other words, provides an opportunity to reconstruct the declinist narrative in a story spanning the comfortably Victorian period from the 1830s to the 1880s, the time when literature was said to overwhelm and to displace religion. In the past decade, however, some problems with this narrative have become clear. Post-Foucauldian historians of authorship and a resurgent discipline of book history have recovered a richer context for the production, distribution, and consumption of printed matter in the nineteenth century, one that suggests ways in which an expanding culture of print often conspired with religion. A shift in focus to readers, for example, has allowed Aileen Fyfe to revise our acceptance of the headlong collision between science and religion during the mid-nineteenth century in favor of attending to how those categories also "related to one another outside the restricted community of specialists" in a broader field of literary consumption defined by popular publishing practices (3). And the most comprehensive studies of nineteenth-century book production, initiated by Simon Eliot, indicate that the religious market for books exceeded or closely rivaled the literary market throughout the 1850s. Add to this general picture the market for Bibles, New Testaments, Prayer Books, hymnbooks, sermons, short religious tracts, and religious periodicals, and one can plausibly claim that religion—not some post-theological literary sphere—was the single largest paradigm for print into the 1870s. It was only in the 1880s and after that the religious market for books became a specialty market outsized by the publisher's category of "Literature."[3]

There is also evidence that authorship and the clerical profession during the nineteenth century overlapped on a scale never seen before or after. According to Richard Altick, in what remains the most detailed study of the sociology of authorship in the nineteenth century, the church was the main extraliterary profession for authors, and the high point of clerical authorship came in the period from 1835 to 1870 (1989: 106). William Hill Collingridge's *Comprehensive Guide to Printing and Publishing* (1869), for example, begins with an appeal to clerical authors. "Amongst authors," Collingridge writes, "the clergy have always held, and still retain, an eminent position with regard to the production of useful books on almost any subject. But more than this: we may venture to assert that no other profession or class produces so many works as the clergy" (1). History does not suggest a choice between the pulpit and the press; history suggests that the pulpit had a privileged connection to the press that became most vital after the mid-century.[4] It was in the midst of the notorious Victorian crisis of faith that religious professionals were most likely to address the community and the nation as authors. For, in addition to relying on a material foundation—tithes and endowments—and a sacramental or symbolic power, the clergy maintained its status by virtue of its literary industry. Literate priesthoods throughout history have attended to archival acts of textual guardianship and exegesis, but the nineteenth-century clergy was distinguished by its profound involvement with varieties of textual production, the publishing of works in no way limited to the devotional or overtly religious.

Once Foucault's ontological question "What is an author?" is checked against the answers to more specific historical queries, some foundational assumptions of literary criticism can take on a character not far short of fabulous. Yesterday's truisms appear, at the least, one-sided. Take J. Hillis Miller's elegant study *The Disappearance of God* (1963), which begins with a familiar notion: "Post-medieval literature records, among other things, the gradual withdrawal of God from the world" (1). Miller adduces good literary evidence for this retreat, but the historical record also provides ample evidence for a counterargument showing that the production and consumption of print during the nineteenth century manifests God's frequent appearance in everyday life; and the representative printer's devil of the nineteenth century was often harried to meet the demands of clerical authors inspired by that manifestation. In these terms, the religious professionalism lurking in the background and emerging in the conclusion of Miller's study has the virtue of quietly compromising his major assumption. Of his five featured writers—De Quincey, Browning, Arnold, Emily Brontë, and Hopkins—two were born to priests, and one was born to be a priest.

In this newer context, Froude's *Nemesis* cannot stand simply as a token of the cult of literature's post-theological nature. It is, just as plausibly, a manifestation of the age's unprecedented confusion—one that was both theoretical and historical—of literary with religious lives. More than a record of the clergyman's displacement by the secular author, the *Nemesis* is also a representative product of what William Whitla and Victor Shea have called "clerical culture" (3–28). Froude's novel and his life story highlighted available tensions between the life of letters and a living in the church, but the weightier fact about clerical culture was its repeated reconciliation of literary endeavors and professional obligations. The novel's key vocational scene is an ambivalent moment coming on the eve of Markham Sutherland's decision to accept—despite religious doubts—a church living. Sutherland does imagine an antipathy between "the Printing Press" and the placeman's pulpit, but at the same time he attributes to authorship a sacred office, one he fears he is unequal to (43–44). Sutherland wants to be an author because he cannot in good conscience be a priest (as defined by those Thirty-Nine Articles), and he wants to be an author because he wants to be a Carlylean priest of the cult of letters. In his perplexed position, Sutherland personifies an important segment of nineteenth-century literary ambition and practice. The Oxford Fellow and clergyman William Sewell, for example, who notoriously tossed a copy of Froude's novel into a fire, was not an unlettered fanatic generally condemning novels to a bonfire of the vanities. He was a prolific author—a poet, novelist, reviewer, polemicist, and children's writer—whose sister, Elizabeth Missing Sewell, wrote widely as well. The pious novels of the Sewell siblings, like those by hundreds of other similar authors, mock the simplistic notions that "novels desanctified the book" (Warner 4) or that the novel is an inherently desanctified literary form.

The scholarly times are ripe, in other words, to write on behalf of the constructionist account but in ways that go beyond the hermeneutic concerns at the core of Coleridgean literary history, concerns that have invited literary historians to dismiss the cultural valence of the established religious professions.[5] Influential accounts of the Coleridgean clerisy, accounts stretching from John Stuart Mill's famous essay (10.117–63) to Ben Knight's study, have encouraged a tendency to view too much of the past in terms of Coleridge's unique position as an influential lay divine, an extraordinary literary apostle to (mostly Broad Church) clergymen. The nineteenth century was in various ways, as Knight's study documents, intrigued by the idea of intellectuals performing religious functions. And the century's emergent idea of the *intellectual* has been linked to narratives of secularization (Heyck 82, 186). But daily life at all levels throughout the nineteenth century was far more conditioned by the fact that so many religious professionals performed functions that would be retrospectively characterized as intellectual. Our attention to a profession in theory, the clerisy, has obscured the literary activity of the actual clerical profession.[6]

This disengagement from certain historical realities is exemplified by the vitality of an emphasis marring many biographies of Matthew Arnold, from the *Anthology*'s sketch to the full-blown *Life*. He was, we are often told, the first holder of the Oxford Chair of Poetry (1857–67) to lecture in English rather than Latin, and this decision, we are reminded, reflected a transitional moment that included the "emergence of 'English' as a separate, organized source of cultural authority" (Stray 1998: 104). In the meantime, however, the other significant innovation of Arnold's professorship is mostly forgotten: it is rarely mentioned that Arnold became the first lay holder of the Chair since its foundation in 1708—and did so only after beating the Reverend John Ernest Bode in a close election. Arnold's professorship recalls how long and how deeply clerical and literary culture had been involved before a prestigious secular profession of letters became widely possible; and the establishment of English studies at Oxford, an event that unfolds in the 1880s and beyond, takes place only as the sequel to this story of ecclesiastical collaboration.[7] As histories of the rise of English studies suggest, this clerical foundation is not limited to Oxbridge. The "first Professor of English Literature" in England, Thomas Dale (1797–1870), was an Anglican clergyman with an appointment at London University (Court 1988 and 1992: 52–67, 87–89). And for proponents of "the Scottish invention of English Literature" (Crawford 1998), it's another clergyman of the Established Kirk, Hugh Blair (1718–1800), who marks the initial point of departure.[8] Moving away from abstract notions of Literature, Religion, and the Author brings us closer to knowing a carnal type, the clerical author, a writer in whom both the literary and religious were embodied at a time when the practical, institutional, and professional links between the religious and the literary were manifold.

But if the clerical author is a figure who must return with the historical author in general, the full story of the nineteenth-century cult of literature must include the post-theological cult as well. This cult features the statistically trifling (though well-documented) deconversion of university-educated males. But it also includes the trials of those who faced legal penalties for their commitments to unbelief. As the work of Iain McCalman (1988), Joss Marsh (1998), Martin Priestman (1999), and others has shown, an industrious irreligious party participated in the nineteenth-century construction of literary authority. And if over 20 percent of the writers selected by Altick from the period 1835–1870 had clerical vocations, over 70 percent did not. In the next generation, the robust clerical character of authorship ended rather suddenly, in a gesture that shadows the best enumerative accounts of publishing trends noted above.[9] Furthermore, contemporary evidence such as Collingridge's in favor of a privileged connection between pulpit and press has to be balanced with studies emphasizing alternative professional foundations for Victorian writing lives. In John Sutherland's study of 878 Victorian novelists, which offers a representative sample out of an estimated total of 3,500 novelists (153), only 12 percent of the male novelists are identified as clergymen, while 23 percent are identified as having careers in law. A sizable 36 percent of all novelists are women.

What about those women? I've suggested above, with mention first of Austen and the Brontë family and then Elizabeth Sewell, that we might think of a tradition of women's writing allied to clerical culture through filial, fraternal, or matrimonial ties. Moreover, a popular writer such as Charlotte Yonge saw her vocation as an extension of the pastoral project of her parish priest, John Keble, and much of her work passed through the parsonage, for correction and approbation, before reaching the larger reading public (Yonge; Jordan, Mitchell, and Schinske). The judiciousness of this argument is strong within the context of respectable nineteenth-century society, which included a range of professional opportunities (theoretically nonexistent) that rendered "clergyman's daughter/wife/sister" into something like a vocation. And yet I also suggested that we might speak of a tradition of women's writing best understood as counterclerical. *Jane Eyre* and *Middlemarch,* two of the century's greatest novels, present heroines characterized by their resistance to clerical tyrants the likes of Brocklehurst, Rivers, and Casaubon. Is it fair to remember Charlotte Brontë as an artist defined by her status as a clergyman's daughter destined to be a clergyman's wife?

Such questions remind us why the dilemma identified at the outset is a tenacious one. The two accounts—the declinist and constructionist—were viable for the nineteenth century precisely because they were widely attested in those times. Some might (many did) remark that literature was usurping religious power; others might (many did) remark that literature at its best and most powerful performed a religious function or expressed religious ambitions. Perhaps the best thing to say is that both reactions simply describe the same event from different perspectives. This compromise position—one that accepts the validity of declinist and constructionist accounts—is in part attractive because it offers a way to deal with a larger problem encountered when writing about a time when the sea of faith was retreating under the desiccating glare of modernity—and a time notorious for its turgid religiosity. It was the best of times and the worst of times for religion; it was the age of Darwin and the age of Newman, an age that begins to draw to an end when we can imagine an esoteric reader in a London flat making his way through Nietzsche, basking in the roseate twilight of the idols, while down on the street the Salvation Army, with brass artillery thundering, wins yet another celestial victory.

In this manner, a history of the religious vocation of literature returns to the purple perplexities of Victorian agnosticism. Despite its attendant virtues, this compromised hermeneutic is doomed to repeat what has been duly noted before, both by the Victorians themselves—"wandering between two worlds," as Arnold put it—and in many post-Victorian books documenting, often with their title pages, the queen's long reign over an age of "faith and doubt."[10] Indeed, it is the queen's reign that must be ignored if one is to say something new about literary authority's religious dimensions in the nineteenth century. And along with the years 1837 and 1901, literary history should cease to pay its respects to 1800. For the same studies that give more historical context for understanding Victorian writers and readers can also undermine the Victorian period itself. Literary critics with historical obligations do not merely need to renounce any steadfast reverence for a Romantic-Victorian border of the 1830s. They need to recognize that the nineteenth century begins in the 1770s, particularly when we look to the history of reading becoming a national enterprise.

Such an unconventional chronology is in part authorized by the newly reopened question of periodization in post-Restoration English literary history and, more specifically, the distress of the discipline of Romanticism.[11] That discipline, as it flourished from the 1960s to the 1990s, was partially challenged from within by historical scholarship, and by the close of the twentieth century it faced external threats as well in the form of unilateral annexations by long versions of both Eighteenth- and Nineteenth-Century Studies. At the turn of the millennium, Romanticism's most pressing topic seemed to be its own survival.[12] But even as Old-School Romanticism is said (by some) to be expiring, one of its traditional articles of faith—the belief that the last quarter of the eighteenth century featured a notable rise in the diffusion and consumption of print—has been given a new historical substantiation.[13] Scholarship of various kinds—on authorship, the legal status of literary property, the rise of literary history, the mechanics of canon formation, the editing of vernacular texts, the history of reading, and book history in general—has provided a revised historical foundation for the point made by Raymond Williams (and others before him) that it was only in the late eighteenth century that our modern sense of *literature*—meaning primarily imaginative writing—began to rival an older meaning which signified learnedness (184–85). In the past, literary scholars were likely to let this semantic shift mark the central self-serving myth of Romanticism: it was a movement fueled by a revolution in thought that elevated the imagination to literary culture's seat of power. We can now connect the institution of *literature*'s primary modern sense to causes less metaphysical. It is now possible to see that the late eighteenth century did not merely witness the evolving cultural preponderance of print. A new culture for print took shape as writing became a new kind of property exchanged by new kinds of writers and new kinds of readers.

The best historical referent for a new culture of print is the 1774 House of Lords judgment on the case of *Donaldson v. Beckett,* which effectively ended a common-law right to perpetual copyright, then normally held by booksellers rather than authors or their heirs. As Trevor Ross puts it, "On February 22nd, 1774, literature in its modern sense began" (1992: 16); and, in the most extensively researched case for the ruling's impact, William St. Clair has not hesitated to characterize it as "the most decisive event in the history of reading in England since the arrival of printing 300 years before" (109). While the importance of the 1774 ruling has always been recognized in histories of British publishing, it took the work of St. Clair, Thomas Bonnell, Ross, and others to establish in detail how the ruling became a key stimulant for both a subsequent explosion in reading in general and the proliferation of a new literary supergenre, the historically organized poetry collection aiming at a comprehensive coverage of the national tradition. Before 1774, "any design to publish a large series of complete texts involving a wide range of authors would have been extremely costly, if not simply impossible, given the difficulties arising from the fragmentary pattern of ownership of the copyright scattered among protective booksellers" (Ezell 126). The first compendious poetry collections—Hugh Blair's *The British Poets* (44 vols., 1773–76); John Bell's *The Poets of Great Britain* (109 vols., 1776–82); *The Works of the English Poets,* with biographical introductions by Samuel Johnson

(68 vols., 1779–81), and Robert Anderson's *The Works of the British Poets* (13 vols., 1792–95)—materially embodied the poetic canon in an unprecedented way; and their rapid journey from bookseller's innovation to cultural staple constitutes one of the great bibliographic transformations of modern British literary culture.[14] Anthologies and literary miscellanies predated that period. But they were rarely organized upon historical principles, and rarely attempted to put forward a canon, focusing instead on entertainment, or, as implied by one title, *Pills to Purge Melancholy* (1719), a kind of therapeutic diversion. The primary connotations of *anthology* today—as an authoritative gathering—suggests how the ancient meaning of the word—a bouquet of flowers—was crushed and obscured by the weighty historical pretensions of those expansive *Poets* of the 1770s and later.

The historical anthology boom of the late eighteenth century is also tellingly coordinated with the so-called reading revolution of the same period. The significant rise in the number of readers and their reading options was a development that seems to have generated as much anxiety as it did self-congratulatory confidence, and the anthologies were in a position to take on the burden of this anxiety. Readers looking to enforce distinctions among participants in an increasingly common activity could offer their attention to historical development as an alternative to the pleasures sought by readers in search of immediate gratification. And aspiring writers could take comfort in the notion that they were addressing a future audience ready to revere the collected works of the past. In the evolving prose apparatus he developed for his poetry from 1800 to 1815, William Wordsworth, who was like Coleridge an avid reader of Anderson's *British Poets* (Wu 3–4), figured his select audience with the ultimately fulfilled hope that he was speaking to anthologizers and anthology readers of the future. At the same time, the increasing affordability of collections pretending to comprehend the "complete" tradition could contribute to the notion that the poetic tradition had been overtaken by the book trade. Bell, for example, not only offered on a grand scale the complete *Poets of Great Britain* in a variety of formats for prices ranging from £8 8s. to £33; he also traded in individual volumes for 1s. 6d. (Bonnell 1987: 138–39; Crawford 2001: 85, 93). A generation later, when Francis Jeffrey reviewed Thomas Campbell's *Specimens of the British Poets* (7 vols., 1819), he was appalled at the prospects of the future anthologizer sorting through his century's "annual supply" of "good staple poetry." If Britain continued "to write and rhyme at the present rate for 200 years longer, there must be some new art of short-hand reading invented—or all reading will be given up in despair" (471–72).

This idea that the late eighteenth century's emergent sense of literary tradition was influenced by an expansion of readers and their options is the basis of Ross's larger study of canon formation (1998). Negotiating among those who have argued about the purported "eighteenth-century invention of Literature,"[15] Ross concedes that a sense of English literary tradition had operated powerfully since the days of Chaucer. But Ross goes on to insist that this tradition was transformed in the last quarter of the eighteenth century. While the older idea of a native literary tradition was primarily used to authorize literary production, the new sense of tradition centered on a kind of appropriate literary consumption; it justified an edifying, patriotic, and at times explicitly difficult experience of reading, one that would eventually call for professional explicators of "English Classics."[16] Such an understanding of late-eighteenth-century literary culture, one owed to recent book history and historically sensitive accounts of literary canon formation, suggests something crucial: when all those Victorian writers made their notorious references to literature taking on or usurping religious authority, they were referring to a literature that was refashioned—theoretically and materially—in the 1770s. That was when the nineteenth-century vocation of literature started to become possible in distinctive ways. And in this new setting, Arnold's high-Victorian plea for readers to compare the stability of Shakespeare with the Thirty-Nine Articles is something more than an illustration of the century's tendency to express literary faith in response to theological stress. Arnold's point was precisely that, but his comment has a history above and beyond his intentions. Most critics are likely to cite Arnold's comparative injunction from the setting of his essay "The Study of Poetry," as it was called when it appeared in his posthumous *Essays in Criticism, Second Series* (1888). There Arnold's famous description of poetry's "immense" future (*CPW* 9.161) seems to be called forth by a religious crisis, one that would find its narration in *Culture and Anarchy* (1869), *Literature and Dogma* (1873), and *God and the Bible* (1875). And in this context, the clearest-eyed prophet of poetry's future is a reader of the Zeitgeist with its looming ethnographic typologies—its Hebrews and Hellenes—and its grand periods of transition: the Renaissance, the Reformation, the Enlightenment, and a Modernism that will shore its fragments against a retreating Victorian sea of faith.

But as Darrel Mansell and Jonah Siegel have both pointed out, "The Study of Poetry" in this guise, like one of its own famous touchstones, appears out of context (Mansell 279). The essay originally served as an untitled introduction to *The English Poets,* a four-volume anthology covering the age of Chaucer up to the present of its initial publication in 1880. This anthology, we can now see, marked an important development in the historical literary anthology as it had been reconceived in the late eighteenth century, for it was the first to include the contributions of many different editors, a collection of readers gathered on the threshold of institutionalized English studies. And the anthology adopted this strategy, according to its general editor, Thomas Humphry Ward, because it was now "impossible" for one critic to do the work properly (v). In these terms, Arnold's late career and its pronouncements need to be reunited with the historic and personal details of publishing literary "classics" in the wake of the Second Reform Bill of 1867 and subsequent educational reforms aimed at the making of a reading nation. The occasion for Arnold's most influential late work on poetry, as Stephen Gill (217–18) and Bill Bell (2002) have shown, was his increasing involvement with the republication of texts compiled from sources no longer protected by copyright. Starting in 1876, under intense financial pressure, Arnold embarked on a new literary career that would include, besides his general introduction to *The English Poets,* the introductory and editorial labor that went into the making of *Six Chief Lives from Johnson's "Lives of the Poets"* (1878), *The Poems of Wordsworth* (1879), *The Poetry of Byron* (1881), and the portions of *The English Poets* dedicated to Thomas Gray and John Keats (1880).[17] "Learning to play the market more effectively while capitalizing on his reputation for occupying a position above such a vulgar pursuit" (Bell 2002: 67), Arnold was living out the paradoxical terms of modern literary culture, those which had established a new connection between "inspiration and merchandise" (Chartier 37). And if we want to understand Arnold's claims about poetry's future in 1880, we cannot simply refer to a vast history of troubled religious belief. Poetry's prospects in 1880 were also determined by the kinds of books that Arnold found himself introducing. The claims made in "The Study of Poetry" about the redeeming function of poetry should be studied with reference to 1774 and what that year can now represent. Both Arnoldian and Coleridgean accounts of culture's mission, in other words, belong to a larger history of the reading nation. The best readers of the best poetry, Arnold and others liked to think, were inevitably on a spiritual quest. But even these journeys had to begin by stepping into the bookseller's shop and taking up the books at hand.

So far, I have described how scholarship of various kinds can both underscore the role of religious professionals in nineteenth-century literary culture and suggest ways in which a history of literature's religious vocation has few reasons to rely on conventional periodization. I now want to describe how a consideration of a new literary authority commencing in the late eighteenth century consolidates arguments stressing clerical culture's influential status despite persistent rumors to the contrary.

In the first place, the eighteenth-century commercialization of literature produced a situation in which the clerical author found his opportunity in both senses—ancient and modern—of the term *profession.* The clerical author was in a unique position to exploit a new demand to have edifying varieties of reading and writing distinguish themselves from purportedly pernicious and materialistic ones. With his professional status, the clerical author was allowed the luxury of appearing to write as an extension of his pastoral duties, or as a seemly expression of excess energy. Even though they certainly wrote for money, clerical authors such as Hugh Blair and Vicesimus Knox—both of whom grew rich in the 1790s from their literary labors—were theoretically insulated from the debasing practice of writing for money. At the same time, the church was more than a convenient veil for obscuring mercenary motives. With the incomes it dispensed—an estimated 11,000 livings worth between £50 and £200 in 1760—the church was an essential financial resource for hundreds of writing lives.[18] Now that Dustin Griffin (1996) has shown how greatly exaggerated were our reports of the death of patronage in the eighteenth century, we might add that the age's great unacknowledged literary patron was the church, an institution that could grant to writers money, status, connections, readerships, leisure, and rhetorical training. And churchmen not only used the church to lead literary lives; they also used literary gestures—most often the dedication of publications to members of the ecclesiastical and aristocratic hierarchy—to advance religious careers. The church was both a source of literary patronage and the institutional occasion for individuals to seek and bestow patronage in ways that were negotiated through the press.

In another way too the late-eighteenth-century rise of modern literary authority leads back to clerical culture; for the setting for the production of literary history at that time was primarily, though not wholly, ecclesiastical. If the nineteenth century featured a golden age for the clerical man of letters, the initial architects of modern British literary history were writers who derived their status and leisure as well as their familiarity with the print market—and oftentimes access to manuscript sources—from their clerical profession. Put simply, the most important writers associated with the "growth of the 'historical sense'" (Wellek 48) that prompted the rise of the new literary history in the 1750s and later were clergymen, figures such as John Upton (1707–60), Robert Lowth (1710–87), Richard Hurd (1720–1808), Joseph Warton (1722–1800), Thomas Warton (1728–90), Thomas Percy (1729–1811), William Mason (1725–97), and Richard Farmer (1735–97). Likewise, the Church of England was home to key figures associated with the rise of new literary values comprehending everything from Wordsworthian to Byronic strains of Romanticism. To name only those well remembered today, we have Edward Young (1683–1765), John Dyer (1699–1757), Laurence Sterne (1713–68), John Brown (1715–66), William Gilpin (1724–1804), Charles Churchill (1731–64), George Crabbe (1754–1832), and

Fig. 1. "Dr. Syntax & Bookseller," 1813, from The Tour of Doctor Syntax in Search of the Picturesque, *3rd ed. (Washington University Libraries, Department of Special Collections)*

William Lisle Bowles (1762–1850). While clerical writers can make up an impressive cast of characters for stories of literary innovation, the church was also home to influential defenders of the Popean line, figures such as William Warburton (1698–1779), who, according to Edward Gibbon, "reigned the dictator and tyrant of the world of Literature" in the 1760s (*Memoirs* 149). And one of the poetic sensations of the 1790s, the dunciadic epic *The Pursuits of Literature* (1794–98), was anonymously authored by the Reverend Thomas James Mathias (1754–1835). All this clerical literary activity prepared the way for the three tours of Dr. Syntax (1812–21), an illustrated series of comic verse featuring a clergyman trying to make some money (fig. 1). *"I'll make a TOUR—and then I'll WRITE IT,"* he tells his wife:

> "You well know what my pen can do,
> And I'll employ my pencil too:—
> I'll ride and *write,* and *sketch* and *print,*
> And thus create a real mint;
> I'll *prose* it here, I'll *verse* it there,
> And *picturesque* it ev'ry where."   (Combe 5; italics in the original)

Immensely popular throughout the century (Savory 102–10), the Dr. Syntax series also inspired a slew of imitations including a tour of Scotland under-

Orthodox Narratives of Literary Sacralization 23

Fig. 2. "Dr. Prosody Correcting His Proof in a Printing office," 1821, from The Tour of Doctor Prosody, in Search of the Antique and Picturesque: Through Scotland, the Hebrides, the Orkney, and Shetland Isles. *(Washington University Libraries, Department of Special Collections)*

taken by a Northumbrian clergyman named Dr. Prosody (1821). His trip (and the book recording it) fittingly ends in a realistically depicted printer's shop in London (fig. 2).

Across the northern border these close relations between clergy and press were the rule as well. As Richard Sher has documented (1985), an influential clerical party of doctrinal moderates set the tone for literary life in Edinburgh and beyond. David Hume and Adam Smith have shaded most recollections of the Scottish Enlightenment as an event tending toward a materialist, utilitarian, and irreligious philosophy that culminates in James and John Stuart Mill. But in practice the Scottish Enlightenment was often a clerical affair. The fame of the "Athens of the North" established in the eighteenth century recalls a long roll of kirk ministers: Thomas Reid (1710–96), Hugh Blair (1718–1800), George Campbell (1719–96), William Robertson (1721–93), William Wilkie (1721–72), John Home (1722–1808), Alexander Carlyle (1722–1805), Adam Ferguson (1723–1816), and James Beattie (1735–1803). Some of these figures named above did not have exemplary religious vocations when judged by the standards of piety set by some contemporaries and by later historians; and this same mentality would not be amused by the bawdy joke put into the Reverend Doctor Syntax's mouth, the one in which the power of his pen is said to be well known by his wife. But in the broader sense of Hanoverian clerical culture, it was precisely the capacity of the church to harbor a variety of writing lives—the variegated worldliness of the clergy—that allowed so much literary activity to come from ecclesiastical hands. The clerical author could be a conventional masculine force integrated into traditional domestic duties; or he could be a rarer character—often homosocially defined—addressing others suffering from an ailment of isolated privilege, one described in *The Bibliomania; or Book-Madness* (1st ed., 1809) by the prolific clerical writer Thomas Frognall Dibdin (1776–1847).[19] With a productive flexibility, the clerical author could pretend that any venture in bookmaking was simply an innocent diversion from graver tasks, or he could devote skills acquired in his professional training to rewarding projects of literary consecration.

The work of J. G. A. Pocock (1999–2003) and David Womersley (2002) on Edward Gibbon helps to conceptualize clerical culture and its dimensions while taking account of important nonclerical and anticlerical writers. Gibbon, at first blush, poses a challenge to the notion that literary achievements, innovative historiography, and religious vocations were predisposed to union in the second half of the eighteenth century. With the appearance of the six-volume *History of the Decline and Fall of the Roman Empire* from 1776 to 1788, Gibbon combined literary and historiographic achievement with a notorious religious infidelity. Astute readers noticed too that the achievement and the skepticism were deeply involved. That is to say, Gibbon staked his rank as a historian—what amounted to his bid for literary fame—on a philosophical skepticism defined as antithetical to religious credulity; and he argued that the major cause of Rome's civic dissolution was the rise and progress of an unlearned, religious sect. If "barbarism and religion" were Rome's nemesis, "literature" was the casualty of their historical assertion. Gibbon's autobiography, first published in 1796, extended this struggle between literature and religion to the history of the reception of his work: disdaining to notice the clerical abuse flowing from the press until his character as an author was questioned, he had stooped to squash one impertinent clergyman, Henry Edwards Davis, in his *Vindication* (1779). Gibbon's own story about his triumph over benighted priestcraft—in antiquity and in his own day—had largely been taken on faith in literary history. But by closely focusing on the recoverable bibliographical facts of Gibbon's life from the 1760s to the 1780s, Pocock and Womersley have shown how the evolution of Gibbon's literary authority was repeatedly influenced and transformed by traditions of clerical historiography and contemporary clerical censure and correction. As Womersley puts it, during the development of Gibbon's history, his clerical critics became "the secret sharers in the business of historical composition"; they became his most consequential "collaborators" (145, 365).

Indeed, the two most interesting cases of literary fame acquired through public controversy in the 1780s—Gibbon's and, posthumously, Thomas Chatterton's—are versions of the same twisted plot in which an ingenious infidel's bid for literary immortality includes his complex identification with clerical writing and clerical culture. Thus Pocock returns us to the mythic scene where Gibbon's masterpiece was conceived, and from there the great author belatedly discovers his destiny to become an ecclesiastical historian: "The bare-footed friars in the ancient temple must move center stage before the *Decline and Fall* could become an Enlightened narrative" (1.378). For Chatterton, the identification with priestcraft has the purity of a perfect impersonation. He sought to enlarge his life and prospects by becoming "one Thomas Rowley, a Priest in Bristol" in order "to convince the World that the Monks . . . were not such Blockheads, as generally thought" (*Complete Works* 1.157, 172). Most recent criticism on Chatterton has focused on creative forgery and its affiliation with licit literary acts; and this association tends to affirm a creed of aesthetic autonomy that would gather strength in the nineteenth century and culminate, as Jerome McGann has suggested (1998: 241), in Oscar Wilde's gospel that life must imitate art. In several ways, however, Chatterton's initial reception history belongs to a clerical context, one the sexton's son ingeniously exploited. Chatterton was, in Walter Scott's colorful phrase, "the beardless youth" who "gull[ed] a whole synod of grizzled deans" ("Chatterton's Works" 217); and the most ardent defender of the antiquity of the Rowley poems was one Jeremiah Milles, the dean of Exeter. According to this early editor of Chatterton's forgeries, doubters were mistakenly dismissing a combination of priestly and literary vocations. They argued "that it was impossible for the fifteenth century to produce an English priest qualified to be the author of these poems." The more glaring implausibility, Milles insisted, was that Chatterton could have composed poetry "perfectly consonant to [the] clerical character" (23).

What is sure is that in the mid- to late eighteenth century, the period in which most scholars locate the rise of modern literary authority (or Romanticism), the sphere of literature had an important ecclesiastical character. Any portrait of British literary activity from the death of Pope to the publication of the *Lyrical Ballads* that featured clerical writing alone would be a caricature. But so too is the standard portrait of literary history during this time—one foregrounding the economic struggles of the secularized denizens of Grub Street—a kind of caricature. Despite ready evidence to the contrary, the rise of modern literary authority is regularly tied to the cessation of church history. Here again, Carlyle is an essential figure for disclosing the extent to which the inception of literature's modern vocation is in fact an argument about the eighteenth-century church, its clerical elite, and their historical relevance. In his 1831 essay on Samuel Johnson, Carlyle invokes a mute inglorious church at the critical moment when our hero of Grub Street must be absolved of his pension, absolved of doing what the modern author must not do: write for patrons. So Carlyle asks readers to compare the value of Johnson's pension to actual Episcopal incomes: "The whole sum that Johnson, during the remaining twenty-two years of his life, drew from the public funds of England, would have supported some Supreme Priest for about half as many weeks ... but who were the Primates of England, and the Primates of All England, during Johnson's days? No man has remembered" (*CE* 28.119).[20] Carlyle is here rephrasing a central article of the faith whose prophet he preeminently was—that modernity's authentic priesthood officiates in a cult of literature. But more than that, Carlyle is helping to endow a tradition in which modern literary authority is postecclesiastical. The modern author is born when the church becomes historically forgettable. This decisive act of literary consecration, which includes the canonization of Johnson, is both bad and good history, a distortion of one portion of the past and a clear picture of another. On the one hand, it averts our eyes from too much actual literary activity. On the other hand, this same aversive behavior is useful evidence of the constitutive repression of the activities of religious professionals in the formulation of an ideology of literary authority. Carlyle's bishops would remain forgotten precisely because they served both declinist and constructionist accounts of the cult of literature. Both for the advocates of a secular culture taking up where religious culture had been argued off and for the advocates of a Romantic literary revival inspiring a religious departure from arid eighteenth-century rationalism, the cessation of a meaningful Hanoverian church history is the primary assumption.

Moving beyond the scheme that pits modern English ecclesiastical and literary culture against one another calls for a confrontation with two powerful historiographic myths, what I call Print Culture's Promethean Dream and the Sleepy Century Before the Dawn. The first is a tradition of scholarship that implicitly affirms that an expanding print culture is inherently heterodox in religion and radical in politics. Here the defining post-Gutenberg experience is the French Revolution and its "fetishism of printing," which often claimed for itself an anticlerical mission. According to this revolutionary mythology, the printing press had an unparalleled capacity to "unmask priests and dethrone kings." As one enthusiast said, "The Old Regime was the age of the priest; the new would be the age of the publisher" (qtd. in Eisenstein 22). Thus, when William Hazlitt described the Revolution "as a remote but inevitable result of the invention of the art of printing" (13.38), he was repeating a revolutionary article of faith. In England, and as Hazlitt experienced firsthand, measures to muzzle print from the 1790s to the 1820s were signs of a recognition by certain political elites of its potentially subversive nature, just as were the less aggressive "taxes on knowledge" (not fully repealed until 1861). Even so, a balanced account of the rise of print culture needs to show how the Protestant establishment in the late eighteenth century and after exploited print. In any long-term understanding of the printing press as agent of change, "enlightened," "revolutionary," or "plebeian" appropriations of the technology have to take their place beside this religious appropriation, one that had liberal and conservative manifestations. In the late eighteenth century, this tradition of interpreting moveable type in terms of religious destiny was only growing and would culminate in the Caxton Exhibition of 1877. During the same period, there were irreligious and radical traditions that appealed to a deadly feud between priestcraft and the printing press. But it was an explicitly religious version of the same contest—one featuring the rise and triumph of a bibliocentric Protestantism—that set the general tone for British cultural life.[21]

My second myth, the Sleepy Century Before the Dawn, is a larger caricature of the eighteenth century that was established during the nineteenth: the eighteenth century had no real politics; and it also, not incidentally, had no earnest religion. The church was static, doctrinally apathetic, the parsonic element of the vacuous polity of corruption and patronage. And like the political placeman, like the pluralist rereading cribbed sermons, the eighteenth-century poet was just going through the motions, following rules prescribed by Pope in the 1730s when he brought English poetry to its modern perfection.[22] But then the nineteenth century dawned (somewhat prematurely in 1789), and the rest is called Romanticism. Post-Namierite historians have rejected the political, theological, and social dimensions of this caricature, and from at least two bitterly opposed perspectives (J. Clark; Colley). But too much literary history still relies on some portion of it. An essay, "Religion and Literature," by Elinor Shaffer, from which I quote in full the opening paragraph, is one example of the ways in which Carlyle's history of a religious decline survives in distinguished academic discourse:

> The close relations between religion and literature in most societies testify to the vital role of imagination in the sphere of human values. The secular terms in which this statement is cast are characteristic of the period from the late Enlightenment critiques of religion to the various forms of nineteenth-century apologetics, although the latter may appear draped in traditional language. The secular agenda and terms still dominate current thinking. This

> period [1780-1830], then, marks a major shift in the relations of religion and literature. It can be expressed by saying that literature becomes the dominant partner; if "religion and literature" would have expressed a clear hierarchy at the beginning of the period, it is of "literature and religion" that we have come to speak. Criticism finds its vocation in negotiating this shift. (2000: 138)

As the extract from Carlyle just cited shows, there is available rhetorical evidence for such a claim about the emergent dominance of literature, one vocationally represented by men of letters usurping ecclesiastical functions no longer being usefully performed. And Shaffer's broader point—made here with a redeeming element of self-consciousness—is illustrated by the career of Carlyle, no less than the career of her central literary hero, a Kant-inspired Coleridge. But, if we bear in mind the best historical reconstructions of the same period's culture of print, the statement that literature at the dawn of the nineteenth century began to dominate religion is, in a word, misleading.

A fatal mistake—one confusing the abstract decay of religion with a political process transforming the state's religious character—is primarily responsible for sustaining the scheme whereby knock-kneed religion, circa 1800, yields the way to hale and hearty literature. Consider the following counterargument (my own) to the one Shaffer just summarized:

> The close relations between religious and literary authority in Hanoverian times testify to the vitality of a theo-political ideology of Anglican hegemony. The long period encompassing the erosion of that hegemony, then, marks a major shift in the authorizing foundations of both religion and literature. It can be expressed by saying that the imagination became the dominant literary value and religion became an expression of private opinion. In our time, literary history is called to narrate the negotiation of this shift by means of, in tandem with, the secularization of the state.

Literature, in other words, rises to a position from which it claimed to rival religion at a time when the religious identity of the state is being transformed. The semantic shift aligning the literary with the imaginative took place just as the religious dimension of political authority was emerging as the age's most productive social question.

Secularization has meant many things to many different people, and in the past two decades there has been a renewed and often critical interest in "the secularization thesis."[23] For the purposes of this study, secularization means something specific. It is a political and legal process that leads to the state relinquishing opinions on theological subjects. This approach to secularization is compatible with the loss of religious faith by individuals and social groups. But it is equally compatible with intense religious enthusiasm. Highlighting secularization's compatibility with various forms of religion and irreligion, however, should not distract us from the moral of an unambiguous story about the fate of one religion during a period of one hundred and twenty years. In the 1760s, conformity with Anglican doctrine (expressed by the Thirty-Nine Articles) was deeply involved with civic rights and access to national institutions ranging from municipal and government offices to the ancient English universities and the primary professions; by the 1880s, (non)conformity with those same doctrines had negligible consequences. But while there is an important story to be told about the declining identity of church and state during the long nineteenth century, we must not confuse this event with a general decay of religion, or even a creeping rot within Anglicanism itself.[24]

Other studies of the modern development of literary sanctity have implicit or explicit rationales for not engaging with this political process of secularization. In David Riede's aforementioned study, for example, which covers the 1790s to the 1870s, there is hardly any attempt to characterize the political history of that eventful period. Names of politicians, policies, legislation, or rulings in legal history are, for the most part, absent. The effect is to focus on a tragic history of critical misreadings as Dante Gabriel Rossetti and Swinburne in the 1860s turn Blake into an ineffectual aesthete, and thus the oracular prophet comes to be venerated within a hierophantic tradition, an orthodox Church of Literature. For Riede and the tradition he ably represents, the lack of reference to religious politics is a silent tribute to the belief that serious intellectual culture had already been secularized. Why discuss the details, stages, and major agents of religious politics when one believes that literary sacralization is a response to unconvincing religion? In another way and for other reasons, Tricia Lootens in *Lost Saints: Silence, Gender, and Victorian Literary Canonization* (1996) disengages the politics of the public sphere, downplaying at the outset any connection between her literary history and a public history of contesting the form and boundaries of religious authority. "Nineteenth-century faith in religious sanctity took its own shapes, and sparked its own controversies," Lootens writes, "but these controversies bore no primary or inevitable relation to the development of reverence toward literary figures" (3). Here religious and literary sanctity are deliberately separated and extracted from any single historical context where they might be related. This tactic is in part a useful alternative to the model which presumes that literary sacralization is primarily a reaction to less-convincing religion. But Lootens's self-referential literary hermeneutic avoids a probable scenario in which developing forms of literary reverence did have something to do with the shifting legal status of the church during the same time. This book issues from the principle that our strategic engagement with either the eighteenth or the nineteenth century is impoverished when we segregate religious and literary history—or forget that they shared the same political context. To put it another way, I focus on moments when religious and literary sanctity appeared interchangeable (or were asserted to be so), and I credit the prevalence of these assertions to the prominence of a political process that culminated in the state's embracing a related disinterest in the boundaries of the sacred and the secular. For it was not an extinction of religious belief that characterized most of what we have come to call secularization; it was, as Mark Canuel puts it, "an altered disposition of government towards belief."[25]

In service to this model for change, four historical theses underwrite my argument that literary sacralization is, on somewhat paradoxical terms, coordinated with a process of political secularization. These theses also confirm the period 1774–1880 as the occasion for our best understanding of the rise of the English cult of literature. They concern (1) secularization's peculiar religious character in British history; (2) its precise historical setting; (3) its status as the primary political event within this setting; and (4) the direct link between these same religious politics and the political institution of a reading nation.

The key to understanding the complicated relation of politics and religion in the long nineteenth century is coming to terms with the counterintuitive fact that mainstream liberalism culminates in a secular state but does so—for the most part—for devoutly religious reasons. The main route to the functionally agnostic state, what came to be called the voluntary system, was graded and paved by religion, most obviously and importantly, as liberal Anglicans and Dissenting Protestants asserted the principle of religious liberty.[26] The formulation and achievement of this agenda has a precise historical setting beginning in the 1770s and ending in the 1880s. In the 1770s liberal Anglicans, Dissenters, and Roman Catholics agitated separately and in concert for what they considered to be a full extension of the principle of religious toleration only partially enacted by the Glorious Revolution. For reformers within the established church, this program centered on a need to revise the Thirty-Nine Articles or to relax the terms of clerical subscription to them.[27] Reformers outside the church tended to focus on relief from various civil disabilities borne by non-Anglican Christians and the terms by which Dissenting ministers were required to submit in nominal ways to the authority of the church. Despite a good deal of clerical support, the attempt to change the Articles, or the terms of subscription required for those entering the church, failed. But the program for extending the terms of toleration to non-Anglicans had successes in the passage of the Catholic Relief Act of 1778 and the Dissenters Relief Act of 1779. The 1780s witnessed widespread, effective agitations for further relief by Dissenters and their allies, and motions for a general repeal of the Test and Corporations Acts in 1787 and 1789 were narrowly defeated. During the reaction to the French Revolution, the reform movement stagnated, and Charles James Fox's 1790 motion for repeal was defeated by a large margin. But the agenda became viable again at the end of the first decade of the nineteenth century. Starting with the triumphant rejection of Lord Sidmouth's Bill of 1811, the passage of subsequent legislation in 1812, and the passage of the Unitarian Toleration Act in 1813 (R. Davis 148–69; Hole 195–99; Watts 2.367–77), the next seventy years saw the piecemeal but near total achievement of an increasingly ambitious (and mostly devout) liberal agenda on religion.

The same period, one needs to concede, witnessed the strength of religiously motivated opponents to this liberal agenda—particularly church-and-state Tories. As James Sack has shown, starting in the 1760s British conservatism most often discovered its coherence in relation to religious issues, and the platform for religious liberty did not advance smoothly or inevitably. But advance, and triumph, it did. By most accounts, this agenda culminates with the passage of the Dissenters' Burials Bill in 1880, and nothing less than a transformation of the basic context of politics (Wiggins). "From the 1880s onwards," as Jonathan Parry writes, "it was evident that the intense evangelical impulse for moral regeneration which had driven the nonconformist political juggernaut . . . was diminishing" (434). And, more than any other cause, the movement's power was sapped by its own success. The cumulative effect of all its reforms was to render the impact of an established church negligible. At that point, the final achievement of a secular state, through disestablishment of the church, became as politically implausible as it was functionally unnecessary, and so it remains today.[28]

The agenda for religious liberty also at times shared reformist goals with a political program calling for a general expansion of the right of adult men to elect representatives in Parliament. But the secular element of the late-eighteenth-century liberal platform was defeated as often as its religious component advanced. Here again, I need to qualify my claims, particularly in sight of the fact that these two movements—one seeking the liberty of devotion, the other the liberty to vote—could overlap. One can emphasize a long nineteenth century dominated by a dynamic of extending religious rights and voting rights. In the 1770s and '80s religious liberals tended to be more disposed toward a larger electorate. And the major religious measures of 1828–29, the Repeal of the Test and Corporation Acts and Roman Catholic Emancipation, gave some force to what became the Reform Bill of 1832, whose reconfiguration of representation in turn empowered some urban areas where Dissent was strong. Similarly, the parliamentary reforms of 1867 inspired (or, perhaps, required) the last great steps forward in the liberal religious agenda in the late 1860s and '70s. The more important point, however, is that the liberal religious agenda and democratization were at odds. Versions of modernization that rely on the synergy between secularization and democratization too often forget that all franchise reforms in the nineteenth century, including the Third Reform Bill of 1884, were crafted as *alternatives* to democracy. Moreover, the failure of a democratic political agenda was in a large part due to the vitality and success of the religious agenda. British politics remained nondemocratic by practicing religious politics in a complicated process, whereby a noninterventionist state developed an agnostic religious conscience so as to allow religion to flourish freely. For these reasons, and by virtue of the repeated defeat of the Chartist agenda, the program for religious liberty is the primary long-term political event of the period under study.

In deciding to focus on the politics of secularization at the expense of a traditional teleology of democratization measured by voting rights, I am emboldened by two other considerations that have helped to determine my chronological scope. In the first place, an implicit teleology of democratization has done much to sustain the independence of the "Lit Crit" disciplines of Romanticism and Victorian Studies and their agreement to use the early 1830s to partition the century. These disciplines are to a significant degree constituted and maintained by different attitudes toward a nonpresent institution of democracy. Old-style Romanticism begins with the formulation of a democratic political agenda and ends with the failure of that agenda signaled by the passing of the Reform Bill of 1832, an event represented as a political tragedy because merely a bourgeois victory. Most Victorianists take up their subject at the same point, but they see it as the installation of a polity dedicated to the achievement of liberal democracy. In the meantime, the primary political story, one of a mainly religious route to secularization, gets subordinated to either the Romantic story of democracy's defeat or the Victorian story of democracy's evolution. Secondly, as I have already suggested, this study foregrounds a teleology of secularization because its final subject—the general claim that literature had assumed a religious function—legitimately directs attention to the fact that the state from the 1770s to the 1880s experienced a radical realignment with religious authority.

Finally, the period 1774–1880 is a device to acknowledge that the evolution of a reading nation in the nineteenth century found its most important obstacles and opportunities in the agenda for religious liberty. Just as the 1880s saw the achievement of an agenda that transformed any possible relationship between the religious and the political, the 1880s also saw the achievement of an educational agenda that transformed the broader cultural context for reading, the process by which the national literary tradition was to be known on a national scale. Along with the Dissenters' Burial Bill of 1880, the other major legislation of that year was an amending Education Act that theoretically instituted compulsory national primary education. After 1880, all children up to age ten were required to attend state-inspected schools; thus literacy, the ability to read, became a kind of right guaranteed by the state. This institution of compulsory literacy was the final step in what is by now a familiar story, the expansion of the reading public. What was exceptional about the reading public after 1880 was its scale. It was the first actual mass reading audience, and entertaining or improving printed matter lay within the economic reach of all but the destitute.[29] The history of the making of this reading audience is often coordinated with the master narrative of democratization extending from the Wilkesite agitations of the 1760s up to the Third Reform Bill. In this respect, Robert Lowe's famous call in 1867 for increased state support for education ("We must educate our masters" [qtd. in Brantlinger, *Reading Lesson* 179]) has been an irresistible tag for those seeing democratization as the nineteenth century's main ideological event. The nineteenth-century politics of becoming a reading nation, however, were more closely determined by movements to secure a liberty of religious devotion. And the notoriously belated institution of a program designed to make reading a national activity required the prior fulfillment of that same political quest.

Here I need to recall that, for most of the nineteenth century, the main obstacles to proposals for systemic state-administered primary education were religious in nature. First, there were fears among Protestant Dissenters that these plans would dedicate state resources to an education biased toward the established church. The increasingly powerful force of political dissent was hardly ready to see national education become a state-funded seminary for the perils of episcopacy. On the other hand, there were Anglican fears that reading the Bible in school without note or comment would raise up a generation of Dissenters—natural sectarians taught early on, and at the state's cost, to cherish unmediated encounters with Scripture. Until the 1880s, Anglicans and Dissenters were locked in debates that were regularly resolved by having the state deal with educational needs in very limited ways.[30] The advocates of what might appear to us an obvious solution—secular education—were few. Most Dissenters and Anglicans (in particular those possessing the property which entitled them to vote) could not imagine elementary instruction without religious instruction and Bible study. It was only with the triumph of the platform for religious liberty, only with the de facto secularization of the state, that Dissenters lost the ability and will to upset plans for universal primary education overseen by the state.[31] Furthermore, it was only when the church recognized itself as one sect among many that Anglican religious functionaries gave up pretensions to being the doctrinally bound educators of the nation's youth. The state was able to require and later ensure that all children become schooled in letters only when the state had developed a secular conscience. Literacy was normalized, and illiteracy pathologized, at the point when the state no longer recognized religious heresies.[32]

By referring to a new pathology of illiteracy, I mean something more specific than its increasing rarity. The 1880 requirement that all children up to the age of ten attend school was part of a new vision of the lives of subjects that demanded that reading would precede work. For while children from ten to fourteen were allowed to work, they could be employed only with certification of achievement in reading, writing, and math (G. Sutherland 125–45). Those who failed to acquire these skills could now be sent to a certified day industrial school, an institution that corrected the defect of illiteracy and directly linked this correction to the normative development of *homo economicus*. This socioeconomic pathologization of illiteracy stands out as a striking event in the history of reading in the British Isles. In 1837, for example, the year of Victoria's coronation, one third of all men and one half of all women couldn't read or write. Hardly considered essential human activities, reading and writing were important indicators of social status. In the space of the next fifty years, however, the literacy rate evens out for men and women and goes beyond 90 percent for the nation as a whole.[33] The conceptual transformation attending this numerical expansion is even more impressive: reading and writing had become, rather suddenly, preconditions for legitimate labor.

A truly national cult of literature, although foretold in the 1770s, did not materialize until the last quarter of the nineteenth century. It was then that the state intervened to make all subjects readers and that English literature became the object of instruction from elementary schools (1876) to the ancient universities. Just as the national reading public envisioned over a hundred years before came of age, the late-eighteenth-century formulation of English literary history became an accredited discipline, a profession, and an inheritance carefully conserved for the nation at large. As Joss Marsh has shown, one index of the rise of literary authority during the 1880s was the refashioning of the theological crime of blasphemy into the literary crime of indecency. At about the same time, and in response to many of the same forces, a newly conceived crime against the word, modern illiteracy, was born in tribute to the disappearance, within the new state's registry, of the old religious crimes of infidelity and heresy. One testament to these momentous changes is the commonplace claim this book aims to recontextualize: the claim that literature had assumed a religious authority.[34] But literature did not assume this authority only after religious experience became less possible. Nor did the cult of literature grow up in a space left vacant by religion. It developed in intimate collusion with religious culture and religious politics. The cult of literature had much business to do with secularization, but not that version of secularization defined as "a growing tendency in mankind to do without religion" (Chadwick 1975: 17). The climacteric of the version of secularization endorsed in this study occurs when the state first smiled kindly on a free trade in paper and in divine inspiration—and when illiteracy became a disease of the unemployable. In this new view of a new nineteenth century, secularization names the emergent political context in which the individual reader, and the evolving reading of the nation, had become sacralized.

2

Zealous Protestants in Literature
Lowth, Warton, and Percy

IAIN MCCALMAN, THE EDITOR of the *Oxford Companion to the Romantic Age* (1999), conducts readers into the book by recalling how he and his planning board had worried whether one could any longer subscribe to such a title: "Was 'Romantic' in fact the most suitable label with which to frame the broad-based cultural history project we had in mind?" (1). To his own question, McCalman answers "Yes"—but mostly, it seems, for reasons of convenience. The opening triad of long articles—"Revolution," "War," and "Democracy"—entices us with traditional themes. But the accounts themselves describe how the "War" was won by the opponents of "Revolution" and "Democracy" in Britain. Saying as much, McCalman squares posthistoricist Romanticism's indeterminate and nonrevolutionary character with the age's fondness for an amiable and indeterminate book. Invoking two antagonistic bibliographic institutions—the *Encyclopaedia* and the *Companion*—McCalman reminds us that it was during the late eighteenth century that the great promise of, and attendant anxieties about, encyclopedic knowledge (authorized by print) became culturally representative. But while the *Encyclopaedia* pursued enlightenment with a faith in universal truths comprehensively represented and rationally organized, the *Companion,* an increasingly popular and ill-defined form, was acquiescent to the individuality of any proposed order of things.

I cite this creative use of book history because it dramatizes a bibliohistorical inaccuracy whenever the *Companion* mentions Thomas Warton's *History of English Literature.*[1] We can all agree with the *Companion* that Warton's *History* is a seminal work, but its correct title was the *History of English Poetry* (3 vols., 1774–81), and no book would be graced with the grand title *History of English Literature* until 1853 (Spalding). Fine scholars have referred to Warton's nonexistent *History of English Literature,* and surely these apparitions have a story to tell.[2] After frankly confessing doubts about the past existence of a Romantic Age, the *Oxford Companion,* for example, might find comfort in recalling that *English Literature* in 1774 had a *History,* one about to feature a distinctive Romantic period as the greatest flowering of literary creativity since Elizabethan times. Similarly, the false title indulges the thought that literary history was a profession in 1774. And so Warton was, as the *Companion* tells us, a "poet, antiquarian, and literary historian" (747). Warton was indeed these things. But the *Companion* remains unable to name Warton's real vocation: it cannot say he was a priest, that he had been ordained in 1754.

In the production of the apocryphal title and the suppression of Warton's profession, we see at work the assumptions of a literary history this study aims to revise. In the following story, I focus on the prominent role played by the clergy in the production of the books associated with the rise of modern literary history, a new history that in several ways advertised the significance of its own consumption by making readers and the reading nation its most consequential entities. And as part of my effort to recall how church history and literary history were deeply involved, the following chapter is more priest-ridden than a gothic novel. Not only was Warton—like Robert Lowth and Thomas Percy—a priest, he was the son of a priest, and his most important intellectual co-conspirator, his brother Joseph, was a priest as well. So too were most of Warton's other important scholarly models, collaborators, and intellectual adversaries. In proposing a narrative in which a national priesthood plays such a role, I need to make it clear that I am not arguing that only the church and its seminaries, the ancient universities, deserve credit or blame for producing what became, over the course of the nineteenth century, the institution of English Literature. I am responding to the fact that the church's role has become obscured—and arguing that a history of the making of the modern British reader needs to include its ecclesiastical chapters.

Poetry and Prophecy in the Age of *Sacred Dramas*

In April 1762 Richard Hurd wrote to his friend and fellow clergyman Thomas Balguy and mentioned that his *Letters on Chivalry and Romance* would be appearing soon. In closing he asked for literary news in a way that boasted of his intimacy with William Warburton, then bishop of Gloucester: "Tell me about (to use a phrase of little Ralph Warburton when he wants to hear a story of a Cock & a Bull) this new Grammar of Dr. Lowth. They say it out sells Tristram Shandy" (*Early Letters* 392).

Hurd's letter is a good core sample of English literary culture in the 1760s. Hurd himself has long been acknowledged to be an important participant in the rise of literary history, and Ian Balfour has called him "one of the most prominent literary figures of his day" (83).³ But the major specimen on display is the father of the inquisitive Ralph, William Warburton, then at the height of his reputation. A self-made man with no university training, Warburton rose into the House of Lords by dint of his voracious literary capacities, and a short list of his major works conveys the stunning scale of the reading material that came from his hand: his *Alliance between Church and State* (1736) remained for more than one hundred years an influential treatise, and his *Divine Legation of Moses Demonstrated* (1st ed., 2 vols., 1737–41) was accepted for many years as proof of his unmatched learning. Having been befriended by Alexander Pope after defending him from charges of deism, Warburton collaborated on the *New Dunciad* of 1742 and its revision of 1743, and several editions of Pope's *Essay on Man* were produced with Warburton's notes and commentary. When Pope died in 1744, he willed to Warburton what amounted to his copyright, a legacy eventually worth between £4,000 and £5,000. It was as Pope's literary confidant too that he reedited the poet's edition of Shakespeare—a venture that earned Warburton £500—in 1747. Finally, in 1751, after a delay that seemed only to increase the public's appetite, appeared *The Works of Alexander Pope*. Between 1751 and 1754, five of Warburton's editions appeared in 10,750 sets, or almost 100,000 single volumes. In the year of the fifth edition, major church preferments began to accrue when he was made a chaplain to George II and a doctor of divinity by the archbishop of Canterbury. A prebendary stall at Durham followed in 1755. Made dean of Bristol in 1757, he was finally consecrated bishop in 1760. As a major literary figure and as a spiritual peer of the realm, he attacked various misinterpreters of the Bible in *Doctrine of Grace* (1763), and in 1765 the fourth edition of the *Divine Legation,* some thirty years in the making, was published.⁴

Both Warburton's status and the literary productivity of the clergy in general are to be gauged by the fact that the best-selling authors mentioned by Hurd—Laurence Sterne and Lowth—were clergymen with consequential relations with Warburton. When Sterne, the heretofore obscure canon from York, brought out the first two volumes of *The Life and Opinions of Tristram Shandy* in December 1759, Warburton cast himself as the provincial author's main metropolitan promoter (Nichol 134). And Sterne certainly had Warburton on his mind as he wrote *Tristram Shandy,* which was, like Warburton's *Divine Legation,* a massive, serial, and encyclopaedic commentary closely identified with its hobbyhorsical author (New). In the final volume of his masterpiece, with his death by consumption looming, Sterne, through Shandy, pondered his literary legacy—his "Posterity"—with a jest that linked Warburton's work and the rollicking satire of another clerical author,

Jonathan Swift's *A Tale of the Tub* (1704): "I say, by Posterity—and care not, if I repeat the word again—for what has this book done more than the Legation of Moses or the Tale of a Tub, that it may not swim down the gutter of time along with them?" (430). Borrowing a cloacal slur from Swift and hurling it at Warburton, Sterne was also capitalizing on Warburton's recent association with inglorious literary consummations, one that had been pointed out by Robert Lowth, the author of the book said to be outselling *Tristram Shandy* in 1762. For, in addition to his *Short Introduction to the English Grammar,* Lowth's major publication in English that decade was *A Letter to the Right Reverend Author of The Divine Legation of Moses Demonstrated* (1765), a polemic that represented a coup in the Republic of Letters. With his *Letter,* which went into four editions in five months, Lowth had cut down the age's reigning literary tyrant and had become, as William Blake's early patron William Hayley would put it, "Pontifex Libertatis" (qtd. in Hall 36).

My discussion of Lowth's contributions to the English cult of literature is initiated here in its clerical context because his appearance in literary history frequently indicates a discomfort with his professional status. This is not to say that Lowth himself has been forgotten by literary history. His lectures as Oxford Professor of Poetry (1741–50), *De Sacra Poesi Hebraeorum Praelectiones Academicae Oxonii Habitae,* were first published in 1753 and had gone to a third edition (1775) by the time they were translated into English in 1787 as *Lectures on the Sacred Poetry of the Hebrews.* And in this guise, as Howard Weinbrot has claimed, the *Lectures* constituted "eighteenth-century Britain's most important extended discussion of poetry" with "Johnson's *Lives of the Poets* (1779–81) excepted" (406–7). Throughout the twentieth century, Lowth was remembered by the academy as an important source for the formulation of Romantic aesthetics and as an influence on literary figures ranging from James Macpherson to Gerard Manley Hopkins. Because Lowth read his Bible as a literary text, one most inspired at its poetic moments, he paved the way for everything from the Blakean faith in the divinity of the imagination to the Arnoldian sacralization of poetry. He is a (if not *the*) great forerunner of the nineteenth-century cult of literature, as James Engell implies with the title of his essay "Robert Lowth, Unacknowledged Legislator."[5]

With this reputation secure in literary history, Lowth's stature as an author is more circumspect. Neither the *New Cambridge Bibliography of English Literature* nor the *Oxford Companion to English Literature* has an entry for Lowth. Citing this last omission, Engell has called for Lowth's "critical restoration" (128), and in service to that project he begins by citing the testimony of the translator of the *Praelectiones,* George Gregory—himself a prolific clerical author—who had assured his readers that it would be a mistake to think that the bishop's subject was an esoteric one. "Although the following Lectures be entitled Lectures on the Hebrew Poetry, their utility," Gregory wrote, "is by no means confined to that single object. They embrace all THE GREAT PRINCIPLES OF GENERAL CRITICISM" (1.v). While I share this desire to see Lowth command more attention, it is a slightly different kind of attention I want to incite. For the appropriation of Lowth as an oracle of general criticism is in many ways another evasion of Lowth's real character as an author, one who cultivated a version of public authority that claimed to reconcile literary and religious values. Literary criticism often seeks to make Lowth intelligible by rescuing him from ecclesiastical history and historical philology, but that history and that historical discipline reveal the full force of his authorial status.

Part of the problem with literary history's appropriation of Lowth is that he is most frequently remembered for what was unremarkable: that is, his acknowledgement that the Hebrew Bible contained poetry. This general proposition is essential to the *Praelectiones*, but it was no innovation.[6] More important, the *Praelectiones* modeled a form of imaginative authority defined by the accommodation of originality with historical mediation. Throughout his career—in his lectures, in his sermons, in his work as a grammarian, in his quarrel with Warburton, and in his mature masterwork, his *Isaiah: A New Translation* (1778)—Lowth articulated a discourse of modern enlightenment predicated on a historical capacity to understand the peculiar virtues of the primitive and simple. In the *Praelectiones*, Lowth thus argued that Hebrew scripture contained a specific kind of poetry, primitive poetry. And while all nations and races had such poetry, Hebrew primitive poetry had peculiar causes for admiration. It was considered the oldest surviving poetry in the world, and it was considered to be inspired by—had its origin in—devotion to an authentic deity. But even as Lowth said that the Hebrew Bible contained "specimens of the primeval and genuine poetry" and emphasized how these specimens "are not less venerable for their antiquity than for their divine original" (1.50), he understood that this poetry was only theoretically present. For the text in which this primal poetry was supposed to be found was corrupted in complicated ways.

Lowth summed up his historicist ends with the formula that "we must endeavor as much as possible to read Hebrew as the Hebrews would have read it" (1.113). It was attention to this proposition about reading—one that relied on both an identification and an alienation—that shaped his career. And Lowth's critical principles were directly influenced by contemporary scholarship regarding the received biblical text. Over and above his goal of appreciating ancient Hebrew poetry, Lowth's vocational program was to produce a more authentic version of the Hebrew Bible and from that text produce a new English translation to replace the Authorized Version of 1611. As Neil Hitchin (esp. 80–89) and Scott Mandelbrote (55–63) have shown, Lowth was a key figure in an Oxford-based, pro-revision ecclesiastical circle of Whiggish dimensions gathered under the patronage and sanction of Thomas Secker, who was bishop of Bristol (1735) and Oxford (1737) and eventually archbishop of Canterbury (1758). After Lowth, the most important member of this circle was Lowth's friend and fellow Oxford divine Benjamin Kennicott, whose *State of the Printed Hebrew Text of the Old Testament Considered* (2 vols., 1753–59) was a call to arms for a project completed with the publication of *Vetus Testamentum Hebraicum, cum variis lectionibus* (2 vols., 1776–80), a new Hebrew text listing thousands of variant readings culled from some six hundred different manuscripts. While Lowth, from the 1750s onward, successfully established himself as Britain's most authoritative reader of ancient Hebrew, he was also frequently advertising the fact that Kennicott was providing the material foundations for a new English version of the remains of ancient Hebrew (fig. 3).[7] And with Secker made archbishop in 1758, Lowth saw the essential institutional development required to commence the project formally. Privately he assured Kennicott that "we sh[oul]d now have the finest opportunity that can be desir'd or expected for procuring a New Translation of the Bible" (qtd. in Mandelbrote 57). Two months after Secker's confirmation, Lowth seized the momentum with a visitation sermon preached before the bishop of Durham, Richard Trevor. Published at Trevor's command, the sermon became an episcopally authorized manifesto for a new English Bible for "an enlightened age" (*Sermons* 91).

Lowth's theme was that the church and the nation were in the midst of a new reformation made possible by learning and commerce, one that was fulfilling the principles of Europe's sixteenth-century Reformation, when Christianity "was, in a manner, republished to the world in its native simplicity" (83). Further intellectual progress was now allowing a more complete return to the "native beauty" of Christianity, "as the most amiable religion that ever was" (88); and the "great progress of learning and useful knowledge" made possible a more accurate translation of the Bible and its worldwide distribution in the wake of "navigation and commerce" (81). This progress also included an anachronistic step closer to the "original" biblical text that allowed readers to set aside theological controversies that could now be seen as later glosses on the text, what he characterized as the accumulated "rubbish of false science" and "the obscure subtilty of scholastic theology" (86). In Lowth's sketch of the corruption

Fig. 3. Robert Lowth, 1777, by John Keyse Sherwin (after Robert Edge Pine). The inspired reader with the first volume of Kennicott's Vetus Testamentum Hebraicum. *(National Portrait Gallery, London)*

of Christianity—something essential to Protestant historiography—the "most pernicious of all heresies" was the heresy of heresy, the "unhappy persuasion . . . that church-communion demands unity of sentiment in the strictest sense; and that all of the same profession should think just alike, not only as to a few plain fundamental articles, but as to many other particulars neither necessarily required, nor clearly revealed" (88). With Christianity's past descent into metaphysical obscurity, "the simplicity and purity of faith was perplexed and corrupted by the subtilty of debate": "Many an absurd opinion, many an over-curious theory and bold decision in matters of doubtful disputation, that would otherwise have sunk into oblivion, and died with its author, gained strength and importance by opposition; till, being dignified with the title of heresy, and perpetuated by an anathema, it was in a manner consecrated, and delivered down as a never-failing subject of strife and division to posterity" (75–76).

Now, with the age's learned return to biblical originals, devout readers could escape from this cycle in which contention consecrated error.

Much of Lowth's sermon can be attributed to a tradition of latitudinarian theology that included John Tillotson, Samuel Clarke, and, most prominently as Lowth came of age, Benjamin Hoadly. The last of these had, as bishop of Winchester, been Lowth's early patron and, among other things, presented to him his first major church preferment, the archdeaconry of Winchester in 1750. And Lowth's debt to Hoadly was something he sought to manage in his major English publication of 1758, his *Life of William Wykeham,* which was published four days after the letter to Kennicott quoted above (27 May 1758). Lowth's *Life* of the medieval bishop of Winchester, founder of both Winchester College and New College at Oxford, pursued the same historicist ends of the *Praelectiones* while also serving as an act of professional piety by the day's most promising Wykemist, as pupils of Winchester College were called. Propriety and past service made Hoadly, the present bishop of Winchester, the obvious dedicatee, but Lowth, who had resigned his archdeaconry at Winchester in favor of the canonry at Durham, also used the occasion to advertise the fact that he had stepped outside Hoadly's orbit. "Having once enjoyed the patronage" of Hoadly, Lowth was "the more ready thus publicly to acknowledge" his obligations now that he was "removed out of the reach of further favors of the like kind" (v).[8] In qualifying his relationship to Hoadly in this way, Lowth was positioning his call for a new English Bible in a less controversial light. Hoadly held, most people believed, unorthodox views on the Trinity and had inspired, among other things, the Bangorian controversy earlier in the century (Sykes 292–96; Young 31–33). And while Lowth's views on related issues were probably similar, he avoided these dogmatic debates. In this pragmatic stance, Lowth at the height of his influence, from the 1760s to the 1780s, was distinguished by his sense of moment. He formulated a powerful discourse of modernity that expressed itself in terms of a right appreciation of the primitive and the simple, and these characteristics became the aesthetic foundations for the amiable and rational Christianity expressed by learned Protestantism. At the same time, he emphasized how the new reformation was unfolding "as a result of the linguistic and theological achievements of members of the established Church" (Mandelbrote 57).

Lowth's consummate statement on the new reformation would come with his *Isaiah: A New Translation* (1778), and much of his success in that performance was founded on his reputation for learning, one that was enhanced and updated in the second and third editions of the *Praelectiones* (1762, 1775). But Lowth was also able to command a well-disposed audience for his *Isaiah* thanks to his *Short Introduction to English Grammar* (1st ed., 1762) and his *Letter*. Lowth's *Grammar,* by far his most widely circulated work, has often played the role of bogey in the story of the rise of proscriptive grammar in the eighteenth century.[9] And Lowth himself claims his approach to be innovative for "teach[ing] us what is right by shewing what is wrong" (xiv). With its title-page epigraph in Latin and many notes containing Greek as well, the *Grammar* was deliberately opaque in selected areas for readers limited to English. But Lowth's appeal to nonvernacular texts, like his treatment of error, was essential to a philological approach that united the grammarian and the theologian.

At the heart of Lowth's theory of English grammar is a conversion of the uninflected nature of the language into a literary virtue of simplicity, an approach that differs from Samuel Johnson's in the "Grammar" included in the prefatory material to his *Dictionary* (1st ed., 1755). There, as Lowth pointed out, the lexicographer had linked the language's lack of inflection to a poverty of regulation, saying "its Construction neither requires nor admits many rules" (qtd. in Lowth, *Grammar* ix). For Lowth, English was not free from a system of rules but "subject to fewer variations from their original Form" (viii). Insisting that English is both uniquely simple and subject to important rules, Lowth defers any extended theoretical defense of that proposition in favor of examples of erroneous usage: "The Notes subjoined to the following pages will furnish a more convincing argument, than any thing that can be said here" (xii). Lowth then closes his preface to the second edition with two final paragraphs that strategically acknowledge exceptions to the rules in a manner that links all learners from the common to the virtuoso. With his "chief end . . . to explain the general principles of Grammar as clearly and intelligibly as possible," he has in his definitions and distinctions preferred "easiness and perspicuity . . . to logical exactness." With the "common Divisions" and "known and received Terms" he has complied, but only "as far as reason and truth would permit"; and "all disquisitions, which appeared to have more of subtilty than of usefulness in them, have been avoided." In these terms, the *Grammar* "was calculated for the use of the Learner, even of the lowest class" (xvi–xvii). To learners of the highest class, the author turns in his final paragraph, paying his compliments "to several Learned Gentlemen, who have favoured him with their remarks upon the former Edition." Having "weigh[ed] their observations without prejudice or partiality," he had endeavored "to make the best use of the lights which they have afforded him. He hath been enabled to correct several mistakes, and encouraged carefully to revise the whole, and to give it all the improvement which his present materials can furnish. He hopes for the continuance of their favour, as he is sensible there will still be abundant occasion for it." The striking thing about Lowth's debt to learning is this submission to a larger economy of perpetual revision in a "system" that "must always stand in need of improvement": "It is indeed the necessary condition of every work of human art or science, small as well as great, to advance towards perfection by slow degrees; by an approximation, which, though it still may carry it forward, yet will certainly never bring it to the point to which it tends" (xviii–xix).

In its deductive principles and its critique of abstraction, the *Grammar* bears traces of its Lockean roots, and the theological nature of this philosophical tradition comes out in subtle distinctions, as when Lowth notes the inherently compromised achievements "of every work of *human* art or science" (emphasis mine). And in defining the parts of speech, Lowth displays grammar's normative function by parsing each word in a sentence about a habit of linguistic perversion, thus suggesting that his current project, like Christianity itself, is a reply to postlapsarian realities: "The power of speech is a faculty peculiar to man, and was bestowed on him by his beneficent Creator for the greatest and most excellent uses; but alas! how often do we pervert it to the worst of purposes?" (9). After naming the nine parts of speech, Lowth then turns to a broader discussion of each one, starting with the article (15–21). This elementary topic characteristically inspires one of his longest footnotes, in which the Greek of the New Testament and its Authorized translation were used to illustrate the distinction between the definite and indefinite article. Citing the centurion's comment following the death of Jesus as recounted in Matthew and Mark ("Truly this was *the* Son of God" [Matt. 27:54; Mark 15:39]), Lowth argues that the proper translation should be "Truly this was a Son of God." While the Authorized Version "supposes, that the Roman Centurion had a proper and adequate notion of the character of Jesus, as the Son of God in a peculiar and incommunicable sense," Lowth's rendering assumed that the centurion "only meant to acknowledge him to be an extraordinary person, and more than a mere man; according to his own notion of Sons of Gods in the Pagan Theology." And he extends the point by crediting the translators with getting right Luke's version of the same event when they have the centurion say, "Certainly this was *a* righteous man" rather than "*the* righteous man" or "*the* Just One" (16–17). The Authorized translators of Matthew and Mark, in other words, had turned the centurion into the world's first Christian, a Gentile who testifies to the divinity of Jesus based on the evidence of his senses: the darkening of the sun, the quaking of the earth, and the opening of graves. Lowth's point is that the testimony of this witness had been anachronistically Christianized.

The centurion was a pagan, and he would, presumably, not have reacted to these extraordinary events by confessing his understanding of a Christological moment influenced by the messianic prophecies of Hebrew poets. Instead, the credibility of the testimony is established by a historically accurate misconception of the godship of Jesus. At moments like this, Lowth is demonstrating how the humble grammarian no less than the learned biblical exegete had to seek the best meaning in a region bounded by "the circumstances of the History" and "the expression of the Original" (16).

Because Lowth so frequently brings to the bar great literary figures such as Shakespeare, Milton, and Pope and cites their breaking of grammatical rules, he has struck some as blind to the flexibility of language.[10] But Lowth's citation of English poets is best understood in a more general philological context that includes his citation of biblical authors, their translators, and even the Prayer Book's prose (134). In this context, one that ranges across notions of secular and sacred canons, Lowth's decision to highlight the erroneous grammar of English poets is an example of his faith in the lessons of history; and he is ready in some cases to credit history's repeated mistakes with a kind of legitimacy. Thus, while he often cites the Authorized Version to point to grammatical errors, he does not hesitate to call that same book "the best standard of our language" (93). After describing the translation as being largely free from a particular verbal "corruption," he goes on to suggest that the error might, in any case, be fully established by "Custom" (93–94). His high literary appreciation of the Authorized Version could be reconciled to his desire to understand its errors and to make himself the chief architect of the new translation that would replace it.

Lowth's *Grammar* is in part a creature of a latitudinarian hermeneutic tradition, but Lowth understood those hermeneutic principles to be derived from the physical realities that beset historical readers and writers. These realities—including a capacity for error—touched the generations of transcribers responsible for compiling and preserving ancient texts as well as modern participants in the expanding market for print. And the most immediate source for the *Grammar* is likely to be found in the desire of the bookseller Robert Dodsley to have on hand a reliable guide for correcting the language and usage of his clients (Tieken-Boon van Ostade). That Dodsley turned to Lowth to produce such a work was a recognition of Lowth's command of literature. That Lowth's literary practice was inextricable from his professional training and duties was a sign of a wider ideal that bound together enterprising booksellers, accomplished ecclesiastics, and the commerce of print.

Lowth's other major publication in English in the 1760s, his *Letter,* is generically unrelated to the *Grammar.* But like the *Praelectiones* and like the *Grammar,* the *Letter* mediated a tone of modern enlightenment with sophisticated gestures toward the primitive and simple as parts of a single story in which the author established a unique literary reputation. The *Letter* was the most memorable contribution to a broader feud over the antiquity of the book of Job. The point became essential to Warburton's argument in the *Divine Legation,* which sought to explode the "natural religion" argument that Christianity had its roots in universal modes of worship and belief. By stressing the unique (and thus unnatural) state of the Mosaic covenant from which Christianity developed, Warburton claimed to prove that Christianity was supernaturally revealed. "Mosaic" religion was manifestly divine because it—unlike the pagan mysteries—included no promise of an afterlife.

The book of Job was a potentially devastating threat to Warburton's chain of argument because it was often dated to a period before the exodus from Egypt and included the evangelically interpreted verses beginning "For I know that my redeemer liveth, and that he shall stand at the latter day upon the earth" (19:25–26). If this passage, as Jonathan Lamb describes the crux, is "read as Job's prophecy of the coming of Christ and the resurrection of the just, then all secrets are out: the Jews are informed from the very first that a future state of rewards and punishments awaits them" (1990: 4). For this reason Warburton was forced to argue that the poem was a post-exilic allegory composed by Ezra in the fifth century BC. Lowth, on the other hand, had argued in his *Praelectiones* that the book was a sublime example of ancient Hebrew poetry, one far older, in any case, than the relatively late days of Ezra. An epistolary feud about this question had broken out privately in 1755 following the publication of the first edition of Lowth's *Praelectiones.* And when Lowth brought out his second edition in 1762 and did nothing to disguise the fact that his views were at odds with the argument of the *Divine Legation,* Warburton made his fourth edition of 1765 the occasion for a typically impertinent attack. This attack then inspired Lowth to publish his *Letter,* which included their earlier correspondence.[11]

The Warburton-Lowth exchange was a theological debate that was relentlessly literary in character. Both Warburton and Lowth were polemical divines seeking title to the highest literary authority, a preeminence earned precisely because it addressed fundamental religious questions. From the start, Lowth knew that he had the advantage of his superior Hebrew, and he would eventually abuse Warburton directly for ignorance on this matter (89). But he did so only after revealing the "true origins and merits of this dispute" by publishing their "Literary Correspondence" on the matter from the previous decade (103–36). By publishing this correspondence, Lowth sought to situate the difference of opinion on personal and literary grounds, emphasizing Warburton's pretension to being the arbiter of "every question in Literature" (13). While Warburton had accused Lowth of duplicity, Lowth emphasized how he had found himself "obliged to differ in opinion from several Writers of great Authority in the Republic of Letters" (104). Rather than being a debate about religious dogma, it was the "dogmatical" air of Warburton that was the sticking point, and Lowth suggested "something more in the spirit of Toleration in Literary matters" was the remedy. The high point of Lowth's earlier defense came as he honored Warburton as "a man of the first rank in letters" but insisted on a personal literary autonomy:

> For myself as a member of the Commonwealth of Letters, I am a true Lover of peace and quietness, of mutual freedom, candor, and benevolence. I detest and I despise the Squabbles that are perpetually arising from the jealousy and peevishness of the genus irritable Scriptorum. I am a staunch Republican and zealous Protestant in Literature, nor will ever bear with a Perpetual Dictator, or an Infallible Pope, whose Decrees are to be submitted to without appeal, and to be received with implicit assent. (131)

The newly composed parts of Lowth's 1765 *Letter* reprise this theme of literary despotism and raise the stakes by adding an attack on Warburton's literary capabilities. Gone were the concessions to Warburton's high rank as a man of letters, and in their place is a framing of Warburton's blunders in the context of an encompassing interpretive liability: the literary tyrant is limited to a demonstrative hermeneutic. Warburton's offensiveness and quickly offended character are linked to a literary praxis in which everything must be, as the final word of Warburton's short title has it, *Demonstrated*. Lowth, in contrast, confesses he can only abide by his opinions and expresses doubts that some points of contention could ever be finally decided.

Throughout the *Letter,* Lowth implies that Warburton's greatest failing is a lack of literary taste, an aesthetic foible based on a blighted historical sense. Wanting to read Job as a "modern" imitation of an ancient poem, Warburton is unprepared to appreciate the authentically primitive. He is unable, as Lowth puts it, to understand that Job was "the Homer of the Hebrew Classics; who, with the venerable air of antiquity, and the force and spirit of original genius, has, at the same time, that elegance of language and beauty of composition, which the more polished and refined ages never surpassed" (80). On this issue Warburton had sought to shut down debate about the dating of texts based on internal stylistic evidence by describing Hebrew as "the narrowest of all languages" and "the most barren of all languages" and "little subject to change" (qtd. on 81). As Johnson would understand English syntax in terms of poverty, Warburton saw the repetitive character of much Hebrew poetry, its paratactic building of parallel images, as a consequence of linguistic dearth: "for when the speaker's phrase comes not up to his idea (as in a scanty language it will not) he naturally endeavors to explain himself by a repetition of the thought in other words" (qtd. on 85). For Lowth, in contrast, Hebrew was elegantly simple, abundant, and evolving, and Hebrew poets repeated "the same thought in other words" because "their language had been copious, and abounded in synonyms and parallel expressions" (85). Warburton wanted to wrestle with a narrow, barren, and static text whose secret meaning could be extracted with the right key. Lowth's Bible has its meaning elucidated through historical understanding.

Defining the Hebrew he knew poorly in terms essential to his aims was a critical error on Warburton's part. Warburton similarly forged the weapons that Lowth would turn on him when he sought to undermine the authority of Lowth's learning by suggesting that it was tainted by the political disloyalty and regressive theology of Jacobite Oxford. In reply Lowth proudly embraced the intellectual tradition of his university and implied that Warburton's attacks on Oxford "prejudices" were inspired by anxieties about his humble origins, his lack of university training, and his disgruntlement at being rebuffed in his attempts to gain an honorary degree (65). Lowth's counterattack is, like Warburton's initial aspersion, essentially personal, but the general opinion that Lowth had refuted this charge was a good sign of a wider cultural transformation that included the failing power of the image of Oxford as the home of seditious theological and political opinions. In contrast to this Oxford, one distinguished by its antipathy to the Glorious Revolution and the Hanoverian secession, the new Oxford was being remade as the place where learning and religion were most powerfully reconciled. And in their union they would provide the essential intellectual arguments on behalf of the emergent Georgian concept of church and king. Lowth proudly identified himself as *A Late Professor in the University of Oxford* on his title page, and he proved to be a good reader of the signs of the time in recognizing that Oxford had shaken off the taint of disloyalty.

This drubbing of Warburton came on the eve of Lowth's elevation to the episcopal bench. He was made bishop of St. David's in 1766 and that same year was translated to the more prestigious see of Oxford. As bishop of Oxford from 1766 to 1777, Lowth was in a position to assist

Kennicott directly, and the third edition of Lowth's now famous lectures, brought out in 1775, further advertised the impending consummation of Kennicott's textual studies. Given the fact that Lowth was, in some cases, polishing lectures written over thirty years earlier, the publication of this edition might seem to have been an unambitious exception to a long period of literary indolence. But, all along, Lowth had been working on a translation of the book of Isaiah that appeared in 1778 as *Isaiah: A New Translation, with a Preliminary Dissertation and Notes Critical, Philological, and Explanatory.* With the translation dwarfed by his "Preliminary Dissertation" and discursive notes, Lowth's *Isaiah* was not only a new version of what was, for most English readers, the central prophetic text of the Hebrew Bible; it was the British Enlightenment's premier document of practical and theoretical hermenuetics.[12] Coming from the holder of the third-highest ecclesiastical office in the land—the author had become bishop of London in 1777—and bearing a dedication to the king, the book was an authoritative prospectus for a new translation of the Bible according to the principles of historical criticism.

Throughout, Lowth operates under the conservative guise of one merely pursuing a "close literal Version." According to Lowth, no translation of Isaiah ancient or modern, from Jerome's Vulgate to the Authorized Version, had been successful because readers had not realized "the real character of the author as a writer" nor "the general character, and the peculiar form of the composition" (i). The cause of this long history of misapprehension was a failure to see that the author (or authors) of Isaiah wrote according to specific poetic conventions. So while "the style, the thoughts, the images [and] the expressions, have been allowed to be Poetical," its character as "Verse" had not been understood. By demonstrating how "the Poetical and the Prophetical character of style and composition" were "really one and the same thing" (iii), Lowth proposes to uncover the plain sense of the text. Calling attention again to the nearly completed work of Kennicott, Lowth allies this project with the prospect of moving closer to the Hebrew original itself. With Kennicott's work "the greatest and most important that has been undertaken and accomplished since the Revival of letters" (lxii), a new and better translation was possible, one unlike "our public Translations in the modern Tongues," which were "in reality only Versions at second hand, Translations of the Jews [sic] interpretation of the Old Testament" (lv).

Even so, as in his *Grammar* and in his *Letter,* Lowth's project of elucidation is balanced against an extended discussion of historical forces that rendered the Hebrew text into a cipher, albeit one quite different from

Warburton's. For, after promising a clear rendering of Isaiah based on an understanding of the author's craft, Lowth describes how biblical Hebrew (as a language) and the Hebrew Bible (as a text) must always remain mysterious in a limited sense. The translator's first challenge is the language itself, which, by virtue of its antiquity, presents problems of understanding: "What we have of it being the scanty relics of a language formerly copious, and consequently the true meaning of many words and phrases being obscure and dubious, and perhaps incapable of being clearly ascertained" (liv). Furthermore, these relics of a wider, lost literary tradition were themselves mediated by ancient editors. So if Kennicott's work returned readers to the idea of a Hebrew Original, the true originals would forever remain at second hand. And nothing could be done to change the fact, which Lowth unanxiously admits, that both the Old and New Testaments were not exempt "from the common lot of other books." All ancient writings were transformed and corrupted as they were copied over hundreds of years, with "the stream generally becoming more impure, the more distant it is from the source." And since "the Hebrew writings of the Old Testament [were] for much the greatest part the most antient of any," one had to concede that they had probably suffered more distortion than other writings of less antiquity (lvii). Detailing the working habits of past biblical transcribers and pointing to particular problems that beset Hebrew orthography, Lowth insists that Scripture must always remain an approximation of what literalist readers understood it to be, a perfect record of God's Word. Purity, simplicity, and authenticity are to be discovered in a text that bore witness to its mediated transmission through history and the ideological commitments of past compilers and transcribers. For this reason, the enlightened biblical reader, in Lowth's mind, sees in Scripture a call to participate in an extension of the past social history of the text. As Ruth apRoberts has put it, the *Isaiah* was an inquiry into "the phenomenology of reading" (130–31). To study and try to get at the meaning of Scripture was to recapture the predicament of the original authors and earliest editors of the writings themselves. And while some had argued that public (i.e., printed) discussion of these problems might "invalidate the authority of Scripture," Lowth insists that a willful ignorance of the problems could cause more bad readings of Scripture (lix).

Lowth's *Isaiah* accommodates yet another element of historical mediation by acknowledging that the Authorized Version has some characteristics—unrelated to its quality as a translation—that deserve preservation. As Lowth says of the Authorized Version, "The Style of that Translation is not only excellent in itself, but has taken possession of our ear, and of our taste," and to have varied from it frequently "would have been to disgust the reader" (lxxii). In being wary of disgusting this English reader, Lowth indicates again his willingness to compromise his theoretical pursuit of originals. The present work of translation called for a return to originals that had been defaced and obscured by ancient editors and varieties of religious sectarianism. But the same translation must also be guided by the stylistic and linguistic precedence of the very document in need of improvement.

Lowth's *Isaiah* reached a fourth edition by 1794, by which time it might sit side by side with the English translation of his Oxford lectures that first appeared in 1787. The *Isaiah* was the central work in a flurry of activity, in addition to the work of Kennicott, by Lowthians such as Benjamin Blayney and William Newcome. Blayney's exemplary translations of Hebrew prophecy—Jeremiah and Lamentations (1784) and Zechariah (1797)—were formatted to indicate that they were part of a series inaugurated by Lowth's *Isaiah:* like that work, they both bore the subtitle *A New Translation; with Notes Critical, Philological, and Explanatory.* And before offering these new translations, he had been responsible for the 1769 edition of the Authorized Version, a work that sought to restore the text of the early-seventeenth-century translation as a preliminary step in establishing it as a standard for linguistic usage. Newcome's *An Historical View of the English Biblical Translations* (1792) was a lengthy and learned endorsement of revision; and in addition to authors such as these writing from within the church, the end of the century was rife with British translation projects by Protestant Dissenters, the Scottish Roman Catholic priest Alexander Geddes, and members of England's small Jewish community. In this larger context, Lowth was repeatedly recognized as the age's key patron for biblical translation (Fuller 28–29; Ruderman 60, 76–87).

Lowth's call for a new authorized translation was not fully answered until 1870, the year when work on the Revised Version officially commenced. The century or so separating Lowth's manifesto and the making of the new translation has been used to confirm Lowth's status as an unfulfilled forerunner in an intellectual context of ignorance or indolence. And thus literary historians have cited Lowth's work as an exception that proves the rule in a story about English parsons passing the port as industrious Germans commence the innovative hermeneutic work of the modern era. But rather than seeing the 1870s and after as the time of the belated arrival of "modern" biblical criticism to British soil, the present study emphasizes how such a revision became politically feasible at that time. By then as well, Lowth's work had been for over one hundred years a catalyst for a variety of experimental literary work, including the scriptural mode employed by Blake starting with the *Marriage of Heaven and Hell* (1790). The fact that Lowth's call was not immediately answered, in other words, does not mean that readers and writers failed to register the impact of his ideas. Lowth was an authoritative inspiration for a wider discussion about biblical translation that increasingly called forth testimony to the literary qualities of the Authorized Version.[13] Along with its near contemporary, Shakespeare's First Folio of 1623, the Authorized Version of 1611 was becoming venerated as a cultural document. And the establishment of the Authorized Version as a literary classic was in part due to the anomaly of its survival as a privileged text during a period when a growing body of criticism detailed its imperfections.

In the late eighteenth century, arguments both for and against revision commonly confused theological and nontheological reading experiences. And a new veneration for the English Bible and the sacrosanct character of its readers would be mapped out in that confusion, all at a time when the Authorized Version "was increasingly the focus of early education and rudimentary learning" (Mandelbrote 46). Vicesimus Knox, for example, in his *Essays, Moral and Literary* (1st ed., 1778), claims that "were the Bible corrected and modernized, it would probably become more showy, and perhaps less inaccurate; but it would lose that air of sanctity, which enables it to make an impression on the common people, the mass of mankind, which no accuracy could produce."[14] Between the lines of Knox's argument—"On the Impropriety of Publicly Adopting a New Translation of the Bible"—there is also a recognition that the Authorized Version was the Bible for the substantial portion of churchgoers who could not (or did not) read the Bible. For these people, the potential trauma of hearing a new, unfamiliar version would be the greatest, "and we should hardly recognise the Bible, were it to be read in our churches in any other words than those which our fathers have heard before us." Beyond this argument, derived from a recognition of the "veneration acquired by time," Knox urges inaction because of the Bible's "intrinsic beauty and excellence" (266–67). In this vein of appreciation, Knox praises the Bible as a book that is ready to gratify readers on terms that are physically sensational. "The poetical passages of Scripture are peculiarly pleasing in the present translation," with a language that is "simple," "natural," "rich," and "expressive":

> Solomon's Song, difficult as it is to be interpreted, may be read with delight, even if we attend to little else but the brilliancy of the diction. . . . The Psalms, as well as the whole Bible, are literally translated, and yet the translation abounds with passages exquisitely beautiful. Even where the sense is not very clear, nor the connexion of idea obvious at first sight, the mind is

soothed, and the ear ravished, with the powerful yet unaffected charms of the style. It is not, indeed, necessary to enlarge on the excellencies of the translation in general; for its beauties are such as are to be recognized by feeling more than by description. . . . In many a cottage and farm-house, where the Bible and Prayer-book constitute the library, the sweet songs of Israel, and the entertaining histories of Joseph and his brethren, Saul and Jonathan, constitute a never-failing source of heartfelt pleasure. (268)

This Bible—sensibility's cherished anthology—becomes an essential resource for writers as well in Knox's essay "On the Advantage which may be Derived to the Tender and Pathetic Style from using the Words and Phrases of Scripture." Here, commentary on the nation's seventeenth-century translation prepares late-eighteenth-century readers for the linguistic reform associated with Wordsworth's "experiment" as described in the *Lyrical Ballads* of 1802. "Florid diction and pompous declamation" are pronounced inadequate "to affect the finer sensibilities of nature," and, to "excit[e] emotions of the tenderest sympathy," Knox appeals instead to "plain words, without epithets, without metaphors, without similes." Those "who would learn to touch the heart" must "become the disciples of Sophocles, Shakespeare, Sterne and Chatterton" (158). Above all else, the "English writer" would find in "our admirable translation" a "diction" unparalleled in "rais[ing] the sympathy of grief" (158–59).

Lowth's impact on Georgian thinking about the Bible and its status as a great literary resource has mostly been recovered by the terms that inspired heterodox literary careers such as Blake's. But a far greater number of readers tasted the fruit of Lowth's thought in works by writers closer in temperament to the liberal clergyman Knox. Another popular and historically representative Lowthian work was Hannah More's *Sacred Dramas; Chiefly Intended for Young Persons: The Subjects Taken from the Bible. To which is added, Sensibility, a Poem* (1st ed., 1782). Following a successful literary career that had thus far peaked with her play *Percy* (1777), this work was a departure for More. It was, as Anne Stott says, "her first literary attempt to reconcile the two halves of her life by publishing in the same volume *Sacred Dramas* and *Sensibility*: the one an attempt to make the Bible familiar to young readers, the other an advocacy of the religion of the heart" (83). More's title-page epigraph from Abraham Cowley—"All the Books of the Bible are either most admirable and exalted pieces of poetry, or are the best materials in the world for it"—refers her volume back to an older critical tradition, but she credits Lowth in "Sensibility" for presently leading the way in the anachronistic project of getting closer to the Bible's theo-poetic inspiration. Playing on the tradition that Roman poets had been inspired by Isaiah, More's poem features the bishop excelling Virgil and his "Pollio":

Illustrious LOWTH! For him the muses wove,
The fairest garland from their greenest grove.
Tho' Latian bards had gloried in his name,
When in full brightness burnt the Latian flame;
Yet, fir'd with nobler hopes than transient Bays,
He scorn'd the meed of perishable praise;
Spurn'd the cheap wreath by human science won;
Borne on the wing sublime of Amos' son:
He seiz'd his mantle as the Prophet flew,
And with his mantle caught his spirit too.   (270)

More had been taught Latin by her father, a schoolmaster whose plans to enter the church had been frustrated, and she considered Lowth's *Praelectiones* to be "a treasure." She was also, starting in the 1770s, very close to Mrs. Kennicott, who kept her informed about her husband's textual scholarship. Of Lowth's *Isaiah*, she was slightly critical when it finally appeared, calling it "a work of great labour and erudition; but better calculated for scholars than plain Christians, as the notes are rather critical than devotional" (Roberts, *Memoirs* 1.137). The devotional readers of her *Sacred Dramas* were thus partially conceived in contrast to a more critical reader courted in Lowth's work. As with Knox's reaction to Lowth's long-unanswered call, More would respond to Lowth in a way that defined a new form of sacrosanct lay reading. And in these terms, her early doubts about the potential popularity of her pious writings were ill founded. After Lowth and other prominent churchmen had urged More to publish the poems that would fill out *Sacred Dramas,* More worried that "the word *sacred* in the title" would be "a damper to the dramas. It is tying a millstone about the neck of Sensibility, which will drown them both together" (Roberts, *Memoirs* 1.138). To the contrary, *Sacred Dramas* inaugurated a new kind of literary career, one that was sacred, sentimental, and exceptionally lucrative.[15]

Treasures of the Gothic Library

Thomas Warton's status in literary history recalls an awkwardly interrupted acceptance speech. Just as Warton, the honoree, begins to thank the gathered audience, up pops the book on which his reputation stands—objecting to the whole affair. By virtue of a consensus long-standing, Warton is a distinguished innovator, "the first historian of English Literature in the full sense of the term," as René Wellek wrote (201); and, as such, he is the author of an unprecedented book, the *History of English Poetry,* which "replaced the old encyclopedic and taxonomic approaches (dictionaries, bibliographies, anthologies or diagrams of literary 'schools') with the first narrative of literary history" (Fairer 1998: 5). And yet this same book has been faulted for too closely resembling those it displaced.

For about two hundred years—ever since the first volume of his *History* was published in 1774—so things stood. Then in 1970 Lawrence Lipking provided a dexterous reading of the Warton problem that attributed this contradiction to the divided allegiances of late-eighteenth-century thought: the *History*'s "era is transitional, its method uncertain, its principle eclecticism; it obeys contradictory impulses and irrational motivations" (355). Since Lipking, our knowledge of Warton has been conditioned and extended in two ways. First, Warton has been a central agent in recent histories of the eighteenth-century "invention" of the English literary canon. Second, David Fairer has repeatedly introduced new evidence about Warton's methods and motivations. In the first case, Warton often plays the unattractive role, as Fairer puts it, of "creating an exclusive historic canon distanced from the reading public" (2000: 61). Fairer's Warton, on the other hand, is an ironist capable of grave jokes and complicated, self-conscious literary gestures; he is even a forger of sorts, strewing his own youthful effusions on the poetic corpus of his departed father (Fairer 1975 and 1978). Most of all, this Warton is an enthusiastic reader, one who extends, rather than retracts, reading invitations.

In the following section, I write on behalf of Fairer's Warton, focusing on how Warton's ambitions as a new kind of reader intersected with his status as a member of an ecclesiastical institution.[16] I show how Warton staked out a representative writing life by relating an innovative English literary history of his own composition to an inherited narrative of religious enlightenment, one that was culminating in the amiable and rational church as portrayed by Lowth, who was Warton's diocesan bishop from 1766 to 1777. By having a career defined by these narratives, Warton did much to enable the future to be eloquently obsessed with various forms of competition and exchange between the literary and the religious; and he helped to endow an aesthetic tradition in which poetic faith and religious faith were the potentially contrary forces that the creative mind had to reconcile in a new paradigmatic allegory of authorship.

Like Lowth, Warton was a child of the clerical intelligentsia, the second son (b. 1728) of Thomas Warton who had held the Oxford Chair of Poetry from 1718 to 1728. In September 1745 this elder Warton, then the vicar of Basingstoke, died. Besides Thomas, the vicar left behind two other children, Joseph (b. 1722) and Jane (b. 1724), who were far from well established in the world. The oldest son, Joseph, had recently received his BA from Oxford and had entered the church, moving around the lowest rungs of his profession by serving as a curate in several places. The younger brother, Thomas, had been at Oxford for less than two years. And, like his brother and his father, he was destined to make his way in the church. About the daughter, we know relatively little, but some familiar elements of the impoverished clergyman's daughter stand out: a vague incapacitating illness, bouts of governessing, and at least one published case of novel writing (Reid 1986). Given their precarious position in 1745, things turned out well for the Warton children. Joseph had the good fortune to succeed to one of his father's livings, and in 1747 he was presented to a further preferment that allowed him to marry and start a family. He was awarded another living close to the cathedral town of Winchester in 1755 and became second headmaster at the college there. In 1766 he succeeded to the headmastership, a position he held until 1793. Thomas ascended the clerical ladder resting on university walls, one that could lead to a comfortable life at the price of avoiding the pleasures of marriage. In 1745 he had won a modest scholarship. This was succeeded by an MA degree in 1750, the winning of a probationary fellowship at Trinity in 1752, and ordination as deacon shortly after. In 1754 he was admitted as a perpetual fellow and ordained priest, and in 1755 his nest was further feathered with a curacy at Woodstock in Oxfordshire. In the next year he was unanimously elected Professor of Poetry and served in that capacity until 1766. In 1771 he was presented by Lord Lichfield to the Oxfordshire living of Kiddington, and in 1782 he was given one of Trinity's perpetual curacies in Somerset. Then in 1785 he was named Poet Laureate and, shortly after, Camden Professor of History at Oxford. Five years later he would die of a paralytic stroke in the Trinity common room.

But back in 1745 the Warton children were young and fatherless, and besides some pressing debts, the departed vicar had left behind some poetry in manuscript; so filial piety and economic necessity suggested the project of publishing by subscription *Poems on Several Occasions, by the Reverend Mr. Thomas Warton,* a volume that would appear in March 1748 (Reid 1999: 278). As much as the Wartons found inspiration in the debts of their father, they were also moved to devise a new aesthetic program to rebuff the formidable shade of Pope, who had died in 1744. A new poetic and critical discourse was emerging in the 1740s, as Robert Griffin (1992), David Fairer, and others have shown, that set itself at odds with the influence and style of Pope; and the Warton brothers, along with other young poets—Thomas Gray (b. 1716), William Collins (b. 1721), Mark Akenside (b. 1722), Christopher Smart (b. 1722), and William Mason (b. 1724)—"were becoming conscious of the rich body of English poetry that predated the Restoration of 1660, when a French neo-Classicism had become preeminent" (Fairer, "Creating a National Poetry" 179). This poetic program was announced in Joseph Warton's *Odes on Various Subjects* (1746), a work that criticized "the fashion of moralizing in verse" and asserted the necessity to cultivate a new poetry of "Invention and Imagination" (3), while Thomas gave the new direction for poetry a more specific name in his "An Essay on Romantic Poetry," an unpublished fragment written in 1745. There, he described a "Kind of Poetry which perhap[s] it would not be improper to call a Romantic Kind of Poetry, as it [is] altogether conceived in the spirit, (tho with more Judgement & less extravagant) & affects the Imagination in the same Manner, with the old Romances" (qtd. in Fairer 1975: 401–2).

By the mid-1750s both Wartons had expanded their suggestive manifestos into substantial works that disclosed how their "attempt to bring back Poetry into its right channel" (*Odes* 3) called for a critical discourse that could value Pope at some level below Spenser, Shakespeare, and Milton. Most famously at the time, Joseph published *An Essay on the Genius and Writings of Pope* (1st ed., 1756), which sought to explain how Pope failed to ascend into the highest rank of English poets. And from the outset in section 1 of the *Essay,* "Of the Pastorals and the Messiah, an Eclogue," he identified Pope's limitations by invoking the authority of Lowth's lectures on Hebrew poetry, which were hailed "as the richest augmentation literature has lately received" (14). He began his discussion of Pope's "Messiah," a poetic synthesis of Virgil's "Pollio" and portions of Isaiah, by crediting the author with understanding "that the Scriptures of God contained not only the purest precepts of morality, but also the most elevated and sublime strokes of genuine poesy"; but Warton then demonstrated how in Pope's adaptations of Isaiah "the dignity, the energy, and the simplicity of the original are in a few passages weakened and diminished by floral epithets and useless circumlocutions" (11). Warton also set Pope down a level by arguing that he had made a poetic compromise in deciding to imitate the portions of Isaiah in which "prosperity and happiness are described." Since "misery and destruction," "distress and desolation" are the occasions for Isaiah's greatest sublimity, Pope passed up his most promising creative resources. By way of contrast, Warton dedicated the remainder of the section to a translation of part of Lowth's lecture 13, including Lowth's version of a portion of chapter 14 of Isaiah (15–18).

Two years before the essay on Pope had appeared, Thomas published his *Observations on the Fairy Queen of Spenser* (1754), a work that advocated appreciating the imaginative achievement of a past poet through historical principles of literary criticism. As a model for criticism based on wide reading in the past, Samuel Johnson recognized the *Observations* as an important breakthrough, telling Warton that he had "shown to all who shall hereafter attempt the study of our ancient authors the way to success, by directing them to the perusal of the books which those authors had read" (*CTW* 27). The *Observations* teem with memorable endorsements of reading itself that became more prominent in the enlarged, two-volume edition that appeared in 1762. The first two sections, for instance, have codas concerning reading that reveal how Warton could invoke a good-humored conflict between readers and critics even as he sketched out a new form of criticism in which reading was the major interpretive key. In the first, Warton resorts to the formalized antitheses that Lipking has discussed (374–77), here with imaginative readers given a delightful excursion even as judgmental critics remain unmoved and unsatisfied: "If there be any poem, whose graces please, because they are situated beyond the reach of art, and where the force and faculties of creative imagination delight, because they are unassisted and unrestrained by those of deliberate judgment, it is this. In reading Spenser if the critic is not satisfied, yet the reader is transported" (1.16). In the second coda, Warton pushes his point a considerable way forward: he denies competent critical taste to anyone who lacks interest in the reading that delighted Spenser. Having shown that "the adventures of [Spenser's] knights are a more exact and immediate copy of those which we meet with in old romances" (1.17), Warton boasts that "many other examples might be alleged, from which it would be more abundantly manifested, that our author's imagination was entirely possessed with that species of reading, which was the fashion and delight of his age." Confident that "lovers of Spenser" will not have found his discussion tedious, Warton acknowledges that "some there are, who will censure what I have collected on this subject, as both trifling and uninteresting; but such readers can have no taste for Spenser" (1.65). In the postscript to the *Observations,* Warton tested the merits of his critical project against the authority of Pope's representation of the Shakespearean labors of Lewis Theobald in the *Dunciad*. Pope had immortalized Theobold as an antiquarian obsessed with "all such reading as was never read," but Warton defends the importance of Theobold's reading and labels Pope's attack "the satire of prejudice and ignorance." The critic's "labour, which so essentially contributes to the service of true taste, deserves a more honourable repository than THE TEMPLE OF DULNESS" (2.264–65). He then goes on to fault Pope for looking down upon William Caxton's barbarisms and ignoring how he had "co-operated in the noblest cause": "In an illiterate and unpolished age he multiplied books, and consequently readers" (2.266).

Besides putting readers and reading at the center of a new critical project, the *Observations* gave shape to what would be Warton's defining topic of speculation, a long-term meditation on the relation of the imagination and learning that extended into an affiliated study of the relation of literary creativity and the fortunes of enlightened religion. In the *Observations,* Warton showed the first signs of his discovery that what he would later call "the present rational principles of protestantism" (*History* 2.430n) were theoretically at odds with the poetic modes he had set out to valorize. In doing so, his work became prescient about the ways in which much of criticism's future authority would be founded on the vocational negotiation of those realms. On these terms, Warton's oblique way into his Spenserean project is telling. In its opening sentences, the *Observations* announced itself as an inquiry into a kink in the story of enlightenment. Why was Gothic literary and cultural dullness so persistent given the revival of learning in Europe? If the revival of learning was dated to the fifteenth or sixteenth century, why did it take until the early eighteenth century for English poetry to reach a classical perfection? And why did Spenser take his cues from Lodovico Ariosto, author of the implausible and episodic *Orlando Furioso,* rather than from Torquato Tasso, author of the more "correct" Christian epic, *Gerusalemme Liberata* (1.1–4)? As Warton sought an account of imaginative fecundity in analytical terms, he came to understand that both Ariosto and Spenser persisted in habits that were equated with those of an unreformed Bible reader, one never satisfied by the plain, literal, or grammatical sense of a text.

This unexpected development took place most importantly in section 10 of the *Observations,* "Of Spenser's Allegorical Character," where Warton gives a clear formulation of the principles of historical criticism. "In reading the works of a poet who lived in a remote age," Warton writes, "it is necessary that we should look back upon the customs and manners which prevailed in that age. We should endeavor to place ourselves in the writer's situation and circumstances. Hence we shall become better enabled to discover, how his turn of thinking, and manner of composition, were influenced by familiar appearances and established objects, which are utterly different from those with which we are at present surrounded" (2.87). In pursuing this program, however, Warton made a fateful connection. The historical reader in Warton's scheme is born to appreciate a poet called "ROMANTIC," as his continuation of the three sentences just quoted makes clear: "Too many readers view the knights and damsels, the tournaments and enchantments, of Spenser, with modern eyes; never considering that the encounters of chivalry subsisted in our author's age; that romances were then most eagerly and universally studied; and that consequently Spenser, from the fashion of the times, was induced to undertake a recital of chivalrous achievements, and to become, in short, a ROMANTIC Poet" (2.87–88). But the same historical reader must confront this poet's affiliated identity as an "ALLEGORICAL Poet" (2.89). Spenser the romantic poet and Spenser the allegorical poet become one and the same.

Warton's portrait of Spenser as an allegorical poet initially emphasizes nontextual origins by calling attention to "public shews and spectacles," pageants, and masques (2.89–90). Spenser not only was writing in the literary spirit of his times; he was representing things he frequently saw. But Warton also notes some problems with Spenser's use of allegory. He frequently introduces allegories "under which no meaning is couched" (2.95); they are often "mere descriptions"; and they can be orphaned from their apparent imaginative scheme when they seem to "contain [either] an improper, or no signification" (2.96). Here his test case is the Blatant Beast and his plunder of the monasteries. If Spenser was "a friend to the reformation, as was his heroine Elizabeth," how could Spenser say "with any consistency" that this beast was scandal? Without answering his own question, Warton then moves on to "another capital fault in our author's allegories" (2.97). Quoting the Abbe du Bos and his condemnation of painters who treat religious subjects too freely ("The facts whereon our religion is built . . . are subjects in which the painter's imagination has no liberty to sport"), Warton faults Spenser for too often "mingl[ing] divine mystery with human allegory." "Such a practice," Warton writes, "tends not only to confound sacred and profane subjects, but to place the licentious sallies of imagination upon a level with the dictates of divine inspiration; to debase the truth and dignity of heavenly things, by making Christian allegory subservient subservient [sic] to the purposes of Romantic fiction" (2.98). This problem of mixing the sacred and the profane, of debasing one by associating it with the other, then leads to a condemnation of Spenser's free use of the Book of Revelations as a literary resource. As "acknowledged falsities," the "extravagancies of pagan mythology are not improperly introduced into a poem of this sort. . . . But the poet that applies the VISIONS of God in such a manner is guilty of an impropriety, which I fear, amounts to an impiety" (2.101).

The centrality of this episode for Warton is confirmed by the fact that the first public notice of the *History of English Poetry* appears immediately after he describes this threshold to poetic impiety. The sentence quoted above is followed by a claim that Spenser in his visionary and allegorical capacity represented the culmination of a native tradition: "If we take a retrospect of english poetry from the age of Spenser, we shall find, that it principally consisted in visions and allegories." And "this subject may," as a note tells us, "be one day considered more at large, in a regular history" (2.101). Warton then provides a summary of that history by sketching a poetic tradition (prone to periodic revivals and relapses) stretching from the ancient British bards to Chaucer, the age of Spenser, Milton, and up to the eighteenth century. The most recent lapse in this tradition was following the age of Fletcher, "when a poetry succeeded, in which imagination gave way to correctness, sublimity of description to delicacy of sentiment, and majestic imagery to conceit and epigram." A literary decadence associated with the rising fortunes of satire ("that bane of the sublime") was ultimately manifested in the age of Dryden by the inability to appreciate "the simple dignity of Milton [who] was either entirely neglected, or mistaken for bombast and insipidity, by the refined readers of a dissolute age, whose taste and morals were equally vitiated" (2.112). And so the section on Spenser's allegorical character comes to a close with a reminder that "allegorical poetry, through many gradations, at last received its ultimate consummation in the Fairy Queen" (2.112).

The topic of allegory had been taken up as a skirmish in Warton's battle to have Spenser properly appreciated by conning his text with something other than "modern eyes." In order to appreciate Spenser it was essential that one understood the gestures of an artist formed by and speaking to a culture steeped in allegory. In the course of explicating Spenser's allegorical practice, however, Warton would deliver two distinct judgments: it was at times blasphemous in its free mingling of the sacred and the profane, and it was the supreme flowering of England's native poetic tradition, one that was eclipsed by a literary decadence linked to the school of Pope. How were Spenser's poetic achievements related to his poetic impieties? Was the eclipse of the imaginative sublime in any way connected to the ending of literary impieties? The *History* is the answer to these questions. And Warton's 1762 *Observations* thus marks the moment in which his successful address of one vocational dilemma—one involving a confrontation between the critic of taste and the avid reader—gave way to his extended involvement with another, one founded on the discovery that the nation's ecclesiastical and poetic histories seemed to have inversely coordinated epochs of consummation.

The *Observations* of 1762 was the central document in a broader mid-century reevaluation of Spenser that included Richard Hurd's *Letters on Chivalry and Romance* (1st ed., 1762). For Warton, his 1762 edition was also a prospectus addressed to the Republic of Letters, and, with this end in mind, it was a decided success. Most important, Hurd responded encouragingly to Warton's hint that he might undertake a "regular history" of English poetry. In addition to his direct encouragement, Hurd passed on William Warburton's approbation of Warton's plans, quickly secured from William Mason a copy of Pope's unpublished plan for a similar history, and later succeeded in getting Thomas Gray to send his sketch for the same project. By November 1762 the thirty-five-year-old Oxford Professor of Poetry had secured endorsements by important literary figures for what was understood to be an unprecedented project. The assistance of Hurd, Mason, and Warburton suggests that Warton managed to prepare a depoliticized field of reception for his intended work, at least among the clerical literati. All three were dedicated Whigs, and Hurd and Mason were Whigs proud of their allegiance to Cambridge intellectual traditions. This support was another sign of the waning of the paradigm in which a theopolitically subversive Oxford was set against a pro-Hanoverian Cambridge.[17] In this sense, the encouragement Warton received from the Warburtonians was related to Warburton's later recognition that it had been a clumsy mistake in 1765 to charge Lowth, and Oxford generally, with crypto-Jacobitism.[18]

Between the announcement of his plans for the *History* and the appearance of its first volume twelve years later, one of Warton's intervening labors—an edition of Theocritus (2 vols., 1770)—appeared, and Warton's search for an authorized dedicatee is a revealing commentary on how Warton and others thought of his career in 1770. Lowth was Warton's first choice, and Lowth granted permission for the dedication, but he advised Warton to seek out a more useful patron, suggesting first William Pitt, the Earl of Chatham, and then Lord North, the actual dedicatee in the end. All three candidates were obviously licensed by the context of Oxford—where Pitt and North had attended Warton's Trinity College—but Warton's initial choice indicated his desire to shore up a literary genealogy for himself as a successor to the Oxford Chair of Poetry (*CTW* 261–64, 272, 276–78). With Lowth as his dedicatee, Warton would also affirm his relationship with the Wykemist tradition of Winchester. For though Thomas had been schooled at home as a matter of economy, he was an honorary Wykemist by virtue of his close connections to his brother, who had attended Winchester College and spent most of his subsequent career in and around the cathedral. Winchester too was the setting for Lowth and Joseph Warton to come to know each other in the late 1750s when Lowth was archdeacon and Warton was second headmaster there. And Thomas Warton's preaching in the 1750s bore Lowthian traces thanks to that relationship. In 1755 Thomas had preached in Christ Church Cathedral his sermon "On Divine Wisdom as shown in the spread of the Gospel," and a major source was his brother's report of a sermon by Lowth on the world's transformation by "Commerce and Printing." Ascribing to a pious rationalism and the belief that "with true knowledge true religion ever resides" (*CTW* 50), the Wartons and Lowth sought to reconcile powerful attractions to versions of the literary past—both the Hebraic and the English—with a modernist discourse. And, as Thomas knew, Lowth had also encouraged Joseph to complete his commentary on Pope "with alacrity and expedition." Writing to Joseph in April 1759, Lowth assured him that such a project was fully compatible with his ecclesiastical station, as it was likely to raise Warton's own "personal credit" as well as "the reputation of the place from whence it comes" (qtd. in Wooll 261). As he devoted his mature years at Oxford to the composition of a new kind of national literary history, Thomas Warton was in a position to know that his own diocesan bishop believed that an honorable literary distinction could only enhance a clergyman's credit. When the first volume of Warton's *History* appeared, he took the time to recognize Lowth's primary work of medieval history, his *Life of William Wykeham,* as coming from "the hand of a master" (1.255).

On its appearance in March 1774, the first volume of Warton's *History* announced itself to be, like the *Observations,* an inquiry into enlightenment, as it promises to trace "the transitions from barbarism to civility" (i) and to "pursue the progress of our national poetry, from a rude origin and obscure beginnings, to its perfection in a polished age" (ii). Warton further embraces a historiography of enlightenment when he attributes a curiosity about the past to his age's "refinement" and the "present improvements in knowledge" (i). Nevertheless, the dominant spirit of Warton's project was a variety of historicism capable of valuing the past on its own terms; and Warton's most important discussion in his preface focuses on his proposed method, one he contrasts with the earlier plans of Pope and Gray. Warton represents these plans as ingenious, but he also represents them as inimical to his current project. The schemes of Pope and Gray

> sacrificed much useful intelligence to the observance of arrangement; and in the place of satisfaction which results from clearness and a fulness of information, seemed only to substitute the merit of disposition, and the praise of contrivance. The constraint imposed by a mechanical attention to this distribution, appeared to me to destroy the free exertion of research with which such a history ought to be executed, and not easily reconcilable with that complication, variety, and extent of materials, which it ought to comprehend. (v)

With the phrase "free exertion of research," we witness an important development of what appeared in the *Observations* as anxieties at being inducted into the Temple of Dullness. In the early 1760s Warton had acknowledged that all his reading could make him the sport of wits, and he had to defend "the business of criticism" as he proposed to conduct it (*Observations* 2.269). In the 1770s the leering wits are not granted the favor of an appearance, and all that reading is given a more exalted name, "research." Valuing intellectual activity over the contrived illustration of received values, Warton's methodological apology explains the character of his text and insists that literary history must engage in formal ways with the recoverable experiences of past readers and writers.

The preface then gives way to two dissertations, "Of the Origin of Romantic Fiction in Europe" and "On the Introduction of Learning into England," that are intended "to establish certain fundamental principles to which frequent appeals might occasionally be made, and to clear the way for various observations arising in the course of my future enquiries" (viii).[19] Starting with the origins of romance was an important substantiation of Warton's basic revision of literary values, his insistence that an appreciation of the native tradition required a fluency in the vernacular romances of Europe; and the most important benefit of a study of romance was a right appreciation of Spenser. So while the first sentence of the preface offers to trace a progressive development, the first dissertation initiates a regressive search for the creative act that will culminate in Spenser. Warton's ultimate answer to the question whence the origin of romance fiction is less important than his assertion that romance is the key to English poetry, and in this conviction the *History* keeps the faith with "An Essay on Romantic Poetry." But the quest for romantic origins now led to a full-scale reevaluation of barbarism itself, achieved through the abandonment of the critical prejudices identified in the preface. "Innumerable and very fundamental errors have crept into our reasonings and systems about savage life," Warton writes, "resulting merely from those strong and undistinguishing notions of barbarism, which our prejudices have hastily formed concerning the character of all rude nations" (d2).[20] Between the composition of the *Observations* and the publication of the first volume of the *History,* Warton's research had allowed him to become one of the first qualified skeptics of a model of history that credited a sudden revival of learning to the sixteenth century. "On the Introduction of Learning into England" thus describes an acquaintance with the classics, mostly within clerical culture, that took place in the tenth through the fourteenth centuries. This prior revival, however, is a false dawn, one featuring an adeptness with the letter but not the spirit of the classics. It was the age of scholasticism, when "visionary theologians never explained or illustrated any scriptural topic: on the contrary, they perverted the simplest expressions of the sacred text, and embarrassed the most evident truths of the gospel by laboured distinctions and unintelligible solutions." The authors of the age were capable of "attempts in elegant literature," but they ended up using their Latin to frame "the flimsy labyrinths of casuistry." Several centuries in advance of the Reformers, the ecclesiastical encounter with classics at this earlier period was "premature." What is most important and innovative about this sketch is the enthusiastic appreciation for the poetic compensation found in the gloom:

> The habits of superstition and ignorance were as yet too powerful for a reformation.... But perhaps inventive poetry lost nothing by this relapse. Had classical taste and judgment been now established, imagination would have suffered, and too early a check would have been given to the beautiful extravagancies of romantic fabling. In a word, truth and reason would have chased before their time those spectres of illusive fancy, so pleasing to the imagination, which delight to hover in the gloom of ignorance and superstition, and which form so considerable a part of the succeeding centuries. (k2)

The preface and the two dissertations establish the thematic circumference of the *History* as a whole. Its primary public allegiance was to an enlightenment narrative endorsing a philologically based religious humanism that had inspired the Protestant Reformation. But by wanting to know something about the history of learning and the history of romance at the same time, Warton found himself documenting the imaginative losses that came with gains of another kind. Having begun his *History* this way, Warton had made it nearly impossible to move beyond the historical period in which the habits of religious superstition continued to flow in poetic practice. A narrative that had intended to reach the age of Addison would reach another premature climax in the second volume of 1778, which concludes (yet again) with two dialectically related chapters on a revival of learning (including the reformation of religion) and the cultural prerequisites for the last great age for romance, the age of Elizabeth (2.407–63). Arriving at the period when learning and true religion had been revived according to the standard Protestant chronology, Warton puts the moment in a striking poetical perspective:

> Setting aside the consideration of the more solid advantages, which are obvious, and not the distinct object of our contemplation at present, the lover of true poetry will ask, what have we gained by this revolution? It may be answered, much good sense, good taste, and good criticism. But in the meantime, we have lost a set of manners, and a system of machinery more suitable to the purposes of poetry.... We have parted with the extravagancies that are above propriety, with incredibilities that are more acceptable than truth, and with fictions more valuable than reality. (2.463)

Preparing to reach the age of the Reformers proper, Warton pauses again to describe the poetic losses that accompanied real reformation.

The *History* was inspired by a desire to understand Spenser's greatness in a national narrative founded on a renewed appreciation for romance, and this mode of inspiration was reaffirmed at its publication when Warton began with a dissertation on romance that points toward and literally concludes with (the word) "Spenser" (12). Nevertheless, the *History* would slowly reveal its incapacity to treat Spenser at length, with the third volume of 1782 ending with an overview of poetry in the reign of Elizabeth but not including any sustained discussion of her pensioned laureate. And the surviving printed portion of the unpublished fourth volume of the *History* is more prologue. In the end, the *History* had become a serial prelude to a work first published in 1754, the *Observations,* a study of Spenser's similarly massive but inconclusive epic. But where the earlier work led to a surprising condemnation of Spenser's habits of impiety, the mature version rhetorically emphasized the poetic price exacted by a tale of enlightenment. Initially promising a story of progress, Warton's project had become, in part, a narrative of decline. What had begun as an investigation into the progress of poetry had become an intermittent elegy for the poetry that was lost to rational inquiry.

Warton's original intention was to ratify with history a literary aesthetic that was the source of a contemporary poetic revival. That project entered the precincts of church history somewhat inadvertently and would proceed at times nervously. Instead of completing the *History,* Warton would devote his energies in the 1770s and '80s to poetry and poetic collections that creatively restated his impasse. Most obviously Warton valorized an imaginative life that seemed to coexist with religious superstitions in *Verses on Sir Joshua Reynold's Painted Window at New College, Oxford* (1782), a poem that features an observer's disavowal of his allegiances to the dim, chaotic, unordered Gothic past in favor of a literally enlightened, classically proportioned future. With such poetry, Warton provided an influential model for the first-person lyric in which the speaker's prudential reclamation of better aesthetic sense is suggestively coordinated with poetic loss. Doing much to institutionalize a poetry skilled in recantation, the poem became an essential model for works such as Samuel Taylor Coleridge's "The Eolian Harp" (first published in 1796), which featured a poetic voice swearing off forms of imaginative license or power in favor of creative codes and situations deemed more reasonable, pious, or useful.

Warton's greatest poetic legacy, however, was his initiation of the sonnet revival of his age.[21] And before the publication of the *Verses,* several of Warton's sonnets, first published in *Poems: A New Edition, with Addi-*

tions (1777; 3rd ed., 1779), addressed what had become Warton's abiding creative topics: the poetic rewards offered to the historical student and the historical potential of poetry. In the sonnets too Warton was ready to turn his status as a reader into his chief characteristic as a writer. "Written in a Blank Leaf in Dugdale's Monasticon" is a vindication of the compilation of William Dugdale's history of England's fallen abbeys:

> Deem not, devoid of elegance, the sage,
>   By Fancy's genuine feelings unbeguil'd,
>   Of painful Pedantry the poring child;
>   Who turns, of these proud domes, th' historic page,
> Now sunk by Time, and Henry's fiercer rage.
>   Thinkst thou the warbling Muses never smil'd
>   On his lone hours?   (*Poems* 77; lines 1–7)

It is characteristic of Warton that what is being celebrated in this poem is both the making of Dugdale's book and the reading of it, the "lone hours" spent in writing or reading.[22] Moreover, the reading of the book has seamlessly given way to a qualified scene of writing, one memorialized by a text inscribed by a writer posing as a reader. Concluding the sonnet with an insistent declaration—"Nor rough, nor barren, are the winding ways / Of hoar Antiquity, but strown with flowers" (lines 13–14)—Warton also makes the final word depart from the rhyme scheme of the sestet (where it is linked to "explores" and "stores") in favor of echoing those same "lone hours" that stand out in the full stop in the midst of line 7. But for those who have long been closeted with old books, the Middle English "floures" and "flours"—words Warton had frequently transcribed in his *History*—can be present in an unwritten (or blank) manner to maintain the rhyme scheme in a fashion. For having explored, in lonely hours, poetic stores, Warton is ready to see and hear, perhaps even smell, flowers and floures.[23] A poem that begins with the isolated pedant ends with an invitation to experience the renewal of spring found on the leaves of old books and in the opening of Chaucer's Prologue to the *Canterbury Tales*:

> When that Aprill with his shours sote,
> The drought of March had pierced to the rote,
> And bathed every vaine in suche lycour,
> Of which vertue engendred is the flour.   (lines 1–4)

If Dugdale composed his monumental text in response to the material dissolution of the seats of religious culture, if he had hoped to preserve in a book what politics and fate had pulled down, this poem insists on carrying on the same antiquarian tradition. To write a sonnet on a "Blank Leaf" was to insert poetry—one of rigorous discipline—into the "historic page" as well as to assert that the historical critic had a poetically rewarding vocation.

"Written in a Blank Leaf" is about monumental loss, the textual and poetic gestures inspired by that loss, and the imaginative compensations available to devoted readers. "Written at Stonehenge," which Warton implicitly paired with it, is about the mystery of the erection of a great structure, one, like a monastery, where the dead might be buried and blessed, the gods worshipped, and learning transmitted. And while the Dugdale sonnet is about a conversion essential to Warton's career, the conversion of the pedantic to the poetic, "Written at Stonehenge" is about writing the history of something—"Thou noblest monument of Albion's isle!" (line 1)—in a manner that leaves the reader unbound by any single account:

> Whether by Merlin's aid, from Scythia's shore,
> To Amber's fatal plain Pendragon bore,
> Huge frame of giant-hands, the mighty pile,
> T' entomb his Britons slain by Hengist's guile:
> Or Druid priests, sprinkled with human gore,
> Taught mid thy massy maze their mystic lore:
> Or Danish chiefs, enrich'd with savage spoil,
> To Victory's idol vast, and unhewn shrine,
> Rear'd the rude heap: or, in thy hallow'd round,
> Repose the kings of Brutus' genuine line;
> Or here those kings in solemn state were crown'd:
> Studious to trace thy wond'rous origine,
> We muse on many an ancient tale renow'd. (*Poems* 78; lines 2–14)

A catalogue or collection, an anthology even, of originary accounts with no attempt to adjudicate between them, the sonnet is a studious reader's storehouse that recalls Walter Scott's appreciative but also critical description of the *History of English Poetry*: it was "an immense common-place book of memoirs to serve for such a history" ("Ellis's" [1804] 153).

Both sonnets are about wide reading in their own way, and they remind us of the full extent to which Warton made this brand of reading essential to his most distinguished creative and critical work. The critical possibilities of old books were similarly reaffirmed in Warton's edition of the shorter poems of Milton, *Poems upon Several Occasions* (1st ed., 1785; 2nd ed., 1791), a work that has been cited as an exemplary instance of the age's invention of the scholarly edition as it survives today (Walsh 200). In some ways the edition was an extension of Warton's *Observations* on Spenser, being a reminder that "when Milton wrote these poems, many traditionary superstitions, not yet worn out in the popular belief, adhered to the poetry of the times. Romances and fabulous narratives were still in fashion, and not yet driven away by puritans and usurpers" (xx). As with Spenser, the key to appreciating Milton's early (and less puritanical) poetry was a familiarity with "coeval books." And Warton thus took issue with Thomas Newton's (then definitive) editions of *Paradise Lost* because the editor "was unacquainted with the treasures of the Gothic library. From his more solid and rational studies, he never deviated into this idle track of reading" (xxi).

Warton's edition of Milton was also a reply to the national literary history collectively included in Samuel Johnson's *Lives of the Poets* (1779–81). In private condemning Johnson as "a specious and popular writer, without taste," Warton declared his intentions "to bring forward every piece of Milton" that had been "depretiated" (*CTW* 518). Warton no more than Johnson admired Milton's anti-episcopacy and republicanism, but rather than placing *Paradise Lost* at the center of Milton's canon, as Johnson did, Warton used his edition to preserve the Milton untouched by "the deplorable polemics of puritanism" (xi). Insisting that Milton could be "reckoned an old English poet" (xxi), Warton also implied that all great English poets now had at their disposal the resources to contribute to the more authentic national tradition. In his note to the lines that culminate with the speaker dissolving "into extasies" in "Il Penseroso" (155–66), Warton predicted (without knowing it) a fair amount of his nation's future preference for the Gothic, both in its literary manifestations and in the coming architectural revival. Reminding readers that Milton had been educated at Saint Paul's school in the days when the old cathedral yet stood, Warton attributed the speaker's desire "to walk the studious cloysters pale, / And love the high embowed roof" to the fact that Milton had been "impressed with an early reverence for the solemnities of the antient ecclesiastical architecture, its vaults, shrines, iles, pillars, and painted glass, rendered yet more aweful by the accompaniment of the choral services" (90). Imagining the nation's Puritan bard perpetually enthralled by such services is one way to acknowledge the ensuing century's fundamental cultural inconsistency: the contemporaneous vitality of evangelical and Catholic revivals.

Ministers, Minstrels, and Redeeming Collection

A collector of outdated and neglected poetry, Thomas Percy has nevertheless long been hailed for his influence over innovative, trend-setting poets. Before studies of that influence were composed from within the twentieth-century academy (K. Sutherland), the poets themselves would acknowledge extravagant debts to the editor of the *Reliques of Ancient English Poetry* (1st ed., 1765), as when William Wordsworth, in 1815, insisted that English poetry had "been absolutely redeemed" by him (3.78). With the scope of Percy's influence uncontested, scholarly interest shifted in the late twentieth century to some form of the following question: Given the fact that Percy had much in common with James Macpherson and Thomas Chatterton, two other contemporary exploiters of the literary past, why did the editor of the *Reliques* earn such an important place in the nation's cultural history, while Macpherson and Chatterton were convicted of the literary crime of forgery?

This question has been raised and answered mostly in response to three critical dispositions: (1) a deconstructive approach to authorship that is prone to elide the distinction between licit literary activity and creative forgery; (2) a historical interest in print culture that sets aside the moral judgments that distinguish literary heroes and rogues in favor of studying how all authors sought status and remuneration through the press; and (3) a general devolution of metropolitan power in modern English literary history that has made Scottish, Irish, Welsh, and provincial (e.g., Bristoweian) elements essential components in a revisionist understanding of what now goes for a *British* literary history.[24] All of these approaches have combined to allow us to think about the relevance of Percy, Macpherson, and Chatterton—at its collective peak in the 1770s through the '90s—in a historical context that is defined by an innovative modernity.[25] My aim in the conclusion to this chapter is to highlight one aspect of the reopened Percy-Macpherson question that has gone largely untouched. With the exception of Richard Sher's suggestive work on Percy and the Ossian controversy (1991), literary history has forgotten how Percy and Macpherson were agents for and subjects of influential religious discourse. Percy and Macpherson have frequently been assembled under the rubric of *Faking Literature* (to borrow the title of K. K. Ruthven's useful study), but not enough attention has been devoted to understanding how the age's debates about literary authenticity were often about religious vocations past and present. As we shall see, some of the most important and consequential claims made by Percy and Macpherson were about imaginative power's capacity to be expressed in an ecclesiastical context: their fates in conventional literary history were determined by the distinctive ways in which they, their adversaries, and their collaborators involved the ambitions of their poetry collections with religious functionaries.

The first son of a prosperous grocer, Percy was born in 1729 in the Shropshire town of Bridgnorth. In 1746 he matriculated at Christ Church, Oxford, having won a scholarship that became important following a reversal in his father's fortunes. Planning a clerical career, Percy took his BA in

1750, remained in residence at Oxford, was ordained deacon in 1751, and took up his first curacies in parishes not far from his birthplace. In 1753 he was ordained priest, took his MA, and received the college living of Easton Maudit in Northamptonshire. Luckily for Percy, the lord of the manor was George Augustus Yelverton, Earl of Sussex, Master of the Bedchamber to the Prince of Wales, the future George III. From Sussex in 1756, Percy received his second living, the rectorship of Wilby; and at the same time he was made the earl's domestic chaplain, which called for Percy to reside in London during the parliamentary season. The earl died in 1758, but the successor to the title remained a loyal patron, and by 1759 Percy was in a position to marry Anne Gutterage. That same year Percy negotiated the first of many literary contracts with the booksellers Robert and James Dodsley. One of these would lead to the publication, in 1765, of the *Reliques,* which was dedicated to Elizabeth Percy, Countess of Northumberland and wife to Hugh Percy, Earl of Northumberland. The dedication was a successful bid for patronage, which included in 1765 a tutorship to young Algernon Percy, followed by Percy's appointment as the family's domestic chaplain. In 1766 George III raised the noble Percys to a dukedom, and their chaplain published *A Key to the New Testament,* a work, like the *Reliques,* that would reach its fourth edition by the 1790s. In 1767 the duke and the duchess stood as godparents to Percy's fourth child, and Anne Percy became wet-nurse to Prince Edward, a form of royal service that earned her an annual pension of £100. In 1769 Percy became a King's Chaplain in Ordinary, followed by the award of a Doctor of Divinity degree from Cambridge. The years 1770 and 1771 saw, respectively, the appearance of *Northern Antiquities,* Percy's translation of a work in French, and *The Hermit of Warkworth,* an imitation antique ballad that went into three editions in its first twelve months.[26] Percy's next major preferment waited until 1778, when he became dean of Carlisle. In 1782 he resigned all English livings and appointments to become bishop of the Irish see of Dromore, which he ruled until his death in 1811.

It is for the *Reliques* that Percy is now remembered, but Percy himself did not always clearly know what the *Reliques* were going to be. And while the project always had a direct relationship with his famous Folio MS, Percy's understanding of how he ought to exploit this resource was evolving (fig. 4). To understand the heterogeneity of Percy's motivations and accomplishments as a literary historian, it is best to recall that he began his publishing career as the editor of a Chinese "novel." In 1758 he had become intrigued by a manuscript of a seventeenth-century Chinese narrative that had been partially translated into a mixture of English and Portuguese. Percy began to touch up the English portions of the manuscript and to translate the Portuguese. *Hau Kiou Choaan; or, The Pleasing History* (4 vols., 1761) was no great success, but it contained a substantial supplementary collection, "Fragments of Chinese Poetry: With a Dissertation" (4.197–256), in which Percy made the first of several public statements about the relation of his work to that of James Macpherson, whose *Fragments of Ancient Poetry, Collected in the Highlands of Scotland, and Translated from the Gaelic or Erse Language* had first appeared in an Edinburgh edition in June 1760. In the "Dissertation" accompanying his Chinese fragments, Percy aligned his literary project with the "extremely literal" translation of "ancient Scottish poetry," as Macpherson's *Fragments* had been described in its preface (6). "The first artless productions of any people will be translated with greater ease and advantage," Percy wrote,

> than those of a nation that is more civilized and refined; as in the one, we expect only the voice of sentiment; in the other the language of study and reflection: in the one the pure effusions of nature; in the other the studied refinements of art. To be sensible of this, we need only compare the literal versions of a psalm of David, and an Ode of Horace: the former will still retain much of the majestic simplicity, which it possesses in the Hebrew: while the latter will be stripped of all those little nameless elegances and graces, which charm us so in the original. This will also inform us, why a late translation of some Erse Fragments appeared so striking and poetical, whereas the most sprightly French song, or the sublimest Grecian ode in a literal prose version, would have been neglected. (199–200)

Implicit too in this definition of a poetry that cannot lose much in translation was a cultural simplicity that precluded the development of complicated religious rites and institutions. Such "poetry will be easy and intelligible to other nations" because it came from a time when religious devotion spoke a natural language, and "the artless beauties of a Lapland song, will have charms for every eye, while the studied allusions to their own customs and mythology, which so constantly recur in the Poetry of the Greeks and Romans, must to a plain unlearned Reader in another language appear intolerably tedious and insipid" (201).

As Nick Groom has pointed out (*Making* 85, n. 89), Percy's Chinese "Fragments" were modeled on the layout of Macpherson's *Fragments* which had been published in its first London edition (April 1761) by Percy's publisher, Robert Dodsley. Percy and Macpherson also shared as the major contemporary source on the sublimity of primitive poetry and its capacities for literal translation the *Praelectiones* of Robert Lowth, who did much of his publishing with the Dodsley brothers as well.[27] According to Lowth, because of the extraordinary simplicity of the Hebrew language,

Fig. 4. Thomas Percy, 1775, by William Dickinson (after Sir Joshua Reynolds). While Lowth led readers back to a text that had been partially obscured by time and transmission Percy redefined national literary origins in terms of his "ancient folio manuscript." (National Portrait Gallery, London)

"a poem translated literally from the Hebrew into the prose of any other language ... will still retain, even as far as relates to versification, much of its native dignity," while "in literal translations from the Greek or Latin," much was necessarily lost (1.71).

From the start, when he first read Macpherson's reported translations in the summer of 1760, Percy had a wide range of responses to the Ossianic phenomenon. But while 1765 marked the appearance of both *The Works of Ossian* and the *Reliques*, we should not confuse these books as rival entrants into the same race. Percy's rival publication with the Ossianic material that appeared from 1760 to 1765 was what he most often called his *Specimens of the Ancient Poetry of Different Nations*, a project that was intended at times to include literal translations of the ancient poetry being edited by Macpherson.[28] As Percy explained the project in 1762 to Evan

Evans, another clerical literary historian and author of *Some Specimens of the Poetry of the antient Welsh Bards* (1764), he had planned for some time to produce "such a work [that] might fill up two neat pocket volumes":

> Besides the *Erse Poetry:* the *Runic Poetry:* and some *Chinese Poetry* that was published last winter at the end of a book called *Hau Kiou choaan or the Pleasing History* 4 vol. Besides these I have procured a MS. translation of the celebrated *Tograi Carmen* from the Arabic: and have set a friend to translate *Solomon's Song* afresh from the Hebrew, chiefly with a view to the poetry. . . . Then I have myself gleaned up specimens of *East Indian Poetry: Peruvian Poetry: Lapland Poetry: Greenland Poetry:* and inclosed I send you one specimen of *Saxon Poetry.* (PL 5.31)

By this time Percy was close to finishing and had printed much of *Five Pieces of Runic Poetry: Translated from the Islandic Language,* a work that would appear in April 1763. Constituting the second installment of his *Specimens,* Percy's *Runic Poetry* now referred to Macpherson's work in a challenging way. Percy admitted his translations were "offered to the public" in part "owing to the success of the Erse fragments"; but while conceding that his translations could not compete with Macpherson's on aesthetic grounds, he also suggested Macpherson had either departed from the commitment to an "extremely literal" translation or done worse. "Till the Translator of those poems thinks proper to produce his originals," Percy wrote, "it is impossible to say whether they do not owe their superiority if not their whole existence entirely to himself" (34). What was most important about the *Runic Poetry* in terms of its influence over Percy's subsequent career was its combination of a deprecation directed at the poetry itself and the articulation of a vocationally grounded admiration for past poetic orders of men: "Poetry [in northern Europe] was once held there in the highest estimation. The invention of it was attributed to the gods, and ranked among the most valuable gifts conferred on mortals. Those that excelled in it, were distinguished by the first honours of the state: were constant attendants on their kings, and were often employed on the most important commissions" (28).

Two years after first telling Evans about his *Specimens,* Percy's Hebrew installment appeared as *The Song of Solomon, Newly Translated from the Original Hebrew: With a Commentary and Annotations* (1764), and this work became another lesson for Percy in the possibilities of addressing problems about authenticity and literary value by way of appeals to a vocational context. As Percy described his goals, he was attempting to rescue the text from the "obscurity and confusion" of former interpretations by establishing the historical and literal sense (*Song* v). While extravagant labor had been expended in pursuit of allegorical interpretations of the *Song,* expositors had come "to neglect that literal sense, which ought to be the basis of their discoveries." Percy's primary interest was in the text as ancient poetry, but he was not trying to challenge the orthodox tradition about its mystical nature, the fact that Christian exegetes had long read it as an allegory about Christ and his "spouse," the church. It was on this major point that Percy invoked Lowth, whom he credits with reconciling the text's status as primitive poetry and as revelation. "For that this fine Eastern pastoral was designed for a vehicle of religious truths," Percy writes, "is an opinion handed down from the earliest antiquity. That it MAY BE so, has been clearly proved by one of the best Critics of the age [a note identifies Lowth]: and that it IS so, may be strongly presumed not only from that ancient and universal opinion, but from its being preserved in a book, all whose other contents are of a divine religious nature." Because his historical interpretation of the text was ultimately dedicated to discovering "what sublime truths are concealed under it" (vi), he hoped he would be pardoned for any appearances of irreverence for "an inspired writer." His comments only applied to the poetry as it was "HUMANLY SPOKEN; relative only to Solomon's poetic powers, no way reflecting on his prophetic character" (vii).

While Percy's *Song of Solomon* was going through the press, his goals were complicated by the appearance of a new edition of Lowth's *Praelectiones* with notes by J. D. Michaelis (1763). Michaelis's first edition of Lowth's lectures came out in 1758, and in this form Michaelis's work seemed to be an aid in Percy's project of literal interpretation. Michaelis's new edition of Lowth, however, prompted Percy to add a postscript. Michaelis now "controverted the position, which is the basis of this whole work, viz. that the SONG OF SOLOMON is a nuptial poem" (99). More than that, Michaelis seemed "to controvert the received opinion of the poem's being a sacred Allegory, and is inclined to look no farther than the literal meaning." But even if Michaelis denied that the Song of Solomon was a sacred allegory, he still "allows it to be a production not unworthy the celestial Muse." According to Percy, Michaelis "thinks it was inserted in the great code of sacred and moral truths, to show that the chaste fervour of wedded love has the express approbation of the Deity, and to obviate the mistakes of such morose bigots, as hold conjugal love inconsistent with the love of God" (103). Perhaps the Song of Solomon did not describe the mystical marriage of Christ to His Church, but it could describe the propriety of a married clergy.[29] A specifically Protestant clerical ideal—one uniting pastor and pater familias—became a solution to a bind for the historical reader of the Song of Solomon.[30]

Even though Percy's collected *Specimens* never appeared, the work can be partially reconstructed by binding together three of Percy's pre-*Reliques* publications, the "Fragments of Chinese Poetry," the *Five Pieces of Runic Poetry,* and the *Song of Solomon.*[31] Like Macpherson's Ossian material, Percy's *Specimens* document a literary vogue for a new species of poetry that could lose nothing in translation, a kind that was liable to explain itself to modern readers. Both Macpherson and Percy sought to capitalize on a notion that the authentically primitive was, ironically, cosmopolitan. On this score, Macpherson was the most successful, with his works gaining popularity in French, German, and Italian versions. Regardless of the question of their antiquity, the poems of Ossian created a literary experience that was accessible to readers across national borders. Percy used similar ideas to explain how poetry from so many different nations could possibly belong together in the same collection. And unlike the first historically organized anthologies of British poetry made possible by the 1774 *Donaldson v. Beckett* ruling, these collections theoretically avoided the topic of literary influence. Macpherson initially had the idea of literary influence so far from his mind that he covered the margins of the first edition of the *Fragments* with parallels to the Authorized Version, Spenser, Milton, Homer, and Virgil, in order to demonstrate that the truly sublime was transhistorical. As the question of Macpherson's sources became controversial, the parallels would be read as impolitic self-exposures. But Macpherson was merely expressing his faith that others would read his book in the spirit he intended, one that made the topic of literary influence moot.

Percy's *Reliques,* in contrast with both his own *Specimens* and Macpherson's translations, was a detailed polemic about literary influence and cultural transmission. And while the contracts for the elements of the *Specimens* were essentially paying for the labor of a translator, the contract with Dodsley for the *Reliques* was about the value and ownership of Percy's MS, a document that referred to a variety of customs that called for learned explication.[32] According to Percy, the *Reliques* were primarily valuable for illustrating "many passages in our ancient English Poets," as he wrote to Thomas Warton the day after signing the contract for their publication (*PL* 3.3). When Percy first wrote to Warton in May 1761, he complimented Warton, as the author of the *Observations* (1754), for recognizing Spenser's use of Thomas Malory's *Morte Darthur,* but he suggested that his own literary research had gone a step further. Percy had discovered the source behind Spenser's source, and in this scheme "the Author of Mort. Arthur (however he came by them in French) only drew up a prose narrative of, and threw together into a regular story the Subject of a hundred Old

Ballads, which had been the delight of our Ancestors for many ages before" (*PL* 3.2). For Percy, in other words, the matter of Arthur first existed in a popular oral canon, one that was fluid while preserving the integrity of characters and situations.

Percy's "striking instance" of this theory is the Arthurian ballad "The Boy and the Mantle," which, according to Percy, confirms that both Spenser and Malory had been translating popular oral traditions into texts. Warton publicized Percy's theory in his second edition of the *Observations* (1762). But Warton produced a source for the source that Percy had put forward, declaring "this fiction is as manifestly taken from an old french piece entitled, *Le Court Mantel*" (1.55). By the time Percy published the *Reliques,* his argument had become bolder, as he presented "The Boy and the Mantle" (which had not "been borrowed from any other writer" [3.1]) directly as the source for Spenser's book 4, canto 5. And in the prefatory material to a modernized version of "The Boy and the Mantle," Percy responded to Warton's 1762 claim that this Arthurian episode was imported, saying "'tis most likely that all the old stories concerning K. Arthur are originally of British growth, and that what the French and other southern nations have of this kind were at first exported from this island" (3.314). Most literary scholars since Percy have, like Warton, insisted on a predominantly Continental origin of the matter of Arthur. But if Percy's attempt to present his Arthurian ballads as traces of England's first literary exports ultimately failed, his speculations about anonymous, oral traditions have been more favorably received. While authors such as Chaucer, Spenser, and Shakespeare were becoming what we today call institutionally canonized authors, Percy cast them as the heirs of a national, bardic line; they became modern artists belatedly reworking preliterary cultural traditions. Percy was writing the key chapter in a literary history that would allow culture to find its legitimacy in a common/communal source. Reconceiving literary authority at the moment of its invention, he made formidable authorial voices indebted to an oral canon. Warton had influentially insisted that scholars must familiarize themselves with the books that Spenser (and other past authors) actually read. And this proposition transformed great authors into readers, a reconfiguration of authorship that extended to the Bard Himself with the publication of Richard Farmer's *Essay on the Learning of Shakespeare* (1767). Percy collaborated with and was influenced by both Warton and Farmer, but he went a step further. In contrast to a purely textual account of literary culture, Percy accounted for the cultural production of literary texts.

Throughout all of this, Percy's essential resource was the order of the minstrels themselves, an exalted vocational paradigm. The argument of the *Reliques* was summed up by the opening sentences of Percy's "Preface" and the essay that immediately follows it, "An Essay on the Ancient English Minstrels." "The Reader is here presented," Percy writes, "with select remains of our ancient English Bards and Minstrels, an order of men who were once greatly respected by our ancestors, and contributed to soften the roughness of a martial and unlettered people by their songs and by their music" (1.ix). "An Essay on the Ancient English Minstrels" then established a more detailed historical relationship between the ancient poets and their heirs:

> The MINSTRELS seem to have been the genuine successors of the ancient Bards, who united the arts of Poetry and Music, and sung verses to the harp, of their own composing. It is well known what respect was shewn to their BARDS by the Britons: and no less was paid to northern SCALDS by most of the nations of the Gothic race. Our Saxon ancestors, as well as their brethren the ancient Danes, had been accustomed to hold men of this profession in the highest reverence. Their skill was considered as something divine, their persons were deemed sacred, their attendance was solicited by kings, and they were everywhere loaded with honours and rewards. (1.xv)

Percy's main claim is twofold. He argues that bardic and scaldic verse survived as popular ballads and that the ancient bards and scalds carried on their vocation, until the end of the reign of Elizabeth I, as the last of the "old Minstrels" (1.xxii). If the ancient English minstrel descended from bards and scalds, genuine minstrelsy descends to modern readers as popular ballads—though not all ballads are bardic relics. Percy's introductory prose distinguishes between "old Minstrel-ballads" and later, nonbardic poetry such as the anonymous verse which was printed in the many "Garlands" that started to appear during the reign of James I. These collections, according to Percy, did not contain old minstrelsy, which was by definition an oral form: "So long as the Minstrels subsisted, they seem never to have designed their rhymes for publication, and probably never committed them to writing themselves: what copies are preserved of them were taken down from their mouths" (1.xxii).[33]

The opening pages of the *Reliques* have the self-effacing gestures common for an introduction of the time, but Percy was making a bold argument. He claimed his oldest ballads were the remains of the old minstrelsy, a type of poetry sung by the successors of an ancient class of poets who served, by the estimate of their audience, a religious function. Percy's divine pretense drew upon classical and biblical sources about the sacred character of primal poets. But his insistence that this same rhetoric could be applied to English poetic history on a sweeping chronological scale was innovative. The claim, however, was soon challenged by the Reverend Samuel Pegge, a prolific antiquarian who denied that the ancient Saxons in particular revered as sacred an order of poets who sang verses of their own composition and played instruments. Essentially arguing that Percy was fusing Celtic, Danish, and Saxon history in order to suit his own purposes, Pegge read a paper at a meeting of the Society of Antiquaries in 1766 that carefully considered the "only two facts adduced, to establish the honour and respectable quality of the minstrels in the Ante-Norman times" (101). These were the suspiciously similar anecdotes about the Saxon King Alfred and the Danish King Anlaff, who were both reported to have disguised themselves as minstrels to reconnoiter opposing military camps. Neither king had disguised his national character; and thus the honor paid to minstrels must have traversed Saxon and Danish borders, confirming the fact, as Percy argued, that "the same mode of entertainment prevailed among both people, and that the Minstrel was a privileged character among both" (1.vvii). Effectively socializing the theory about the transnational nature of primitive poetry, Percy had his representative minstrels earning the rapt attention of audiences across cultural borders in times of war. Pegge, on the other hand, suggested that the stories themselves were apocryphal, with Anlaff's deeds likely based on the story about Alfred. Even admitting the events to have taken place as described, however, Pegge proceeded to turn Percy's context of veneration on its head. It was not a "sacredness" of character or a "mark of dignity," Pegge argued, that allowed these disguised poets a privilege of movement, but a far less exalted trade in pleasing idle men massed in camps: "for there never was an army in the world that was not attended with minstrels of various sorts," and "it was natural for this sort of men to follow a camp" (104–5). Thus Alfred most probably assumed "the character of a mimic, a dancer, a gesticulator, a bastleteur, or jack-pudding, who commonly made use of some instrument of music for the purpose of assembling and drawing people about them" (106).

The degradation of Percy's sacred profession was steep. In Percy's argument, the minstrels had privileges that exceeded regal ones. Pegge insisted that these same figures were merely afforded the privileges of "jester[s] and antick[s]" (106); and he suggestively linked them to prostitutes, another common profession of camp followers. In the second edition of the *Reliques* (1767), Percy carefully answered Pegge's arguments without directly acknowledging them, swelling the "Essay on the Ancient English Minstrels" to twenty pages (from some nine in 1765), and adding thirty-two notes, several of them miniature essays, that added another thirty-eight pages (B. Davis 155).³⁴ Percy now made it clear that his minstrels were medieval—or post-Conquest—figures, revising his first sentence to read: "The MINSTRELS were an order of men in the middle ages, who united the arts of poetry and music, and sung verses to the harp of their own composing." And where Pegge had tried to degrade this order's mission to physical antics, Percy sought to elevate gesture, emphasizing how the minstrels "accompanied their songs with mimicry and action" and "practised such various means of diverting as were much admired in those rude times, and supplied the want of more refined entertainments" (1767: 1.xix). On this issue Percy wisely conceded much, admitting that the term *minstrel* "was sometimes applied by our old writers to such as professed either music or singing separately, and perhaps to such as practised any of the sportive arts connected with these" (1767: 1.xlii). But Percy still insisted that there was an honored order of performers who "united the powers of melody, poem, and dance" (1767: 1.xli); and the process by which "the name of Minstrel [was] at last confined to the Musician only" was the history by which the revered profession fell into disgrace (1767: 1.xlii). Percy also made it much clearer that his minstrels were the successors to a Teutonic tradition. While he still referred to the ancient British (or Celtic) bards, the argument was now firmly directed at a Gothic (or Germanic) past and a reverence for poets that was epitomized, Percy claimed, "by none more than by our own Teutonic ancestors" (1767: 1.xix–xx). And in a new note, he absolves English minstrelsy of any Celtic debts, limiting his argument to tracing

> the Descent of the French and English Minstrels only from the itinerant oral Poets of their Gothic ancestors the Franks and Saxons, and from the Scalds of their Danish brethren in the North. For though the Bards of the ancient Gauls and Britons might seem to have a claim of being considered as their more immediate predecessors and instructors; yet these, who were Celtic nations, were ab origine so different a race of men from the others who were all of Gothic origin, that I think one cannot, in any degree, argue from the manners of the one to those of the other. (1767: 1.lxvi)³⁵

Most important of all, in the 1767 edition Percy used the church to remove minstrelsy from the proverbially immoral context of camp followers. In a long note on the various etymologies of minstrel and in scattered places through the expanded apparatus, Percy exploited a range of linguistic confusions regarding *minstrel, minister,* and *minster,* the last a medieval name for a monastery, a monastery church, or any important church (*OED*). According to Percy, it was not simply the case that these words resembled each other: the minstrel's sacred character was suggested by "the clerical appearance of the Minstrels, who from the middle ages downwards seem to have been distinguished by the Tonsure, which was one of the inferior marks of the clerical character." Percy's minstrels were fully incorporated into an ecclesiastical sphere, and "sometimes assisted at divine service." Citing an account of the enthronement of Archbishop Neville in the 1460s, Percy said that "Ministers seems to be used for Minstrels" in the direction, "'Then all the Chaplyns must say grace, and the Ministers do sing'" (1767: 1.xxxix–xl).

In addition to clericalizing the minstrels, Percy dexterously relied upon a tradition of clerical invective aimed at the practitioners of worldly musical entertainments. It was this tradition, after all, that "relate[d] many curious particulars concerning the profession and arts of the Minstrels" (1767: 1.xliii). Percy cited evidence of ecclesiastical animosity toward the minstrels, but in doing so he suggested that much of it originated in a theological severity recognizable—to moderate Protestant eyes—as a pejorative, Roman Catholic monasticism. "Notwithstanding this clerical appearance of the Minstrels," Percy wrote, "their sportive talents rendered them generally obnoxious to the more rigid Ecclesiastics, and to such of the religious orders as were of more severe discipline." Noting that it was a morose ecclesiastical paradigm that had abhorred minstrelsy, Percy also suggested that opposition between ecclesiastical orders and poetic orders—as recorded by the monks—was sometimes born in a rivalry for noble patronage. And thus the writings of rigid and hypocritically worldly clerical types "commonly abound with heavy complaints of the great encouragement shewn to these men [the minstrels] by the princes and nobles" (1767: 1.xl–xli).

From the broadest historical perspective, we can recognize Percy and Pegge as carrying on a tradition in which English ministers became the natural historians of the minstrels. Before Warton would document at length in his *History of English Poetry* how the English monasteries were not "the retreats of illiterate indolence" but rather "the only respectable seminaries of literature" (f2), Percy emphasized a theoretical and pragmatic collaboration between poetry and religion that was initially pagan (and pre-Christian) but also extended into medieval Catholicism and beyond as Percy produced the key source for England's redeeming poetic revival. Percy's minstrels stood out in 1767 as more complex characters. But he did not back down from the bold argument as it appeared in the first edition. If anything, he made the theological element stronger, adding as the threshold to his central vocational sentence—"Their skill was considered as something divine, their persons were deemed sacred, their attendance was solicited by kings, and they were everywhere loaded with honours and rewards"—the statement that the origin of the scaldic art "was attributed to Odin or Woden, the father of their Gods" (1767: 1.xx). Composing an ambitious literary genealogy, Percy linked his Folio MS to nothing less than ancient Teutonic theophany. He wrote a *mythos* of the cultural conservation of the *logos* that passed from Odin to ancient bards, from the bards to the medieval minstrels, and finally from the minstrels to the poetic relics themselves.

In their capacity to be revered and to be vehicles for entertainment (that was neither indecent nor immoral), Percy's revised minstrels reflected his status as an author who had given his time to "a parcel of OLD BALLADS" as he described it in the Preface to the first edition which continued to be printed in later editions. "To prepare it for the press," Percy wrote, "has been the amusement of now and then a vacant hour amid the leisure and retirement of rural life, and hath only served as a relaxation from graver studies"; and he hoped "he need not be ashamed of having bestowed some of his idle hours on the ancient literature of our own country, or in rescuing from oblivion some pieces (tho' but the amusements of our ancestors) which tend to place in a striking light, their taste, genius, sentiments, or manners" (1.xiv). Percy thus advertised his ability to edit poetry as an amusement and as a respite from more serious labors that were conscientiously carried out. And a clerical interest in native song was allied to a vocational ideal eager to distinguish itself from the celibate and ascetic one associated with Roman Catholicism. Just as there had been for the minstrels of old, there was an important link between entertainment and vocational duty. In the late eighteenth and early nineteenth centuries, with the value of clerical incomes steadily growing, the ideal parish priest became a professional version of the genteel Protestant father, a virile figure capable of presiding over a festal board and retiring to a drawing room where his daughters would display accomplishments on the piano.

Ideally too this drawing room was at a convenient distance from the father's study, a place where, in addition to the investigation of national antiquities, biblical studies were pursued. Constituting a graver task, such studies were not, however, cloistral in character. Percy's *Key to the New Testament* (1st ed., 1766), which roughly kept pace with the call for further editions of his *Reliques,* was a project that linked the labors of the study to a nation of Bible readers on the move. It also reflected Percy's interest in the material history of books in two very different ways. On the one hand, it emphasized the necessity of becoming fluent in how the various documents making up the New Testament came to be, giving, as its fuller title puts it, *an account of the several books, their contents, their authors, and of the times, places and occasions, on which they were respectively written.* But the *Key* was also produced with an eye to present bibliographic realities. Disclaiming any pretensions to critical originality, Percy advertised the fact that his small, duodecimo *Key* is "chiefly extracted from two eminent Writers," J. D. Michaelis and Nathaniel Lardner. The first's *Introductory Lectures to the Sacred Books of the New Testament* (1761) had appeared in an anonymous translation "published in one volume quarto," while Lardner, a Presbyterian minister, had released a second edition of *A History of the Apostles and Evangelists* the year before in "three Volumes 8vo." "But as their works are not of portable size," Percy had decided to "give a short abstract of their respective contents . . . reduced within a small compass for the pocket" (vi–vii). There is nothing heroic about Percy's project of cramming into a duodecimo the Protestant Enlightenment's commitment to a historical understanding of Scripture. But this type of labor was usefully applied elsewhere. Whether it be directed at the nation's minstrelsy or Scripture, Percy's work in his study was fundamentally related. In both cases, a pragmatic and commercial reality was linked to a prior context of inspiration now to be seen on an authenticated, printed page.

A significant vocational context also explains the addition of a note to the second edition of the *Reliques* that gave a tepid personal testimony to the authenticity of Macpherson's poems. In citing the past social status of the ancient British bards, Percy noted that "no pieces of their poetry have been translated, unless their claim may be allowed to those beautiful pieces of Erse Poesy, which were lately given to the world in an English dress by Mr. Mac-Pherson: Several fragments of which the editor of this book has heard sung in the original language, and translated vivâ voce, by a native of the Highlands, who had, at the time, no opportunity of consulting Mr. Macpherson's book" (1767: 1.xlv). Despite Percy's earlier statements of doubt surrounding Macpherson's works, he had been persuaded by his fellow clergyman Hugh Blair to add this note following a visit to Edinburgh in October of 1765. Percy had traveled there as the chaperone of Algernon Percy, son of the dedicatee of the *Reliques,* who was attending the University of Edinburgh and boarding with Blair, already well known for his lectures as Professor of Rhetoric and Belles Lettres. With these professional and personal ties binding Percy (domestic chaplain to the noble Percys) and Blair (the major promoter of Macpherson), it had become almost impossible for Percy not to appear cautiously receptive to the general claims made in Blair's *Critical Dissertation on the Poems of Ossian,* which had just appeared in its third edition as part of the 1765 *Works of Ossian.*[36] Percy's addition of the note was an act of compromised solidarity with the idea of honorable clerical orders. But the note and its subsequent erasure in the third edition of 1775 would eventually only call attention to a fundamental difference separating the editorial labors of Percy and Macpherson. Percy's *Reliques* and all of Macpherson's Ossianic publications were produced by a similar vocational desire to define and describe a formerly prevalent kind of authorship. But where Percy repeatedly used religious vocations to authenticate his publications and the time he spent on them, Macpherson—despite his essential relationship with Scotland's clerical literati—had come to rely on a priestly void as the best proof for his claims about antiquity.

From the start, Macpherson's promoters were tempting readers to think that the extreme antiquity of Ossian's poetry was revealed by a religious absence, beginning with an explicitly Christian one described in *Fragments of Ancient Poetry* (1760). It was this void that John McGowan stressed when he, on 21 June 1760, sent a copy of the *Fragments* to William Shenstone, one of Percy's literary confidants. Sending off what was one of the first printed copies of the book to reach England, McGowan suggested that

> perhaps their date may reach back beyond the time of Christianity being preached in our Islands, Hence it will follow, that our Ancestors were rising by surprizing efforts to catch the fairest flowers of Parnassus, while the polite Regions of Europe resounded with Polemick Theology & Monkish nonsense, this becomes the more probable, when we reflect, that scarce any trace of Xtianity is to be found in their pieces, & no trace of the names that prevailed after the Ninth Century, instead of which the names appear entirely pagan. (qtd. in M. Smith 153)

As Blair had put it in the preface to the *Fragments,* the argument for their "most remote antiquity" was based on their style, their silence on the clan system, and the "remarkable" fact that "there are found in them no allusions to the Christian religion or worship; indeed, few traces of religion of any kind."[37] "One circumstance seems to prove them to be coeval with the very infancy of Christianity," Blair went on, bringing the poems back to the start of the third century: "In a fragment of the same poems, which the translator has seen, a Culdee or Monk is represented as desirous to take down in writing from the mouth of Oscian . . . his warlike atchievments and those of his family. But Oscian treats the monk and his religion with disdain, telling him, that the deeds of such great men were subjects too high to be recorded by him or any of his religion: A full proof that Christianity was not as yet established in the country" (5). With the publication of *Fingal* in December 1761 (dated 1762), it became clear that Macpherson's claim to extreme antiquity would rest on a history of two British priesthoods. The Ossianic scene evolved into a historical epoch bordered by the fall of the Druids and the subsequent rise of the Christian Culdees. And the salient conflict was not simply one between oral poets and religious figures skilled in letters. It was a conflict between Irish and Scottish canons of Ossianic verse (O'Halloran; Kidd 229–32; Trumpener 4).

The contested antiquity of Macpherson's translations centered on a Hiberno-Scottish debate about the origins and homeland of the true Gael in the British Isles. A tradition of Irish scholarship insisted that Highland Gaelic culture was the trace of past Irish conquest. But the Scots held that the Irish had never conquered Scotland, and that the monuments of Irish traditional culture were degraded versions of Scottish originals. As Macpherson would explain in his preface to *Fingal,* Irish bards regularly attributed their poems to the older and Scottish Ossian in a bid for their own authority. With Irish bards singing songs "by" Ossian that featured the exploits of Fingal in Ireland, the tradition grew up that Fingal was Irish rather than "of the ancient Caledonians." At issue was not an anachronistic geographical question ("Did Ossian come from Ireland or Scotland?"), for both Irish and Scottish historians agreed that the ancient Celtic territory spanned the Irish Sea, and that in the days of Fingal, as Macpherson put it, the Caledonians and the Irish were "almost the same people" (37). The question, rather, was one about the present location of the purest—and thus oldest—versions of Ossianic song.

For Macpherson, who had recovered the bulk of his material in the Highlands on his well-advertised trip in August of 1760, the clearest sign of the antiquity of his poems was their near total silence about Christianity. And the belatedness of similar Irish material was disclosed by its frequent depiction of Saint Patrick and other hints of ecclesiastical history. Besides being born in England, Patrick was a Roman citizen, a "South Briton" in Macpherson's terminology, and he could not play a prominent role in the epics of those Caledonians who always managed to stay "beyond the pale of empire" (37). By insisting that the purely preserved epics were to be found in the Scottish Highlands, Macpherson had to define the historical Ossian as a figure not only predating Patrick's mission to Ireland, which took place in the mid-fifth century; he had to make Ossian precede the first Christian missions to Caledonia, dated to the early fourth century. And since Ossian sang nostalgically of the deeds of his father, Fingal, and others before him, it was a matter of course that Ossian and the history he told were from the second and third centuries. Presented as Scottish originals distinguished from later Irish rivals, Macpherson's poems had to become some fourteen hundred years old. Macpherson struck the pose of dealing with the Hiberno-Scottish debate in short scope and alerted readers to a fuller treatment in a forthcoming work, what would appear in

1768 as *Critical Dissertations on the Origin, Antiquities, Language, Government, Manners and Religion of the Ancient Caledonians,* the author (John Macpherson) being none other than the father of the highland singer Percy had heard in 1765. But *Fingal* brought a great deal of attention and replies from Irish historians, and Macpherson in the introduction to *Temora* spent a good deal of time explaining again how St. Patrick can only appear in spurious or corrupted Ossianic poetry.

In a dissertation concerning the antiquity of the poems prefixed to *Fingal,* Macpherson also turns to a pre-Christian Caledonian priesthood in order to round off the historical period that was illuminated by authentic Ossianic poetry. Following standard classical sources on the Celts, Macpherson describes the ancient Caledonians as a society ruled by "a mixture of aristocracy and monarchy" and Druids. Moving beyond this generalization, however, Macpherson made his Druids into priestly usurpers of political power: "The esteem of the populace soon increased into a veneration for the order; which a cunning and ambitious tribe of men, took care to improve, to such a degree, that they, in a manner, ingrossed the management of civil, as well as religious, matters" (44).[38] From this position of supreme power, Macpherson noted a decline "in the beginning of the second century" (45). The Druids had become estranged from the lay hierarchy as a result of the wars of the Caledonians against the Romans, a social stress that prevented the nobility from frequently initiating themselves into the priestly caste. This produced a wider rupture between the martially responsible aristocracy and the priesthood, which had held "the extraordinary privilege" of appointing in times of danger a "temporary king, or Vergobretus" who was to "lay down his office at the end of the war." When the estranged order of Druids sent a delegation ordering one such Vergobretus to yield his office, that chief magistrate—Trathal, the grandfather of Fingal—refused and thereby caused a "civil war" that "ended in almost the total extinction of the religious order of the Druids." Those who survived retired to their groves and caves, where they more slowly dissipated into obscurity (45). Macpherson then makes "an inferior order" of the Druids, the bards, responsible for preserving the ancient Caledonian poems. For even though the wars fought by Fingal's grandfather eradicated the Druids, the chiefs realized they needed the bards to keep their names alive. As the surviving "disciples of the Druids, [who had] had their minds opened, and their ideas enlarged, by being initiated in the learning of that celebrated order," Macpherson's bards are a defrocked priesthood devoting the remnants of druidical skills to the celebration of heroic patrons (48). A precise historical setting for Ossianic culture had thus been constructed, one summed up in Blair's

Critical Dissertation: "The Druidical superstition was, in the days of Ossian, on the point of its final extinction; and for particular reasons, odious to the family of Fingal; whilst the Christian faith was not yet established" (Macpherson 355).

In *Temora, An Ancient Epic Poem in Eight Books* (1763), which appeared soon after the first edition of Blair's *Dissertation,* Macpherson included "A Specimen of the Original of Temora. Book Seventh." But the publication did little to assuage Macpherson's critics. If he could produce this "original," why not publish all of the recovered corpus so that the republic of letters could study his translation in detail? Moreover, when Macpherson admitted that he had not always followed "the erroneous orthography of the bards" (330), he created a graphic image of himself correcting ancient manuscripts; the bad spelling of the bards was the writing on the wall that Macpherson had deemed it impossible to fall back onto a defense based on the purely oral preservation of the poems.[39] That matters only got worse following the publication of the "originals" was the view of Blair's friend and countryman David Hume, who was concerned that Blair's focus on aesthetic vindication would be unpersuasive to posterity. What the poems needed were "testimonies," not "arguments" (D. Hume 1.399), and for these Hume urged Blair to turn to his "connexions among [his] brethren of the clergy":

> You may easily learn the names of all ministers of that country [i.e., the Highlands], who understand the language of it. You may write to them, expressing the doubts that have arisen, and desiring them to send for such of the bards as remain, and make them rehearse their ancient poems. Let the clergymen have the translations in their hands, and let them write back to you, and inform you, that they heard such a one (naming him) living in such a place, rehearse the original of such a passage, from such a page to such a page of the English translations, which appeared exact and faithful. (1.400)

The result was an appendix to the second edition of Blair's *Dissertation,* which was republished, with few changes, in the 1765 *Works.* What the "Appendix" most effectively memorialized, however, was the fact that the Scottish clergy was the only profession that was able to undertake such a national survey. If, as Richard Sher has demonstrated, the Ossianic project was promoted by a mostly non-Gaelic-speaking clerical party in Edinburgh, with Blair at its head, the clergy was also the order of men that bridged metropolitan modernity and Highland parishes. The church was the setting from which one could draw a number of men who had the linguistic expertise (needing to span English and Gaelic) and an active involvement with the authority of print. While Gaelic was primarily an oral language with few printed resources, the Scottish clergy was home to the greatest number of bilingual, literate Gaelic speakers. Gaelic lexicographers were often clergymen, and such linguistic expertise was acquired and maintained *because* of professional duty, a desire to be able to preach the Gospel in Gaelic and to disseminate it in print for the smaller number of Gaelic readers, as with the first complete Scottish Gaelic New Testament that appeared in 1767.[40] It was to the kirk's parish clergy, then, that Blair appealed in what amounted to his most exacting test for external evidence: having individual Gaelic reciters perform the works of Ossian before clergymen "who would compare what they rehearsed with the printed version" (406). The scene repeated throughout Scotland in the fall of 1763—one featuring a Gaelic singer (possibly illiterate) performing before the parson while holding the latest Edinburgh edition of Ossian—is a good figure for the clergyman as the age's medium of a cultural ideal poised between tradition and innovation, antiquity and modernity, orality and textuality.

The clerical authentication of Ossian's poetry was an odd climax to a bold literary venture launched with a retelling of a fable in which a monk is refused his request "to take down in writing" the songs of Ossian. The two imaginary exchanges together capture the historical realities of the Ossianic vogue and its scandal. The power of Ossian's reported disdain for the technology of writing was most palpable to those who held in their hands a fashionable book conveying this confrontational tale. But, in the end, the Gaelic-speaking clergy, according to most observers, was essential only for proving what nobody doubted: that there was a living tradition of heroic balladry in the Highlands. As Hume had told Blair, "Nobody questions, that there are traditional poems in that part of the country where the names of Ossian, Fingal, and Oscar and Gaul, are mentioned in every stanza" (1.400). The pressing point remained the issue of antiquity, that Macpherson's translations were of poems preserved "during a course of fourteen centuries," as Hume said (1.399).

When Macpherson gave a more or less final form to his Ossianic labors in *The Poems of Ossian* (1773), neither the "Appendix" nor the "original specimen" of *Temora* was reproduced. Instead, the order of the poems was rearranged "so as to form a kind of regular history of the age to which they relate" (409), as Macpherson put it, and this new order implicitly declared that a narrative about priestcraft—one construed as a response to Irish counterarguments—would be the basis for Macpherson's final claim to antiquity. The poem that concluded volume 1 of the collection, "The Battle of Lora," drew the Ossianic age to an end by having the blind and dying poet address a newly arrived Christian missionary. Ossian thus sings to a "Son of a distant land, who dwellest in the secret cell," in the hopes that the psalm-chanting monk will not forget the heroism of the pre-Christian Caledonians (119).[41] It is a slim point of contact between the poetic and the ecclesiastical in Macpherson's work, and it by definition had to be a terminal moment. Macpherson never backed down from his claims about the antiquity of the poems he had translated. But to do so, he became a historian of priestcraft. The common etymology of the surname Macpherson—Son of the Parson—would have its revenge upon the young man who had refused to make his university studies the threshold to the church. Religious orders of men—druids, culdees, monks, and ministers—were the essential resources for Macpherson's most controversial claims, those of purity and remote antiquity.

Some critics have tried to establish a subaltern orality as the best context for Macpherson's authorship. In this scheme, Macpherson's exploitation of oral tradition was doomed to remain unintelligible to a logocentric, print-obsessed English literary scene. Nevertheless, mostly non-English antiquarians dueling across the Irish Sea determined the historical contours of Macpherson's claims as they took their final form in 1773. And Macpherson's own confused appeals to old manuscripts, his willingness to publish original specimens, and his reference to the orthographically challenged bards make him an unconvincing theorist of orality. A Tory pensioner who dedicated his works to the earl of Bute and sought wealth in an imperial adventure in Florida, Macpherson is a cracked-voiced prophet against political or ideological empires.[42] But he does stand out as Walter Scott's great predecessor as a Scotsman who earned a fortune by exploiting a new British cultural context through the press. Macpherson was a pioneer in discovering how print was a medium in which one could vividly imagine the consolations of orality.

Closely following the 1773 *Works of Ossian*, the third edition of Percy's *Reliques* appeared in 1775 with the pro-Ossian note dropped: the printed gesture of solidarity with the "vivâ voce" witness had been canceled. The year 1775 also saw the publication of Samuel Johnson's *Journey to the Western Islands of Scotland*, a work that contributed to a process that made Anglo-Scottish cultural difference the preponderant context for understanding the Ossian scandal. This context became irresistible thanks to James Boswell and his obsession with recording his English hero's oral presence. After testing the market for his veneration in 1785 with *The Journal of a Tour to the Hebrides, with Samuel Johnson, LL.D.*, Boswell gave the world his *Life of Johnson* in 1791. There, in what would be regarded as the greatest biography of the first modern English man of letters, the Ossian controversy assumed its iconic profile. The battle was between London's cudgel-wielding lexicographer and an evasive cheat from the misty Highlands, all featured in a book by a Scotsman entranced by the vehemence of his English subject's anti-Scots prejudices.[43]

Johnson's 1775 *Journey* had marked the beginning of the eclipse of the Hiberno-Scottish aspects of the Ossian controversies. But there were occasional reminders of the more substantial Irish challenges to Macpherson, as with Charlotte Brooke's *Reliques of Irish Poetry* (1789), a work that invoked as its editorial model the labors of Percy, who, as bishop of Dromore, subscribed for two copies (Preface, xiv). An earlier tribute to Percy's influence had come in *The Execution of Sir Charles Bawdin,* a poem first published in May 1772. Said to be written by "a Priest in the 15th Century" (iii), the ballad was now dedicated to the "Dutchess [*sic*] of Northumberland . . . behind whose illustrious name the Reliques of Ancient English Poetry were with propriety introduced to the world." The poem had in fact been composed by the young Thomas Chatterton, who had trod Percy's poetic path by having minstrels and monks mingle their art in one solemn song:

> The Fre'rs of Seincte AUGUSTYNE next
>   Appearedd to the Syghte
> Alle cladd ynne homelie Russett Weedes
>   Of godlie Monkysh Plyghte:
>
> Ynne diffraunt Partes a godlie Psaume
>   Moste sweetlie theye dydd chaunte;
> Behynde theyre Backes syx Mynstrelles came,
>   Whoe tun'd the strunge Bataunte.   (*Execution* 18)

One hundred years later this poem would appear in a typographically altered form in Walter Skeat's *Poetical Works of Thomas Chatterton,* included in the Aldine Edition of the British Poets. This edition marked the full canonization of Chatterton, despite his forgeries, as a great English poet. And Skeat insisted in transliterating Chatterton's language back into standard English as much as possible. Thus the "Fre'rs of Seincte Augustyne" accompanied by "syx Mynstrelles" became the "Friars of Saint Augustine" followed by "six Minstrels" (2.12). The fact that Skeat was both a clergyman and one of the day's foremost authorities on Old and Middle English was another sign of the pervasive collaboration between English poetic and religious orders during the period under consideration.

I have focused in this chapter on three clerical writers, but the remainder of the book—with the important exception of John Keble—features lay figures, all of whom in different ways addressed converging relations between literary and religious authority in the past and present. I begin with a reappraisal of the commencement of the literary career of Walter Scott, a writer whose early success owed a great deal to his understanding of how figures such as Warton, Percy, Chatterton, and Macpherson had created new opportunities for the modern author.

3

Entertaining Salvation
Scott's Jovial Priests

WALTER SCOTT HAS INSPIRED harshly discordant appraisals of his significance to modern religious authority. In the late 1830s the clerical leaders of England's Catholic revival eulogized the departed author as a primary source for their movement. John Keble, the age's most widely read poet-priest, claimed that Scott's "love of the marvellous and supernatural, [was] not simply . . . employing his fancy"; it was "exercising the principle of faith within him." Coming in his review of John Gibson Lockhart's *Memoirs of the Life of Sir Walter Scott* (7 vols., 1837–38), Keble's comments were part of a broader attempt to credit Scott's writings with disposing readers to look with reverence on "ancient institutions" of all kinds, including the church: "His rod, like that of a beneficent enchanter, has touched and guarded hundreds, both men and women, who would else have been *reforming* enthusiasts" (*OPR* 75, 67). John Henry Newman would echo Keble in the same periodical, the *British Critic,* saying that Scott, "by his works, in prose and verse," had been "stimulating" the "mental thirst" of readers and "silently indoctrinating" them in Catholic principles. Compared to the writings produced by "popular writers of the last century," Scott's works "stand almost as oracles of Truth confronting the ministers of error and sin" (*Essays* 1.268). At about the same time, the young Mary Ann Evans, to be better known as George Eliot, was in the process of losing her evangelical faith, and she would later confess that "the unsettlement of her orthodox views" could be attributed to the influence of Scott (Cross 1.529). In this scheme, Eliot's reading of Scott's novels stimulated the development of a historical faculty that would reject the claims of supernatural Christianity. Like the Anglo-Catholic one, Eliot's appropriation might seem gratuitous, but her reaction has been born out by Scott's distinguished place in Marxist accounts of the modern novel, where Scott's historicism represents a great turning point in the direction of the secular (Lucáks 19–63).[1]

According to some, then, Scott deserves credit for playing a role in a post-Enlightenment religious revival, one that makes a new literary sensibility essential in recovering from the assaults of Voltaire, Hume, and Company. According to others, Scott is a pioneer of literature's post-theological commitment to the world at hand. Or, as John Stuart Mill might have said after writing his essays on Bentham and Coleridge (1838 and 1840), Scott could fairly be seen as a contributor to both Benthamite and Coleridgean cultural formations: he could entertain those engaged in the worldly reformation of human society—even as he could prove to be a potent resource for religious believers. This chapter shows how Scott's early work endowed such a divided reception. In this reading of his career, Scott establishes his literary fame at the turn of the century with a series of ballads and a metrical romance, *The Lay of the Last Minstrel* (1805), that ambiguously represented poetry's vocational status. Often reminding his audience that the modern author's duty was merely to entertain, Scott defined his relationship with readers in frankly materialistic terms. But this overt context for Scott's writing and its avid consumption was set against repeated references to poetry's sacred task in a devotional strain that partially explains Scott's Tractarian reception. Setting his poetry in a Debatable Land where the sacred and the profane were demarcated by a contested line, Scott courted readers with a sensational confusion of good and evil that was at the heart of much popular writing we now call "gothic." At the same time, thanks to his historical ambitions and his attention to a vocational theme, Scott transformed his early work into a commentary on poetry's potential alliance with religious authority.

In presenting this account of the achievement of Scott's literary fame, I pay close attention to the pertinent bibliographic facts as they have been recovered by William Todd, Ann Bowden, and Jane Millgate in particular.[2] And by doing so I want to establish why it is foolhardy to seek to choose (definitively) between either the Tractarian Scott or the Scott as read by Eliot and other post-theological intellectuals. I also want to distinguish my reading of the early books themselves from readings constrained by Scott's creative autobiography, a sprawling, dislocated work that began to appear in the late 1820s. This narrative—made up of introductions by Scott and an editorial apparatus by Scott and Lockhart—was first collected in the Magnum Opus edition that included the twelve-volume *Poetical Works* (1833–34); and "our understanding of the early reception of Scott's poetry," as Millgate has shown, "continues to be shaped by the editorial apparatus of that edition, especially as supplemented by the narrative account embodied in Lockhart's 1837–8 *Memoirs*" (1993: 187). An important subject in its own right, this imposing story about the age's most prolific author is nevertheless a deceptive guide to the first decade of Scott's poetic career.[3] In this sense, scholarship on Scott's poetry will have a fruitful revival in this century only when attended by a development parallel to the one that has accompanied the revival of interest in Scott's novels. Just as the Edinburgh Edition of the Waverley Novels is seeking to give to readers of today the texts "as they were presented to their first readers" (Daiches), future readers of the poetry need to reach back beyond the massive Victorian monuments to grasp the books themselves.

Scott began writing the *Lay* in 1801 when it was designed to conclude the collection of ballads published as *The Minstrelsy of the Scottish Border* in two volumes in February 1802.[4] The larger project had been conceived in the fall of 1799 when Scott was still smarting from his failure to make his way in London as a fashionable playwright and man of letters in the mold of Matthew Lewis, whose *Castle Spectre* had been the hit on Drury Lane the previous season. It was on the strength of Scott's translation of G. A. Bürger's ballads "Die Wildjager" and "Lenore"—published as *The Chase and William and Helen* in 1796—that Lewis sought out Scott in the summer of 1798 and soon invited the young advocate to contribute similar ballads to a poetry collection published, after long delay, as *Tales of Wonder* (1800). More immediately, Lewis arranged for the publication of Scott's translation of J. W. Goethe's play *Goetz of Berlichingen,* which earned him the substantial sum of fifty guineas. Hoping to capitalize on momentum granted by the appearance of that work, Scott made his first adulthood trip to London, putting most of his energy into a gothic drama of his own, *The House of Aspen.* In any event, John Kemble refused the chance to produce the play, and when Scott returned north he redirected his attention toward what would become the *Minstrelsy*.

Much has been written about the intimate relationship with Lewis on the eve of Scott's turn to the *Minstrelsy*. Scott himself devoted an extraordinary amount of space to the subject in 1830, some thirty years after the events, in his "Essay on Imitations of the Ancient Ballad" (*PW* 4.44–53, 71–76, 79–87); and Michael Gamer has argued that the Scott-Lewis relationship comprised an implicit context for literary production, a mode of authorship that stands in stark contrast to the one embraced by Scott in the *Minstrelsy* and in the romances and novels that flowed from that project. For Gamer, Scott produced the *Minstrelsy* as part of an effort "to transform himself from disciple of Lewis to antiquarian scholar and national bard"; and this authorial transformation "involves a full-scale appropriation and recasting of popular gothic materials into a respectably historical, national, masculine, and poetic mould" (26, 165). This attention to Scott's active involvement in the construction of his own literary career is well placed. But there is a limitation to such an account, which is, after all, a direct translation of what Scott himself and Lockhart, his son-in-law and authorized biographer, said about the early poetic career (Lockhart, *Memoirs* 1.253–264, 299). The early works themselves tell a more complicated story that is about a sustained vocational dilemma, not its resolution. Scott did briefly play the role of protégé to Lewis, but both before and after meeting Lewis, Scott understood himself to be a poetic follower of Thomas Percy, whose fourth edition of the *Reliques* (dated 1794) had come out in 1795. To the extent that any notable disciple must adopt and adapt the teachings of the master, Scott was Percy's most successful disciple, and in his early ballads and metrical romances, he would find his poetic inspiration in Percy's fruitful confusion of ministers and minstrels.[5] Unlike his fellow Scotsman James Macpherson, who would try to authenticate his Ossianic poetry with a double rupture between poetic and priestly vocations, Scott's wider cultural resonance was a tribute to his initial understanding of how modern British readers could remain the legatees of ancient ecclesiastical endowments.

Even so, it was in the 1780s and 1790s that a peak in the debates about both the Rowley and Ossian poems had most prominently raised the question of Percy's integrity as an editor. Just as Scott came of age, Percy was being recognized as the father of a great literary revival, but his status in this new literary history was haunted by a charge of fraudulence; there were even rumors that various literary foundlings were the bishop's natural sons. It became common to describe Thomas Chatterton's forgeries as logical extensions of the project inaugurated by the *Reliques*. And when William Henry Ireland confessed to his Shakespeare forgeries, he traced his literary crimes to his instantaneous infatuation with the same unforgettable book: "Nor has the infinite gratification I experienced on its first perusal diminished even to the present moment," he would write in an autobiography first published in 1796 (10). As the editor of poetry with pretensions to antiquity—particularly his *Sir Tristrem* (1804)—and as the author of imitations of ancient poetry, Scott in the first decade of his writing life was treading on potentially venerable ground. But that same ground was also associated with the age's greatest creative frauds, and Percy, like no other figure, lived out the age's paradoxical association of literary veneration and literary scandal.[6]

The intimate terms of the Percy-Scott relationship have been partially preserved in a correspondence beginning in 1800. Scott, age twenty-nine, began the exchange with the seventy-year-old bishop thanks to the offices of the Scottish man of letters Robert Anderson, who had recently edited

The Works of the British Poets (13 vols., 1792–95), one of the period's pioneering collections made feasible by the *Donaldson v. Beckett* judgment (1774). In June 1800 Anderson informed Percy about an "ingenious friend" who "will soon appear as Editor of a Collection of Border ballads . . . upon the plan of 'The Reliques,'" and he also passed along two poems by Scott— "Glenfinlas" and "The Eve of St. John"—"in the style of the ancient Scottish Ballad" (*PL* 9.29). Percy sent back his thanks for "the most obliging Present" and only gingerly embraced such literary activity, saying, "I am too much wedded to the pleasures (I believe I should rather say *Follies*) of my youth not to have a strong predilection for such Compositions" (*PL* 9.34).

Scott would write directly to Percy in October 1800. Acknowledging the bishop's present distance from the world of old ballads and their modern imitation, he also took up the theme of continued interest in these bygone literary habits. He "would not have intruded" upon Percy, Scott says, "had I not been assured . . . that notwithstanding your present more important Studies & avocations your Lordship still retains some attachment to those pursuits which procured the Editor of the first & only classical collection of ancient poetry a place among the highest of our English Literati" (*Letters* 12.167). Percy wrote back, apparently with further approbations, and Scott, in his second letter, paid an elaborate compliment in return. "I shall not trouble your lordship," Scott began,

> with an attempt to express the pleasure I felt at the receipt of the letter with which you honored me, because the task would be equally difficult to me, and disagreeable to your Lordship. Were I to compare it to anything, it would be to the sensation I felt when the Reliques of Ancient Poetry were first put into my hands, an era in my poetical taste which I shall never forget. The very grass sod seat to which (when a boy of twelve years old) I retreated from my playfellows, to devour the works of the ancient minstrels, is still fresh and dear to my memory. (*Letters* 1.108)

Scott would rewrite this scene at least twice in texts addressed to posterity. The first (quoted below) was written for an aborted autobiography composed in 1808 and described the impact of becoming "acquainted with Bishop Percy's Reliques of Ancient Poetry":

> I remember well the spot where I read these volumes for the first time. It was beneath a huge platanas tree in the ruins of what had been intended for an old fashioned arbor. . . . The summer day sped onward so fast that notwithstanding the sharp appetite of thirteen I forgot the hour of dinner, was sought for with anxiety and was still found entranced in my intellectual banquet. To read and to remember was in this instance the same thing and

henceforth I overwhelmed my schoolfellows and all who would harken to me with tragical recitations from the ballads of Bishop Percy. (*Scott on Himself* 27–28)[7]

In recalling his encounter with ancient poetry and its inspired imitations, Scott identifies himself with the perished race of minstrels in a temporal exile figured both by his retreat from youthful company and by his sequestered reading in the redundantly aged arbor. Abstaining from conventional food, the young Scott devours the songs of antiquity as the singer and the song become one. Transformed into what he has been supping on, he becomes, like Samuel Taylor Coleridge's Ancyent Marinere, a possessed speaker addressing an overwhelmed audience. His defining youthful moment as a reader, in other words, was an act of communion with ancient poets, an initiation into an order that knows the secrets of the grave. And throughout the first stage of his poetic career, from the days of his translations and imitations to the extraordinary success of the *Lay*, Scott faithfully returned to the scene of his first reading of Percy: a chilling and thrilling conversation with the dead.

This same complex discourse on poetic pleasures, death, and death-defying poetic moments is the inspiration behind the two ballads—"Glenfinlas" and "The Eve of St. John"—that Scott submitted to Percy's inspection. Scott had privately printed these two ballads in 1799, and they would be published, along with "The Fire-King," "Frederick and Alice," and "The Chase" (retitled as "The Wildhuntsman"), in *Tales of Wonder*. They would also appear in all editions of the *Minstrelsy* (Todd 5Aa, 6A, 7Aa, 8Aa). All of these poems were what Scott defined as "romantic" ballads featuring marvelous events, and they grew directly out of the literary mode that included Scott's first venture at authorship, his free adaptations of Bürger's ballads published as *The Chase and William and Helen*. The first of these ballads features an earl who refuses to stay his passion for the hunt on "God's own hallowed day" (*W* 5.352). Advised by a "young and fair" horseman to join in "devotion's choral swell," the earl prefers the advice of a "dark-browed friend": "To muttering monks leave matin-song, / And bells, and books and mysteries" (353–54). After violently trampling with horse and hound his peasants, their livestock, and their crops, the earl and his headlong retinue come to a "sacred chapel," where he is beseeched again to stop the hunt:

> All mild, amid the route profane,
>   The holy hermit poured his prayer;—
> "Forbear with blood God's house to stain;
>   Revere his altar, and forbear!"   (358)

The earl refuses, concluding, "Not God himself shall make me turn!" (359), and an awful voice thus utters the terms of a perpetual curse:

> "Be chased for ever through the wood;
>   For ever roam the afrighted wild;
> And let thy fate instruct the proud,
>   God's meanest creature is his child." (560)

The second ballad in Scott's first publication features the fair Helen (an anglicization of Lenore) awaiting the return of William from the Holy Lands. Prone to assume the worst, Helen is sure his prolonged absence means he must be "false or dead" (*PW* 6.293, st. 1), and when William does not return with the main body of the crusading host, Helen rejects the consolations of prayer:

> "Why should I pray to ruthless Heaven,
>   Since my loved William's slain?
> I only pray'd for William's sake,
>   And all my prayers were in vain." (296, st. 15)

To her mother's entreaty to "take the sacrament," the daughter replies,

> "No sacrament can quench this fire
>   Or slake this scorching pain;
> No sacrament can bid the dead
>   Arise and live again." (296, st. 17)

She then retreats to her lonely bower where the regretted William himself soon appears, demanding that they "Mount and away! for ere the day / We reach our bridal bed" (300, st. 34). At the conclusion of a furious nocturnal ride, the bridal bed is revealed to be a distant grave, and Helen finds herself embracing a ghastly skeleton. Her wedding becomes her funeral and the occasion for the assembled spirits to reveal the poem's moral: "E'en when the heart's with anguish cleft, / Revere the doom of heaven" (306, st. 46).[8]

Bürger's "Lenore" struck a nerve with British writers and readers in the late 1790s, and no fewer than five translations, including Scott's, were published in 1796 alone.[9] As Scott well knew, however, Bürger's ballads (and those of other German poets) were inspired by the ballad revival as popularized by Percy. "Lenore" in particular had strong debts to "Fair Margaret and Sweet William," "Sweet William's Ghost," and "Margaret's Ghost" (by David Mallet).[10] These and other ballads in the *Reliques*—including "Lord Thomas and Fair Annet," "Lord Thomas and Fair Ellenor," "Corydon's Doleful Knell," "The Lady's Fall," and "The Bride's Burial"

(Groom, *Making* 54–55)—featured lovers dying in grief, and most of them are animated by the confusion of weddings and funerals, with unconsecrated, flesh-devouring graves displacing hallowed conjugal beds. Bürger and others composing in this mode remained committed to a linguistic creed of simplicity as had been popularized by Percy, but they emphasized how the erotic tragedies inspired statements against the conventions of good and evil.[11] Bürger's ballads also brought to the fore, in a complicated way, the institution of the church. By the witness of impassioned and impious speakers, the ballads contained and conveyed critiques of ecclesiastical power; and by subjecting these sources of blasphemy to punishments outside the normal channels of penance, the prerogatives of the sacred are maintained by fiendish means. The earl's unyielding lust for the hunt, for example, causes him to be perpetually hunted. And Helen's initial assumption—that William is either false *or* dead—precedes the appearance of a false *and* dead William as part of a lesson about God's ruthless power.

Bürger had, as Scott wrote in 1806, "borrowed liberally, and without acknowledgment" from Percy ("Herbert's" 221). And when Scott made the transition from translating and imitating German ballads to composing ballads of his own, he was consciously retranslating the innovations of Bürger, Goethe, J. G. Herder, and others back into their native dialect. He generally preferred implicit impieties to repeated blasphemies, but the representation of ineffectual or distorted sacramental power remained central. This was the theme in "The Eve of St. John," a poem that begins with a baron, prepared for combat, departing for three days. Upon his return, he asks his page to report on his lady's conduct, and the page recounts how she had each evening ascended the beacon hill, where she had been joined by a knight. During their third meeting, the page had heard the lady bid the knight come to her bower the next midnight, the Eve of St. John. The knight initially refused and reminded her of the priest in the tower, but the lady assured him the cleric had been called away (*W* 3.232–33). When the page names the visiting knight as Sir Richard Coldinghame, the baron insists the story must not be true, for Sir Richard was slain three nights before (234–35). After this disturbing interview, the baron and his lady are reunited, they prepare for bed, and the Baron falls asleep. Sir Richard then appears as commanded, and the lady urges him to fly. But he calmly tells her how he had been treacherously slain by the baron, now sleeping by her side. He was then doomed to wander the beacon height. When she inquires after the state of his soul, whether he be "saved" or "lost," Sir Richard does not answer directly but doubly rebukes the baron's homicide and the lady's illicit desire, as he uses his ghostly hand to scorch a wooden beam in the tower and the lady's wrist:

> "Who spilleth life, shall forfeit life;
>   So bid thy lord believe:
> That lawless love is guilt above,
>   This awful sign receive." (238)

Like "The Chase," "The Eve of St. John" climaxes with the delivery of a summary moral; and a sense of moral rectification is buttressed by the adoption of penitential religious vocations. The "Lady gay" becomes a "nun, who ne'er beholds the day," and the "bold Baron" becomes a "monk, who speaks to none" at the poem's close (239). At the same time, the poem has a countertheme about sacramental efficacy departing from the church. That power now seems to be invested in a cursed spirit who delivers his lesson "at the lone mid-night hour when bad spirits have power." And the comings and goings of this spirit are carefully sketched in relation to the church's main representative in the poem, the tower's absent priest. Scott is able to suggest several layers of depravity when he has Sir Richard initially reject the lady's invitation on account of the priest. Rather than being a reminder of the sin she proposes, the priest, to the lady, is a physical obstacle already overcome. He has been called away to say masses for a slain knight, and he need not be "fear[ed]" (233). Laughing scornfully, Sir Richard replies, "He who says the mass-rite for the soul of that knight / May as well say mass for me" (236). For the Baron too, reality dawns as he becomes aware of an ecclesiastical farce he has initiated. When the page reports his wife's meetings, the baron wants to be incredulous, because he has slain Sir Richard himself, and the church is a witness to that death: "For the Dryburgh bells ring, and the white monks do sing / For Sir Richard of Coldinghame!" (236). Haunted by an unauthorized resurrection that he is keen to doubt, the baron insists that Sir Richard's grave "cannot give up the dead!" (237). But the poem is indeed about a man who rises from the grave, albeit not in the manner promised by the musical monks. No less than the fair and faithless Helen—who understands her prayers to be fruitless and vain—Sir Richard is a witness to the vanity of the church's rites. And readers, in the end, are witnesses to a sacerdotal parody. The prayers and masses taking place in the consecrated abbey are rendered worthy of Sir Richard's scorn, while the bower of the baron and the lady—desecrated by murder and a conspired fornication—becomes an effective confessional.

"Glenfinlas" is also about infidelities (both marital and theological), implicit necrophilia, and a general confusion of gifts and curses, prayers and spells. With its title meaning "The Green Ladies of the Glen," the poem features two chieftains, Ronald and Moy, enjoying the postprandial pleasures of the hunt. The host, Ronald, turns to his guest from Ireland to suggest that they should crown their pleasures by seeking the company of the sisters Mary and Flora, daughters of proud Glengyle (*W* 3.308–9). Moy declines the invitation, foreseeing a tragic end to Ronald's quest. Not to be deterred, Ronald departs in search of Mary, leaving Moy the sole occupant of their lodge. Then, at midnight, Flora appears before Moy, and requests his aid in returning to her "father's towers" (315). Moy, realizing the lady does not come from "mortal blood," refuses her reiterated pleas and dismisses the spirit by playing his harp. In a violent climax, the tempting spirit flies away, "mingling" with a "rising storm" that demolishes the hut around Moy. Following "loud bursts of ghastly laughter," the detached arm and "gasping head" of Ronald, in a shower of blood, come crashing down into the hissing fire (317–18).

"Glenfinlas" was a breakthrough text for Scott because in it he featured a poet as the poem's central character, Moy, who is a prototype of the minstrel in the *Lay*. As with the poet at the center of the 1805 best-seller, Moy's poetic gifts are fundamentally "tragical"; and his vatic power— "the gift the future ill to know"—is classically balanced against its origins in "the last dread curse of angry heaven" (310). But his harping also invites misappropriation by nonheroic consumers in search of an evening's entertainment. For Ronald, who entreats Moy to distract the elder sister, Flora, with "a melting tale," Moy's power of song ought to serve a plot of seduction made urgent by a bout of drinking (309–10). The speaker of the poem, in contrast, emphasizes how Moy's music is prophetic and necromantic:

> 'Twas Moy; whom in Columba's isle
>   The seer's prophetic spirit found,
> As, with a minstrel's fire the while,
>   He waked his harp's harmonious sound.
>
> Full many a spell to him was known,
>   Which wandering spirits shrink to hear;
> And many a lay of potent tone,
>   Was never meant for mortal ear.
>
> For there, 'tis said, in mystic mood,
>   High converse with the dead they hold,
> And oft espy the fated shroud,
>   That shall the future corpse enfold. (307)

The central action of the poem thus rests on Moy's mystic minstrelsy. For it is by flinging "his wildest witch-notes on the wind" that he is able to dismiss the spirit in the form of Flora (317). As with Sir Richard's powers to mark and reform mortal sinners, Moy's potent song is represented in relation to the church and its rituals. At first, and as a test, Moy asks Flora to "three times tell each Ave-bead, / And thrice a Pater-noster say; / Then kiss with me the holy reed." To this challenge, Flora gamely replies that Moy ought to change his bonnet for a "monkish cowl" (315). With her refusal to perform them, prayers and liturgical rites signify Flora's ghastliness, and a religious vocation is her taunting name for Moy's lack of gallantry. But it is a resource semi-ecclesiastic and semi-poetic that is Moy's salvation:

> He mutter'd thrice St. Oran's rhyme,
>   And thrice St. Fillan's powerful prayer;
> Then turn'd him to the eastern clime,
>   And sternly shook his coal-black hair.
>
> And, bending o'er his harp, he flung
>   His wildest witch-notes to the wind;
> And loud, and high, and strange, they rung,
>   As many a magic change they find.   (316–17)

In its original published form in *Tales of Wonder,* "St. Oran's rhyme" is only slightly glossed by an earlier note on "St. Oran's rule" that says the holy man "was a friend and follower of St. Columbus, and was buried in Icolmkill"; and about the other saint, Scott gave another uninformative note, saying, "I know nothing of St. Fillan, but that he gave his name to many chapels, holy fountains, &c. in Scotland" (Lewis 1.127, 134). As presented in the nonantiquarian context of *Tales of Wonder,* Moy's invocation of the saints might be read as evidence of his orthodox religion. In the *Minstrelsy of the Scottish Border,* however, Scott expands both notes considerably (*W* 3.321–22), and the biography of St. Oran gained more details in the notes to "The Cout of Keeldar" (*W* 3.300), one of the modern imitations by Scott's major collaborator, John Leyden. The new note to "Glenfinlas" shows how Scott found in his editorial practice an opportunity to carry on a blasphemous discourse that Bürger had featured in his verse. Any simplistic confrontation between a fiendish spirit and a religiously empowered minstrel is complicated in the *Minstrelsy* as readers learn more about a "dubious" saint renowned for his "rigid celibacy":

> According to the legend, he consented to be buried alive, in order to propitiate certain dæmons of the soil, who obstructed the attempts of Columba to build a chapel. Columba caused the body of his friend to be dug up, after three days had elapsed; when Oran, to the horror and scandal of the assistants, declared, that there was neither a God, a judgment, nor a future state! He had no time to make further discoveries, for Columba

caused the earth once more to be shovelled over him with the utmost dispatch. (*W* 3.321)

Like Sir Richard's tale, the legend is a parody of the orthodox resurrection, which the editor, a connoisseur of such diablerie, has typographically unearthed. Readers are also invited to pay attention to a distinction between "rhyme[s]" (attributed to St. Oran) and "prayer[s]" (associated with Fillan). Moy appeals to the apparatus of the church—the ave-beads, paternosters, and the cross—but it is prayer *and* the rhymes of a sainted blasphemer that rid the hut of the fiend.

As portions of the *Minstrelsy,* "The Eve of St. John" and "Glenfinlas" have their interests in the sexual and the supernatural given the authority of history and tradition. Readers of gothic writing of this period struck some contemporary commentators as the victims of a modern disease. But Scott's collection documents how ballads focused on the related themes of forbidden knowledge and sexual enchantment were traditional forms. Scott's key historical figure in these terms was Thomas of Ercildoune, who had lived during the thirteenth century and was "celebrated as a prophet, and as a poet" (*W* 3.169). In "Thomas the Rhymer, in Three Parts" (*W* 3.166–226), readers thus encountered the historical inspiration for a figure such as Moy. What Thomas shares with Moy—who has held "converse with the dead"—St. Oran, and Sir Richard is an experience of death that evades the conventional postmortem destinations of Heaven or Hell. In part 1 Thomas accepts a sexually charged invitation from a "ladye bright" (173), and after kissing the "rosy lips" of this Elfin Queen (174), he is shown "the path of righteousness," "the path of wickedness," and a third "road to Elfland" (175–76). Accompanying his lady to this last destination, Thomas discovers it is no bower of bliss but a dark space running with blood:

> It was mirk mirk night, and there was nae stern light,
>   And they waded through red blude to the knee;
> For a' the blude, that's shed on earth,
>   Rins through the springs o' that countrie. (176)

Eventually they come to "a garden green" where Thomas is offered an apple that Scott unambiguously identifies as "the produce of the fatal Tree of Knowledge" (176, 178). Following his return to earth at the end of his seven years of service to the Queen of Elfland, Thomas and his capacities for prophecy and poetry are the subjects, respectively, of parts 2 (186–212) and 3 (213–26). Part 2 is Scott's versification of some prophecies attributed to Thomas and printed in 1615; part 3, what Scott calls an "attempt to commemorate the Rhymer's poetical fame," is wholly of Scott's own composition. It represents Thomas as the host of a feast where his "witching tale" is the captivating entertainment (217). Later that evening, in "minstrel guise," Thomas departs from his ancestral tower, never to be seen again (222–24).

The poet of Thomas's disappearance, Scott was also the primary author of the Rhymer's modern return in books that included his edition of *Sir Tristrem* (1804), once intended, like the *Lay,* to form a part of the *Minstrelsy*. An unremarkable Middle English metrical romance, *Sir Tristrem* was a work that Scott on little evidence attributed to Thomas, who is represented as having received the story from the last Celtic bards to survive in Britain (*W* 4.xxi–xlv). This work, in which "the original priestly poet-historians of Percy's formulation, are brought to life" (Matthews 64), was not prized, even by Scott, as poetry; it was valued as confirmation of the legend that Thomas had indeed been a poet. A text about the construction of a great British poet from the Borders, it would go into second, third, and fourth editions from 1806 to 1819 because it had been, as the title page notes, "Edited from the Auchinleck MS. by Walter Scott, Esq." (Todd 13Aa–e).[12]

Scott's poetry in the *Minstrelsy* would become increasingly involved with an antiquarian apparatus. But that apparatus—which would also take up one third of the *Lay*'s printed pages—did nothing to obscure Scott's obsession with ventriloquizing dead voices. Scott's imagination was most animated by circumstances that equated a perilous poetic necromancy and the historical resuscitations of the devoted antiquarian. An interpretive model that sets historical or antiquarian ambitions at odds with gothic or creative modes is doomed to miss the complexities of Scott's brand of historicism, one calculated to please a variety of contemporary readers.[13] Scott's antiquarian ventures, with their emphasis on "the accumulation of material without subordination to system or theory," were, as Susan Manning says, "ideologically promiscuous" (104). And editorial gestures were authorial opportunities in a deliberately hybridized career that "integrate[d] sensation and folklore" (Watt 132). "Writing in a culture under pressure," as Robert Crawford has argued, made it natural for Scott to assume a mode of authorship in which collection and framing were "bound up"—not opposed to—"creative endeavor" (2000: 113). At the same time, the tendency for some of Scott's work to take implicitly anti-ecclesiastical forms could be explained by orthodox Protestant historiography, which was eager to document the gloom of superstition that spread over the British Isles before the Reformation. Such a posture, for instance, would have been the excuse for the publication in 1784 of "Black Sanctus, or monke's hymn to Saunte Satane" in Thomas Evans's *Old Ballads,*

Historical and Narrative (3.242–44), a collection that Scott considered to be the era's most important supplement to Percy's *Reliques*.

In several respects, the ballads Scott forwarded to Percy in 1800 were formulaic productions in a deliberately sensational genre. Sent to the venerable prelate with the implicit message that he was ultimately responsible for their composition, they elicited from Percy qualified approbation. Despite Percy's hint that such poetry and his ecclesiastical vocation were at odds, the ballads pointed toward the *Lay* as a book that would link vocationally ambitious poetry to the musical mutterings of monks. Scott would thus win his fame, as we shall see, with a text that is fated to conclude with an eruption of ecclesiastical lyricism.

The poet of the *Lay* is the dispossessed heir of Thomas and Moy, the last of a race doomed by history itself. In a number of ways—most blatantly as a victim of the rise of print culture—the minstrel is sacrificed at the hands of an unappeasable modernity; and he addresses an audience that has been forcibly resigned to the new cultural and political context inaugurated by the Glorious Revolution. Even so, Scott's poem is energized by its amended commitments to the initial Percyean creed about the minstrels in their primitive splendor: they were creatures of a time, as Scott put it in 1806, when "the history, the laws, and even the religion of barbarous nations" were "expressed in verse" ("Ellis's" [1806] 387). For all of Scott's attention in the *Lay* to the historical forces that render the past and its ways obsolete, his creative ingenuity is also dedicated to the minstrel's capacity to retain the power to perform religious rites. And if, by Scott's own definition, the minstrel is the last of his race, the minstrel is also the vehicle for Scott's claim to have inherited, against all historical odds, the primal poetic vocation. About a clash between bardic culture and book culture, a story to be read across borders separating men and women, English and Scots, village churls and mighty earls, a feudal past and a commercial present, the *Lay* comprehends an impressive array of historical and conceptual dualities. But all of these divisions, conflicts, and uneasy marriages are subordinate to Scott's bid to have his representative poet entertain the idea of salvation for an audience suffering from a modern malady eliding boredom and mortality. Recognizing Scott's poetic achievement in the *Lay* depends on our ability to appreciate the doomed minstrel's triumph as well as the related fact that Scott's bright literary future was built on his identification with an obsolete mode of aesthetic production.[14]

Such an appreciation first has to overcome the tradition, heeded in Peter Murphy's representative reading of the *Lay* (140–72), that the poem is a haphazard work, that a major character, the goblin page, is an inexplicable interpolation, and that the entire sixth canto is an undisciplined addition. That the poem's reception has been determined by this catalogue of flaws is understandable given the fact that Scott himself endorsed them.[15] He gave a biographically compelling form to them in the "Introduction" to the poem for his *Poetical Works* of 1830 (6.5–31), a "narrative of happy accidents," as Jane Millgate calls it (1984: 16), emphasizing how the author took up the subject of the goblin page in courtly fealty to the wishes of the enchanting Countess of Dalkeith (see also J. Sutherland 1995: 98–105). This history of the poem's genesis, composed a quarter century after the event and after the death of the duchess, was adopted in Lockhart's *Memoirs,* which also printed a letter from 1805 (1.388–89) in which Scott assumed his famously cavalier stance toward his craft. "The sixth canto is altogether redundant," Scott gladly admitted, "for the poem should certainly have closed with the union of the lovers, when the interest, if any, was at an end. But what could I do? I had my book and page still on my hands, and must get rid of them at all events. Manage them as I would, their catastrophe must have been insufficient to occupy an entire canto; so I was fain to eke it out with the songs of the minstrels" (*Letters* 1.243). This disregard would become an important element of Scott's authorial charm. But it is naïve to take it at face value.[16] *Eke*-ing it out, for instance, was also the casually bold figure Scott used to describe the origin of many poetic epigraphs found in his fiction. They came initially from his reading, Scott explained, but finding it "too troublesome" to consult his books, he first quoted from memory and "when that failed, eked it out with invention." Not to be troubled and ready to fail, the writer here can seem careless and carefree. At the same time, he is an author claiming as his own the power to forge "scraps of poetry" across the full range of British literary history (*Prefaces* 78).

There is, in fact, much evidence, old and new, suggesting that Scott partially invented what became the standard account of the *Lay*'s making. Scott's goblin plot certainly has an extensive intertextual relationship with the *Minstrelsy of the Scottish Border,* the collection the *Lay* was originally intended to conclude. With that work's keen interest in "sundry classes of subordinate spirits" (*W* 1.cxcix) and poems that featured just such a mischievous sprite, the idea that the goblin page was put into Scott's head is perverse.[17] And Celeste Langan's revisionist reading of the *Lay,* in concert with a broader reconceptualization of the anthology as a creative form, allows us to understand the final canto, with its collection of British minstrelsy, as something more than padding (56, 63–70; see also Eller 51–54). Scott's determined feudalization of the poem's origins in 1830, as both Richard Cronin and Jane Millgate have shown, now appears to be a representative repetition of his initial success with the *Minstrelsy*. That work rendered into a luxurious commodity songs that were (theoretically) owned in common by all readers (Cronin 864–65). Scott's description of the aristocratic (and implicitly nonmercenary) inspiration for the *Lay* was a similar sleight of hand: faced with the expiration of its copyright in 1830, Scott provided the poem with yet another creative frame as a way to extend proprietary rights over the book that marked his initiation into a writing career that was lucrative on an unprecedented scale (Millgate 1989).

The book itself of 1805 has a plot that is elegant and elaborate, more overdetermined than haphazard, and relentlessly self-referential. The main poetic plot of the 1550s—which is the subject of the minstrel's late-seventeenth-century song—takes place over the space of three days, following a tripartite scheme of funeral-wedding-funeral. It begins under the shadow of a termination, the slaying in 1552 of Sir Walter Scott, the head of the Buccleuch clan, who has been killed in a feud with the Kerrs. As the story opens in Branksome Tower, this man's widow, Lady Janet Beaton, is dedicated to maintaining the feud and to perpetuating the rituals of mourning. The lady's skill in occult studies, however, has revealed to her the potential eruption of a comic plot of youthful union, since her daughter Margaret is conducting a secret affair with Henry, Lord Cranstoun of the Kerr clan. To prevent its progress, she requires the further aid of a Mighty Book buried with the wizard Michael Scott in Melrose Abbey. William of Deloraine is sent to retrieve the book, and he arrives there as canto 1 ends. Deloraine wrests the book from Scott's grave in canto 2 and sets out to return it to Branksome Tower. In canto 3 he crosses paths with Cranstoun and is wounded near to death. Cranstoun orders his page—a mysterious dwarf—to bear the wounded knight on to Branksome Tower, but before doing so, the page reads a spell from the book that grants him powers of physical transformation. After returning the unconscious Deloraine, the page encounters Margaret's younger brother, the heir of Buccleuch, and leads him into the woods, where he is abandoned. There the young Buccleuch is captured by a party of English come north to avenge an earlier raid by Deloraine into the English marches. Canto 4 depicts the English converging before Branksome Tower and demanding, with the heir of Buccleuch as their hostage, that the lady hand over Deloraine. It is then decided that a test of single combat will determine the fate of both Deloraine and the young Buccleuch. In canto 5, Cranstoun—aided by the spell imparted to his page—disguises himself as Deloraine and defeats the English champion Musgrave, thus reuniting the lady and her son. Disclosing his true identity, Cranstoun wins the hand of Margaret. Canto 6 features the wedding and the ensuing feast where well-honored minstrels entertain. As one of the minstrels closes his song, the long-dead Michael Scott appears, calling away the mischievous page. With their revelry interrupted in this ghastly way, the wedding party vows a pilgrimage to Melrose Abbey "for the sake / Of Michael's restless sprite" (6.27; *W* 5.196). The poem's (once) conclusive wedding then gives way to a final requiem mass for Michael Scott in the abbey, a ritual that brings to an end the strife that cost Sir Walter Scott his life.

The final funeral pilgrimage to Melrose, which ends the action of 1552, takes place as a reply to an earlier pilgrimage vainly undertaken in the hope of ending the feud (1.8; *W* 6.21). By closing with another funeral rather than the wedding—that is, by ending where he began—Scott balances his commitment to history's repetitions with the *Lay*'s more overt advertisement of history's unavoidable progress. History's tendency to repeat itself is also suggested by Scott's persistent attempts to make the late-seventeenth-century frame and the mid-sixteenth-century story reflect each other (Goslee 1988, 22–23). The minstrel's striking entrance accompanied by an orphaned boy, for example, is echoed at the end of his song by the grand departure of Michael Scott and his adopted charge, the goblin page. And like Branksome Tower of 1552, Newark Castle, where the minstrel arrives in 1690, is defined by an absent patriarch and a lady in mourning. She is Anne Scott, the first Duchess of Buccleuch, who presides over a court mourning the death of her husband, James Scott. Better known as the Duke of Monmouth, this Scott was a natural child of Charles II and was executed in 1685 after he sought, as a Protestant, to wrest the throne from his uncle, the Catholic James II. Like the lady of his song, like the lady he is to entertain, and like the orphaned boy bearing his harp, the minstrel too is defined by a patriarchal absence of dynastic proportions, the eclipse of the House of Stuart.

Many of these creative repetitions move across the expansive temporal borders separating the sixteenth and seventeenth centuries, but Scott also employs this motif of repetition and reversal on a smaller scale: the transformation of the goblin page into a likeness of the boy is recalled and revised by the English threat to turn the boy into a page (4.21; *W* 5.120). And in a poem that infrequently exploits the synchronic resources of metaphor and simile, the diachronic and spatial resource of chiasmus becomes Scott's distinctive linguistic gesture. It is no accident that one perfect chiasmus ("For love is heaven, and heaven is love" [3.2; *W* 5.74]) is the vehicle for alluding to a subject matter that claims the reader's attention in both of the poem's major historical settings of 1690 and 1552. Early in the poem, we learn that the sixteenth-century feud will not cease "Till pride be quelled, and love be free" (1.17; *W* 5.28). And Scott also has the minstrel address his present audience's frustrated desires "to hear a melting tale, / Of two true lovers in a dale" (2.29; *W* 5.63). When he claims at this point that he "may not, must not, sing of love" (2.30; *W* 5.64), one is invited to consider how the characters in the minstrel's song, its fictional audience, and Scott's real readers share the potential fate of being stopped short when love *is* sung. Indeed, it is the lady's announcement that "pride is quelled, and love is free" (5.26; *W* 5.159) toward the end of canto 5 that has prompted the claim that the remaining forty-odd pages of poetry are superfluous. But this premature climax suggests that the *Lay* is about something else after all. Like Coleridge's "The Rime of the Ancyent Marinere" (1798), another poem inspired by Percy and his German imitators, the *Lay* is overtly dedicated to the illustration of a comforting truth. One assures us that God equally loves the "great and small" (*CW* 16:1.418, 615); the other shows us the rewards for setting love free. Just as much as the "Rime," though, the *Lay* presents its central platitude in a slightly unconvincing manner, and it too, being a poem about literary possession, has a will other than its own. Not love but blood—a substance equally vital to the course of life and death—moves the *Lay* along its way.

Appearing in some form over fifty times in the text, blood stains the threshold of the poem's telling—where we are reminded that the duchess "had wept o'er Monmouth's bloody tomb!" (Intro.; *W* 5.13)—and the threshold of the story told, which begins with the lady swearing vengeance over Walter Scott's "bloody bier" (1.11; *W* 5.22). And just as blood literally opens the book at the center of the minstrel's poem (3.9; *W* 5.79), blood discloses the *Lay*'s secret ambitions to perform those rituals of revival which the church and its priestly initiates claim as their own. Scott never lets readers forget that blood transformed from communion wine had been the central sign of the church's authority, one that was linguistic and textual, embodied in both an order of men and an extraordinary book. But the blood that so copiously flows throughout the text is not simply a substance to be produced by violence or to be transformed by hierophantic thaumaturgy. Even as it heralds life's violent termination and its miraculous revival, blood is also summoned in the creation of new life engendered by aroused flesh coupled in love, and Scott deploys an extensive "semiology of sensibility" focused on blushing heroines and sentimental readers (Goslee 1993: 77). Precisely because it is associated with the primal and the terminal, with love and war, with birth, death, and rebirth, blood, its transformation and its transforming agency, is the author's sign of power and becomes intimately involved with both the oral art of minstrelsy and the crafts of reading and writing.

In *English Bards and Scotch Reviewers* (1809), Byron charged Scott with a Gothic dullness by recalling that the *Lay* featured "high-born ladies . . . / Forbidding Knights to read who cannot spell" (qtd. in J. Wordsworth iv). Referring both to the lady's instructions to Deloraine concerning Michael Scott's book—"Be it scroll, or be it book, / Into it, Knight, thou must not look" (1.23; *W* 5.32)—and to Deloraine's reassuring affirmation of illiteracy, Byron struck at one of Scott's major themes, the questionable status of skill in letters, "gramarye," or "glamour" as it is called in the *Lay* (Goslee 1988: 19; Fielding 44–73; Langan 58–59). To Byron, Deloraine's illiteracy renders the lady's speech superfluous, and this gibe can stand for a critical tradition that makes Scott the language's most prodigious spendthrift. For Scott, however, the episode is an occasion to recall a context in which reading, a threatened life's potential redemption, *and* ecclesiastical privileges are involved, here in the institution of the Benefit of Clergy to which Deloraine alludes when he refers to his "neck-verse" (1.24; *W* 5.32). Together, the lady and William voice gramarye's ambivalence in the *Lay*: reading in this poem is both an avenue to damnation—"If thou readest, thou art lorn!" the lady warns (1.23; *W* 5.32)—and a path to salvation.

The poem's dedication to this topic is announced in the first stanza of canto 1, when the lady retires "to her secret bower," which is, as depicted in an early illustration (fig. 5), a transgressive reading closet including an idol and hermetically inscribed texts:

> Her bower, that was guarded by word and by spell,
> Deadly to hear, and deadly to tell—
> Jesu Maria, shield us well!
> No living wight, save the Ladye alone,
> Had dared to cross the threshold stone.   (1.1; *W* 5.17)

As the minstrel invokes this protection, Scott invokes a textual confrontation between the book that tells the story of Jesus, son of Mary, and the type of book consulted in the bower; and the lady's reading habits are depicted with a persistent ambivalence as they seem to be both potentially fiendish and inherently ecclesiastic. On the one hand, the lady's studies are given an ecclesiastical genealogy, since she learned the art from her father, "a clerk of fame," the historical Cardinal Beaton, as Scott's note suggests.[18] But the church is learning's complicated sanctuary. The lady's father is pictured in "studious mood" in "St. Andrews cloistered hall" where he too practices "the art that none may name" (1.11; *W* 5.24). This strange power of letters is the major theme in canto 2 as Deloraine seeks the book of Michael Scott within the precincts of Melrose Abbey. There Deloraine

Fig. 5. The Lady in Her Secret Bower, 1809, from an illustrated edition of The Lay of the Last Minstrel *published by John Sharpe.*

encounters the same warning about the dire consequences of becoming familiar with the book's contents (2.5, 13–15; *W* 5.46–47, 51–53) from the "ancient priest" (2.3; *W* 5.45) who attended Michael Scott at his death and buried him. Having heard from the wizard a final confession, the man, who once had been a "warrior bold" (2.7; *W* 5.47), assumed his present cloistered profession and now wears the stones in penance "For knowing what should ne'er be known" (2.5; *W* 5.47).

Frequently associated with an apparently heterodox and fatal occultism, the book is also identified with the sacred, and Deloraine's journey to Melrose is an urgent pilgrimage to a holy site on the Eve of St. Michael, the same liturgical date on which Michael Scott was buried (2.15; *W* 5.53). Disclosed on this night alone by moonlight "kiss[ing]" a devotional window, Michael Scott's grave is touched by both a tender holiness and the aestheticized traces of that primal feud between Satan's rebellious forces and the loyal angelic host:

> The silver light, so pale and faint,
> Shewed many a prophet, and many a saint,
>> Whose image on the glass was dyed;
>> Full in the midst, his Cross of Red
> Triumphant Michael brandished,
>> And trampled the Apostate's pride.
> The moon-beam kissed the holy pane,
> And threw on the pavement a bloody stain.   (2.11; *W* 5.50–51)

When the secret tomb is opened, a light breaks forth "gloriously" and it shines "like heaven's own blessed light," and the benignant character of this energy "issuing from the tomb" (2.18; *W* 5.55–56) seems to be in accord with Michael Scott himself, who is well preserved, dressed as a pilgrim, and grasping a silver cross. But while the light of the bloody cross points toward the wizard's grave, the status of his book remains unresolved. Deloraine is still seeking, as the monk puts it, "What heaven and hell alike would hide" (2.5; *W* 5.46).

The luminous stain that points to the book is a temporary representation of blood. To open the book itself, and to give us the poem's first overt representation of reading, real blood is needed. On his return, Deloraine fights Cranstoun and is wounded by him in a scene that toys with the relations between sexually and martially summoned blood. Scott figures Cranstoun's erotic capacities in terms of his power to draw forth the tinting and swelling blood of the aroused body, the arterial mechanics of tumescence, quickened heartbeat, and dilated pupils: "Dreaded in battle, and loved in hall," Henry to fair Margaret is a sight to behold, one that

> Lent to her cheek a livelier red;
> When the half sigh her swelling breast
> Against the silken ribband pressed;
> When her blue eyes their secret told.   (2.28; *W* 5.62–63)

Perversely, however, the meeting between the two lovers promised to the audience at the close of canto 2 is only a flirtatious prologue to the more intimate meeting between Deloraine and Cranstoun. With "the mystic Book, to his bosom prest / . . . like a load upon his breast" (2.24; *W* 5.60), Deloraine will collide with Cranstoun in a scene that again features silk, bosoms, blood, secrets, and penetration:

> But Cranstoun's lance, of more avail,
> Pierced through, like silk, the Borderer's mail;
> Through shield, and jack, and acton, past,
> Deep in his bosom broke at last.   (3.6; *W* 5.76–77)

With Deloraine lying "senseless as the bloody clay" (3.7; *W* 5.77), Henry orders his page to attend the foe back to Branksome. And as Cranstoun rides away, Deloraine—despite a well-advertised illiteracy—is for the second time represented in relation to the habits of a clergy defined by a culture of letters. When the page discovers under the knight's "corslet" the Mighty Book, "Much he marveled, a knight of pride / Like a book-bosom'd priest should ride" (3.8; *W* 5.78). Initially the page assumes that the knight's wounds and the book are not closely connected: "He thought not to search or staunch the wound, / Until the secret he had found" (3.8; *W* 5.78). But it is the blood of the same wound that will reveal what is every book's primary secret: how to open it. Though it will "not yield to [the goblin's] unchristened hand," smearing "the cover o'er / With the Borderer's curdled gore" opens the book and leads to the poem's central reading experience:

> A moment then the volume spread,
> And one short spell therein he read.
> It had much of glamour might,
> Could make a ladye seem a knight;
> The cobwebs on a dungeon wall
> Seem tapestry in lordly hall;
> A nut-shell seem a gilded barge,
> A sheeling seem a palace large
> And youth seem age, and age seem youth—
> All was delusion, nought was truth.   (3.9; *W* 5.79)

The glamour of grammar is confirmed here by the complex pun on "read" at the start of the passage. Linked to the verb "spread," "read" ends a couplet that rhymes both aurally and visually. At the same time, this "read"—directly following the application of Deloraine's gore—links reading and blood via the homophonic suggestion of the (in)visible sanguinary adjective. Both "read" and "red" have become signs for the same sound in a metapoetic plot that has been unleashed by (and on) the page, a word Scott uses duplicitously as he makes gestures that have to be seen in print and heard by the ear (Goslee 1988: 38–40; Langan 56–58). And thus the art of the lady's father to "chang[e] his mortal frame" (1.11; *W* 5.24) is handed over to the page of the knight seeking the hand of the lady's daughter.

For Nancy More Goslee, the goblin's brief possession of the book speaks to the poem's anxieties about an inappropriate female literary power. It is "the first step in a process of conservative correction" to chasten the lady as an "intellectually aggressive woman"; and the manner of revealing the book's words reveals affiliated anxieties about impersonal reading experiences featured in a modern culture of print where books "randomly available to any reader" are "almost demoniacally free of [the] social constraints imposed" on oral authors. "Smearing his book with blood," as Goslee suggests, "this anarchic goblin may represent both an author's imagination escaping all normal constraints and a nightmare vision of the 'ideal reader' attracted by such violence. Because the blood is that of the illiterate Deloraine, in some sense his wound marks a sacrifice to the 'unchristian' anarchy of a culture dominated by writing" (19–20). But it is not only the borders between male and female, oral and written that are being suggestively crossed. The more important borders are those between the sacred and the profane, the living and the dead. Just as the lady's character is defined by her perilous initiation into a class of clerical erudition, the book she has summoned into circulation is ambiguously hierophantic. By yielding to the blood of Deloraine, the book becomes associated with the desires of an ill-willed sprite, a "distorted" character who exploits the book's powers of distortion (2.31; *W* 5.65); and this literally useful blood has been shed by violent anarchy, the feud between clans equally just in their pursuit of vengeance. Yet that blood also recalls an essential lubricant of priestly power, sacrificial blood, which may upset the antithesis between life and death. Showing blood that is a sign of his mortal peril, Deloraine has also been promised a deliverance, based on his faith in the spilling of Christic blood, from death's curse. And in a similar capacity, the shape-shifting dwarf has his own ambiguous "ministry" (3.32; *W* 5.66).

The opening of the mighty book, like the opening of Michael Scott's grave, is a bloody affair in which the signs of death and life are confused in a "strange scene of death" (2.20; *W* 5.57).[19] And at the close of canto 2, as we are preparing to see the goblin read the book brought out of the grave, the minstrel's revival—a transformation of his cadaverous appearance—begins to assert itself as Scott's primary topic. The minstrel gives his page the sign—a faltering in his voice—that he is ready, with the help of a poetic type of blood, to raise himself from his own doubtful state of animation:

Full slyly smiled the observant page,
And gave the withered hand of age
A goblet, crowned with mighty wine,
The blood of Velez' scorched vine.
He raised the silver cup on high,
And, while the big drop filled his eye,
Prayed God to bless the Duchess long,
And all who cheered a son of song.
The attending maidens smiled to see

116 *Entertaining Salvation*

> How long, how deep, how zealously,
> The precious juice the Minstrel quaffed;
> And, he emboldened by the draught,
> Looked gaily back to them and laughed.

Here the minstrel starts his bid for a personal and vocational redemption that rivals the mighty book's capacity to make age seem youth, a trick that will get over-shadowed by the power to make the dead live again. Drinking wine in a eucharistic moment associated, like Michael Scott, with Spain, a land of occult learning, the minstrel revives himself with and within his own performance. The blessing offered by the minstrel to the Duchess might strike some as less impressive than the gifts extended to the Christian communicant. Scott nevertheless displays a poetic faith that calls for the two to look and sound alike. The "silver cup" raised "on high" echoes the "silver cross" in Michael Scott's hand; and the couplet containing the cup and rhyming "high" and "eye" will be echoed in a couplet where a "holy Friar" raises a "crucifix on high" before the "darkening eye" of a parting soul (5.23; *W* 5.156). There is something contrived and glib, even tactless in this sacramental parody, but Scott is restrained by no sense of decorum as he continues in a manner that confirms other bloody confusions:

> The cordial nectar of the bowl
> Swell'd his old veins, and cheer'd his soul;
> A lighter, livelier prelude ran,
> Ere thus his tale again began.   (2.coda; *W* 5.68–69)

The "cordial" drink refers us again to the heart, chest and bosom, that corporeal zone in which love and war trace their tales. And Scott's cup runneth over, perhaps, as Margaret's "swelling breast" has given way to the old man cordially revived to "livelier" song followed by the penetration of Cranstoun's corslet and the violation of his "bosom'd" book.

The careful reader will want to join the observant page in slyly smiling at this performance. For the minstrel immediately opens canto 4 with an accomplished revival that makes one wonder if he has been limping on purpose all along. The *Lay* opens with the entrance of an aged and infirm creature, the sole survivor of a perished poetic race:

> The way was long, the wind was cold,
> The Minstrel was infirm and old;
> His withered cheek, and tresses gray,
> Seemed to have known a better day;
> . . . .

> For, well-a-day! their date was fled
> His tuneful brethren all were dead.   (Intro.; *W* 5.11)

And toward the conclusion of canto 2, the minstrel will reclaim the narrator's words to remind his audience what they can plainly see: "My hairs are gray, my limbs are old, / My heart is dead, my veins are cold" (2.30; *W* 5.64). In the opening of canto 3, however, the manner of the minstrel's initial entrance is disavowed:

> And said I that my limbs were old;
> And said I that my blood was cold
> And that my kindly fire was fled.
> And my poor withered heart was dead.   (3.1; *W* 5.74)

With the minstrel's poetic revival at the end of canto 2 and the start of canto 3, a new subject becomes possible that addresses and transforms the initial subject about the relationship between skill in letters and the authority of the church. The *Lay* becomes a poem about the power of letters, the power of the church, *and* a poetic authority that claims to encompass them both. A son of song has assumed the power to change mortal frames, and he does not hesitate to feature his own body as a central character in this tale about revival. The minstrel's performance, which increasingly refers to his own private history, becomes, as well, increasingly confused with the plot of the 1550s and its themes of death, mourning, and the return of the dead. Slowly but surely, the power of transformation instilled in the mighty book has been appropriated by the minstrel and his song.

In cantos 4–6 Scott repeatedly raises the question of how poetry—like religion itself—can respond to mortality. As forces loyal to the Buccleuch clan and English foes converge on Branksome Tower in canto 4, the events present the lady with a dilemma posed by her political and domestic identities. By initially refusing to exchange Deloraine for the heir of Buccleuch, the lady seems to put her political identity first, but she is in a good position to be haughty toward the English—"who war on women and on boys," as she goads (4.23; *W* 5.121)—because her studies have revealed to her the direct arrival of ten thousand Scots. Before the English can be gulled into this broader conflict, however, they too learn of the approach of the relieving force and wisely propose the alternative of a trial by single combat. The lady's loyal retainers entreat her to accept these superficially favorable terms, and because her "art" is one "she might not name" (4.30; *W* 5.128), she must do so.

With these terms secured, the minstrel suspends the plot of the 1550s and closes the canto with a digression about his own art's power to relate the events of the past truthfully, a retrospective theme that mirrors the lady's recently challenged ability to see into the future. Preparing to describe the upcoming duel as one fought on foot (rather than on horseback), the minstrel invokes the authority of his dead master, the "jovial Harper." This paternal figure not only taught his protégé that the duel so happened; he had once fought a deadly duel with another poet, the Bard of Reull, who had questioned this historical detail. And the sign of the song's authenticity is the same substance that earlier pointed to and opened up the mighty book in the song: "tuneful hands were stained with blood" (4.31; *W* 5.130) in a poetic feud that exonerated the harper's account even as it cost him his life when he was judicially executed for slaying the contrarian bard. From the image of this "rival's grave" (4.32; *W* 5.130), the minstrel turns attention to his master's grave, asking, "Why should I tell the rigid doom, / That dragged my master to his tomb?" But the minstrel refuses to sing of his master's death, claiming that his "jealousy of song is dead" now that all his "minstrel brethren [have] fled" (4.35; *W* 5.130–31). And so the song pauses.

The closing frame of canto 4 thus begins at the intriguing moment when the minstrel has shifted his attention from recounting past poetic glories—to be attested by a form of poetic martyrdom—to his own present poetic incapacity, a deadness to song that makes him put off the supreme poetic topic, the death of a master poet. And at this point, the audience, led by the duchess, consoles him with praise for his ability to revive the past in terms that are both necromantic and textualized:

In pity half, and half sincere,—
Marvelled the Duchess how so well
His legendary song could tell—
. . . .
Of chiefs, who under their gray stone
So long had slept, that fickle Fame
Had blotted from her rolls their name,
And twined round some new minion's head
The fading wreath for which they bled;—
In sooth, 'twas strange, this old man's verse
Could call them from their marble hearse.

The minstrel is reportedly well pleased by this "half sincere" praise, but the narrator calls it merely "the vain tribute of a smile" (4.coda; *W* 5.131–32).

Canto 5 then suddenly opens with the minstrel making an ambitious claim about the poet's ability to orchestrate a perpetual tribute to his own passing:

Call it not vain:—they do not err,
  Who say, that, when the Poet dies,
Mute Nature mourns her worshipper,
  And celebrates his obsequies.   (5.1; *W* 5.136)

This landscape culminates a local sepulchral motif that includes the grave of the master's rival, the grave of the master, the many graves of the master's disciples, and the past society called forth from the tomb. The minstrel's last word in canto 4 is "dead"; in canto 5, it is "grave," and from the end of canto 4, Scott belatedly discloses an unwillingness to move thematically beyond canto 2 where Deloraine and the monk sat on a "marble" tomb preparing to open another (2.12; *W* 5.51). The fifth canto's greatest poetic effect is therefore the burial of Musgrave, and in that act the minstrel closes the gap between his art and its subject by literally performing a requiem mass. Suspending his lyrical output, the minstrel weaves together nature's perpetual service of mourning (invoked at the outset of canto 5) with a funeral service, including a "full choir," played out over the warrior's grave. With this close, the minstrel is no longer, as he was earlier, engaged in oblique parodies of ecclesiastical rituals; he is performing a solemn rite. Scott's staging of this musical triumph finds its reception in the audience's most blatant misreading of the minstrel's values: the ladies ask why he does not take his musical talents to "the more generous southern land" where his "skilful hand" would be "well requite[d]" (5.coda; *W* 5.165). Not liking to hear his harp ranked above his poetry, "Less liked he still, that scornful jeer / Misprized the land, he loved so dear" (5.coda; *W* 5.166). It is this doubled dislike that inspires the minstrel to utter his most famous lines about one's "native land" and the breath of the body and the death of the soul (4.1; *W* 5.169).

While some are tempted to read the *Lay* as a story about the alienated poet's successful wooing of an audience (Cronin 868), the situation is more complicated and conflicted than that. Even as the minstrel's audience becomes increasingly responsive, cantos 4 and 5 represent a progressive misreading of things in a series of interactions that link poet and audience through difference. The tribute to the preservation of the past, for example, is met with a patronizing assumption that song is a locally affective rather than a broadly effective cultural legacy. Believing song to be the noblest monument and threatening all the "unsung" with obscurity (5.2; *W* 5.137), the minstrel is praised for bringing back to life those who have been forgotten by written history, "blotted from" the rolls of Fame. The minstrel has raised his craft to a (technically) heroic level by recounting how bloodied hands defended oral tradition's accuracy, but his audience must resort to the ink-stained hands of the annalist to note this achievement. And while the minstrel celebrates a primal attachment to the land of one's fathers, his audience is implicitly more familiar with the (relatively modern) notion of national ties. Much as the singer of the *Iliad* exemplified the heroic ethos by ending his epic with the return of Hector's body to his Trojan father, the Scottish minstrel's tribute to this native ideal is best paid with returning the Englishman Musgrave to his father's grave across the border. When that solemn musical journey elicits the advice that the minstrel should cross the same border to earn money with his harping, Scott represents a clash of values that he would exploit throughout his career.

Within the *Lay* this clash also takes the form of a tension existing between the minstrel's increasingly sepulchral poetics and the subject demanded by the sixteenth-century plot: the celebration of the spousal rite to be followed by feasting, mirth, and revelry. At the opening of canto 6, the promise of a brighter future built on youthful union makes up the minstrel's theme, but both the aged and the dead will dominate the close of the poem. Following the initial frame in which the minstrel orchestrates his own dramatic death by exposure—"Still lay my head by Teviot stone, / Though there, forgotten and alone, / The Bard may draw his parting groan" (6.2; *W* 5.171)—we return to the plot of 1552 in stanza 3, with an eruption of minstrelsy that conveys a boisterous poetic energy:

> Not scorned like me! to Branksome Hall
> The Minstrels came, at festive call;
> Trooping they came, from near and far,
> The jovial priests of mirth and war;
> Alike for feast and fight prepared,
> Battle and banquet both they shared.
> They sound the pipe, they strike the string,
> They dance, they revel, and they sing,
> Till the rude turrets shake and ring.   (6.3; *W* 5.171–72)

Replying to the tercet closing stanza 2, the closing tercet in this stanza is the most active verse in the poem. Where "lay" and "may draw" governed the elegiac end rhyme of "stone," "alone," and "groan" in the previous stanza, the tercet of stanza 3 features an abundance of agents, verbs, and objects, and the all but shrill emphasis of "string," "sing," and "ring." This initial poetic revival is a sign of how little attention will be paid to the explicitly ecclesiastical portion of the spousal rite, which the minstrel glosses over in two stanzas only obliquely focused on the event itself (6.4–5; *W* 5.172–73). Far more keen to perform the rites attending death, the minstrel gives up the chance to perform a wedding mass and instead recalls a poetic debate about whether or not the lady, given her practice of "such dangerous art" (6.5; *W* 5.173), was able to approach the altar. This is the minstrel's penultimate return (see also 6.28; *W* 5.197) to the ultimately unresolved question of gramarye's status. Shrinking from the spousal rite—in a manner that parallels the lady's contested history during the same event—the minstrel suggestively embraces a "faithful truth" (6.5; *W* 5.173) as opposed to the truth itself.

The remainder of the canto is driven by the actions of the poem's mischievous reader, the goblin page. Circulating through the hall, the page threatens to convert the wedding feast into a scene of butchery (6.7–9; *W* 5.175–79), and the lady bids the minstrels to begin their entertainment "lest farther fray / Should mar the concord of the day" (6.10; *W* 5.179). As Scott brings his story to this end, he has the last minstrel become the first—albeit oral—anthologizer of ballad poetry (6.10–13; *W* 5.179–92). As the creative imitator, collector, and preserver of three separate pieces of minstrelsy by Albert Graeme, Fitzraver, and Harold, the minstrel becomes an ironic model for Scott's own career, one who must disappear to allow his latter-day heir to resurrect him on the page. Each of the poems, just as in Percy's *Reliques* and Scott's own *Minstrelsy,* is prefaced with a historical introduction that places the style and form of the poetry into a narrative of literary development on a scale ranging from the rude to the polished. Albert Graeme, from the Borders, is a singer of "a simple lay"; while Fitzraver, the English minstrel, has mastered more complex forms—"sonnet, rhime, and roundelay" (6.13; *W* 5.182)—and looks forward to a written and printed poetic tradition that shows Italianate influence. Harold, from the Orcades, synthesizes the contrasting simplicity and sophistication of the first two bards. Because of his origins in the extreme north, he carries on an ancient Nordic tradition considered uncouth, but one that has been tempered by time into a "milder minstrelsy" (6.22; *W* 5.189).

Scott's close attention to the distinctive origins of different kinds of minstrelsy is balanced against a commitment to having the poems remain thematically unified. Drawing on the aesthetic primitivism that inspired the ballad revival, the anthology assembled here is at once locally specific (literally provincial) and theoretically universal. The minstrel collects from across the British Isles culturally distinctive versions of the same tale about love's promise and death's reign. Recycling elements of the minstrel's main plot, these songs also reaffirm the *Lay*'s connections to the gothic ballads that initiated Scott's poetic career. Graeme's ballad, for example, by featuring a refrain in which "Love will still be lord of all," recapitulates the *Lay*'s overt plot about setting "love free." But as with Scott's gothic ballads, it is treachery that dominates the action. When an English lady is to marry a Scottish knight, the lady's brother poisons the new bride with his wedding gift of a flask of wine. The knight, made a husband and a widower in one day, then kills the brother in fealty to love's lordship: "So perish all would true love part." This true love reaps more death yet as the knight takes up the "cross divine" and "die[s] for her sake in Palestine" (6.12; *W* 5.181). Starkly and repeatedly, the eight quatrains of Graeme's lay feature the rule of love in a story where gifts are fatal, murder comforts the broken-hearted, and dying to kill others in Palestine is a parody of the Atonement.

Fitzraver's song takes up the *Lay*'s theme of occult studies. It depicts the doomed Earl of Surrey—to be murdered by Henry VIII—having the image of the Lady Geraldine conjured up in a "vaulted room of gramarye" (6.17; *W* 5.185), a scene that gives the reader an analogous glimpse of the lady's secret bower where the minstrel began his poem in canto 1. Like the *Lay* with its elaborate reflections of plot and theme across the temporal borders of 1552 and 1690, Fitzraver's song is complexly self-reflective as it features the apparition of Lady Geraldine in a mirror, where she appears partially clothed on a couch reading from an ivory tablet "the raptured line" of the noble poet, Surrey, now looking at her (6.19; *W* 5.186). As the song draws to its rapid conclusion, the sensuous sentimentality shifts back to the darker theme of the gothic ballads—tyrannical desire, sacrilege, and beds fouled by violence and deceit—here all coordinated with a historically despotic Henry VIII: "The gory bridal bed, the plundered shrine / The murdered Surrey's blood, the tears of Geraldine!" (6.20; *W* 5.186).

In a stunningly efficient self-referential gesture, Scott models the last piece of minstrelsy, Harold's song, on "Sir Patrick Spens," the first traditional ballad printed in the *Minstrelsy* (*W* 1.3–14). In Scott's version, Rosabelle ignores various omens and the warnings of a "gifted Seer" (*W* 5.190) and crosses stormy seas to be at a ball with a young lord. The predictably gloomy result is that "now the sea holds lovely Rosabelle!" The poetic compensation offered is the suggestion that this watery grave will outlast the famous chapel holding the graves of "twenty of Roslin's barons bold." Carrying out the claim that the poet is the figure to render the landscape into a lasting monument, Scott then ends Harold's song with a juxtaposition of the church's rites and nature's (implicitly) more availing song:

And each St. Clair was buried there,
   With candle, with book, and with knell;
But the sea-caves rung, and the wild winds sung
   The dirge of lovely Rosabelle.   (6.23; *W* 5.192)

The minstrel's performance of these three songs signals the beginning of the culmination of his poetic revival. He himself has come alive through the course of his song, and now he has revived the tuneful brethren earlier pronounced dead. This poetic revival in its full bloom, however, calls for the minstrel to reject the advice given by the dark friend to the blasphemous earl in "The Chase": "To muttering monks leave matin-song / And bells, and books and mysteries" (*W* 5.354). For mysteries, books, and bells will be appropriated in a ritual that engenders the poem's high point of social union as all parties join together in a pilgrimage to Melrose Abbey to celebrate a funeral mass for Michael Scott, the eloquent corpse who appears just as Harold's lay ends. Like many of Scott's own grandly self-deprecatory gestures, the minstrel's summoning of Michael Scott into his song seems oddly self-defeating, highlighting, as it does, minstrelsy's inability to keep the peace. As long as the page remains at large, the minstrels can only briefly forestall the conflict doomed to erupt, and thus it seems to take the appearance of a wizard, a man of books, to unite the community in a common dread of the animated dead. But the sudden and brief appearance of Michael Scott—described in three long stanzas that dramatically stall the poem's time (6.26–28; *W* 5.194–97)—is the concluding episode that substantiates the minstrel's claim to be a master of the grave, to be able to officiate at calling forth the dead. Sending lords and warriors, in sackcloth and barefooted, up the aisle toward the altar in Melrose Abbey, the minstrel has the mighty figures of the past tread the same path that brought *him* into the *Lay*: "Gone was their glory, sunk their pride, / Forgotten their renown; / Silent and slow, like ghosts, they glide" (6.30; *W* 5.198).

His "lay, so light and vain" then ends in a way that is anything but. Meditating on a post-apocalyptic fate that renders puny the historical and cultural ruptures of the sixteenth and seventeenth centuries, the minstrel confronts his audience with the world's last event. Chanting his rendition of the "Dies Irae" as sung by "the Holy Fathers," the minstrel surreptitiously adds to his creative anthology one last song that reunites the poetic, priestly, and prophetic vocations:

That day of wrath, that dreadful day,
When heaven and earth shall pass away,
What power shall be the sinner's stay?
How shall he meet that dreadful day?
When, shriveling like a parched scroll,
The flaming heavens together roll;
When louder yet, and yet more dread,
Swells the high trump that wakes the dead;
O! on that day, that wrathful day,

> When man to judgement wakes from clay,
> Be THOU the trembling sinner's stay,
> Though heaven and earth shall pass away!   (6.31; *W* 5.200–201)

If it is the case, as Jerome McGann has said in a different context, that "the anthology format opens the doors of one's perception to changes of many kinds" ("Introduction" xix), what do we gain by recognizing that the *Lay*, initially intended to conclude a poetic collection, ends with an anthology of sorts, one that includes British minstrelsy and Catholic hymns?

On the one hand, the *Lay* gives a portrait of the artist as a Romantic prophet in response to the currents of unification that characterize collective projects. The poem begins with a wearied figure who "seemed to have known a better day" (Intro.; *W* 5.11) only to end with the reminder of the "dreadful day" awaiting all. And to an earlier question posed by a well-pleased audience (had he "No son, to be his father's stay / And guide him on his rugged way?" [3.coda; *W* 5.98]), we have the patiently delayed counterquestion: "When heaven and earth shall pass away, / What power shall be the sinner's stay?" In these terms, the minstrel's world-weary entrance heralds his habitation of the bleak space, the poem's true threshold, where being begins and ends. The words that begin the *Lay* ("The way was long") announced a figure who does not come from somewhere as much as he simply comes, and the text's primary substantive of entrance ("way") reappears, transformed into a directional preposition, as the minstrel's parting word ("away"). As he comes, so he goes, singing a song to the end of time. An outcast on several levels, Scott's minstrel is a figure of extraordinary experiences; but his terminal conviction is that his state is universal. Like other masterworks of European Romanticism—and like Scott's other bloody poems of blasphemy and inspiration—the subject of the *Lay* is thus the fate of poetry, the fate of the creative imagination, standing before death and its aftermath.

At the same time, invoking the material heterogeneity (rather than the synthetic ambitions) of the collective form, Scott creates a work in which its grandest internal metaphysical claims are peripherally deflated. In the final closing frame, the narrator of the whole recounts how the minstrel has retired to a nearby "simple hut" where he entertains travelers and waylaid huntsmen before his "cheerful hearth." And so the Creator's wrathful fire is put off by hospitality's welcome "blaze" (6.coda; *W* 5.20). This slightly fey setting for the minstrel can stand for Scott's conventional place in past literary histories where he reigns, as Thomas Carlyle put it, as the age's "great intellectual *restaurateur*." "He might have been numbered among the Conscript Fathers," Carlyle wrote in 1827: "He has chosen the worser part, and is only a huge Publicanus" (qtd. in L. Frye 39). It is not my intention to deny wholly that Scott deserves such an estimation but rather to emphasize how Scott also entertained readers with the prospect of the poet's power to wake the dead, a power that Scott unforgettably experienced when he first opened Percy's *Reliques*. Thus the *Lay* concludes, characteristically of Scott at large, with an ambivalent representation of the minstrel. He is part apocalyptic prophet, part boon companion, a cosmic wanderer, and a pub bore in the making. In wavering as he does, Scott confuses related discourses of salvation and entertainment. This is one specific way to recognize how Scott's extraordinary career issued from a model of authorship that was estranged from the ideal as articulated by Coleridge in his *Biographia Literaria* (1817). That work was a protest against a scenario of modern cultural degeneration in which books and authors devolved from "religious oracles" into "entertaining companions" (*CW* 7:1.57). While Scott too would invoke that devolution, he did so comically, prepared to reunite the two extremes with a sensibility that was most serious when most playful. No less than the mighty book at the center of the *Lay*, the works of Scott were sent into the world with the disarming warning that different readers might put them to quite different ends in a historical process that would always be repeating and reversing itself.

While some commentators on Scott's writing life stress important moments of authorial transformation, it is more useful to recognize Scott's extraordinary consistency, his willingness to sustain the very same productive tensions this chapter has described. In *Waverley* (1814), for instance, we have another text that has served to mark several personal and historic watersheds: one can choose among (1) the period of Scott's poetic dominance giving way to the era of Byron, (2) Scott's poetic career giving way to one in prose, or even (3) the invention of the modern historical novel.[20] On the other hand, the book seems to confess a tenacious allegiance to the vocational paradigm outlined here as the novel's true hero, the Baron Bradwardine, retreats to his "hole" following the failure of the uprising of '45. Reading his Livy, his mighty book of potent delusions, and using his knife to cover the interior of his small cave with "Latin proverbs and texts of Scripture," the baron is defying a rebel's death by his internal exile to the heart of his dispossessed lands (304). The commentary that he engraves on his sanctuary tells the story of his ability, in part founded on his obsessive reading, to evade the dictates of political time. The comparable English situation, as Scott reminds us, is an explicitly ecclesiastical place, "The Priest's Hole" to which Mr. Pembroke, infatuated with his own unpublishable manuscripts, must retire (330). But it is the baron's den of privation that becomes the scene for a kind of reading and writing that is miraculous. Calling the hole the baron's "Patmos" (303, 315), Scott's apt allusion construes a mode of reading and writing that is absurdly but resolutely apocalyptic even as it is literally salvific. And it is no coincidence that the central ritual of the baron's religion is a communal taking of wine from a golden goblet "wrought by the command of Saint Duthac, abbot of Aberbrothock" in tribute to "another baron of the house . . . who had valiantly defended the patrimony of that monastery." Like Edward Waverley himself, this cup has been on a journey that spans the "mystical and supernatural" (46) and the bathetically materialistic as it comes to be temporarily enshrined in a pawnshop, sold off as a spoil of war by that unrivaled agent of demystification, Mrs. Nosebag (339). Fortunately for Saint Duthac, the baron, Mrs. Nosebag, and the pawnbroker, the celebrated cup can be restored to its historical environs at a price acceptable to all parties.

The baron's religion, nevertheless, affords him "rapture" in the end (338); it is a parody that insists on the privileges of authenticity. For similar reasons, the shadow of Scott's career, particularly when the question of the modern author's religious significance is raised, falls over a staggering range of events in Britain's great age of print. An extraordinary number and variety of readers in the nineteenth century found in Scott's works everything from the precious seeds of spiritual renewal to a cordial antidote for ennui or illness.[21] For some, Scott pointed toward the *Tracts for the Times* (1833–41) and the resurgent sacerdotalism of the Catholic revival. And before Keble had recruited Scott to the Catholic cause in his influential review of Lockhart's *Memoirs*, *The Christian Year* (1st ed., 1827) turned to the *Lay* in the liturgically central poem "Easter Day" (140). Readers also had a chance to incorporate Scott's poetry into pious devotions with works that had nothing to do with High Church campaigns, as was the case with William Bengo Collyer's *Hymns, Partly Collected and Partly Original* (1812), the first of many nineteenth-century hymnals to include Scott's version of the "Dies Irae."[22] For the freethinking writer Harriet Martineau, just as surely, Scott had "done more towards exposing priestcraft and fanaticism than any influence of our time" (1.36). And for the future novelist George Eliot, Scott's historicism pointed the way to the conclusions of D. F. Strauss's *Das Leben Jesu*. Scott's jovial priests even lived on in the heterodox tradition that culminated in the work of James Joyce, who would open *Ulysses* (1922) with a eucharistic parody followed by a blasphemous ballad about a queer young fellow who rose from the dead (3–4, 18–19). This most inventive heir of Scott would pay similar respects at the opening of *Finnegans Wake* (1939), where readers are told a story that had been "retaled early in bed and later on life down through all christian minstrelsy" (3).

4

Common Things Hallowed
Keble and Macaulay

TWO OF THE NINETEENTH CENTURY's best-selling books of verse—John Keble's *The Christian Year* and Thomas Babington Macaulay's *The Lays of Ancient Rome*—are all but unread by scholars of the age's poetry. With no comment we pass by the vast majority of published poetry for reasons pragmatic and aesthetically sane. In the case of these two books, however, we don't read them at the cost of forgetting a distinctive dynamic in which the history of the reading nation converged with religious and political history. Interpreted as central poetic gestures in larger literary campaigns, *The Christian Year* and the *Lays* stand out as related interventions in a voluble debate about reading, one that had assumed a distinctive profile in the late 1820s. This debate, as we shall see, subsumed arguments about national education, controversies about reading the literary remains of antiquity, and contested readings of the literary tradition in English that had been reconceived in the late eighteenth century thanks, in part, to the efforts of figures such as Lowth, Warton, and Percy. Keble and Macaulay held opposing views on all of these topics, and both authors stood at opposite extremes in the political culture of their maturity. But these same antagonistic political commitments compelled them to create books that involved their readers in a process whereby liturgical texts were either conserved and revered or manufactured and demystified. The vast readerships acquired by these books, in other words, had much to do with their common ground: a bibliographically incisive response to the act and idea of reading itself.

More specifically, this chapter aims to show how both Keble and Macaulay had a complicated relationship to parody that reflected this study's larger topic, a prevalent confusion of the religious and the literary. In the 1820s Keble, somewhat to his own surprise, found himself writing in a pious parodic mode. Conscious that parody was a rising political agent of modern infidelity, he also understood how it was related to the reading practices that were essential to preserving what he considered to be the Catholic faith. At around the same time and in response to similar pressures, Macaulay also practiced a parodic mode of writing, but his parodies were attempts to claim the privilege of historical impartiality. An essential component of Macaulay's own personal historiographic accreditation, this disinterested mode was ultimately related to his understanding of the liberal state's necessary apathy toward theological distinctions.

Broughamism, the German Threat, and Milton's Heresy

The story of the making of *The Christian Year* and the *Lays* begins in 1825 when their authors published anonymous periodical essays that would later be put forward as important documents for understanding their literary careers. In June 1825 Keble's essay "Sacred Poetry" appeared in the *Quarterly Review* (31: 211–32), and as one critic has said, it "might be read as an extended preface to his forthcoming book of poems" (J. Griffin 38). Macaulay's contemporary manifesto was his essay "Milton," which followed in August in the *Edinburgh Review* (42: 304–46). "I derived so much pleasure," Henry Brougham wrote at the time, "from seeing the true faith so inimitably preached by so young a disciple" (qtd. in Clive 90). Exercises in cultural politics that aimed to guide post-Peterloo Britain in nearly opposite directions, "Sacred Poetry" and "Milton" were also commentaries about a reading crisis that would assume a distinctive profile in 1825 with the clarification of Broughamism, the threat from Germany, and Milton's heresy.

Broughamism was the name that John Henry Newman gave in 1841 to the age's faith in the power of reading to redeem the middle and lower orders. Coming from his satire *The Tamworth Reading Room* (LD 8.544), the label was an insult bestowed on the Tory leader Robert Peel for his adoption of the liberal values of Henry Brougham, the Whig politician who had recognized the young Macaulay as a disciple.[1] But as far as Broughamism was a public agenda to espouse or oppose, it had been born in the spring of 1825. At that time Brougham, then MP for Winchilsea and coeditor of the *Edinburgh Review,* had established himself as the major national patron of the Mechanics Institutes movement, the Society for the Diffusion of Useful Knowledge, and what would become London University.[2] And while Broughamism was, for Newman at least, a derogatory label for a kind of materialism, Broughamism also was, from the start, potent and controversial because it had inescapable theological dimensions. Take for example Francis Jeffrey's 1825 review of *Practical Observations upon the Education of the People* (1825), the best-selling tract in which Brougham outlined the mission of the Mechanics Institutes. A "review" of a pamphlet based on an article published in the previous number, Jeffrey's real task was further advertisement for his liberal co-worker's views, and to that end he gave a fine example of Broughamism, claiming, "Since the time when the Scriptures were first printed and circulated in the common tongue, there has been no such benefit conferred on the great body of the people, as seems now to be held out to them in the institutions which it is the business of this little work to recommend and explain." Jeffrey then closes, "We have only to add that the work is very short, and very cheap" ("Education" 508, 510). The bathetic plunge to the "very short, and very cheap" was just the kind of turn exploited by satirists of Broughamism, but Brougham and his allies were invited to speak in ways that gave scriptural qualities to cheap tracts because all previous attempts to educate the people on a national scale—all attempts to establish a national readership—had been frustrated by religiously inspired barriers erected, at different times, by both Dissenting and Establishment forces.

As early as 1808, Brougham had become a proponent of the monitorial system devised by the Quaker schoolmaster Joseph Lancaster, and he had been a founding member of the Royal Lancasterian Association, which in turn became the British and Foreign School Society in 1814. Rather than achieving their goal—that of granting most children the chance to learn their letters at a reasonable cost—Brougham and his associates inspired the formation in 1811 of the National Society for Promoting the Education of the Poor in the Principles of the Established Church, a body that endorsed the competing Madras system devised by the Anglican clergyman Alexander Bell. The issue that inspired advocates of either system was whether or not the Bible should be read and taught with note or comment. The British and Foreign School Society offered nondenominational education featuring the Bible itself, while the National Society integrated the Anglican Prayer Book and its catechism into its instruction. And it was on the strength of some variety of this disagreement that a centralized system of national primary education was put off until the 1870s and after (R. Stewart 121–2).

Brougham in 1816 revived his reforming efforts with a new tactic, that of providing better documentation of the dismal status of popular education. He managed to have himself appointed chair of a select House Committee to inquire about the state of education among the poor in London, and the committee's activities expanded into an investigation of educational charities throughout England and Wales. Prying into these clerically dominated bodies brought forth a fair amount of clerical opposition, but in gathering all his information, Brougham developed a new respect for the church's institutional scope. Receiving information from some 11,200 clergymen, Brougham, the statistician and information-hungry reformer, discovered that "the working parish priests" of the nation were the ready answers to many needs. All of this led to an Education Bill introduced on 28 June 1820, one that created a parish-based system of elementary schools "united and knitted" with the "Protestant establishment," as Brougham told the House (*H* 2.73). He even suggested that his bill would extend clerical power, since "a parson was a clerical schoolmaster, and a schoolmaster was a lay parson" (*H* 2.74). By limiting religious instruction to "the Scriptures alone," Brougham believed that "none but very squeamish Dissenters" would balk at the opportunity (*H* 2.77–78).[3] But, on this account, he was wrong, and the bill "was abandoned in the face of Dissenters' outcry against the provision which entrusted religious instruction to the Church of England" (R. Stewart 127).

Only after encountering these frustrations did Brougham redouble his faith in books themselves. "The education of the people," he wrote in 1826, "is chiefly to be accomplished by reading; . . . the main reliance, therefore, of all who desire the improvement of the body of the people, must ever be on books" ("Diffusion" 197). Consumers of print were both the means and the ends of Broughamism. And, as Brougham frankly admitted, affordable works had also to be short to be of use in the lives of working people. Brougham's advocacy for the Mechanics Institutes in 1825 was thus intimately connected to his sponsorship of the Society for the Diffusion of Useful Knowledge (SDUK), an organization eventually responsible for the publication of thousands of tracts, its own weekly periodical, *The Penny Magazine* (1832–45), *The Penny Cyclopaedia* (1833–43), and many other cheap texts. The SDUK grew out of a meeting convened by Brougham in April 1825 that included George Birkbeck, the founder of the London Mechanics Institute. Also present at the meeting in April was George Grote, who was likewise a key organizing force behind the third major institution associated with Brougham, London University, a seat of higher learning designed to extend the benefits of Broughamism to the middle classes. In January 1825 Brougham had hosted a dinner where the idea of starting a nondenominational, nonresidential university was first planned, and by May, Brougham had introduced a bill in the House to obtain a charter. Mostly for religious reasons—i.e., opposition to the opening of advanced degrees beyond the terms of Anglican control—the bill was rejected. But Brougham and his allies forged ahead, and the university, unchartered, began instruction in 1828. As with the Mechanics Institutes and with the SDUK, Brougham's support for a nonresidential university in London was founded on a faith in the efficacy of diffusing knowledge in accessible and affordable forms. The institution was structured as a matter of economy that would open the university experience to a layer of society that could not afford the estimated "three hundred pounds a year" required to maintain a gentleman scholar at either Oxford or Cambridge (Brougham, "High Church" 223).

Most adherents of Broughamism asserted the piety of their reliance on books. Their commitment to the printed word was represented as an extension of a history of modern enlightenment that began with the Reformation, and Brougham himself repeatedly endorsed the study of Scripture—without note or comment. Brougham was also a key supporter of the successful candidacy of an Anglican clergyman, Thomas Dale, for London University's first Professorship of English Language and Literature (Court 1992: 52–53); and directly after taking the appointment in January 1828, Dale would describe his faith in "the noble art of PRINTING" in a sermon published to benefit the Printers' Pension Society (Dale 16). Many observers nevertheless interpreted Broughamism in terms of a national religious crisis. "What are all these Mechanics Institutions, Societies for spreading Knowledge, &c.," Samuel Taylor Coleridge asked, "but so many confessions of the necessity and absence of a National Church?" (*Inquiring* 411). The most determined critics of Broughamism saw it as a concerted agenda to usurp ecclesiastical authority; and in the church's place, Brougham was offering the compensatory institution of reading itself, a gesture summarized by his commitment to reading Scripture without the assistance of church formularies. Similarly, while England's ancient residential universities (theoretically) cultivated gentlemen through a series of pastoral relationships, Brougham's vision of a university featured students copying lectures, retiring to their own dispersed lodgings, and preparing for exams with books and a growing list of cram materials. The clergy was at the core of the ancient residential universities, where colleges were headed by priests and home to celibate Fellows, most of them required to take holy orders. For the new version of higher learning, there was a faith in print and in the individual reader.

Neither the history of modern British educational reform nor the history of the philanthropic dissemination of improving reading material begins with Brougham or these three institutions—the Mechanics Institutes, the SDUK, and London University—that took shape in 1825. But Broughamism became an identifiable cultural and political program as a result of Brougham's notorious energy and his ability to turn public speech and public writing into mutually supporting acts of promotion. "In the midst of an Election contest," as William Hazlitt would put it in his 1825 portrait, "he comes out to address the populace, and goes back to his study to finish an article for the *Edinburgh Review;* sometimes indeed wedging three or four articles (in the shape of *refaccimentos* of his own pamphlets or speeches in parliament) into a single number. Such indeed is the activity of his mind that it appears to require neither repose, nor any other stimulus than a delight in its own experience" (11.139). Not merely an advocate for the flow of what Carlyle would describe as "that huge froth-ocean of Printed Speech we loosely call Literature" (*CE* 5.163–64), Brougham was the feverishly active agent in the diffusion of his own views about the redemptive value of cheaply reproduced speech. "He was a kind of prophet of knowledge," as Walter Bagehot, writing in 1857, would say. "His voice was heard in the streets. He preached the gospel of the alphabet; he sang the praises of the primer all the day long" (3.169). At a time when a campaign for a free press and an end to all "taxes on knowledge" was being waged by radicals (Wiener), Brougham became the primary spokesperson for a centrist ideology of print that rejected alternatives to the political left and right. An object of scorn and satire by religious Tories as well as plebeian radicals, Brougham's place in succeeding cultural history was determined by the variety and volume of contemporary opposition to his projects.[4] But he more than any other figure was responsible for making the nation at large produce so much printed material about reading.

If Broughamism names a controversy about an expression of faith in books, "the threat from Germany" names a controversy about a scholarly creed, reportedly foreign, that held that all ancient books had to be read in the same manner.[5] In the June 1825 issue of the *Quarterly Review,* the first important notice of this threat came in an essay by the Oxford-educated clergyman Thomas Arnold, who introduced British readers to Barthold Niebuhr, the author of a *History of Rome* that had first been published in German in 1811. Niebuhr argued that the early Roman annals—as recorded in works by Livy and others—were a mixture of reliable history and myth and partially drawn from poetic traditions. By calling attention to this divide, he made the critic's first task the identification of mythical narratives. Once identified, they were given a historical interpretation based on available external evidence. In the process of denying the historicity of narratives by Livy, Niebuhr compared them to Greek poetical narratives as well as scriptural narratives. Most controversially of all, he compared Mosaic genealogies to mythical dynasties of the Greeks; and he suggested that the division of the life of Moses into three equal parts, like the Gospel genealogies of Christ, was a numerical symmetry typical of primitive myths. Despite these positions, Arnold cautioned against any "sweeping charge of 'German folly and infidelity,'" and he hailed

Niebuhr's work as the expression of an "inquiring" yet faithful historical mind ("Early Roman History" 86–87).

Several other works and events of 1825 signaled the awareness of a new school of historical interpretation that had two hallmarks: it leveled the epistemology of "revealed" texts with those of purely human origin, and it had a distinctive Teutonic character. At Cambridge, the Reverend Hugh James Rose condemned "German Rationalism" in lectures published as *The State of the Protestant Religion in Germany;* while Connop Thirlwall, a fellow at Trinity soon to take orders, translated into English a key work of German biblical criticism, Friedrich Schleiermacher's *Ueber die Schriften des Lukas. Ein kritischer Versuch* (1817). Anonymously published as *A Critical Essay on the Gospel of St. Luke,* Thirlwall's book included a long introduction from his own hand summarizing various theories of the origins of the Gospels, theories that were, as he put it, "equally and decidedly irreconcilable with that doctrine of inspiration once universally prevalent in the Christian Church" (xi). The same year Thirlwall, Rose, and Arnold were either attacking, defending, or promoting German historical criticism, the young E. B. Pusey traveled from Oxford to Göttingen, and he would go on to study at Bonn as well as Berlin where he came to know Schleiermacher. When he returned to England from the second of two periods of foreign study, Pusey published *An Historical Enquiry into the Probable Causes of the Rationalist Character lately Predominant in the Theology of Germany* (1828), a book that defended pious versions of historical criticism and faulted Rose for lumping together all German critics into one category. Rose was perturbed and replied with *A Letter to the Lord Bishop of London, in Reply to Mr. Pusey's Work on the Causes of Rationalism in Germany* (1829), and a second, enlarged edition of his 1825 work (retitled as) *The State of Protestantism in Germany* (1829). Pusey, now on the defensive and accused of holding rationalist tendencies himself, then brought out *An Historical Enquiry into the Causes of the Rationalist Character lately Predominant in the Theology of Germany. Part II* (1830).[6]

Pusey, Rose, and their reviewers were beginning a protracted debate about the significance and causes of a form of criticism that explicitly spanned classical and biblical philology. With the publication, from 1828 to 1833, of an English translation of Niebuhr's *Roman History* by Thirlwall and J. C. Hare, responsible participation in this debate was no longer limited to readers of German. As these translations were extensively reviewed, Niebuhr was being acclaimed, on the one side, as an ingenious, innovative historiographer. On the other side, he was being called, as John Barrow put it in the *Quarterly Review,* "a pert dull scoffer" whose work was "pregnant with crude and dangerous speculations" (9). According to the *British Critic,* Niebuhr attached "little or no credit to the History of the Old Testament, beyond what every ancient document, in which there is a mixture of truth and fiction, is entitled to receive" ("Niebuhr's History" 367). Hare and Thirlwall then challenged their critics in *A Vindication of Niebuhr's History of Rome* (1829).[7] In the midst of this heated debate, a Niebuhrian interpretation of the Old Testament appeared in the form of Henry Hart Milman's *History of the Jews* (1829). A popular poet in his own right, and holder of the Oxford Chair of Poetry (1821–31), Milman carried on the Lowthian tradition of treasuring what were taken to be the simple and amiable truths of Christianity; and in his history, he emphasized how early Old Testament narratives had their origin in a primitive society. By stressing this context, Milman interpreted many biblical miracles as the impressions typical of a credulous, poetical mind-set. The controversial reception of his work was both a product of what he said, and the fact that he, a clergyman with impeccable establishment credentials, should say it. He had written his history, as the Dissenting *Monthly Repository* said, "with a liberality and rationality . . . hardly to be expected from an orthodox Oxford Professor at the present day" (G. Lee 377). Orthodox Oxford was, in general, less pleased. In February 1830 Godfrey Faussett, the Lady Margaret Professor of Divinity, denounced his colleague in an Oxford sermon published as *Jewish History Vindicated from the Unscriptural View of it Displayed in the History of the Jews.*

The debate about historical criticism in the late 1820s and after had important features that distinguish it from a longer history of theological controversy that stretched back through the eighteenth century to the philosophical attacks on revealed religion. First, it was primarily an intramural battle fought by Anglicans, most of them ordained priests, rather than a struggle between the church and external assailants. Secondly, this debate took place during the "constitutional revolution" of 1828 to 1832, which undermined the Anglican hold on political and cultural power. Some leaders of a new dogmatic party in the church were convinced that recently imported critical tendencies were reacting dangerously with the traditional agents of Whiggery. Newman, who had closely observed the debate between Rose and Pusey, recalled that Rose

> had been the first to give warning . . . of the perils to England which lay in the Biblical and theological speculations of Germany. The Reform agitation followed, and the Whig government came into power; and he anticipated in their distribution of Church patronage the authoritative introduction of liberal opinions into the country. He feared that by the Whig

party a door would be opened in England to the most grievous of heresies, which never could be closed again. (*Apologia* 45)

Eventually this perceived threat compelled the delineation of an earlier Germanic source for all the trouble: Friedrich August Wolf, whose *Prolegomena ad Homerum* (1795) had denied Homer's solitary authorship of the *Iliad* and the *Odyssey*. Starting in the late 1820s, Wolf was on his way to becoming one of the century's grand heresiarchs, and Niebuhr, who had briefly studied under Wolf, was recognized as his most influential heir. The increased attention to Wolf reminds us just how little anxious attention was paid to his theories during the first two decades of their publication. The German threat did not exist in English minds until the late 1820s, and before then the nationalized source of subversive free thought was France. For those most anxious about the new Teutonic threat, the fact that a corrosive theological liberalism had two German classicists—Wolf and Niebuhr—at its roots suggested that the source of theological error was a habit of reading itself. That this tendency flowed from the geographic homeland of Protestantism raised the idea that it was the Protestant faith in the individual reader's private judgment that was the cause of the problem. What Newman would define as the heretical doctrine of liberalism—the belief that "there is no existing authority on earth competent to interfere with the liberty of individuals in reasoning and judging for themselves about the Bible and its contents" (*Apologia* 261)—was not fathered by heretics per se, but by readers undisciplined by any respect for ecclesiastical authorities or traditions. The day's most dangerous intellectual trend, to some observers, was a new kind of blasphemy that expressed itself as doubts about Rome's early history and the authorship of the Homeric poems.

As Broughamism and the threat from Germany were making self-consciously modern reading practices into subjects of political and religious controversy, a resonant illustration of the consequences of unmediated Bible reading was made public in the summer of 1825 in Charles Richard Sumner's edition of John Milton's long-lost treatise on Christian doctrine. The newly recovered manuscript had been, by royal command, translated by a well-placed clergyman later to become a bishop; and its publication as *A Treatise on Christian Doctrine: Compiled from the Holy Scriptures Alone* was intended to be an event that would bind together more surely the nation's religious and literary foundations. But, as the publication of what turned out to be Milton's heresy called forth over fifty critical reviews in the following year, readers witnessed an evolving cult of national literary veneration colliding with the doctrines of orthodox Protestantism.

Beginning with an epistolary introduction addressed "to all the Churches of Christ" (1.1), Milton began by identifying reformed religion—and its pure doctrines—with the independent Bible reader. "I thought fit," he says, "to scrutinize and ascertain for myself the several points of my religious belief, by the most careful perusal and meditation of the Holy Scriptures themselves" (1.2). Such dedication to the *sola scriptura* principle was not cause for scandal. But, for most observers, when Milton sat down to read his Bible without note or comment, he clearly rose up a heretic, endorsing in the newly published *Treatise* a wide range of heterodox positions, including a denial of the orthodox Trinity. Before 1825, Milton's religious and political views had long been the object of scrutiny and debate, apology and accusation. But even Samuel Johnson, a good hater of Milton's politics, had pronounced the poet to be "untainted by any heretical peculiarity of opinion" (qtd. in Mineka 1943: 116). And the English public sphere from 1688 on was in theory and practice construed to tolerate Milton's anti-episcopacy. The religiously tolerant Protestant monarchy was based on the assumption of a peaceful cohabitation between the established church and orthodox Protestant sects, all of them nonepiscopal. Mainstream Protestants considered the church's Thirty-Nine Articles to be divided between doctrinal articles and the less essential articles on "Church Government." Milton's anti-episcopacy fell into this last category. His confirmed Arianism, however, was a form of theological dissent of another order.

One opportunistic reader of Sumner's edition was Henry Hetherington, author of *Cheap Salvation; or, An Antidote to Priestcraft*. An advocate of cheap print and eventually an indicted blasphemer, Hetherington used the occasion of one of his imprisonments in the early 1830s to stage a mock theological debate with the Reverend D. Ruell, the chaplain of Clerkenwell Prison. Inspired by Ruell's advice to commit his religious thoughts to paper, Hetherington replied with a parodic "religious tract" that showed how the moral religion of Jesus had degenerated into the "expensive, corrupt, hypocritical, timeserving lip worship" of "Priestianity" (7), and Sumner's edition of Milton was a useful resource in this endeavor (14). Hetherington, however, was not truly interested in Milton's extensive theological distinctions as much as in a general drift of anticlericalism that had always been a portion of the legacy of the poet who had written about "the paw / Of hireling Wolves whose Gospel is their maw" ("Sonnet 16: To the Lord General Cromwell" lines 13–14). Of the three main avenues of public reception by those interested in the doctrinal details—those of the established church, orthodox dissent, and rational dissent—it was the last, the small but influential Unitarian community, that was best prepared to greet the publication warmly. Though Milton did not assert the common humanity of Jesus, he gave "the Unitarian sense of most of the texts alleged by Trinitarians," as the *Monthly Repository* put it (qtd. in Mineka 1943: 131). The only complaint that Unitarians had about the *Treatise* was that it was not likely to circulate widely given its price, and the young Harriet Martineau was commissioned to extract the most pertinent parts in *John Milton's Last Thoughts on the Trinity* (Mineka 1944: 84–97).[8] Publication of the *Treatise* was most awkward for orthodox dissent, those confessions that had long venerated Milton for both his poetry and his theology. Thus, in periodicals such as the *Evangelical, Methodist,* and *Congregationalist* magazines and the *Eclectic Review,* "bitter sorrow and regret" were the most common reactions (qtd. in Mineka 1943: 120). From the perspective of the establishment periodicals, those like the *Edinburgh Review,* the *Quarterly Review, Blackwoods,* and their more overtly religious counterparts, the *British Critic* and the *Quarterly Theological Review,* the disclosure of Milton's heresy was, on the face of it, less disturbing. The poet had always been either a theological and political rebel, according to conventional Tory wisdom, or tainted with an excessive Puritan zeal, according to the standard Whig correction. A quintessential moderate response to the new Milton of 1825 came in the *Quarterly* from Henry Hart Milman. He admitted that Milton commenced his study on sound Protestant principles, but in Milman's forgiving portrait of the poet's error, Milton's reading of the Bible was undone by its peculiar intensity. While Milton discovered his religion in heroically diligent scriptural study, he had forgotten that the Gospel had been originally preached to the unlettered (445–46). In the end, Milman subordinated Milton's theological opinions to a more important celebration of his literary immortality. Describing an inevitable future when the English of Shakespeare and Milton should "become extinct in the vicissitudes of ages," Milman insisted that "the perpetual and devotional study" of their "untranslatable" poetry would be the surest vehicle for preserving the beauties of the language (456–57).

Milman was, as we have seen, sympathetic to the historical criticism at the heart of the threat from Germany. This scholarly inclination, along with his literary accommodation of Milton's theological errors, explains why he—despite his continued association with the *Quarterly*—has been placed within an influential group of "liberal Anglican" ecclesiastics that included Thomas Arnold, Richard Whately, Renn Dickson Hampden, Connop Thirlwall, and others (Brent 139–41; Forbes). A more strident Toryism, however, was what many readers expected to see on the pages of the *Quarterly*. One such reader upset at the kindly disposition shown toward Milton was Richard Hurrell Froude, who was, as he wrote to his fellow clergyman John Keble, horrified "at finding [Milton]. . . styled 'the great religious poet of the Christian world.'" To Froude the portrayal of Milton was out of the *Quarterly*'s character, particularly given the fact that the previous June number had included an article expressing the position that "it was to be regretted that even a person of Milton's talent should have undertaken a religious subject." "Disgusted at this gross inconsistency," Froude claimed he "could not read the [Milman] review through" (188). Froude's disgust provides evidence that, for some readers at least, as far as the *Quarterly* maintained a coherent position on Milton in 1825, that position was shored up by Keble: he was the author of the June article, "Sacred Poetry," that had rendered Milman's piece grossly inconsistent. Once Froude discovered Keble's authorship, he was doubly surprised given Keble's "aversion to reviews" and the fact that this one "did not come up to" Keble's "standard of aversion to Milton" (190). Noting this double aversion was a shrewd tribute to his former tutor, for "Sacred Poetry" is an essay about a complicated form of authorship that coordinated a denigration of Milton with a disdain for a contemporary literary sphere dominated by eager readers, opinionated critics, and writers seeking the approval of both.

Keble's theological poetics would get more prominently advertised in his capacity as Milman's successor as Oxford Professor of Poetry (1831–41), and his poetic theology would inflect his contributions to the *Tracts for the Times* (1833–41). But all his essential ideas on poetry, religion, and their relations were expressed in this anonymous publication of 1825. "Sacred Poetry" begins by pretending to review one "little volume" of religious verse, Josiah Conder's *Star in the East* (1824). Even so, the opening paragraph speaks in an idiom that links the contentious topic of widespread reading, the periodical industry of "criticism," and theological debate:

> There are many circumstances about this little volume, which tend powerfully to disarm criticism. In the first place, it is, for the most part, of a *sacred* character: taken up with those subjects, which least of all admit with propriety, either in the author or critic, the exercise of intellectual subtlety. For the *practical* tendency, indeed, of such compositions, both are most deeply responsible; the author who publishes, and the critic who undertakes to recommend or censure them. But if they appear to be written with any degree of sincerity and earnestness, we naturally shrink from treating them merely as literary efforts. To interrupt the current of a reader's sympathy in such a case, by critical objections, is not merely to deprive him of a little harmless pleasure. It is to disturb him almost in a devotional exercise. The most considerate reviewer, therefore of a volume of sacred

poetry, will think it a subject on which it easier to say too much than too little. (OPR 81)

Keble here registers the central complaint of the dogmatic revival that was at the heart of what would soon be known as Tractarianism, Puseyism, the Oxford Movement or, most generally, the Catholic revival: things of a sacred character, things such as Scripture, the church, and its priesthood, were being irreverently handled by censorious criticism. And this trend, so the argument ran, was summarily embodied by the dual claim that Scripture ought to be read like any other book and that the individual reader, not any profession of faith, was the key to biblical interpretation. These concerns—centered on "the current of a reader's sympathies"—lead to Keble's elaboration of a form of literary exchange involving authorless books and critically disarmed readers. For the book under review, as Keble put it,

> bears internal evidence, for the most part, of not having been written to meet the eye of the world. It is vain to say, that this claim on the critic's favour is nullified by publication. The author may give it up, and yet the work may retain it. We may still feel that we have no right to judge severely of what was not, at first, intended to come before our judgement at all. This of course applies only to those compositions, which indicate, by something within themselves, this freedom from the pretension of authorship. (OPR 81)

Keble goes on to demonstrate the superiority of Edmund Spenser's allegorical mode over Milton's direct treatment of sacred subjects in an argument that aims to show how Spenser is England's preeminent sacred poet. If some readers in the early nineteenth century would reject allegory as part of a shift identified with literary Romanticism and its high valorization of symbolic modes (Kelley), Keble was a notable dissenter from this trend. But he registered its existence by his readiness to admit the "disadvantages" attending an elaborate allegorical project; and he argued that Spenser would have weighed these himself before embarking on a poetic journey so qualified. In this scenario, Spenser carried out his plan with "the hope of being seriously useful, both to himself, and his readers": "To himself, because the constant recurrence to his allegory would serve as a check upon a fancy otherwise too luxuriant, and would prevent him from indulging in such liberties as the Italian poets, in other respects, his worthy masters, were too apt to take." "Far more indulgent" than either Shakespeare or Milton in his temperament, Spenser wisely set "himself a rule, which should make it essential to the plan of his poem to be always recommending some virtue; and remind him, like a voice from heaven, that the place on which he was standing was holy ground." And no less than the epic author here, Keble's readers are called to practice a form of discipline:

> A good deal surely is to be gained from the mere habit of looking at things with a view to something beyond their qualities merely sensible; to their sacred and moral meaning, and to the high associations they were intended to create in us. Neither the works nor the word of God; neither poetry nor theology; can be duly comprehended without constant mental exercise of this kind. The comparison of the Old Testament with the New is nothing else from beginning to end. And without something of this sort, poetry, and all the other arts, would indeed be relaxing to the tone of the mind. The allegory obviates this ill effect, by serving as a frequent remembrancer of this higher application. (OPR 99–100)

Spenser, in these terms, outshines Milton because his epic is conducted on a plan that reaffirms Scripture's allegorical nature. Where the Puritan poet seized a subject drawn from Scripture, the more divine poet chastened his imagination by adopting a scriptural mode of writing and reading. In having Spenser triumph over Milton in this way, Keble was challenging the essential point of historical criticism that Scripture must be read like any other book. In contrast, "Sacred Poetry" defined a kind of reading that escaped the pernicious effects of an intellectual pride that was, at once, embodied in modern print culture, the historical tendencies of Protestantism, and the timeless temptations of "the Author of Evil himself" (OPR 103).

Despite its setting, Keble's "Sacred Poetry" expresses a religiously inspired aversion to the abundance of periodical reviews. Macaulay's famous essay on Milton from the same year, by way of its reception, illustrated the new powers attributed to periodicals and their contributors. "Like Lord Byron," Macaulay "awoke one morning and found himself famous," wrote his nephew G. O. Trevelyan about the stir created. At the time, John Murray reportedly had "declared that it would be worth the copyright of 'Childe Harold' to have Macaulay on the staff of the Quarterly" (Trevelyan 116–17). The gauge of fame here might seem odd, comparing the amorous lord's poetry of exile to the periodic prose of an evangelical saint's son. But as Lee Erickson has demonstrated (71–83), the 1820s were a time when poetry, as a vocation and as a publisher's venture, was being harried by the periodical writing that was Macaulay's forte. Thus, Macaulay's central contention in the essay—that Milton's poetic achievement was a triumph against "that most orthodox article of literary faith, that the earliest poets are generally the best"—had an important contemporary resonance. By admiring Milton's poetry as the greatest exception to the rule "that, as civilization advances, poetry almost necessarily declines" (*WLM* 5.4), Macaulay was underscoring the primary rationale for the ascendancy of the prosaic vehicle for his own ensuing fame.

The essay in its first five paragraphs gives an account of the discovery of the manuscript of the *Treatise,* commends the labors of its editor and translator, and quickly enumerates the most controversial "heterodox opinions" made public in it. Macaulay then dismisses any real theological import to the event, writing that "the book, were it far more orthodox or far more heretical than it is, would not much edify or corrupt the present generation. The men of our time are not to be converted or perverted by quartos." And he goes on to diminish the weight of the treatise from the substantial setting of "quartos" to varieties of semiotic transience. "For a month or two," Macaulay predicts, the *Treatise* "will occupy a few minutes of chat in every drawing-room, and a few columns in every magazine; and it will then, to borrow the elegant language of the play-bills, be withdrawn, to make room for the forthcoming novelties" (*WLM* 5.3).

The full flippancy of this gesture is developed in the next paragraph, which contains a warning that the Puritan hero will also be relished according to Cavalier principles. "The dexterous Capuchins never choose to preach on the life and miracles of a saint," Macaulay writes, "till they have awakened the devotional feelings of their auditors, by exhibiting some relic of him—a thread of his garment, a lock of his hair, or a drop of his blood. On the same principle, we intend to take advantage of the late interesting discovery, and while this memorial of a great and good man is still in the hands of all, to say something of his moral and intellectual qualities" (*WLM* 5.3). Macaulay's dismissal of theological quibbling, in other words, goes beyond the conventional endorsement of a manly, rational Christianity. He insists that the *Edinburgh Review*'s wisdom—his wisdom—is born in an understanding of the contiguity between playbills entreating audiences to the fleeting spectacles of the stage and the relics used to awaken the feelings of devotion in an ecclesiastical audience seeking the blessings of eternity. Macaulay is not simply recycling a trope about the essential equality of stagecraft and priestcraft; he was embracing both in a bid for performative power that allowed enthralled auditors—put here in theater seats and pews—to live on as periodical readers. Macaulay exhibits the new book, compared to a bogus relic, in order to preach on the (ironically) more permanent nontheological aspects of the author's life: "to commemorate, in all love and reverence, the genius and virtues of John Milton, the poet, the statesman, the philosopher, the glory of English literature, the champion and the martyr of English liberty" (*WLM* 5.3). In this way, Macaulay subsumed the transient scandals of the press into another element of his own mastery of the rising literary form, one that became the day's most fitting setting for a celebration of the author of the *Areopagitica*.

As with Keble's "Sacred Poetry," Macaulay's "Milton" is a creative response to the forces that made reading itself into a pressing topic of literary discourse. Keble in "Sacred Poetry" urged readers to avoid becoming critics of writing on sacred subjects, and he went on to explain how the nation's greatest sacred poet had similarly restrained himself by adopting an allegorical discipline. Macaulay, on the other hand, presented himself as a rhetorical opportunist eager to exploit a publishing scandal that had—he would insist against much contrary evidence—no important religious significance. Returning to Macaulay's essay looking for useful criticism on Milton and *Paradise Lost,* we are apt to share some of the disappointment expressed by Matthew Arnold in the 1870s (*CPW* 8.165–87). But if we return to the essay sensitive to the day's urgent discourse about reading, Macaulay's impact on his initial audience can be understood as something other than a response to the author's style. Likewise, Keble's essay can do more than illustrate the other-worldly character of its retiring author and his attraction to antiquated patristic hermeneutics. It has been shown how Keble's high valuation of Spenser's "veiled" method is related to the Tractarian doctrine of reserve and mystical modes of biblical interpretation (G. B. Tennyson 66–67, 105–9; Fraser 36–37; W. Shaw 67–74).[9] But the allure of these retiring modes and the Tractarian hermeneutic program was paradoxically modern in its close attention to the age's debates about reading.[10] Past histories of this terrain have stressed the clash of clerical parties inspired by theological differences, with the Oxford Movement in particular taking center stage in a drama of conversion, apostasy, or professional martyrdom. But these parties and these theological differences were prompted by close attention to the promise and peril of becoming a nation of independent readers. In Keble's representative poetry, as we shall see, "A reader is persuaded by what is not said" (Armstrong 72), and this peculiar circuit of authorial communication was a diligent commentary on the nation's destiny in readerly terms. What is certain is that both Keble and Macaulay were addressing the options and challenges facing intellectual elites living in the age of Broughamism, the threat from Germany, and the abundantly printed testimonies to Milton's heresy. And it is in this context that "Sacred Poetry" is one cultural moment's indispensable companion to Macaulay's "Milton." This history certainly suggests why 1825 was the year when Keble was persuaded to abandon his initial commitment to posthumous publication of the poems that make up *The Christian Year.* As Keble wrote to J. T. Coleridge in March 1825: "I will tell you a secret; which is that after all my backwardness (which I suppose was chiefly affectation) on such subjects, I am in a fair way to commence author" (qtd. in Coleridge 1.117).

Ways of Reading History

One is tempted to collect into a book, rather small, the poetic gems strewn throughout *The Christian Year*. There are unforgettable similes—"Like sailors shipwreck'd in their dreams"—and grand epiphanies—"He watch'd till knowledge came / Upon his soul like a flame"—and idyllic retreats where "The secret lore of rural things" calls to us "in this crowded loneliness," "the ever-moving myriads" swayed in "this loud stunning tide / Of human care and crime." And there are excursions to lands of lotos where "Bright maidens and unfailing vines" tend to desire, as well as moments of recoil from these idle dreams, revealed to be "Poor fragments all of this low earth." Then there are the fitting memorials to an unrelenting despair: "We in the midst of ruins live"—"Such thoughts, the wreck of Paradise."[11] In order to attract readers in the twenty-first century, what we would want to avoid are the arid stretches of theology in which these relics of the imagination are buried.

I propose this book only as a provocative travesty, for, as Kirstie Blair has reminded us (2003), Keble's poetic accomplishments are abundant.[12] But there is value in thinking about *The Christian Year* as a book that needs to be saved for the present time through the making of another book: that is the complex situation in which *The Christian Year* came to be. Unlike the vast majority of nineteenth-century religious poetry, *The Christian Year* was not simply a book of poems on sacred topics. It was a poetic liturgy that, as G. B. Tennyson has explained in detail (75–82), "parallels or mirrors the Book of Common Prayer throughout" (81).[13] In these "times of much leisure and unbounded curiosity," as Keble wrote in his advertisement, "when excitement of every kind is sought after with a morbid eagerness," readers have forgotten the merits of the liturgy, its provision of "a sound rule of faith" and "a sober standard of feeling in matters of practical religion." And thus Keble's premise for publication was to help others in bringing their "thoughts and feelings into more entire unison with those recommended and exemplified in the Prayer Book" (v–vi). But *The Christian Year* also became a potentially ambiguous commentary on the contemporary agency of the book it set out to recommend. That the troubled priest must seek support in poetry was a lesson that slightly grated on the main goal of the volume; and as the author of a book that, in several senses, mimicked the Book of Common Prayer, Keble understood how his literary project resembled other less pious, imitative acts.

Keble noted the problem in a commonplace book entry—"Parodies of things Sacred"—dated 12 August 1822: "Besides what is real and truely distressing in this way, I apprehend there is a good deal which is merely imaginative and fanciful. Now, to avoid needless vexation from this, (and perhaps it may answer other good purposes,) it seems a good rule always to consider; Whether the case does not admit of our regarding the common thing as hallowed, rather than the sacred one profaned" (OPR vi). From 1818, the date of the composition of its first poems, to the early 1820s, when most of the poems had been completed, *The Christian Year* was nurtured during a great age of sacred parody (Marsh 22–77, 100–104). While new attention to the literary value of Scripture gave the Bible renewed prestige as a model and resource for original literary composition, writing in sacred modes also became an opportunity to exercise a form of duplicity grounded in the author's intentions. Close to the time when Keble made his entry into his commonplace book about parody, Byron had exploited this ambiguity in *Cain: A Mystery* (1821), a closet drama that was indeed blasphemous even though the author invoked the Bible as his primary source. And immediately before Byron's work appeared, the plebeian parodist William Hone captured the nation's attention with a series of liturgical parodies that became the centerpieces of a widely reported, ultimately unsuccessful trial for blasphemy (Grimes; Shock 78–112). Keble, in other words, had good reason to fear that "a prejudice against" sacred poetry had arisen "out of its abuse" (OPR 92). He was writing at a time when both aristocratic and plebeian strains of sacred parody were resonating with a broader anticlerical sentiment that had been statistically embodied in John Wade's *The Black Book; or, Corruption Unmasked!* (1820).[14]

Keble's recognition of his own exceptional relation to parody explains a striking point in his lectures on poetry delivered in the 1830s. In lecture 35, Keble suggests that the most famous epic of unbelief, *De rerum natura* by Lucretius, invited a parodic reading that could redeem it. Like a "contaminating stain," there is a fundamental impiety running through the poem. But many of its lines "cast their testimony in favor of sound and sincere piety." "Not one of [the heathen poets] has left more numerous passages," Keble said, "which any one, perhaps changing here or there a word or two, but yet maintaining the general tenor of the whole, can quote on the side of goodness and righteousness. Such a method of quotation is technically called a 'parody': but that word is generally used only of comic and humorous adaptations; and yet that it is of force even in grave subjects will be universally allowed" (2.349–50). Before this remarkable pronouncement, Keble had rephrased the entry "Parodies of things Sacred" in "Sacred Poetry" where Spenser emerges as Keble's central poet, in part because the *Faerie Queene* remains sacred even while it shares procedures common to parody. According to Keble, there is "a disposition,—the very reverse of that which leads to parody and caricature,—which is common indeed to all generous minds, but is perhaps unrivalled in Spenser. As parody and caricature debase what is truly noble, by connecting it with low and ludicrous associations; so a mind, such as we are now speaking of, ennobles what of itself might seem trivial." "His was a mind," Keble asserts, "which would have shrunk more from the chance of debasing a sacred subject by unhandsome treatment, than of incurring ridicule by what would be called unseasonable attempts to hallow things merely secular" (*OPR* 100, 102).

In all of these cases, Keble confronted an issue that was at the center of his writing life as the "Author of the Christian Year": a potential to confuse writing piously submissive to sacred codes and writing that critically mocked the sacred.[15] Addressing an audience that often had unorthodox or irreligious equations between sacred and profane texts pointed out, Keble helped to make such equations intelligible to readers with the great success of his own poetic liturgy. In *Past and Present* (1843), for example, Carlyle would level gift-book anthologies, the textually digestive ventures of Broughamism, and the Anglo-Catholic reverence for the Prayer Book and church councils. "The Liturgy, or adoptable and generally adopted Set of Prayers and Prayer-Method," Carlyle writes, "was what we can call the Select Adoptabilites, 'Select Beauties' well-edited (by Œcumenic Councils and other Useful-Knowledge Societies) from that wide waste imbroglio of Prayers already extant and accumulated, good and bad" (*CE* 10.130). Indeed, a good deal of evidence suggests that *The Christian Year* could become a household liturgy in its own right, and "the sanctity of the Book of Common Prayer" was often intermingled with or even transferred to Keble's book (G. B. Tennyson 82). And Keble would have the problematic position pointed out for him by others, including those within the church liable to criticize the High Church's veneration for the "real martyrdom" of Charles as an offensive debasement of the passion of Christ (*OPR* 119–20).

For all of the above reasons, "King Charles the Martyr" (399–401) stands out as *The Christian Year*'s consummate exercise in a project that sought to reconcile ancient Scripture, the nation's liturgy and history, and the reading of modern poetry. Addressing a self-consciously problematic topic, the poem makes elaborate bibliographic gestures as it discloses how Keble finds his most comforting writing subject to be a specific kind of reader. Made up of ten quatrains rhymed *abab* that are divided into two parts of five stanzas each, the poem begins by figuring Charles's death as an extension of a tradition of martyrdom that begins with the apostles, as readers are reminded in the epigraph from an epistle by the most famous apostolic martyr (1 Peter 2:19). With this history in mind, the poem finds it a blessing that, here, "Far in the North," no less a man than a king suffered death for the sake of his faith. In stanzas 4 and 5, the persistent presence of Charles is remarked throughout the land, as the "trace" of him is to be found on "the haunted ground / Lone battle-field, [and] crumbling prison hall," and the "aching solitary breasts" of those "Whose widow'd walk with thought of thee is cheer'd" (st. 4–5). The martyred king and his mourning subjects are then brought even closer in the poem's second half, beginning in stanza 6, which convenes an intimate meeting in a maternal church, followed by a reunion on the page of the Prayer Book itself:

> True son of our dear Mother, early taught
>   With her to worship and for her to die,
> Nurs'd in her aisles to more than kingly thought,
>   Oft in her solemn hours we dream thee nigh.
>
> For thou didst love to trace her daily lore,
>   And where we look for comfort or for calm,
> Over the self-same lines to bend, and pour
>   Thy heart with hers in some victorious psalm.   (400)

At this point the most intimate "trace" of the king, earlier described in the first line of stanza 4, is readily available to all ready to "trace," on the Prayer Book's page, the daily service. The "solemn hours" of the church, the appointed times of the service, are not only times past when the devout Charles worshipped; they are present and future times when the reader will be closest to Charles over the "self-same lines." In stanza 7, in particular, King Charles (as a reader), any reader of the Prayer Book past and present, and the reader of Keble's poetry are brought together in a syntactical elision that bridges the past tense of the first and last lines and the present tense of the interjected clause that takes up, almost wholly, the second and third lines. The "pour" in the third line technically speaks to the past, being part of a compound predicate that includes "didst" from the first line. At the same time, it almost passes to the ear for a present command to "pour" out the heart in a gesture that mingles royal and readerly experience.

The comforts offered by these repeated tracings are answers to a failure to trace the *liber naturae* as described in a poem much earlier in the sequence, "Dimness" (4th Sun. in Advent), which begins by noting failures of connection and discernment—"How little can the heart embrace!" and

"I know it well, but cannot trace"—and goes on to describe an impeded reader:

> Mine eye unworthy seems to read
>   One page of Nature's beauteous book:
> It lies before me, fair outspread—
>   I only cast a wistful look.   (21)

In "King Charles the Martyr," the faithful reader finds abundant traces of Charles despite his violent removal from this world. But the speaker in "Dimness" struggles to see the landscape itself: "The distant landscape draws not nigh / For all our gazing" (24). These failures are reconceived in "Septuagesima Sunday," one of the most aggressively textualized poems in the collection, which begins with two stanzas that refer to God as a universally legible author:

> There is a book, who runs may read,
>   Which heavenly truth imparts,
> And all the lore its scholars need,
>   Pure eyes and Christian hearts.
>
> The works of God above, below
>   Within us and around,
> Are pages in the book, to show
>   How God Himself is found.   (79)

The goal of such a poem—one achieved equally in its composition as well as its reading—is a gracious state in which a pious form of reading overwhelms human authorship of any kind. The speaker of the poem thus becomes a reader ready to rely on an external source for a "heart" that becomes the essential visual organ:

> Thou, who hast given me eyes to see
>   And love this sight so fair,
> Give me a heart to find out Thee,
>   And read Thee every where.   (81)

In both "Dimness" and "Septuagesima," books and reading are traditional tropes. But in "King Charles the Martyr," reading itself provides comfort and calm in ways that deal more directly with history and bibliographical realities. Readerly synchronicities in "King Charles the Martyr" are most comforting, somewhat surprisingly, at the point where the poetry is interrupted by a footnote. Stanza 8 concludes, "Straight to the Cross she turned thy dying eye," as Charles's faithful mother, the church, repays his loyal love with timely comfort. At this moment too the reader is asked to turn her eye to the bottom of the page to read a quotation from Thomas Herbert's *Memoirs,* in which Keble recalls how on the day of Charles's death, Bishop Juxton read to the king a chapter from Matthew, "which relateth the Passion of our Blessed Saviour." As the story goes, when the king asked the bishop if he had chosen the reading himself, the bishop replied that it was "'the proper lesson for the day, as appears by the Kalendar;' which the King was much affected with, so aptly serving as a seasonable preparation for his death that day" (401). In this way, Charles, the Prayer Book reader, and the reader of *The Christian Year* are shown how his death was to be a glorious victory. "King Charles the Martyr" is thus about a day that recalls a series of temporal relations: the "solemn hours"—in both their secular and ecclesiastical sense—and "daily lore" that bind past and present worshippers. And "the proper lesson for the day" is available—as it was available to Charles in 1649—to any contemporary reader ready to be grateful for "the seasonable preparation" for a "funeral way" to be traveled by both royal saints and common sinners.

The penultimate stanza—with its initial "And yearly now" concluding in "earthly fears" that have followed on the interspersed "tears" and "dear"—is an accomplished aural and visual distillation of the ideology of the book as a whole. It minutely sounds the same rhyme that begins with the book's title—*The Christian Year*—and ends with "Fear" (412), its final word:

> And yearly now, before the Martyrs' King,
> For thee she offers her maternal tears,
> Calls us, like thee, to His dear feet to cling,
> And bury in His wounds our earthly fears. (401)

The book's perennially seasonable lesson is thus a warning not to be ruled by dim readings of the earthly year but to submit, through a pious fear of sin, to the eternal cycles of the liturgical year.

In poems like "King Charles the Martyr," *The Christian Year* conveys a temporality of reading that is allied to the synchronic nature of allegory and typological modes of interpretation. This model for reading is also directly antagonistic to what Keble defined as a corrupt form of historical reading. In one of his sermons on the martyrdom of Charles, "Danger of Sympathising with Rebellion," preached on 30 January 1831, for example, Keble describes how the monarch was murdered for the sake of a pathological love of liberty. But he is well aware that "there is a way of reading history, and watching the turns of passing events, which would make men indifferent to all this, and teach them to regard it as a matter of course" (117). As he puts it later, "We are told over and over again, that the season had come round, in a kind of moral cycle, when there could not but be a revolution: that the King was in some sort fairly punished for not understanding the times better: that it was indeed much to be regretted, but could not be helped, and had better be bourne with, in consideration of greater benefits ensuing" (122). This way of reading, Keble argued, which has little reverence for the traditions of the past, was doomed to become an apology for collective crimes, a justification of regicide in 1649 and a present justification of what Keble would call "National Apostasy" in his famous sermon of that name preached on 14 July 1833. Similarly, in his most famous contribution to the *Tracts for the Times,* "On the Mysticism Attributed to the Early Fathers of the Church" (1st ed., 1840), Keble went out of his way to defend those patristic reading habits that were "the likeliest to startle and scandalize a mere modern reader" (40).

Keble's antihistoricism was also featured in his lectures on poetry. In his inaugural lecture, delivered on 7 February 1832, he defended the study of ancient poetry "at a time of national peril." Because "the functions of noble poetry and good citizenship" were "closely intertwined" (1.13–14), Keble assured his young audience that his subject was neither an irresponsible luxury nor a politically neutral act. And in lectures 6–16 he supported this claim with a politically charged commentary on the Homeric poems and the question of their origin.[16] Keble began the Homeric lectures with a critique of the historical criticism associated with Wolf and Niebuhr, then leaning toward a consensus that the Homeric poems had no single author. With others explaining the origin of the poems in terms of the evolution of the Greek nation, Keble advised his Oxford audience to ignore "the farfetched and too clever speculations of certain contemporary would-be critics, whose constant theme is that the age, not the writer, is the real author of all that is written." And he went on to caution against "assign[ing] so great weight to the age and time, whether in literature, politics, manners, or daily life, as to ignore that far more and much greater influence is awarded by a kindly Providence to each man's character, strength of will and patient industry" (1.99). The critical process that converted ancient works of individual genius into anonymous cultural artifacts ultimately undermined the feasibility of revealed, historically transcendent moral commandments. In the historicist view of the world, Keble claimed, individual moral responsibility was apt to be compromised in deference to a history of progress, a way of reading history favored by the Broughamite Whigs and Benthamite Radicals who were collaboratively betraying the nation.

Keble's criticism, from the lectern, of the historical approach to the Homeric text is identical to his denunciation, from the pulpit, of the historical justification of regicide, of the "too fashionable notion of I know not what fatal necessity, suspending, as it were, men's accountable agency, when they yield to the 'spirit of the times'" ("Danger of Sympathising" 123). All his writings were contributions to a single, synchronic portrait of rebellion, a reoccurring history that began with man's disobedience in the Garden, repeated itself in the Old Testament history of broken covenants, the murder of Charles I, and the dismantling of the Anglican state that began in 1828. In all cases, the sacred ways of the past were repeatedly under attack by innovators who invoked the spirit of the times and the "specious plea of public welfare" (*Lectures* 1.123).

In addition to poems such as "King Charles the Martyr," a work of achieved reconciliations, *The Christian Year* also contains poems that speak in a less assured way. Like Tennyson's *In Memoriam* (1850), Keble's book features a form of eloquent poetic skepticism as it questions poetry's capacity to serve humanity's fundamental complaints.[17] And Keble's poetic voice frequently returns to a dilemma about the propriety of devoting his time and attention to poetic composition. "Palm Sunday" (113–15) addresses this dilemma in a creative fashion: it is a poem written by one whose need of the liturgy's discipline is best evidenced by unfulfilling poetic composition. "Palm Sunday" takes up directly the question of the poetic vocation's relation to "God's own work," the relationship of the ministry and minstrelsy. It begins by recognizing in the poet's work a sign of divine sanction and inspiration as well as a cause for particular caution. Those "whose hearts are beating high / With the pulse of Poesy," are "Heirs of more than royal race / Fram'd by Heaven's peculiar grace" (113). But this poetic race by virtue of its "chosen" status is susceptible to more galling acts of apostasy, and the poem underscores the paradoxical propinquity of the sacred and the profane: "Should bards in idol-hymns profane / The sacred soul-enthralling strain" (115). Written sometime during the winter of 1820, Keble no doubt had Byron and the newly identified "Satanic School" in mind, and with this specter of a perverted power raised, the present poetic speaker turns his comparative poetic weakness to a strength. Though the present poet is "of meaner birth" and "in that divinest spell / Dares not hope to join on earth" those of a higher rank (114), the closing four lines show how a superior poetic faith abides in a performance in which pious intentions outweigh achievement:

> Childlike though the voices be,
>   And untunable the parts,
> Thou wilt own the minstrelsy
>   If it flow from childlike hearts.   (115)

Common Things Hallowed   151

In "Easter Day," a poem first composed in 1822, Keble directly wonders what will be the poetic response to the liturgically central day that marks the first Christian resurrection: "Oh! day of days! shall hearts set free / No 'minstrel rapture' find for thee?" (140). The allusion to Scott's *Lay of the Last Minstrel* turns to the opening stanza from canto 6 where the minstrel asks, "Breathes there the man, with soul so dead, / Who never to himself hath said, 'This is my own, my native land!'" Scott's answer is a good example of his habit of exploiting the potential for the poet to be elevated into an agent of immortality, one doubly denied to any unpatriotic man:

> If such there breathe, go, mark him well;
> For him no minstrel raptures swell;
> High though his titles, proud his name,
> Boundless his wealth as wish can claim;
> Despite those titles, power, and pelf,
> The wretch, concentered all in self,
> Living, shall forfeit fair renown,
> And, doubly dying, shall go down
> To the vile dust, from whence he sprung,
> Unwept, unhonoured, and unsung.   (6.1; *W* 5.169–70)

Keble's similarly grave poem also features and documents how on Easter "the base world" itself had been transformed, "ennobled" and "glorified":

> No more a charnel-house, to fence
> The relics of lost innocence,
> A vault of ruin and decay
> Th' imprisoning stone is roll'd away.   (142)

Scott goes from the repeated question about the endurance of a man's breath—"Breathes there the man" and "If such there breathe"—to a punitive denial of the minstrel's inspired celebratory powers. Keble's revision moves in the opposite direction. He begins by partially doubting the presence of poetic inspiration (the questioned "'minstrel rapture'"), then follows with the climatic evocation of a moment of speech in which the Son of Man, risen from the grave, breathes a humble name:

> Oh! joy to Mary first allow'd,
> When rous'd from weeping o'er his shroud,
> By his own calm, soul-soothing tone,
> Breathing her name, as still his own!   (142)

"Easter Day" thus succeeds in subordinating its own poetic questions to the commemoration of its liturgical raison d'être, one that elides poetic affect and the "soul-soothing tone" of the Christic word, which in this case is "Mary" according to the Gospel of John (20:16) and a "joy to Mary" in the poem.

"Sixth Sunday after Trinity," a poem written in 1826, is a text in which prayer and poetry coexist in a relationship that ultimately has the earthly minstrel become the subject of a contrite prayer that acknowledges yet again a universal "dreadful day." The poem invokes the biblical David in both its epigraph (2 Samuel 12:13) and an identified allusion to the fifty-first Psalm, and its subtitle, "The Psalmist Repenting," thus speaks doubly to a past act of repentance and a present act of defining poetry's insufficiency should it lack a heart won in prayer:

> If ever, floating from faint earthly lyre,
> Was wafted to your soul one high desire,
>   By all the trembling hope ye feel,
>   Think on the minstrel as ye kneel:
>
> Think on the shame, that dreadful hour
>   When tears shall have no power,
> Should his own lay th' accuser prove,
> Cold while he kindled others' love:
> And let your prayer for charity arise,
> That his own heart may hear his melodies,
>   And a true voice to him may cry,
>   "Thy God forgives—thou shalt not die."   (220–21)

As with "Easter Day," Keble seeks to write a poem in which the poetic remains categorically something other (and something less) than the soul of the poem itself. And as Keble's national reputation grew, the experience of reading "Sixth Sunday after Trinity" was conditioned by an identification of "the minstrel" with Keble, appearing here as a poet whose melodies will be audible only with the help of the prayers of his legion of readers. Keble's thoughts on David, in other words, are directly transferable to his readers' thoughts on Keble, and in both cases a psalmist is redeemed by prayer, not poetry.

Keble remained officially—one might say ostentatiously—reticent as a poet, never in his own life adding his name to the title page of *The Christian Year*. But he was an active disseminator of a body of work that could be taken as an extended guide on how to read the volume of poems that sold so well for so long. With a reader's sense of time and timing at the heart of what Keble took to be the difference between pious fidelity and grave error, *The Christian Year* was a powerful alternative to the fashionable literary annuals that rose to prominence along with Keble's volume in

Common Things Hallowed   153

Fig. 6. "*Hursley Churchyard with Porch and Vicarage,*" *1867, from* The Birth-Place, Home, Churches, and Other Places connected with the Author of "The Christian Year," Illustrated with Thirty-two Photographs, *2nd ed. True to Keble's economy of reserve, this work of extensive and meticulous documentation refrained from naming its subject on the title page.*

the late 1820s and throughout the 1830s.[18] Particularly since it shared the fate of the secular annuals of being a conventional gift book, *The Christian Year* deserves recognition as the age's best-selling antihistoricist annual. While secular annuals attracted buyers with the literary novelties of each year, *The Christian Year,* like the Anglican liturgical calendar and Keble's view of theopolitical history, was simply repeated. Its title reminded readers that the Christian year—unlike the fickle productions of restless poets—did not simply pass away but returned again and again by virtue of its divine derivation. The unchanging date appended to the end of the advertisement, "May 30th, 1827," therefore served as the signature line to a book that had no named author. Reading *The Christian Year* on these terms recalls the coherence of Keble's work and explains how the retiring "Author of the Christian Year" became such a potent cultural authority even as that authority physically emanated from the rural vicarage of Hursley (fig. 6). Encouraging the devoted reading of books distinguished by a freedom from the pretension of authorship, he was nevertheless, as Newman called him, "the true and primary author" of the Catholic revival within the church (*Apologia* 28). As we noted at the opening of chapter 3, Keble would try to give similar credit to Walter Scott in 1839. Keble's designs on

154   Common Things Hallowed

Scott were willfully partial, but Newman's appraisal of the scope of Keble's influence was comparatively well balanced.

The Making of Liberal Scripture

In the 1820s Keble practiced an unconditional "filial piety" (Moor 13) that would be celebrated in the many works that honored him following his death in 1866. Macaulay during the same time was moving away from the religion of his father, Zachary, a prominent member of the evangelical Clapham Sect. And, as John Clive has put it, "that the strain between father and son never became a break was primarily due to the son's continued willingness to yield, at no little cost to his own inclinations, when confronted by the paternal wrath" (54). Clive concluded his study of the shaping of the historian by suggesting that the mature Macaulay's torrential conversational powers were to be explained by this habit of yielding: "The bottled-up energy that exploded in his conversation was due, in part, to the repressed hostility which, like so many sons of Evangelical fathers, he could not possibly have dared to express openly" (499). But there is also much evidence to suggest that Macaulay was born to declaim: during a visit in 1807 to Hannah More's rural retreat, Barley Wood, a seven-year-old Macaulay had mounted a chair to preach to astonished laborers summoned from the fields; and the prodigy came away with a bank note for £10 to be applied to the purchase of books (*LM* 1.6, n. 3). More had run a school in Bristol where Macaulay's mother, Selina, had been both a student and a teacher; and it was through More that Macaulay's father had met his future wife. So More looked on Thomas, their firstborn, as a hatchling of her own. And she eventually bestowed on young Thomas the substantial legacy of her personal library.

In August 1832, however, More, with her death approaching, disinherited Macaulay. By that time, the precocious preacher had grown into an orator of a different order, a young MP of advanced Whiggish principles. And many were convinced that Macaulay had given up the religious faith shared by his parents and More.[19] Macaulay seems to have recognized the bibliographic price for his evolving views. In 1831 when his mother spoke of sending one of his speeches to More, Macaulay replied, "Oh no, don't send it; if you do, she'll cut me off with a Prayer-book alone" (*LM* 1.277, n. 3). One result of Macaulay's muted disavowal of his religious patrimony was his extended practice of ironic literary imitation, a mode that allowed the son to drift while staying attached. Macaulay's published and unpublished poetic compositions in the 1820s in particular are dominated by parody, burlesque and ironic imitations; and his most famous book before the appearance of the *History of England* (4 vols., 1848–55), the *Lays of Ancient Rome,* was a collection of ballads "recovered" through creative literary imitation. Though he did not publish the *Lays* until 1842, Macaulay had effectively begun the book in 1834, and its triumphant appearance marked the culmination of Macaulay's struggle to discover the terms of a literary vocation that would be shaped by his evangelical upbringing even as it constituted a significant departure from it. And no less than *The Christian Year,* the *Lays* was a book that sought to disseminate particular reading habits.

Initially Macaulay wrote in the pious tradition for which the Bible was both a source for subject matter and a model for expression; and, in this sense, he was for some time Hannah More's legitimate heir. She, with works such as *Sacred Dramas,* had helped to make poetic adaptations of Scripture into popular vehicles for recreation for young readers and writers. Like Keble, though, More was wary of treading on sacred ground, and close to the time when Keble recorded his comments on parodies of things sacred, More would note in a preface to *Bible Rhymes* (1821) a new ambivalence about her poetic projects. If afforded the reception intended for them, works such as *Bible Rhymes* were designed "to excite an increasing interest in the Bible, by inducing the readers to search it for themselves." But she also registered a growing concern about the potential misapplication of her own writing. At some points in her 1821 preface, she verges on denouncing aesthetically accomplished writing in a sacred vein, saying that "the dignity of the Sacred Volume is so commanding, its superiority to all other compositions so decided, that it never gains any thing by human infusions: paraphrase dilutes it, amplification weakens, imitation debases, parody profanes" (1.63).

More was rephrasing similar qualifications expressed in December 1821 in the *Christian Observer,* the evangelical quarterly that had been edited by Zachary Macaulay from 1802 to 1816 and that remained an organ of his influence. In a review of John Jebb's *Sacred Literature,* a work that applied Robert Lowth's ideas about Hebrew poetry to a reading of the New Testament, the *Christian Observer* approved the premise of the book and admitted that several passages in the New Testament "breathe the very spirit of ancient poetry." But there were potential dangers in this approach to Scripture. "Whatever curiosity and amusement there may be in thus speculating upon the language of the New Testament," the reviewer went on, "it may be thought that there is little use in these refined niceties, and some danger of being seduced by them from the plain doctrine of revelation, into an unprofitable admiration of the artificial beauties of its composition; and that the sacred writers may thus become to us, not a savour of life unto life but a song of one that hath a pleasant voice, and can play well on an instrument."

In the end, Jebb's work was judged to be "most favorable to theological science" ("Jebb's *Sacred Literature*" 762, 770–71). But it was necessary to pause and point out the inherent dangers of such a venture.

More's preface to *Bible Rhymes* and the review of *Sacred Literature* recall how, within the world where Macaulay came of age, literary endeavors instinctively confessed their potential corruption or had them carefully drawn out. And in Macaulay's poetry of the 1820s we see him writing in a way that needed to include a rationale for the literary activity itself. In some instances, he seems to have composed verse on terms that could please his father and his increasingly conservative benefactor More. In other cases, he seems to have exploited this habit of vindication. Two of Macaulay's earliest poetic publications, both of which appeared in the *Christian Observer,* mark a transition across these affiliated modes, one that was designed to lead readers back to Scripture and a fuller appreciation of it, and one that used Scripture to vindicate aesthetic activity. The first poem, "Paraphrase of the Prophecy of Nahum," was published in March 1820, and it was a straightforward attempt to make a noncontroversial Hebrew prophecy more immediately accessible to contemporary readers. Signed "Adolescens," it was a writing exercise that was about careful Bible reading, the devotion of time and talent to spiritually profitable ends, and an iteration of the Bible's poetic excellence. In September 1820, the *Christian Observer* carried a biblical adaptation of another order, "The Lamentation of the Virgins of Israel for the Daughter of Jephthah: a Hebrew Eclogue," which Macaulay had sent to his father. Rather than being a paraphrase, the thirteen stanzas of this poem constituted a creative response to the brief passage in Judges describing how Jephthah, returning from a military victory, had sacrificed his daughter in order to keep a vow to the Lord (11:29–40). In the letter covering the poem, Macaulay tells his father about his "continued and regular reading which I have been practising with great success of late" as the start of what turns out to be a burst of praise for ancient Greek as "incomparably the best vehicle both for reasoning and for imagery that mankind have ever discovered." "Deep in Plato, Aristotle, and Theocritus," Macaulay was "particularly charmed" by the latter, and he "had several times thought of translating or imitating some of his Idyllia." But rather than pay tribute to the Grecian Muse, Macaulay turns back to Scripture to recall "that Palestine is the land of pastoral poetry." "In that delightful country," Macaulay writes, "flowing with milk and honey, abounding in rich landscape and fertile plains, and enjoying an almost radical degree of liberty before there were any Kings, while 'every man did that which was right in his own eyes,' many of the visions of Arcadian beauty and freedom were probably realized" (1.146).

The transition to the disquisition on Palestinian pastoralism appears to have been carefully planned. For the son in that transition was implicitly invoking the incontrovertible word of the father: the premise of Macaulay's poetic labor—that the Bible and its landscapes were uniquely connected to pastoral modes—stood out in the *Christian Observer*'s 1815 review of Byron's *Hebrew Melodies,* a collection that included "Jephtha's Daughter."[20] In that review, perhaps by Zachary Macaulay himself, the poetry was generally praised, but the reviewer closed by regretting that the collection "had no one poem of a decidedly pastoral character, not any properly pastoral allusion": "Surely, a Hebrew melodist sacrifices one of his greatest natural advantages, when he wholly neglects this ground. No book, ancient or modern, exhibits the pastoral life in such amiable and attractive colours as the Bible" ("Byron's *Hebrew Melodies*" 547). Knowing much of the *Christian Observer* chapter and verse, since he had been its indexer at the behest of his father, Macaulay knew his praise of biblical pastoral was authorized by the magazine that would see fit to print his poem.[21] But in its details, the son's pastoral does not much resemble the mode as described by the *Christian Observer,* which had focused on biblical pastoral in terms most endearing to Christians, i.e., the tender care of good shepherds ("Byron's *Hebrew Melodies*" 547–48). Macaulay's pastoral is faithful instead to the eroticized elements of Theocritean verse, with the emphasis falling on thwarted love and the mourning of the dead, dance and song, and the strewing of flowers. With Jephthah's daughter a female Daphnis, it is her virginity as much as her death that is mourned in a lush poem that treads the convoluted line where the celebration of maidenhood is part of a larger fertility rite. Macaulay's poem also captures, at its scriptural core, the complexities of his relationship with his father, who cultivated his son's genius even as he was bent on training it toward pious ends. A poem that speaks about the "daughter of a father's tenderest care" who is also the "victim of a father's cruel faith" (589) succinctly describes—with the change of one word—Macaulay's role as the hero of his own Oedipal romance.

Macaulay also found a duplicitous opportunity in his emphasis on the political conditions associated with pastoral poetry, said to flourish in the days of the Judges when the lack of a monarchy was the precondition for the enjoyment of "beauty and freedom." The "Hebrew Eclogue" indeed obliquely marked the anniversary of the Peterloo massacre in September 1819, which Macaulay had denounced with a vehemence that had worried his parents. This potential meaning of the "Eclogue" was recognized by his father, who included in the *Christian Observer* a chastened prose introduction drawn from his son's letter. Where young Macaulay had described a country "enjoying an almost radical degree of liberty before there were any kings," the *Christian Observer* pointed to a country "where the people, at least in the earlier stages of their history, enjoyed an extraordinary share of political freedom." And where the son had described the probable realization of "the visions of Arcadian beauty and freedom," the *Christian Observer* excised the "beauty and freedom" to emphasize the fictional nature of those visions: "Many of the visions of Arcadian fable were probably realized" (*LM* 1.146; "Lamentation" 587). Having been annoyed the year before at being called to affirm that he had not been secretly "initiated into any democratical societies" at Cambridge (*LM* 1.132), Macaulay made his father midwife to a sexually charged, antipaternalist allegory that, among other things, echoes Byron's Manfred when he noted "pipes in the liberal air" after commenting that "here the patriarchal days are not / A pastoral fable" (*Manfred* 1.2.49–50). In this sense, the "Hebrew Eclogue" was a literary hoax, and it is related to "Tears of Sensibility," what Macaulay called "a burlesque on the style of the magazine verses of the day" (*LM* 1.167) that he had managed to foist onto the pages of the *Morning Post* in November 1821.[22]

"A Radical War Song," a poem dated to 1820 but first published in 1860, gives another example of an early text in which religion, politics, sex, and irony are the young poet's materials. Borrowing directly from British counterrevolutionary iconography, the song includes stock images of the criminal justice likely to be practiced by radicals ("The peer shall dangle from his gate, / The Bishop from his steeple"); and there is a vivid retribution promised to the conniving practitioners of lawyer-craft and priestcraft:

> We'll strap the bar's deluding train
>   In their own darling halter,
> And with his big church bible brain
>   The parson at the altar.

All of which culminates in a Cockney's spirited vision of a coming age of free love and tax-free gin:

> No discontented fair shall pout
>   To see her spouse so stupid;
> We'll tread the torch of Hymen out,
>   And live content with Cupid.
>
> Then, when the high-born and the great
>   Are humbled to our level,
> On all the wealth of Church and State,

>   Like aldermen, we'll revel.
>   We'll live when hushed the battle's din,
>   In smoking and in cards, sir,
>   In drinking unexcised gin,
>   And wooing fair Poissardes, sir.   (*WLM* 8.546–47)

"A Radical War Song" is a clearly ironic paean to the pleasures of radical liberty, and thus it might have pleased the father who had been worried about his son's overzealous sympathy for the martyrs of 1819. But despite what we can imagine to be approbation for its political position, it seems unlikely that the father would have been amused by any poem building up to such a drunken orgy. Furthermore, Macaulay's predominant model in "A Radical War Song" was the reactionary, parodic poetry of the *Anti-Jacobin,* which had infamously abused the family patroness Hannah More and her educational projects from 1800 to 1802 (Stott 231, 238–52). In these terms the antiradical political commitments of the poem function as a cover for anarchic, sexually charged poetic expression. And like its poetic contemporary "Hebrew Eclogue," "A Radical War Song" includes a duplicitous, self-referential project of vindication. If scriptural study exonerates a lush excursion to Arcadia in the one case, politics exonerate a Pisgah site of the philandering golden age to come.

These poems of 1820 belong in the context of several other surviving exchanges on the topic of a brilliant son's literary habits, including an episode from earlier that year when Macaulay was called to respond to the report that he had become known as a "novel-reader" (*LM* 1.140–41). The most contentious conflict came in 1823, when Zachary Macaulay expressed shock at his son's involvement with *Knight's Quarterly Magazine,* a short-lived periodical published by Charles Knight, who would soon become associated with Henry Brougham and the SDUK and other "popular literature" ventures. Knight relied heavily on a band of contributors from Cambridge for his *Quarterly Magazine,* which was presented as the effusions of a convivial "knot of young men," their labors being dedicated to a tutelary deity, "the Lady Mary Vernon, the Mistress of all Harmony, the Queen of all Wits, and the Brightest of all Belles." Promising to avoid all heaviness in their devotions to her, they would go "forth to the world once a quarter, in high spirits and handsome type, and a modest dress of drab, with verse and prose, criticism and witticism, fond love and loud laughter; every thing that is light, and warm, and fantastic, and beautiful, shall be the offering we will bear" (2). Macaulay's character in this fraternity was "Tristram Merton," who is prone to erupting into a ceaseless flow of similes and historical parallels that were fired by his "omniscience" or remarkable memory (7–8). Most readers today would be put off by the erudition of the magazine, but it was the gallantry—the quest for "the thanks of pleasant voices" (2)—that caught the attention of Tristram Merton's father. After seeing the first number, Zachary pronounced *Knight's* to be "a loose, low, coarse and almost blackguard work." "Where there is less of coarseness," the father wrote to his wife, "there is still a strain of voluptuousness and even licentiousness which is quite intolerable" (*LM* 1.187, n. 3). Zachary was particularly worried by the son's poems "Oh Rosamond!" and "By Thy Love, Fair Girl of France." The first is a three-stanza lyric that begins with the (only slightly) sublimated sexual energy of a summer's dawn:

> Oh Rosamond! how sweet it were, on some fine summer dawn,
> With thee to wander, hand in hand, upon the dewy lawn,
> When flowers and heaps of new-mown grass perfume the
>   morning breeze,
> And round the straw-built hive resounds the murmur of the bees;
> To see the distant mountain-tops empurpled by the ray,
> And look along the spreading vale to the ocean far away.

A lover for all seasons, the speaker then closes with a description of the domestic pleasures to be had on "winter nights":

> How gay would be the fireside light, how sweet the kettle's moan,
> Joined to the lustre of thy smile, the music of thy tone!
> How fondly could I play for hours with thy long curling tresses,
> And press thy hand and clasp thy neck with fanciful caresses,
> And mingle low impassioned speech with kisses and with sighs,
> And pore into the dark-blue depths of those voluptuous eyes. (219)

This unmistakably English story—which mingles a lover's voice and the "kettle's moan"—is rephrased "By Thy Love, Fair Girl of France." But "Laughter, blushes, sighs, caresses," "lips," and "tresses" are given the added allure of the "varied wiles" practiced in France, including the utterance of "those foreign accents dear / Whose wild cadence on mine ear / Still in slumber lingers" (220).

In his defense of his involvement with *Knight's,* Macaulay was not above deception, giving what Thomas Pinney calls a "misleading" account in which he pretended that "a bookseller of whom we knew nothing [had] coupled improper productions with ours in a work over which we had no controul" (*LM* 1.188, n. 1).[23] The father was not moved, and in June 1823 Macaulay withdrew his services. "My father, in particular, is, I believe," Macaulay wrote to Knight, "generally known to entertain, in their utmost extent, what are denominated evangelical opinions." And, although Macaulay insisted that he did not partake of these same scruples, "Gratitude, duty, and prudence alike," as he put it, "compel me to respect prejudices which I do not in the slightest degree share." But Macaulay was careful to leave a window open for return, describing his withdrawal as "for the present" (*LM* 1.189).

Macaulay got back onto the pages of *Knight's* with "Moncontour," a poem published, along with "Ivry," as "Songs of the Huguenots" in the January 1824 issue (33–35). A lament by a devout Huguenot soldier following a defeat in 1569, "Moncontour" was also Macaulay's bid to have his father rescind objections to his association with *Knight's;* and "confin[ing] himself to historical subjects," as Jane Millgate has suggested, was one way for Macaulay to forestall the parental objection to "the two conventional love lyrics" (1973: 12). What hasn't been noted is the way in which Macaulay combined the turn to history with an implicit commentary on the episode that made the historical mask desirable in the first place. Macaulay's answer to his creative bind was a sequence of historical lyrics that first turns away from the erotic landscape that had opened "Oh Rosamond!" and offended the father. "Farewell to thy fountains, farewell to thy shades," sings the true believer, defeated and departing for exile in 1569:

> To the song of thy youths, and the dance of thy maids,
> To the breath of thy gardens, the hum of thy bees
> And the long waving line of the blue Pyrenees.

The Huguenot then claims a spiritual triumph more significant than the immediate reality of defeat, and the poem concludes with an unequivocal expression of faith:

> Farewell, and for ever. The priest and the slave
> May rule in the halls of the free and the brave;—
> Our hearths we abandon;—our lands we resign;—
> But, Father, we kneel to no altar but thine.

Macaulay carefully paired this poem of triumph in defeat and liberty in bondage with "Ivry," a poem celebrating a Huguenot victory a generation later in 1690. As its concluding stanza puts it, the battle at Ivry has reversed the situation lamented in "Moncontour":

> For our God hath crushed the tyrant, our God hath raised the slave,
> And mocked the counsel of the wise, and the valour of the brave.
> Then glory to his holy name, from whom all glories are;
> And glory to our Sovereign Lord, King Henry of Navarre.

The poem thus begins by recommencing the dancing and singing that had been bidden farewell in "Moncontour":

> Now glory to the Lord of Hosts, from whom all glories are!
> And glory to our Sovereign Liege, King Henry of Navarre!
> Now let there be the merry sound of music and of dance,
> Through thy corn-fields green, and sunny vines, Oh pleasant
>   land of France!

Throughout this episode, history—or at least a particular Protestant version of it—is a useful consolation for the poet's father. Within that story, however, the son has composed a metanarrative about the silencing and subsequent revival of youthful, sexually promising song, "the merry sound of music and of dance." In part, the author of "Oh Rosamond!" and "By Thy Love, Fair Girl of France" returned to *Knight's* as the prodigal son kneeling before the father. But the son's true measure of freedom comes from his ability to control the reception of a text that is both a concession and a rebuttal to the father's disapprobation. As in the story of Jephthah's daughter, there was a critique of the father's moral compass even as the child practiced an obedience beyond reproach.

These paternal issues are confirmed when we read the "Songs of the Huguenots" as the second installment in a larger performance that begins with "Scenes from 'Athenian Revels,'" a closet drama that immediately precedes the poems on the pages of *Knight's* (17–33). And in both cases—in seventeenth-century France and in fifth-century Athens—history is a medium for the construction of a representative sequence about poetic responses to paternal authority. Like "Songs of the Huguenots," "Athenian Revels" has a dyadic structure with two distinctive but clearly related scenes. It is set on the eve of the expedition to Sicily led by Alcibiades, a military quest that became overshadowed by the infamous mutilation of the Hermae, a type of sacred statuary scattered throughout Athens. The identity of the perpetrators of this profanation remained a matter of debate, but the event was attributed to Alcibiades and his closest companions, a reportedly impious coterie eventually charged with performing unauthorized initiations into the Eleusinian mysteries. In Macaulay's version, the hand behind the mutilations is not clearly revealed, but the mock initiations do seem to have taken place.

The drama opens, however, with a conventional domestic conflict between an overscrupulous father and a financially dependent son. The conservative father is Callidemus, while the son, whose vocational ambitions waver between poetry and politics, is Speusippus. "So, you young reprobate!" says Callidemus, opening the scene with a list of charges that culminates in the licentiousness Zachary had detected in *Knight's* (17). Callidemus seems to rant over much in the first scene, but the son is destined in the second scene to find himself disturbed by Alcibiades's impiety as it moves from words to deeds. What was totally original in Macaulay's reconstruction was his precise account of why Alcibiades calls for the illicit initiation: it is a stunt to express a romantically inspired lyrical faith, a gesture to confirm Alcibiades's claim that he will return from the battles of history to an Arcadian scene of music and dance.

Recalling the revels of the briefly reconciled triumvirate in *Antony and Cleopatra,* the second scene of "Athenian Revels" takes place in the house of Alcibiades, who presides over a gathering that is simultaneously decadent and heroic. "Bring larger cups" is the opening command of the dashing young leader, who announces, "This shall be our gayest revel." But he goes on to acknowledge the price that he and others are prepared to pay: "It is also probably the last—for some of us at least" (24). Alcibiades is up to maintaining the light tone, but his young love Chariclea finds it impossible to be cheerful, and thus Alcibiades makes a promise that he will return. Breaking out into poetry of his own composition, he sings of the ways in which their reunion shall be celebrated:

> Then for revels; then for dances,
> Tender whispers, melting glances.
> Peasants, pluck your richest fruits:
> Minstrels, sound your sweetest flutes:
> Come in laughing crowds to greet us.
> Dark-eyed daughters of Miletus;
> Bring the myrtles, bring the dice,
> Floods of Chian, hills of spice. (25)

The lyre then goes round the room and comes to Chariclea herself, who chooses to "sing an old Ionian hymn, which is chanted every spring at the feast of Venus, near Miletus." Like "Oh Rosamond!" the hymn is a three-stanza love lyric that recycles many of the earlier poem's conventional tropes:

> Let this sunny hour be given,
>   Venus, unto love and mirth:
> Smiles like thine are in the heaven;
>   Bloom like thine is on the earth;
> And the tinkling of the fountains,
>   And the murmurs of the sea,
> And the echoes from the mountains,
>   Speak of youth, and hope, and thee. (27)

With these themes of youthful passion amid a setting of sunshine, fruitful flora, mountains, and the sea, the pseudo-Miletian hymn generally recalls "Oh Rosamond!" More specifically, it translates the object of desire in the earlier poem—meaning *rose of the world*—in the line "Bloom like thine is on the earth," an allusion that gets confirmed by the hymn's last line, which speaks of "The long curls of rose-crowned hair" (28).

Macaulay alludes as well to the earlier sequence by having Alcibiades's fateful decision to initiate Charlicea recall the "foreign accents dear" in "By Thy Love, Fair Girl of France." With a foreign-born mother, Chariclea is barred from initiation into the mysteries of the state's cult. But Alcibiades throws over this rule in tribute to a Keatsian aesthetic where beauty is truthfully native to poetic eyes. "Surely we ought to say to every lady," Alcibiades declares, "'The land where thou art pretty is thy country.' Besides, to exclude foreign beauties from the chorus of the initiated in the Elysian fields is less cruel to them than to ourselves" (30). To this plan, Speusippus objects, proving to be his father's son in his genuinely shocked appeal: "In the name of all the gods—" (31). Alcibiades, though, is dismissive of the hesitations expressed, and he delivers a detailed charge of hypocrisy. Incredulous that his companions are "taken with a fit of piety" (32), Alcibiades also speaks like Macaulay himself, who in "Moore's *Life of Lord Byron*" (1831) would write that "we know no spectacle so ridiculous as the British public in one of its periodical fits of morality" (*WLM* 5.391). In the end, "Athenian Revels" remains an amphibious literary creature. It is susceptible to being read as a didactic representation of the consequences of impiety. But it also records and alludes to a series of impieties, profanations, and full-blown blasphemies.

In the next issue of *Knight's*, Macaulay extended a similar historical and poetic project in "Songs of the Civil War: I, The Cavalier's March to London, and II, The Battle of Naseby," a sequence that revisits the historical strategy behind "Songs of the Huguenots" and carries on the suggestive religious and sexual themes of "Athenian Revels." As with the Huguenot songs, these two are chronologically sequenced: the first one recounts an anticipated Cavalier victory in 1642, and the second records a Roundhead victory in 1645. Like all the works discussed here, the Cavalier song has an erotic plot at its core, with the conquest of London repeatedly troped by rapacious references to "maiden's shrieks," the cries of "London's dames, in wilder fear," and the unavailing screams of a "sweet Precisian" (321–22). This leads to the poem's concluding foresight of a nocturnal celebratory rite of wine, women, and song. Imaging "a glorious pyre" made of "tons of rebel parchment," the Cavaliers marching toward London predict the destruction of the rebellion's sanctimonious and sacred texts: "Petition, psalm, and libel / The Colonel's canting muster-roll, / The Chaplain's dog-ear'd Bible"—all will "crackle in the fire." And by the glare of this semi-blasphemous light, in part kindled by striking a rhyme with "libel" and "Bible," he tastes the battle's rewarding vintage:

> We'll tread a measure round the blaze
> >   Where England's pest expires,
> And lead along the dance's maze
> >   The beauties of the friars:
> Then smiles in every face shall shine,
> >   And joy in every soul.
> Bring forth, bring forth the oldest wine,
> >   And crown the largest bowl.
>
> And as with nod and laugh ye sip
> >   The goblet's rich carnation,
> Whose bursting bubbles seem to tip
> >   The wink of invitation;
> Drink to those names,—those glorious names,—
> >   Those names no time shall sever,—
> Drink, in a draught as deep as Thames,
> >   Our Church and King for ever!

"The Battle of Naseby" then enacts an audacious juxtaposition: having closed the first poem with the vision of a Cavalier orgy, Macaulay commences the Puritan poem with references to an altogether different "vintage," one that primarily comes from the prophetic poetry in Isaiah (especially 41:25, 63:2–6):

> OH! wherefore come ye forth, in triumph from the North,
> >   With your hands, and your feet, and your raiment all red?
> And wherefore doth your rout send forth a joyous shout?
> >   And whence be the grapes of the wine-press which ye tread?
>
> Oh evil was the root, and bitter was the fruit,
> >   And crimson was the juice of the vintage that we trod;
> For we trampled on the throng of the haughty and the strong,
> >   Who sate in the high places and slew the saints of God.   (323–24)

The vengeance called down upon the Royalists in "The Battle of Naseby" is represented as punishment for the licentiousness vigorously confessed in "The Cavalier's March to London"; and in this sense, the poem is literally puritanical in ways that might have pleased Zachary Macaulay. But the more important message of the songs read together—and read against each other—was a particular historical perspective that ventured to equate the bibulous tread of Cavaliers with the biblical grapes of wrath invoked by Obadiah. Macaulay "was showing his mastery of the cultural and ideological materials of history, all within a religious context" (Edwards 10–11); and his latter-day prophet's scriptural appropriations suggest how the Cavalier song was just as surely a theopolitical tract. Despite its bacchic character, that song is a hymn in praise of the victories won for "Church and King" no less than Obadiah's song violently and devoutly derides "the mitre and the crown."

A form of historiographic impartiality similarly convenes a conventional antithesis when "The Cavalier's March to London" is recognized as a reworking of "A Radical War Song," which it resembles in diction, imagery, and structure. The seventeenth-century Royalist would seem to have little in common with the post-Peterloo plebeians, but they do in fact speak similarly.[24] These congruencies show how Macaulay was initiating himself into different political enthusiasms and rising above them by understanding their structural similarities at their violently climactic moments. In a context of dealing in opposites, Macaulay exercised rhetorical and poetic power even as he illustrated a precept at the heart of his liberal statecraft. As represented in his speeches on the Reform Bill, this statecraft is the expression of a political will able to reconcile opposing social forces in an act that allows the polity to survive a social revolution that has already occurred or is under way. Macaulay's work in *Knight's Quarterly Magazine* thus records at least two forms of duplicity. History was a kind of cover that allowed Macaulay to make poetic expressions that evaded parental censure. The uncontexualized lyrics "Oh Rosamond!" and "By Thy Love, Fair Girl of France" forced Macaulay to withdraw from *Knight's*. With his historicized dramas and poems, he was able to recommence a literary career in spite of his father's scruples. At the same time, such a turn to history was inspired by Macaulay's conviction that the impartial historian had to embrace imaginative resources in order to comprehend political culture's oppositional dualities.[25]

The duplicitous gestures of Tristram Merton in *Knight's* found their consummation in the *Lays of Ancient Rome*, a collection of ballads that narrated early Roman history as recorded in the prose works of ancient historians such as Livy and Polybius. The divided allegiances of these Roman ballads connect them to Macaulay's earlier poetic imitations, parodies, and hoaxes as well as to his penchant for pendent texts. But the *Lays* was far more ambitious, conveying a commentary on classical and biblical philology, contemporary English constitutional politics, and their convergence. By the late 1830s, when most of the *Lays* had been written or drafted, Macaulay had discovered how his private experience as an author of duplicitous texts was a model for a public poetic discourse addressed to a nation with two major political classes, one the party of conservative traditions, the other the party of progress and change. Invoking the authority of Thomas Percy's *Reliques of Ancient English Poetry* as well as Walter Scott's *Minstrelsy of the Scottish Border,* Macaulay exploited strategic possibilities peculiar to the ballad book as a literary form, one that allowed invention and innovation to hitch their fortunes to acts of historical conservation.

Macaulay began composing his Roman ballads in the summer of 1834 in India, where he had obtained a position on the Supreme Council for India, and his lucrative post (worth £10,000 a year) was a reward from the Whig magnates for his important rhetorical services. So while Macaulay later recalled that the plan for the *Lays* "occurred to me in the jungle at the foot of the Neilgherry hills" (*LM* 4.66), the poet found himself in an Asian jungle, to a large degree, because of his speeches in favor of Reform. In the first of these speeches, he gave a theory of revolutions that made an analogy between Roman and British social conflict. "All history," Macaulay argued, "is full of revolutions, produced by causes similar to those which are now operating in England. A portion of the community which had been of no account expands and becomes strong. It demands a place in the system, suited, not to its former weakness, but to its present power. If this is granted, all is well. If this is refused, then comes the struggle between the young energy of one class and the ancient privileges of another. Such was the struggle between the Plebeians and the Patricians of Rome" (*WLM* 8.17). The reference to Roman history in 1831 was a key element of Macaulay's pro-Reform rhetoric, and that same pro-Reform rhetoric provided the essential plan for his pretended recovery of Rome's oral poetry, which came in four separate ballads, each with its own independent preface, and a general introduction to the whole. The individual prefaces described the political context of the period when the ballad was supposed to have been composed and the earlier time when the events portrayed in the ballad were supposed to have happened. "Horatius" was composed in 394 BC and described how an Etruscan attack on Rome in 514 BC was turned back. "The Battle of the Lake Regillus" was composed in 303 BC and described the defeat of a Latin army in 496 BC. "Virginia" was composed in 372 BC and described the attempt of a Patrician to exploit a plebeian sexually in 449 BC. "The Prophecy of Capys" was composed in 275 BC and described the disclosure of a prophecy to Romulus in 753 BC—the traditional date of Rome's foundation.

In all of these ballads, Macaulay showed how performances of historical poetry in ancient Rome were involved with a series of constitutional reforms including the Licinian Laws (367 BC), a reform that liberal historians of the 1830s often compared to England's constitutional changes of 1828–32. These laws required one of the two annually elected consuls to come from plebeian ranks and removed religious and civil disabilities placed on the plebeians, disabilities that Macaulay compared to those borne by Roman Catholics in the United Kingdom before 1829. The ancient Roman aristocracy had resisted the calls for reform but "at length, the good cause triumphed":

> The results of this great change were singularly happy and glorious. Two centuries of prosperity, harmony and victory followed the reconciliation of the orders. Men who remembered Rome engaged in waging petty wars almost within sight of the Capitol lived to see her mistress of Italy. While the disabilities of the Plebeians continued she was scarcely able to maintain ground against the Volscians and Hernicans. When those disabilities were removed, she rapidly became more than a match for Carthage and Macedon. (*WLM* 8.514)

The removal of plebeian religious and civil disabilities thus led to "a turning-point in the history of the world" (*WLM* 8.528), the historic *translatio imperii* represented by the Roman eclipse of Greek and Carthaginian power.

To at once bear and illustrate this political message, Macaulay invented a canon of Roman poetry in which internal and external conflicts were fused. The poetic texts of "Horatius" and "The Battle of the Lake Regillus," for example, describe the Romans defeating other Italian armies in 514 and 496 BC, but Macaulay's prose introductions describe how internal, domestic conflicts influenced the performance or composition of these ballads in 394 and 303 BC. Macaulay's collection also set the event of his fictional poetic recovery against a history of aesthetic displacement. So while Macaulay's four ballads pretended to recapture Rome's oral traditions ("a literature truly Latin, which has wholly perished" [*WLM* 8.448]), his prose documented their demise by uniting the assumptions of the modern ballad revival with the old idea that Rome's political domination of the ancient world coincided with her cultural subjugation to the Greeks. The first ballad, "Horatius," "is meant to be purely Roman." "The Battle of the Lake Regillus" from ninety years later "has a slight tincture of Greek learning and of Greek superstition" (*WLM* 8.485); and the final ballad, "The Prophecy of Capys," represents "the latest age of Latin ballad-poetry" (*WLM* 8.530). In this sense, the last Roman minstrel anachronistically descends from Thomas Percy, who had dated the final demise of the English minstrels to the rise of Elizabethan literary culture, which also coincided with England's heroic age of global navigation; and Macaulay's account of the eclipse of Latin minstrelsy was, ultimately, a complex tribute to an imperial destiny driven by domestic political transactions. He offered the partners of what would become known as the Victorian compromise a reassuring historical analogy that favored religious toleration and an expanded franchise. Just as Rome's emergence as a Mediterranean power was traced to the constitutional reforms that made plebeian vitality available to imperial endeavors, England's destiny expanded with the admission of the middle class, Catholics, and Dissenters to the privileges and responsibility of citizenship. Translating the historical rationale for the constitutional reforms of 1828–32 into a poetic text, Macaulay then addressed this text to England's post-Reform readers, a book-buying public that was politically indebted to the historical rhetoric versified in the *Lays*.

Historians today still find themselves rephrasing Macaulay's arguments for political liberalization. Macaulay's pro-Reform rhetoric, in other words, survives as a standard interpretation of how and why those changes took place. In her study of the constitution of modern British national identity, for example, Linda Colley portrays Catholic emancipation, the decisive ideological break of 1828–32, as a military bargain, saying, "As far as the governing elite was concerned, the main solvent of traditional Protestant intolerance was war and its demands" (326). The *Lays*, however, was conceived in an atmosphere in which there was an alternative to liberalism, and liberalism was understood to be something more than a utilitarian plan to make Catholic peasants into imperial soldiers. The triumph of liberalism did make it possible for all, regardless of their religious beliefs, to become loyal patriots, but before liberals could refashion the state into a kind of agnostic police agency, they had to dismantle the sectarian state. Macaulay contributed to this process directly as a politician, orator, and essayist who regularly provided vigorous formulations of the liberal theory that the state should be indifferent to theology. As the author of a volume of primitive national poetry, he advocated liberalization in a more complicated fashion. With the *Lays*, Macaulay sought to popularize the historical criticism that Keble, Newman, Pusey, and others had recognized as the most important internal solvent of the sectarian ideology that had united church and state on doctrinal (rather than merely pragmatic) grounds.

That is to say that the *Lays* was the most widely read mid-century vehicle for "the threat from Germany." It openly acknowledged itself to be an application of the principles of Barthold Niebuhr, who had argued that

Rome's earliest annals were based on a lost canon of epic songs. And Macaulay's university-educated audience was sensitive to the way in which the *Lays* had implications for interpreting Scripture. Niebuhr was a notorious figure precisely because he demanded that all ancient texts, whether they be the ancient annals of the Greeks, Romans or Hebrews, should be read in the same historical manner. The underlying assumption of the *Lays* was the classical version of the idea that early Hebrew history, as recounted in the Old Testament, was based on a variety of different source materials—including poetry—that were conflated, combined, and redacted by a succession of priestly scribes. More specifically, the ancient Roman annals were derived from two competing canons of aristocratic priestly documents and popular oral traditions, a general division that rephrased the conviction that the Hebrew Bible was a synthesis of distinctive priestly and prophetic traditions. This idea about the two main sources of early Roman history was conveyed in Henry Malden's *History of Rome* (1830), a work that was published by the SDUK and which Macaulay had read and corrected in manuscript (*LM* 1.249). Summing up Niebuhr's theory, Malden had described how early Roman history was composed "from two distinct sources, which correspond to the two orders of the people":

> In nations where an hereditary or exclusive priesthood has maintained itself, the early history is commonly nothing but an arbitrary chronological outline, in which are comprehended memorials of institutions and events connected with religious observances. Where the mind of a people has not been cramped by such a dominant order, the native early history has commonly developed itself in the form of popular traditions, and often of popular poems. The twofold state of Rome possessed both kinds of history. The religious books were the property of the Patricians; the traditionary poems were probably cherished by the Plebeians or Commons. That the two streams of history were at first separate and independent will appear still more probable, when in the course of the history the distinction between the Patricians and Plebeians shall have been more developed. As by the progress of civil institutions the two orders were blended into one people, so in the annals of the first historians the two kinds of materials were compounded into one narrative. (60–61)

The *Lays,* then, was a sly essay about the origin of national scripture and its liberal (that is, historical) interpretation. The four contemporary historians cited in Macaulay's preface (Connop Thirlwall, Henry Malden, Thomas Arnold, and Barthold Niebuhr [*WLM* 8.447]), were all liberals, but the *Lays* did more than invoke the authority of liberal historians. It bore the message that men like Thirlwall, Malden, and Arnold were liberals because they practiced a particular type of historiography that was the essence of nondogmatic theology.

Macaulay's analysis of the origin of national scripture and its modern interpretation begins with the most basic hermeneutic crux, the interpretation of two conflicting narratives in "Horatius." As Macaulay describes it, there are two main traditions narrating the efforts of Horatius to save Rome from an Etruscan attack. In one, followed by Polybius, Horatius single-handedly defends a bridge over the Tiber and perishes when he finally plunges into the water. In the second version, followed by Livy, Horatius fights with two others and safely swims ashore. According to Macaulay, the two traditions reflected political differences within the Roman nation-state. One version, sung by Macaulay's plebeian bard, "was preferred by the multitude, the other, which ascribed the whole glory to Horatius alone, may have been the favorite with the Horatian house," an ancient Patrician tribe (*WLM* 8.464). Far from being an interpretive problem, these conflicting narratives endorse Macaulay's conclusion that ancient Roman history was a series of class conflicts wisely resolved by liberal reforms.

In his next ballad, "The Battle of the Lake Regillus," Macaulay shows how the political reconciliation of patrician and plebeian called for the literal synthesis of the religious documents controlled by the constitutional elite and the oral poetry cherished by the common people. Macaulay's primary interest is not the Roman military victory over the Latines in 496 BC but rather the political crisis of 303 BC that occasioned the composition and performance of the poetic narrative. As Macaulay tells the story, the republic was saved from revolution in 303 BC by two censors, one a patrician, the other a plebeian, who instituted a series of "reforms" including "a remodeling of the equestrian order" that was accompanied by a new equestrian ritual, the *transvectio equitum*. "Determined to give to their work a sanction derived from religion," the reformers "ordained that a grand muster and inspection of the equestrian body should be part of the ceremonial performed, on the anniversary of the battle of Regillus, in honour of Castor and Pollux, the two equestrian Gods." Given the success of these reforms, there "can be no doubt," Macaulay said, that Rome's patrician clergy acted in concert with the reformers, and "it is probable that those high religious functionaries were, as usual, fortunate enough to find in their books or traditions some warrant for the innovation" (*WLM* 8.488–89). This divine sanction then finds its way into the prophetic close of "The Battle of the Lake Regillus" as sung by Macaulay's fictional bard. There, the High Pontiff Sergius gives an inspired command that the equestrian muster take place to commemorate the assistance of Castor and Pollux (st. 40; *WLM* 8.511). In other words, the bard's rhapsody set in 496 BC ends with the prophetic institution of an equestrian ritual first performed in 303 BC, a religious ceremony that is anachronistically instituted by the recitation of the poem. The text is a pious forgery and illustrates how the crisis-diverting act of blending "the two orders . . . into one people" was literally a matter of compounding "two kinds of materials . . . into one narrative" (Malden 61).

Macaulay's third ballad, "Virginia," is supposed to have been sung in 372 BC, about seventy years before the reforms that gave rise to the composition of "The Battle of the Lake Regillus." The filicidal violence recounted in "Virginia" represents Rome's class conflict at its worst, just before the passage of the Licinian Laws. And the fact that it survives in fragments is formally suggestive of the potency of the domestic violence that is its subject. The intensity of the conflicts depicted in "Virginia" sets the stage for a dramatic resolution of internal political tension in Macaulay's final ballad, "The Prophecy of Capys," which is also the last episode in a series of epic scenarios in which some form of divination is associated with military conflict. In "The Battle of the Lake Regillus," as we have just seen, the associated act of scriptural interpretation is a politically expedient postscript. In his opening ballad, "Horatius," Macaulay invented a disastrous act of Etruscan divination. Before marching on Rome, "thirty chosen prophets" from the Etruscan confederation search their scriptures for a sign about the upcoming war:

> Evening and morn the Thirty
>   Have turned the verses o'er,
> Traced from the right on linen white
>   By mighty seers of yore.

These inspired exegetes find texts propitious of victory and tell Lars Porsena, "Go forth, beloved of Heaven; / Go, and return in glory" (st. 9–10; *WLM* 8.468). But Roman swordcraft proves more potent than Etruscan priestcraft, and the "pale augurs, muttering low" have their prophecy confounded (st. 46; *WLM* 8.478).

At the time of the performance of "The Prophecy of Capys" in 275 BC, Rome has once again won a military victory by defeating the Greeks at Tarentum. But instead of recalling a scene of scriptural interpretation in the poetic text (as in "Horatius") or in the introductory prose (as in "The Battle of the Lake Regillus"), Macaulay closes his ballad book with an ambitious regress to the original moment when the divine promise was given to Romulus in 753 BC. The poetic text is a prophecy of national greatness that is uttered to Romulus after he and Remus have taken their revenge and murdered their uncle King Amulius and the priest Camers:

> Now slain is King Amulius,
>   Of the great Sylvian line,
> Who reigned in Alba Longa,
>   On the throne of Aventine.
> Slain is the pontiff Camers,
>   Who spake the words of doom:
> "The children to the Tiber;
>   The mother to the tomb." (st. 1; *WLM* 8.531)

While marching around with the severed head of Amulius, Romulus comes across the priest Capys, who is, understandably, trembling from "head to foot." Capys atones for the earlier priestly sentence by predicting a glorious future and declaring the known world to be Rome's promised land. The ballad, in other words, is a rendition of the imperial revelation given to Aeneas in the sixth book of the *Aeneid* and a version of the Lord's promise to Abraham that "I will make of thee a great nation" (Gen. 12:2). The revelation to Romulus, as Macaulay puts it, "was likely to be a favorite theme of the old Latin minstrels. They would naturally attribute the project of Romulus to some divine intimation of the power and prosperity which it was decreed that his city should attain. They would probably introduce seers foretelling the victories of unborn Consuls and Dictators, and the last great victory [at Tarentum] would generally occupy the most conspicuous place in the prediction" (*WLM* 8.527). The book as a whole thus ends with a prophetic vision of a sacred city in the midst of a triumphal procession:

> Blest and thrice blest the Roman
>   Who sees Rome's brightest day,
> Who sees that long victorious pomp
>   Wind down the Sacred Way,
> And through the bellowing Forum,
>   And round the Suppliant's Grove,
> Up to the everlasting gates
>   Of Capitolian Jove. (st. 30; *WLM* 8.539)

Synthesizing biblical discourse about the New Jerusalem with a liberal's faith in the fruits of free trade, Macaulay's Rome is a materially apocalyptic city. Whereas the Jerusalem glimpsed in Revelations is built of gold and girded by walls of precious stones and pearly gates that never close,

174 Common Things Hallowed

Macaulay's Rome, with its "everlasting gates," is an emporium for the world's treasures:

> Hurrah! for the great triumph
>   That stretches many a mile.
> Hurrah! for the rich dye of Tyre,
>   And the fine web of Nile,
> The helmets gay with plumage
>   Torn from the pheasant's wings,
> The belts set thick with starry gems
>   That shone on Indian kings,
> The urns of massy silver,
>   The goblets rough with gold,
> The many-coloured tablets bright
>   With loves and wars of old,
> The stone that breathes and struggles,
>   The brass that seems to speak;—
> Such cunning they who dwell on high
>   Have given unto the Greek.   (st. 28; *WLM* 8.538)

And once again, as with the other cases of prophecy in the *Lays,* this greatest of all moments of Roman divination is subordinated to the social and political forces that require its narration. But while national theology was formerly in the hands of a hereditary priesthood, the series of constitutional reforms described in the *Lays* has expanded the mythic franchise of Rome and yielded Roman theology to the nation—or at least the crowd-cheered bard speaking for it. By virtue of the resolution of the conflict between plebeians and patricians, the nation now has one narrative. The patrician and plebeian versions of the revelation to Romulus are identical because that revelation is the transcendent fiction that unifies all Roman classes.

In the context of antiquity, the *Lays* can be said to end with a rousing celebration of Roman religion. In the context of modernity, however, the *Lays* ends with a national theology understood in purely earthly terms. Macaulay is, after all, interested in Roman revelation to the extent that he can show that it is a mythic tradition about a historical process determined by respectable revolution. The religion that promises internal concord and promotes external expansion is, according to the thesis of the *Lays,* the religion that most easily represents the evolving aspirations of its believers. Using the same principles that could make ballads seem like national scripture, he made the liberal state appear to be history's consecrated polity.

In 1835, near the time when Macaulay first conceived of the *Lays,* John

Gibson Lockhart would identify this demystifying poetic project in the *Quarterly Review*. Describing the impact of innovative biblical criticism coming from Germany, Lockhart cited what he considered a misappropriation of the antiquarian labors of his father-in-law, Walter Scott. "Everything lofty, and everything tender, was alike smoothed away and obliterated," Lockhart wrote, "and the Bible had become in the hands of these *Christian* commentators a mere *Minstrelsy of the Jewish Border*—a patchwork of wild old ballads, connected by extracts from barbarous chronicles, antiquarian notes, and editorial excursus" (23). These same scholars explained "the history of the Patriarchs as a series of *mythi,* and the Gospel of St. Luke as a mosaic-work of *volk's-lieder*" (33). Deeply infused with the spirit of the modern ballad revival and fresh from reediting the first posthumous edition of Scott's *Minstrelsy of the Scottish Border* (1833), Lockhart nonetheless intended to mock the import of the higher criticism by claiming that it reduced Scripture to folklore, a word to be coined in 1846 (*OED*).[26]

Understanding the *Lays* in this context can explain why a philosophical radical such as John Stuart Mill was so well disposed toward the volume in the *Westminster Review.*[27] Mill understood how the *Lays* took a comparativist look at religion in the ancient world; and this significance of the *Lays* was recognized by James Frazer, who would open *The Golden Bough* (1890) with an epigraph from "The Battle of the Lake Regillus," which speaks of the shrine at Aricia where "The ghastly priest doth reign, / The priest who slew the slayer, / And shall himself be slain" (Frazer 1.1; compare *WLM* 8.495). But this skeptical strain in the *Lays* will not explain why it was also hailed enthusiastically in the *Quarterly Review* or *Blackwood's*. The *Lays* enjoyed such a wide popularity among all kinds of readers, from liberal to conservative, from the devout to the freethinking, because Macaulay carefully exploited historicism's complex genealogy. Macaulay invoked a Germanic historicism that had been (at least since 1825 for many readers) identified with antisupernatural aims. But Macaulay also invoked Scott and Percy as the creative patrons of his poetic and historical experiment. And the *Lays* implicitly recalled how the reportedly destructive tendency of historical criticism had grown out of the nationally redeeming labors of British ballad collectors and literary historians.

As a book that found a good purpose in acknowledging debts to Scott, the *Lays* stands out as yet another creative appropriation of the posthumous authority of the Wizard of the North, who had been presented in Lockhart's *Memoirs* (1837–38) as Britain's most significant man of letters since Samuel Johnson. With Lockhart's work frequently compared to James Boswell's *Life of Johnson,* Macaulay, both a devoted Boswellian and a great reader of Scott, was the *Edinburgh Review*'s obvious candidate to review the biography. But Macaulay declined the job. Instead, and probably with far greater effect, he made his *Lays* into an homage to Scott that disseminated the moderate reading of his influence. While the Tractarians under Keble's leadership insisted that Scott's career provided a thrilling moral about revived obligations to the past, Macaulay's *Lays* gave a Whiggish interpretation to Scott's historicism in terms that were mostly inoffensive to mainstream Tory sentiments. Macaulay in the *Lays* thus went out of his way to pledge a double allegiance to the Laird of Abbottsford and his posthumous retainers when he extended praise to Lockhart's work as a ballad translator in his *Ancient Spanish Ballads* (1st ed., 1823). The compliments to Scott and to Lockhart probably had the direct benefit of having Lockhart, then editor of the *Quarterly Review,* give the task of reviewing the *Lays* to Henry Hart Milman, the most liberal clerical man of letters associated with the Tory organ.[28] As with his earlier poetic publications, though, Macaulay in the *Lays* was reveling in speaking with a forked tongue, for even as the *Lays* pledged allegiance to instances of Tory balladry and to Tory antiquarianism, it was just as surely a vehicle for the ballad revival as a poetic reconquest of texts and traditions that had been dogmatized by ecclesiastical types. In political terms, this meant that the *Lays,* like the *History of England* that followed it, blends "the romantic and the utilitarian, Burkean Toryism and philosophical radicalism" (W. Thomas 275).

Despite their elements of conservatism, Macaulay's patriotic bards did threaten the theological foundations of the Anglican state because they were creatures of a critical movement willing to concede the legendary and literary character of Scripture. And in the generation to come, historical critics would narrate the origin of Scripture in the same Niebuhrian terms that Macaulay had popularized. In Rowland Williams's contribution to the controversial best-seller *Essays and Reviews* (1860), for example, the author discussed how it now seemed clear that the book of Daniel was neither by Daniel nor from the time it was supposed to be from, the sixth century BC. Instead, it was from the second century and, rather than being prophetic, was a form of history written in the guise of prophecy. "The truth seems," Williams wrote, "that starting like many a patriot bard of our own, from a name traditionally sacred, the writer used it with no deceptive intention, as a dramatic form which dignified his encouragement of his countrymen in their great struggle against Antiochus" (193–34). Like "The Prophecy of Capys," the prophecy of Daniel was a backdated national legend inspired by contemporary events. In Samuel Wilberforce's condemnation of *Essays and Reviews,* the major error of its contributors was described in terms that similarly recall the critical procedures enacted in the *Lays*. In the hands of the essayists, Wilberforce said, the inspired

Fig. 7. "The Lament of the Hebrew Minstrel," 1859, by John Tenniel, from The Lays of the Holy Land, *a profusely illustrated book containing poetry from hands as ideologically diverse as Lord Byron and Hannah More. Here the minstrel figure initially elevated by Percy is fully integrated into the biblical tradition.*

essence of the Bible had become uncomfortably elusive; it was something "embedded in the crust of earlier legends, oral traditions, poetical licences, and endless parables,—a certain residuum, which may be considered, in a certain sense, as the record of revelation; whilst what is legend, and what the more noble residuum, must be determined for himself by every man" (269). In the end, Wilberforce accused the essayists of trying to force a question with no attractive answer, asking "whether Holy Scripture can withstand the assaults of the remorseless criticism now turned upon it—, or, whether the human mind, which with Niebuhr has tasted blood in the slaughter of Livy, can be prevailed upon to abstain from falling next upon the Bible" (293). This orthodox disdain for such a literary Bible was similar to the discomfort expressed by the positivist Frederic Harrison in the *Westminster Review*. Harrison did not share Wilberforce's religious faith, but he agreed with the formidable bishop that it was a contradiction to be both a Christian—not to mention a Christian minister—and a reader of a Bible that is merely "a medley of legend, poetry, and oral tradition, compiled, remodeled and interpolated by a priestly order centuries after the times of the supposed authors" (310).

In the past, *Essays and Reviews* has often been represented as a volume that unleashed new concepts on an unwary audience, most of it ignorant of modern trends in reading Scripture. The present study has made it clear that *Essays and Reviews* was a notable climax to a long clerical debate that has been dated to 1825, the year when Thomas Arnold introduced British readers to the historical criticism of Barthold Niebuhr—and the year when John Keble published his antihistoricist manifesto "Sacred Poetry." In the end, however, it is important to remember that the combined force of Wilberforce's characterization of theological error and Harrison's charge of self-serving latitudinarianism falls short of accounting for the habits of the larger reading public. This public also included readers who were simultaneously enthusiastic about both *The Christian Year* and the *Lays;* and a broad channel of reception existed for books such as *The Lays of the Holy Land* (1859) that heterogeneously united a veneration for Scripture, poetic sensibilities, and potentially intense religious faith (fig. 7). Another book in line with the *Lays,* albeit in different ways, was George Gilfillan's *Bards of the Bible* (1st ed., 1850). The most popular work by the prolific Scots minister of a Secession congregation, *Bards of the Bible* is evidence of an increasing interdependence, for some readers, between the poetic and the scriptural. The book itself aspires to bardic levels by virtue of being "a Prose Poem, or Hymn, in honour of the Poetry and Poets of the inspired volume" (Preface); and its central contention is that all of the Bible is essentially poetic and that all of Scripture's most important historical agents are bards, including the "transcendent poet who died on Calvary" (191). At times unintentionally hilarious—as when the Apostle Peter is called "the Oliver Goldsmith of the New Testament" (231)—Gilfillan's book nevertheless had its devoted readers, and in the rush of Gilfillan's poetic enthusiasm, Macaulay takes his place alongside authentic biblical bards: "What Macaulay's 'Lays of Ancient Rome' have done for the fabulous legends and half-true traditions of Roman story, have Jasher, Iddo, Deborah, and David, in a higher and holier manner, done for the real battles and miracles which stud the annals of God's chosen people" (80–81).

In the next chapter, we will see another case in which the border between sacred and profane canons was traversed by William Ewart Gladstone. Prime minister an unprecedented four times, Gladstone, like almost all devout Anglicans, was deeply attached to *The Christian Year,* but he also noted "lik[ing]" the *Lays* "very much" (*GD* 3/11/42); and in his political maturity, Gladstone would adhere to Keble's Anglo-Catholic theology even as he acquiesced to the reality of Macaulay's theory of the state. This personal accommodation is one way to understand his ability to dominate an era in which a declining reliance on the idea of national religious conformity coexisted with, in some cases inspired, vigorous religious devotion. "For fifty years he was so closely associated with the public affairs of this country," James Bryce said in 1903, that "the record of [Gladstone's] parliamentary life is virtually an outline of English political history during those years" (400). Or, as Colin Matthew put it more recently, "To a curious extent, . . . an assessment of Gladstone is a personification of an assessment of Britain's moment in world history" (645). To make such an assessment, it is essential to come to terms with this man's passion for the greatest of all the bards, Homer.

5

Primitive Traditions and Modern Readers
Gladstone's Homer

IN MAY 1870 *Punch* noted the recent literary achievements of William Ewart Gladstone and Benjamin Disraeli, the age's incompatible stars of parliamentary politics who were in the first round of twice alternating premierships between 1868 and 1880 (fig. 8).[1] Driven out of office in 1868 largely by Gladstone's pledge to disestablish the Irish church, an agenda that revived charges that the Liberal leader was in secret a Roman Catholic, Disraeli sought satiric revenge in *Lothair* (1870), a novel about a young aristocrat who narrowly avoids the twin temptations of revolutionary republicanism and Roman Catholicism.[2] Gladstone's contemporary work, which had appeared in August 1869, was *Juventus Mundi: The Gods and Men of the Heroic Age,* part revision, part sequel to his earlier *Studies on Homer and the Homeric Age* (3 vols., 1858).

Very different books coming from very different men, *Lothair* and *Juventus Mundi* nevertheless exhibit a common belief in the topicality of ancient, non-Christian religions. In Disraeli's story, his eponymous hero is briefly snared by what are presented as two semi-pagan revivals: a pantheistic brotherhood bent on overthrowing Europe's national monarchies and a Roman Catholic conspiracy to establish universal papal authority. With a materialistic worship of nature depicted as the true creed of the republicans, the Catholic conspirators—led by cunning Jesuits—are portrayed as latter-day Roman imperialists. Eventually disenchanted with both extremes, Lothair is shown the way back to the Church of England thanks to the tutelage of Paraclete. This mysterious native of Palestine is what Disraeli liked to consider himself, a Jewish Christian (or Christian Jew) disdainful of the religious dogmas pronounced by foreign—that is, Greek and Italian—ecclesiastical councils; and his lesson for Lothair, delivered as the two survey Jerusalem from the Mount of Olives, concerns the providential nature of national distinctions. "'In My Father's house are many mansions,' says Paraclete,

> and by the various families of nations the designs of the Creator are accomplished. God works by races, and one was appointed in due season and after many developments to reveal and expound in this land the spiritual nature of man. The Aryan and the Semite are of the same blood and origin, but when they quitted their central land they were ordained to follow opposite courses. Each division of the great race has developed one portion of the double nature of humanity, till after all their wanderings they met again, and, represented by their two choicest families, the Hellenes and the Hebrews, brought together the treasures of their accumulated wisdom and secured the civilisation of man. (316)

Gladstone's *Juventus Mundi* also spoke about Hebrews and Hellenes. But where Disraeli was mostly interested in nations as racial entities, Gladstone had what turned out to be loaded textual interests. From the start, his career as nineteenth-century Britain's most famous reader of Homer was motivated by his belief that some features of the "Olympian religion" corresponded "with the Hebraic traditions, as conveyed in the books of Holy Scripture, and also as handed down in the auxiliary sacred learning of the Jews" (*Juventus* 202). Portraying a historic national faith, the *Iliad* and the *Odyssey* for Gladstone also bore traces of God's revelations to the ancient peoples of the Near East. And no less than Disraeli, Gladstone would find personal and political bearings by seeking to reconcile contending but related strains. For in addition to being at or near the center of parliamentary life for some sixty years (1833–96), Gladstone starting in 1847 was the author of five books and over forty articles on Homer and the Homeric Question, the debate about the authorship, unity, and historical value of the Homeric poems.[3]

Disraeli the racial theorist has been of interest to scholars of nineteenth-century constructions of ethnicity; and critics pass easily from *Lothair* to a work like Matthew Arnold's *Culture and Anarchy* (1867)—another contemporary text about Hebrews and Hellenes—with little concern about evaluating the validity of the racial categories themselves (Brantlinger, "Disraeli" 101–5; Cheyette 55; Ragussis 211–33). But when it comes to having something to say about Gladstone's Greeks and Jews, a different scholarly tale emerges. Gladstone's notion that Homer's poetry is infused with a divine light has led commentators to label his Homeric writings eccentric and amateurish. Since 1975, various kinds of historians have called Gladstone's work "absurd" (Lloyd-Jones 123, 124); "crack-brained"

Fig. 8. "Critics," Punch, 14 May 1870: 193, by John Tenniel. Gladstone growls, "HM!—flippant!" while Disraeli snorts, "HA!—Prosy!"

(Shannon 1.317); "fantastical," "unscholarly," and "bizarre" (Jenkins 14–15, 181). The late Colin Matthew did not dismiss that work so quickly, but his final verdict emphasized what it tells us about the author, not the age.[4] Gladstone's Homeric writings have been approached most productively by scholars such as Frank Turner in the broader context of nineteenth-century Hellenism. Even then, though, Gladstone's scholarship remains "nonetheless perplexing" (1981: 166).[5]

Primarily seen as a psychological curiosity, Gladstone's Homeric work has become divorced from its public context: politically significant debates about the origin and interpretation of ancient texts, debates that bridged sacred and secular canons. And instead of paying close attention to the history of these debates, critics most often use the Homeric avocation to illustrate something about Gladstone's extraordinary mind as his public life becomes a spectacle that ultimately reflects a unique inner life. An intensely religious man whose first period of parliamentary activity (1833–45) was just as intensely conservative, he drifted toward liberalism in the second part of his career (1847–65), and emerged in 1868 as prime minister of the greatest of all Victorian reforming governments (1868–74). During the long evening of his career, he returned three more times to be prime minister (1880–85, 1886, and 1892–94) and developed a close bond with portions of the increasingly large electorate. He late in life made granting home rule to the Irish a moral mission and with this mission seemed intent, so his critics said, on breaking up the British Empire. To these critics, Gladstone's zealous, crusading style of politics was a sign of an unbalanced mind, one ruled by an uncontrollable principle of self-assertion hidden behind a grandiose penchant for public moralizing. He was a hypocritical reformer who would also manage to persuade himself that his long-term habit of interviewing prostitutes was based on a love of their souls rather than a fascination with their flesh. Gladstone's eccentric scholarship thus becomes another illustration of the remarkable character of a man who would declare in 1888 that he had two remaining worldly ambitions: "One is to carry Home Rule—the other is to prove the intimate connection between the Hebrew and Olympian revelations!" (M. Ward 2.78). He was just the type (so goes this caricature) to take upon himself, Moses-like, the task of delivering the Irish from their captivity even as he concocted a new defense against unbelief formulated with ingredients gathered on his dauntless excursions to the summits of Helicon and Sinai.

While Gladstone's Homeric work is most often subordinated to some version of this narrative of an extraordinary, psychologically complicated life, this chapter aims to show how that life and that mind were representative of the age's developing social and political conditions. At the outset, it is important to understand how the most frequently derided aspect of Gladstone's views—his ideas about corrupted revelation—were once commonplace. Both Samuel Taylor Coleridge and John Henry Newman, for example, believed that "heathen" religious traditions contained elements of true revelation corrupted, and both believed that various non-Christian religious traditions contained traces of the revealed mystery of the Trinity. On these matters, Gladstone was a conscientious student of the two men who are by some accounts the guiding spirits, respectively, of Anglican and Catholic religious thought in nineteenth-century Britain. In 1829, while at Oxford, and probably inspired by a visit of "Cambridge men" including Arthur Hallam (GD 26/11/29), Gladstone "began Coleridge's Friend" (GD 30/11/29), where he would have read that "the earliest Greeks took up the religious and lyrical poetry of the Hebrews; and the schools of the Prophets were, however partially and imperfectly, represented by the mysteries, derived through the corrupt channel of the

Phoenicians" (*CW* 4: 1.503–4). Several years later, Gladstone studied the departed sage's *Literary Remains* (*GD* 26/2/36), which, among other things, discussed "patriarchal tradition" and traced the manner in which Asiatic and Greek mythologies were connected via the Samothracian Mysteries bearing "a distorted reflection of the Mosaic scheme" (1.185). This same 1836 edition contained a lecture delivered in 1825 to the Royal Society of Literature that made similar points about the Samothracian Cabiri, an ancient trinity often cited in discussions about the connections between true and corrupt religion (2.323–59; compare *CW* 11:2.1251–301). What might well have struck Gladstone about these extra-scriptural channels of revelation was the fact that they were accepted in both the incipient Broad Church theology associated with Coleridge and the sacerdotal theology promoted by Newman. Thus, in 1834 (*GD* 9/3/34ff) Gladstone had read in Newman's *The Arians of the Fourth Century* (1st ed., 1833) that "there is nothing unreasonable in the notion, that there may have been heathen poets and sages, or sibyls again, in a certain extent divinely illuminated" (82). "It is unquestionable," Newman said in the same work, "that, from very early times, traditions have been afloat through the world, attaching the notion of a Trinity . . . to the first Cause" (90).

The case of Coleridge in particular illustrates why noncanonical revelation was so widely discussed for much of the nineteenth century. As a Unitarian in his politically radical days, Coleridge saw heathen trinities as evidence of Trinitarian Christianity's corruption, as he would argue in his 1795 "Lectures on Revealed Religion," where he traced out the way in which "Christians had permitted themselves to receive as Gospel the idolatrous doctrine of the Trinity" (*CW* 1.212). When Coleridge found his way back to the established church, he decided that the Trinity was the keystone to orthodox belief, and thus he saw some extra-scriptural mysteries as the refracted light of true revelation. This same argument was made in a popular manual of Anglican orthodoxy, Bishop Tomline's *Elements of Christian Theology*. Having reached its sixteenth edition by 1826 when Gladstone studied it at Eton, Tomline's work discussed heathen trinities at length, concluding that "the discovery of the existence of this doctrine in the early ages, among [other] nations . . . , has been of great service to the cause of Christianity, and absolutely refutes the assertion of infidels and sceptics, that the sublime and mysterious doctrine of the Trinity owes its origin to the philosophers of Greece" (73).[6]

If we take the time to read what Gladstone read, not only does his acknowledgment of corrupt revelation appear theoretically orthodox (in the sense of standard); it becomes clear that competing theories of theological corruption were essential to supporting or challenging the self-declared orthodoxy of the established church. Gladstone's ideas about theological corruption were in common circulation, and they were often put into circulation in order to maintain the good credit of a politically privileged creed. Anglicans, Dissenters, Roman Catholics, Unitarians, non-Christians, and nonbelievers never agreed on how to distinguish true and false religions or true and false dogmas. Instead, the British ruling classes gradually decided that the state would be indifferent to religious dogmas. And with the waning of an apologetic tradition that was the learned rationale for theological discrimination, Gladstone's ideas about corrupt theology did become eccentric. But this eccentricity was a consequence of the agreement to make any detailed Christian theology politically irrelevant. The once pervasive discourse about theological corruption had become what Richard Rorty would define as "an entrenched vocabulary which has become a nuisance" (9).

The prevailing inability or unwillingness to see how Gladstone's ideas about Homeric religion were based on a massive body of related writings comes from the tendency to judge periods of cultural conflict almost solely by the assumptions and criteria of the victors. Such a historiography merely illustrates a history of ideas that gets resolved preliminary to investigation. This chapter, in contrast, seeks to understand the commencement of Gladstone's Homeric career with a history of his reading; and the following narrative is chiefly indebted to the *Gladstone Diaries* (1825–96), the century's most remarkable bibliographic document and an unparalleled record of an individual's reading. Reconsidering Gladstone's career as the century's most prolific Homeric scholar, I argue that his reading of ancient epics as corrupted Scripture was a representative legacy of the period when the state's claim to legitimacy shifted to pluralistic foundations. And while this new version of Gladstone's literary activity remains deeply interested in what is by any measure a fascinating biography, this biographical dimension does not negate the social relevance of the story told. Gladstone is indeed a personification of the Victorian age, as others have argued, but not simply because he would eventually become British liberalism's Grand Old Man. Just as important, Gladstone is representative because he, as we shall see, reluctantly became a liberal in the 1840s and found himself thereby dedicated to a literary avocation haunted by its insoluble religious ambitions.

The first memorable bibliographic event in Gladstone's life is further testimony to the influence of Hannah More. As Gladstone was fond of recalling in his old age (Roberts, "Bookworms" 163–64; Quaritch), he still possessed a copy of the evangelical matriarch's *Sacred Dramas,* presented by the author herself in 1815 with a verbal preface: "As you have just come into this world, and I am just going out of it" (qtd. in Morley 1.12). Gladstone forgot what had followed, but he took to heart the reminder of the way of all flesh. For Gladstone's life and his life-long relationship with books were dominated by his faith that this worldly existence was an act of preparation. Ten years after receiving More's memorable gift, Gladstone began the diary that was to become a central part of his daily life and his preparation for the next. Normally composed at night before prayers, the diary was a reckoning of what Gladstone called the "all-precious gift of Time" (qtd. in Morley 1.205), and the catalogue itself indicates that when not talking, eating, sleeping, or praying, Gladstone was most likely to be reading, writing, or, as the constant expansion of his collection often called for, "working" on his books. What sets Gladstone apart from other bibliophiles, however, is the industry and care he devoted to recording his reading. As early as December 1825, Gladstone writes, "Began to make list of books which I have read" (GD 22/12/25), and he continued to work on that same list—one that includes some 21,000 titles (including periodical pieces) and some 4,500 identified authors—for over seventy years.[7]

Among other things, this list of books documents Gladstone's sense of guilt for having entered politics when he had convinced himself that he had a higher calling in the church. During Gladstone's studies at Eton, it was understood that he would make his profession in law and from there enter public life. Before matriculating at Oxford in 1828, however, he became attracted to the church as well. Things reached a crisis in the summer of 1830, when he wrote to his father to announce that he had been "inclined to the ministerial office for what has now become a considerable period" (Morley 1.636). John Gladstone wisely suggested that the son might be choosing the easier path, saying "that the field for actual usefulness to our fellow-creatures . . . is more circumscribed and limited in the occupations and duties of a clergyman" (Morley 1.641). More important, the young Gladstone was reconciled to the parliamentary path because domestic politics had taken on such a religious tone at the time when he came to the age of vocational decision. Shortly after he had matriculated, the Repeal of the Test and Corporation Acts was given Royal Assent, to be followed by the House narrowly passing a motion favoring Catholic emancipation (GD 15/5/28); and much clamor about "the Catholic Question" continued until April 1829 when a Roman Catholic Relief Bill finally passed. It was not these measures, though, that inspired the politician in Gladstone, but rather the issue of parliamentary reform that followed. Gladstone was in favor of Roman Catholic relief well before such a measure could pass the House of Lords, and like many others he considered these acts to be extensions of religious toleration, not the erosion of religious values. But the Reform Bill struck Gladstone as a catastrophic mistake, an innovation that "threatens not only to change the form of our Government, but ultimately to breakup the very foundations of social order," as he successfully moved in a famous speech made at the Oxford Union (GD 19/5/30). And even though Gladstone left the university before the "official" start of the Oxford Movement (in 1833), he was inspired by the broader debate about a new strain of "rationalism" gaining ground within the clergy. He read Hugh James Rose's work on dangerous tendencies in German thought (GD 3/10/30); and he had heard Godfrey Faussett preach his harsh sermon on Milman's *History of the Jews,* a controversy he would also follow in the *British Critic* (GD 28/2/30, 13/5/30; see above 232). His friend Benjamin Harrison, who would enter the church and contribute to *Tracts for the Times,* was inspired by the threat seen in Milman's work in particular to take up his Hebrew studies under E. B. Pusey's guidance. In these "Milmanic days," as he told Gladstone in 1830, the Old Testament needed new defenders (Add. MSS 44204.3). Gladstone's theological interpretation of the concurrent intellectual and political crisis thus allowed him to conceive of a parliamentary career that satisfied what had been ecclesiastical ambitions.

The week before he started cramming for exams at Oxford in October 1831, the distress had become apocalyptic in Gladstone's mind; "the actual signs of the times," he wrote, "are such as should make us ready for the coming of our Lord" (GD 22/10/31). Despite these distractions, an exhausted Gladstone left Oxford with a rare Double First and a reputation for being the university's most fluent young opponent of Reform. Still unsure of his future but reconciled to the fact that it would not be in the church, Gladstone embarked in February 1832 for a restorative trip to the Continent. Six months later, he was in Italy when he received "the disastrous but expected news" that the Reform Bill had passed the House of Lords (GD 16/6/32). A letter soon followed inviting him to stand for a seat in Parliament under the auspices of the Duke of Newcastle, and Gladstone was elected to Parliament in December 1832. The first dozen years of his political life were a mixture of profound political disappointment and uncommon success. The successes included holding office as Junior Lord of the Treasury (1834) and Under Secretary for War and the Colonies in Sir Robert Peel's short-lived government of 1834–35; and by 1843, at the age of thirty-two, he held his first cabinet post as President of the Board of Trade. The disappointments were mostly founded on the fate of the theories put forth in his first two books, *The State in its Relations with the Church* (1st ed., 1838; 4th ed., 1841) and *Church Principles considered in their Results* (1840). Speaking of both books, Colin Matthew describes their political moment as "the last point at which a general defence of Anglican hegemonic nationalism could be attempted. If conservatism was to be more than a Fabian defence against, and consequently a pragmatic accommodation of the liberal, pluralist, and industrial state—if it was to be an ideology rather than a reaction—Gladstone's position, or something like it, had to be held" (41).

In April 1839 T. B. Macaulay reviewed the second edition of *The State in its Relations with the Church* for the *Edinburgh Review,* and he made a similar point about Gladstone's conspicuous dissent from more practical views. Calling him "a young man of unblemished character, and of distinguished parliamentary talents," Macaulay nevertheless insisted that Gladstone had become an instrument for reactionary interests; he was "the rising hope of those stern and unbending Tories who follow, reluctantly and mutinously, a leader [i.e., Robert Peel] whose experience and eloquence are indispensable to them, but whose cautious temper and moderate opinions they abhor" (*WLM* 6.326). Six months later, John Keble, reviewing the same book in the *British Critic,* would dismiss the attack by Macaulay, calling him the maker of "ludicrous analogies" and the "deviser" of "facetious sayings" (363). Recasting Macaulay's stiff-necked Tory into a more heroic witness in the wilderness, Keble made it clear that Gladstone was not someone to fight a battle only because likely to win: "We find him writing in a tone, not indeed of despondency, but of very deep and serious alarm; not as one who would gave [sic] up the defence of a place, but as one who thought the time was come for making a last effort, and calling out those who would not shrink from a forlorn hope" (356).[8]

Gladstone's books on church and state were concerned with a central political problem that, in the wake of 1828, inspired many other works, among them Coleridge's *On the Constitution of the Church and State, according to the Idea of Each* (1829); Thomas Arnold's *Principles of Church Reform* (1833); Edward Osler's *Church and King* (1837); Thomas Chalmers's *Lectures on Church Establishments* (1838); F. D. Maurice's *The Kingdom of Christ* (1838); and William Palmer's *A Treatise on the Church of Christ* (1838).[9] And all of these books addressed a wider debate about the nature of the state. As Gladstone framed the question: "It begins to be a common inquiry, why if all sects be recognised as legally competent to serve the State, the State is to render its reciprocal service to one form of religion only?" (1841: 2.258). The state, according to Gladstone, could continue to identify itself with one Christian sect and, at the same time, continue to be tolerant of a certain amount of religious heterodoxy. By maintaining this position, Gladstone was challenging what he called the liberal theory which "exclude[s] all functions which assert or imply the superiority of truth in religion to error, or the relevancy of any man's religious creed to his principles of moral conduct" (1841: 2.379). The "concurrent action of political liberalism" and "religious liberalism" (1841: 2.274) was leading people to embrace godless, utilitarian political principles. Many were denying "that religion is the great sanction of civil society," and attempting "to substitute an universal education or general culture at the expense of the state for the universal spiritual culture by the church" (1841: 2.397–98). In Gladstone's mind, this agenda, as far as it found the support of sincere Christians, was inspired by the unchecked supremacy of private judgment. The liberal theory of government was a political concession to a specific literary scenario: the free and easy circulation of Scripture, which was subject only to a plurality of interpretations. To avoid the inevitable results of this alliance between an antireligious, Benthamite elite, nonconformists, and a broader body of liberal Christians, Gladstone insisted that the state should support one religion based upon the truth of its doctrines; and the only way to assure the church's conservation of theological truth was to reassert its creedal foundations on the principle of "Catholic consent," which meant that the preliminary guide to biblical interpretation was a body of traditions represented by the writings and confessions of the primitive church. This dogmatic foundation, Gladstone argued, was essential for preventing the heretical interpretations of the Bible that inspired nonconformity or infidelity.

Almost sixty years later, Gladstone looked back at the time when he wrote his first books and explained what had been the cause of his taking a position that would eventually appear so extreme. "The land was over spread with a thick curtain of prejudice," he wrote in 1894: "The foundations of the historic Church of England except in the minds of a few divines were obscured. The Evangelical movement with all its virtues and merits had the vice of individualising religion in a degree perhaps unexampled" (*Prime Ministers' Papers* 1.246). And in this turn to historic and institutional foundations, Gladstone was in accordance with the larger Catholic revival, which was reasserting the idea that the church was a supernatural institution. John Stuart Mill, in the winter of 1839, provided a private sketch of this agenda in a letter to the French positivist Gustave d'Eichthal. This "Oxford School," as Mill called it,

> has revived & reasserted the old Anglican doctrine that the English Church is the Catholic Church—that the Church of Rome since the council of Trent is schismatic—& it claims in behalf of the Church a real Spiritual Power, similar & almost equal to that which was exercised by the Catholic Church before the Reformation. The depository of this Spiritual Power

is, according to them, the body of ordained Clergy, that is, ordained by Bishops deriving their authority by apostolic succession from Jesus Christ. The principal peculiarity of this school is hostility to what they call ultra-Protestantism. They recognise tradition, & not the Scriptures merely, as one of the sources of Christianity. . . . They reprobate the "right of private judgement" & consider learning rather than original thinking the proper attribute of a divine. . . . Among others of their proselytes it is said that Gladstone, the only rising man among the Tories, is one; the man will probably succeed Peel as Tory leader, unless this prevents him. The principal chiefs are Dr. Pusey, an Oxford Professor, & Mr. Newman. (12.415–16)

Mill's placing of Gladstone in this sacerdotal context is canny, for Gladstone's books were partially born in his attempts to pursue his aborted church vocation in the political arena. And he composed them at a time when he was engaged in forms of spiritual discipline that were worthy of a monk. Both before and after happily marrying Catherine Glynne in 1839, fasting and devotional reading and writing were his main weapons against temptations that seem to have been fundamentally sexual. In March 1839 on Easter Eve, for example, Gladstone's Lenten diet—"a cup of tea to breakfast, coffee to lunch with two or three mouthfuls of oatcake to qualify it" and a "restricted dinner"—gave him "a glimpse of understanding, how fasting might be sweetened to the heart," but his eyesight was suffering and he was anxious about having the strength to speak in the Commons. Deliberate physical taxations—which included "the habit of prayer with arms extended"—were effective, but he realized he needed "stronger animal support" in order to serve the great causes of the day. "Shall I ever be a man of study and of prayer, a man of the cell and of the lamp, of the chair, of the altar, shall I ever cast the burden from my shoulder and flee away and be at rest," he was to ask himself (GD 30/3/39). Such entries suggest that it was not simply the ideas conveyed by Gladstone's church-and-state books that were important to him; the activity of their composition was itself purposeful. His pious ends sanctified his time at his lamp—his reading and writing—and those same ends provided a rationale to moderate his acts of self-denial to a degree that would allow him the strength to debate, read, and write.

The extent to which Gladstone devoted time and energy to the contemplation of spiritual discipline can be gauged by his substantial memorandum from March 1838 on a "Third Order" to be composed of "brethren, both clerical and lay" who would live in "separation from the world" (CCR 2.433–37). This prospective brotherhood, for which Gladstone drafted forty-nine rules governing daily conduct and different levels of initiation, was in part a dream about formalizing an aspect of his life that would remain important throughout the 1840s when he participated in "the Engagement," a confidential Tractarian brotherhood under Keble's pastoral supervision (Matthew, "Gladstone" and 1997: 22, 90–92). Since 1835, his two most important relationships outside his own family were with Henry Manning and James Hope, who had both been, like Gladstone, tutored by Charles Wordsworth while at Oxford. Manning had entered the church, while Hope had taken up law, and the three eventually saw themselves as jointly pursuing a religious quest, with their variegated professional expertise amounting to a sum greater than its parts. Hope vetted Gladstone's books on legal matters, while Manning shored up the author's program at its theological crux: its devotion to the test of Catholic consent and the embrace of the traditions that had been recognized *quod semper, quod ubique, quod ab omnibus*—always, everywhere, and by everyone—as the church father Vincent of Lerins had put it.

For Gladstone and other Anglo-Catholics, the major flaw of liberal hermeneutics rested on their antipathy to primitive church traditions, those religious ideas that were not written in the Bible itself but spread by word of mouth, words that issued from the apostles and found their way into the nonscriptural writings of the church fathers. John Keble had placed *traditum,* or tradition, at the center of contemporary theological debate in his sermon *Primitive Tradition Recognized in Holy Scripture* (1st ed., 1836), which had reached a third edition in 1837 when a postscript was added and Manning's corroborating *Tract 78* was "subjoined." Dozens of controversial works about tradition followed, peaking in 1839.[10] For Gladstone and others, the importance of tradition at this time extended beyond the limits of a conventional theological doctrine. Tradition was a consequential epistemological principle that defined a mode of reading and writing that linked the present to antiquity. Manning's oft-cited *Tract 78*—its fuller title being *Testimony of Writers of the Later English Church to the Duty of Maintaining, Quod semper, quod ubique, quod ab omnibus traditum est*—illustrates this as much with its contents as with the authorship required for its production. It was a doubly and deliberately derivative work, a compilation of a tradition of witness to the concept of tradition. Mill's comment that the Oxford School "consider[s] learning rather than original thinking the proper attribute of a divine" was more than an ironic insult. For Gladstone and others, Catholic faith was maintained by a form of disciplined reading regulated by the early church's oral traditions.

Gladstone's church-and-state books had him branded as the rising hope for an intolerant Toryism, and some of the details of his quest for spiritual and social order were extreme. But the learned bookishness of this quest distinguished his conservatism and allowed him to join what we would now consider the broader clerisy or intellectual elite. In July 1840, for example, he participated in the foundation of the London Library (*GD* 18/7/40), the private circulating library that was the brainchild of Thomas Carlyle. While Gladstone had intimate connections with an increasingly controversial Tractarian clergy, his long-standing involvement with the London Library linked him to an intellectual world that included philosophical radicals such as George Grote and John Stuart Mill as well as liberal divines such as Henry Hart Milman. The London Library in the 1840s was thus a highly circumscribed forerunner of the liberal state's educational institutions: it could serve the interests and working habits of men like Grote and Mill, even while its collection in ecclesiastical history would be selected by the High Church Tory Gladstone (*GD* 7/1/41, 20/2/41; Baker, 1992: 62–72).

Nevertheless, by the time the fourth edition of *The State in its Relations with the Church* came out in 1841, Gladstone's theopolitical principles were becoming more scandalous than extreme. Some of the clerical leaders of the Catholic revival were no longer trying to strike a via media between Protestantism and Catholicism; an attack on Protestantism itself increasingly seemed to be the goal. Gladstone was prepared to face the arguments of Whigs and Radicals in the House. Having his arguments compromised by the theology of the Oxford Movement was more unsettling. In July 1838, for example, as Gladstone was putting the final touches on his manuscript, the annual grant to Maynooth College, a Roman Catholic seminary in Ireland, was proposed in the House. Gladstone in debate—as he had done in his book—pointed to the grant as one of those inconsistencies in government policy that "contravened and stultified the main principle on which the Established Church of England in Ireland was founded." As a Roman Catholic seminary, Maynooth College was dedicated to the propagation of religious error, and it was therefore a dangerous precedent for the state to fund it, despite the argument that a more loyal Roman Catholic priesthood was thereby cultivated (*H* 44.817). Viscount Morpeth replied to this position by turning the theology of the Oxford Movement against Gladstone. "If they were to be always talking of the objectionable doctrines taught at Maynooth," Morpeth said, "they must not be surprised if they sometimes heard of the not very satisfactory doctrines which had recently become fashionable at Oxford." Morpeth then read extracts from the *Remains of the Late Reverend Richard Hurrell Froude* (4 vols., 1838–39), a work jointly edited by Newman and Keble, which included Froude's notorious comment, "Really I hate the Reformation and the Reformers more and more, and have almost made up my mind that the rationalist spirit they set afloat is the pseudoprophetes of the Revelations" (*H* 44.817–18).

Gladstone had stood up to defend the Establishment on doctrinal grounds and then found himself confronted by a Whig reading Oxford attacks on Protestantism. This same scenario was repeated in March 1841 when a bill was proposed to allow Jews to hold municipal office. Gladstone objected because it would prepare the way for non-Christians to serve in Parliament, and this would make a mockery of House statutes that required MPs to begin each session with prayers and a declaration to preserve the one true religion (*H* 57.754–60). Macaulay replied by attacking the notion of any consensus about religious truth, saying that "there was as much difference already in the House on the subject of true religion, as there was between the Jew and the Christian. The Roman Catholic differed from the Protestant, and the Unitarian differed from the Trinitarian, as to what was the true religion. Whichever of them was right, there must be a great deal of false religion in the House of Commons" (*H* 57.761–62). The shifting theological terrain can be mapped by the fact that two years after his initial review of Gladstone in the *Edinburgh Review*, Macaulay now added a strong appeal to the ways in which theologians within the church were themselves becoming either religious dissenters or hypocrites. He reminded the House that the authority of oaths was being undermined most creatively by clerics such as Newman, who had recently argued in "Remarks on Certain Passages in the Thirty-Nine Articles" (or *Tract 90*) that those articles, while unquestionably "the offspring of an uncatholic age," were "through GOD'S good providence, to say the least, not uncatholic, and may be subscribed by those who aim at being catholic in heart and doctrine" (3–4). Responding to arguments like this, Macaulay said,

> He had of late seen so much proof how little articles and forms were able to bind the ingenuity of casuists, that he should be sorry to see the House again occupied in framing such cobwebs. He could only wish for that which would put an end to this bill and all such bills—enlightened toleration; but if learned persons elsewhere would teach the Jews some of their own ingenuity, there could not be the slightest doubt but that, as those ingenious persons swallowed confession and absolution, so these tests might also be swallowed by the Jews without the slightest hesitation. He would venture to say, that a better gloss could be found for a Jewish declaration than other glosses which he had seen, and that not merely for the purpose of obtaining civil offices, but in order to hold the faith of Rome with the endowments of the English Church. (*H* 57.764)

The year 1841 would prove to be an important turning point for the nation at large; for Gladstone it had been a "disastrous" year (*GD* 25/11/41).

The reign of Whiggery was over, and the Conservatives were back in power under the leadership of Peel. But the religiously inspired resistance to liberalism was breaking up from within. From the publication of the first volume of Froude's *Remains* in 1838 to the publication of *Tract 90* in 1841, the Oxford Movement underwent its most important transformation (F. Turner 2002: 313–403; Nockles 234–46). During this period, the Tractarians went from being the leaders of a coalition that insisted on the authority of religious creeds to being an increasingly isolated collection of theologians forced to invoke a new liberty of interpretation. In April 1841 the *Eclectic Review* pronounced Gladstone's *Church Principles* to be "one of the most dangerous" of "all the publications of the Pusey school." "It is lamentable," the reviewer concluded, "to find a layman, one belonging to a class generally considered the great bulwark against the encroachments of priestcraft, servilely following wherever the clergy lead" ("Gladstone on *Church Principles*" 369, 396). Gladstone also knew that his sister Helen and his friend Robert Williams were seriously considering the competing claims of the Church of Rome. When it was rumored in January 1842 that the bishops were about to convene in order to pass an official condemnation of the *Tracts* and their authors, Gladstone composed a long letter to the *Times* defending the Catholic character of the Church of England (*CCR* 1.270–78). Despite the clamor against "Puseyism," Gladstone pointed out that "Catholic principles" were derived from the "Prayer-Book, the Articles, and the Canons" of the church. The Oxford writers would never desert the church as long as the church preserved its Catholicity (*CCR* 1.276–78).

The *Times* refused to print the letter, and Gladstone's predictions about the fidelity of the Oxford writers were in several instances proven wrong. Three months later, in May 1842, his sister formally converted to Roman Catholicism, an act that provided an embarrassing chance for others to argue that Oxford principles led to Rome. According to the *Christian Observer,* her conversion "was the natural and just effect of the doctrines propounded" in her brother's writings ("Publications" 500–501). In October 1843 Gladstone's analysis of the strained situation appeared as "Present Aspect of the Church" in the *Foreign and Colonial Quarterly Review,* an article that sought to give a balanced history of the movement that was now showing so many signs of stress. When he sent the article to his friend Benjamin Harrison, he was urged to avoid such public analysis. "What we seem to me to want," Harrison wrote, "is to have 'the Tracts', if possible, forgotten" (Add. MSS 44204, 16/11/1843). By that time, too, Gladstone had learned of Newman's probable abandonment of the Church of England. Newman confessed to Henry Manning that he had become convinced since 1839 that the Church of Rome was the true church, and Manning passed the news on to Gladstone. Gladstone counseled Manning to write back describing "the fatal results to all Catholic progression in the Church, which his fall . . . would produce—results which I may seriously illustrate by the effects that the horrors of the French Revolution produced in a most violent reaction against democratic principles in England" (*CCR* 1.285).[11] A few days later, Gladstone wrote again to Manning proposing that they draw up a declaration, "an united protest on the part of those whom the public voice has associated with Newman, declaring together with their adherence to Catholic principles their loyalty to the actual English Church and their firm resistance to the actual system and claims of Rome." The times called for "something fresh, positive, emphatic, and adapted to the greatest crisis and the sharpest that the Church has known since the Reformation—for such I do, for one, feel would be the crisis of the apostasy of a man whose intellectual stature is among the very first of his age, and who has indisputably headed the most powerful movement and the nearest to the seat of life that the Church has known, at least for two centuries" (*CCR* 1.286–87).

During the winter of 1843, besides getting more hints of Newman's possible conversion, Gladstone and his other close confidant, James Hope, were also particularly alarmed by Newman's *Lives of the English Saints,* a serial dictionary of national hagiography that had been announced in September (Ker 281–82). In a correspondence largely shared with Gladstone, Hope was urging Newman to take up only "easy 'Lives'" that did not press the miraculous too much or too often mention the Pope's authority. Newman was defiant. "I will not limit certainly the degree of disgust which some people will feel towards it," he wrote back, speaking about the idea of the Pope's supremacy, "but do they feel less towards the notions of monks, or, again, of miracles? Now Church History is made up of these three elements—miracles, monkery, Popery. If any sympathetic feeling is expressed on behalf of the persons and events of Church history it is a feeling in favour of miracles, or monkery, or Popery, one or all" (*Correspondence* 282). Newman eventually desisted from his proposal in a kind of deference to the opinions of Gladstone in particular, who had gone over proof sheets of the life of Saint Stephen Harding (*GD* 3/12/43, 7/12/43). But as Newman wrote to Hope, learning that so devout a man as Gladstone was not willing to support this project was a good sign that he, Newman, might be in the wrong communion. "I assure you," Newman wrote, "to find that the English Church cannot bear the Lives of her Saints (for so I will maintain, in spite of Gladstone, is the fact) does not tend to increase my faith and confidence in her" (*Correspondence* 286–87).

At the end of 1843, in his yearly birthday entry in his diary, Gladstone recorded his own realization of the impossibility of resisting liberalism on the terms he had initially conceived. "Of public life," he wrote, "I certainly must say every year shows me more & more that the idea of Christian politics can not be realised in the State according to its present conditions of existence" (GD 29/12/43); and in May 1844, signs of Gladstone's coming political conversion were confusingly disclosed. Gladstone had begun a course of reading on Unitarianism in preparation for an upcoming vote on the Dissenters Chapels Bill (P. Butler 111–12; Chadwick 1966: 1.391–95; Machin 1977: 165–69). This bill, introduced by Peel's government, sought to secure the title of certain Unitarian congregations to their property, which was now being legally contested because the congregations had begun as Trinitarian Protestants. The opponents of the bill claimed that it put the government in the position of encouraging heresy. Gladstone surprised everyone by claiming that the question was not one of heretical and orthodox doctrine. Rather than considering the truth of either Trinitarian or Unitarian Christianity, Gladstone gave a history of the hermeneutic tendencies of Protestant Dissent. By losing their faith in the doctrine of the Trinity, Gladstone argued, these Dissenters were maintaining their adherence to their fundamental belief that Scripture individually interpreted was the basis of the Christian faith. The doctrinal history of these Dissenting chapels only illustrated the argument that Gladstone had set out at length in his books. The original endowers of these chapels had an "idea of Christianity, as a shifting, changing advancing subject" (H 75.369). They were struggling with the "two great antagonistic principles" of interpretation: "One of them was the authority of religion—the view that religious truth is something permanent and immutable. The other was that which relied exclusively on the supremacy of private judgement. These two principles were struggling against each other. The supremacy of private judgement, and the disinclination to tolerate, in any form, human interpolations of Scripture, were practically gaining the upper hand over the old principle." By identifying the chapel founders as opposed to "all Creeds and human compilations," Gladstone argued that they could find in their original theology "the seeds of all those progressive changes which had since been developed" (H 75.369–70). The Irish MP Sheil rose after Gladstone and predicted that Gladstone would soon "become the advocate of the most unrestricted liberty of thought" (H 75.377). In Gladstone's mind, however, he was simply citing the rationale for his own Catholic principles, ones that had led him, in a circuitous fashion, to support measures also favored by liberals.

Gladstone's political crisis came to a head in February 1845. It was a crisis, in its purest sense, about books and the government's role in regulating their interpretation. Peel had pledged to increase and make permanent the government grant to the Roman Catholic seminary at Maynooth, convinced that this was a good way to avoid the politically wasteful debates about the grant each year. What most disturbed Gladstone and other opponents to Peel's Maynooth bill was something that might strike us as an overrefined distinction, one separating annual grants from permanent endowment. Earlier grants had been given to Maynooth on a technically exceptional basis because they had to be annually approved. Making the grant permanent transformed the character of the state's funding; the state would now be permanently committed to paying for the indoctrination of Roman Catholic priests. The measure, as Gladstone described it, would "provid[e] ease and leisure, the means of reading and of meditation, with a view to the maintenance of the faith which they [i.e. Roman Catholics] profess" (*H* 79.529). During 1845, 10,253 petitions bearing almost 1.3 million signatures were submitted to the House in opposition to the new Maynooth measure (Wallis 547).[12] Gladstone, then serving in Peel's cabinet as President of the Board of Trade, eventually decided to resign his office over the matter. He did so, as he explained to the House, because he felt he could not share responsibility for a government measure that so clearly contradicted his church-and-state theories (*H* 77.77–81).

Many hoped that Gladstone's resignation would allow him to assume leadership of those Tories who had had enough of Peel's liberalizing. But Gladstone was instead preparing to admit that his church-and-state principles could no longer guide his decisions as a politician. On 11 April 1845, to the astonishment of many, he spoke as a private member of Parliament in favor of and voted for the Maynooth measure that had been the source of his resignation. The most popular objection to the bill was the argument "that this country is a Protestant country," and the state's endowment of a Roman Catholic seminary would constitute "a breach of our religious obligations" (*H* 79.536). But Gladstone refused to oppose the bill on the principle of Protestantism; he could not adopt Protestantism "as a principle of the Constitution, or as a principle of religion." The type of Protestantism being invoked to oppose the Maynooth grant was "an undefined and negative idea," a protest against the Church of Rome, not a positive body of doctrine (*H* 79.541). This Protestantism was "a most delusive appellation, of which we are totally unable, as a Legislature, either to fix the meaning, or to check the variations" (*H* 79.542).

Some accused Gladstone of a self-serving political opportunism, while others have cited the episode as a recognizable Gladstonian exercise in ornate casuistry. More simply, Gladstone was making it clear that he held nothing in common with the popular objections to Peel's measure. These objections were conveyed to the House on the same day as Gladstone's speech in a petition from the Dublin Protestant Operative Association that called for Peel's impeachment for "high crimes and misdemeanors against the laws and the constitution of the realm" (*H* 79.499). Peel's proposal, the petitioners claimed, was "highly unconstitutional, indicative of a man who means to subvert their national liberties, and calculated to involve in peril the Throne and the Constitution." Britain was by law a Protestant kingdom, and it was subversive for the British Parliament to fund a seminary of Roman Catholic doctrine, "such principles being, according to law, false, idolatrous, and anti-Christian" (*H* 79.496).

An Oxford-based theological controversy was again a decisive influence on Gladstone's political development. Ten days after giving his February speech in Parliament to explain his resignation, Gladstone traveled to Oxford to attend a meeting of convocation to vote on proposals to condemn W. G. Ward's *Ideal of a Christian Church* (1844), to strip the author of his degrees, and to censure Newman's *Tract 90*. Gladstone had been urging people to leave Ward undegraded because he only represented an extreme expression of otherwise legitimate Catholic principles. Gladstone disagreed with Ward's conclusions, as he made clear in a review of Ward's book that appeared in the December *Quarterly Review* (149–200). But it was unfair for Oxford to condemn Ward when the extremist conclusions of the Evangelical party were left uncensored (Newsome 294). If the church was going to tolerate extreme expressions of its Protestant principles, it ought to tolerate (so went Gladstone's logic) extreme expressions of its Catholic principles.

The censure against Newman was vetoed by one of the proctors, but the motions against Ward passed with Gladstone voting in the minority. The scene at Oxford convinced Gladstone that popular Anglicanism was mostly sustained by a revulsion from Catholicism.[13] The voluminous "out of doors" agitation against Peel's Maynooth measures was to be expected. For the elite, predominantly clerical constituency of Oxford, however, Gladstone had higher hopes for a recognition that the church indeed had an essential "Catholic"—though not Roman Catholic—character. But in the end, the hundreds in Oxford lined up with the millions elsewhere. The Maynooth controversy and the Oxford vote of 1845 combined to mark a critical juncture in Gladstone's long evolution from Tractarian Tory to Liberal statesman. The character of the popular opposition to the Maynooth motion and its resemblance to the anti-Catholic proceedings at Oxford convinced him that his theory of the state's religious conscience—one based on doctrinal truth derived from Catholic consent—had no political legs. All the while, though, Gladstone's belief in the authority of Catholic consent remained fundamental to his own religious affiliation.

During the same time that Gladstone was disentangling himself from his church-and-state principles, Newman had started writing his *Essay on the Development of Doctrine* (1845), the book with which he disentangled himself from the Church of England. In their anti-Protestantism, Newman's essay and Gladstone's speeches of 1844–45 were similar. Gladstone had told the House that Protestantism could not be the basis of either a sound faith or a sound theory of the state's theological identity. Newman said, "Whatever be historical Christianity, it is not Protestantism" (72). Maintaining that Roman Catholicism was the true religion and the Church of England was the church in error, Newman relied on a simple reversal eloquently elaborated. He argued that what were described by Anglican theologians as the corruptions of Roman Catholicism were legitimate developments. In a fashion that would seem to later observers to resemble the major ideas of Charles Darwin, Newman made his final break with a bibliocentric Christianity by claiming that dogmas could evolve (Culler 107).

Newman became a Roman Catholic on 9 October 1845, and Gladstone got word of his conversion in Germany, where he had gone to try to persuade his convalescent sister Helen to return to England. Helen's faith in the Church of Rome had remained vigorous, but her health was deteriorating and her addiction to opiates was intensifying. For most of the month of October, Gladstone remained in Baden-Baden supervising his sister's care—which mostly consisted of bleedings and the application of leeches. While presiding over this scene, Gladstone was also experiencing a crisis of sexual temptation, which resulted in a long memoranda on his "chief besetting sin," the reading of what he considered pornographic works. To his wife and Henry Manning he was writing about his eagerness to read Newman's newest book, a text he expected would be the catalyst for a fresh round of "perversions" (Shannon 1.183; Purcell 1.312–13; *CCR* 1.348–50). To himself, Gladstone was confessing the perils of ribald reading. Particularly suspicious of his habit of stumbling upon salacious works or passages, he made a solemn pledge not "to look over books in bookshops except known ones" and decided to keep a record of his reading sins as a way to regulate them (*GD* 26/10/45). Three weeks later, Gladstone was in a bookshop and recorded the "purchase of theological books," but, as his supplementary record of sinful reading indicates, he looked into more than theology on this Sunday (*GD* 16/11/45).

This cataloguing of sinful reading must inform any understanding of Gladstone's more conventional bibliographic labors. Gladstone's ability and willingness to spend significant funds on the purchase of texts and his intense involvement in the controversies of his time contributed to the rapid growth of a private archive of books, pamphlets, and papers. And as early as 1837, he had decided to attack it systematically, producing his memoranda, "Of Keeping Books and Papers" and "Mechanical Rules to assist in Keeping Papers," which are still to be found in the massive collection of the Gladstone Papers in the British Library. So while "labouring to reduce my papers into order," Gladstone composed two more papers and preserved them for the rest of his life (GD 25/11/37; Add. MSS 44727.256–57). In July 1845, three months before carefully analyzing his regrettable reading noted above, he had similarly sought the stabilizing value of arranging and cataloguing books. During the summer recess after his resignation over Maynooth, Gladstone began working on a catalogue of his books, and his three major categories of theology, English secular literature, and foreign secular literature reflected what would prove to be a long-term interest in accommodating, if not reconciling, the national, the secular, and the sacred in his public and private life. Gladstone also revealed the complicated motives behind much of his bibliographic work when he called his first mature catalogue "a formidable undertaking but one that I can carry on when not enough settled for steady work" (GD 26/7/45). This entry invests the concise phrase "Worked on books" (or some variation of it), which appears so often in the diaries, with its easily overlooked importance. Wary of the sinful thoughts that visited him when he was idle, Gladstone's bibliographic projects offered a type of labor that he could prophylactically take up when he was either too tired or too agitated for other work. In attacking what he often called the "chaos" of his books and papers, Gladstone was also faithfully following a commandment expressed in Thomas Carlyle's monastic fantasy *Past and Present* (1843) whose hero, the monk Samson, would serve as St. Edmundsbury's "Librarian, which he liked best of all being passionately fond of Books" (*CE* 10.72). "Wheresoever thou findest Disorder," as Carlyle put it in a passage which Gladstone marked, "there is thy eternal enemy; attack him swiftly, subdue him; make Order of him, the subject not of Chaos, but of Intelligence, Divinity and Thee!" (*CE* 10.201).

Newman's new book also spoke of the eternal, and Gladstone received a copy on 28 November, shortly after his return from his mission to tend to his sister. Moving immediately to the work's conclusion, Gladstone read Newman's closing challenge: "And now, dear Reader, time is short, eternity is long. Put not from you what you have here found; regard it not as mere matter of present controversy; set not out resolved to refute it, and looking about for the best way of doing so; seduce not yourself with the imagination that it comes of disappointment, or disgust, or restlessness, or wounded feeling, or undue sensibility, or other weakness. . . . Time is short, eternity is long" (448). Gladstone believed in eternal punishment just as devoutly as Newman did, but he got to work resolved to write against Newman. His greater hope was that his friend and now archdeacon Henry Manning would produce a more definitive reply, one worthy of a professional theologian. Gladstone was particularly anxious to see Newman refuted on High Church principles in order to prove that those principles did not necessarily lead to Rome (Purcell 1.313–16; Newsome 315–16). The failure to answer Newman on such terms would be yet another victory for the type of indefinite, negative Protestantism that Gladstone had been criticizing.

Gladstone was working on his own reply to Newman until 17 December, when he was interrupted by a political crisis. Peel's support for Corn Law reform created enough Tory dissension to tempt Russell and the Whigs into trying to form a government. They failed, and when Peel formed a new Tory government, he asked Gladstone to join as Colonial Secretary. Gladstone accepted the offer and was sworn in on 23 December. Consumed with cabinet work, he now had to leave off his writing on development, though he did continue to read a steady stream of works about Newman's book. In the March 1846 *Quarterly Review* (404–65), for example, Gladstone read Henry Hart Milman's answer to Newman, and it was just the type that Gladstone thought insufficient. Milman attacked the sophistry of Newman's analogical method, and pointed out that the only argument that Newman produced on behalf of the necessity of doctrinal infallibility was its desirability. Most important, Milman simply concluded that the doctrinal points that captured Newman's imagination were not essential to Christianity. Milman, in other words, answered Newman with the liberal theology that Gladstone did not value. "The offensive parts able, the positive unsatisfactory," was Gladstone's comment (GD 10/4/46).[14]

Peel's government and—as it turned out—the Tory party fell apart in July 1846, a year of theopolitical rupture for the national churches of England, Ireland, and Scotland (S. Brown 324–410). By the end of his second administration, Peel had committed his government to the permanent funding of Maynooth College and the repeal of the Corn Laws. A pragmatic approach to religious issues and a belief in open markets, the twin pillars of centrist liberalism, had become features of Tory policy under Peel; and the shock of becoming functionally liberal literally broke up the party. Gladstone left London in July of 1846 looking forward to a six-month vacation. With the loss of his cabinet seat, Gladstone was now a private citizen, and he entered a political wilderness from which he would not emerge until August 1847 when he was reelected to the House as a member from Oxford.[15] He had recently watched both the Oxford Movement and the Tory party explode from within, and he now had a year to find his bearings. In the meantime, Gladstone's hopes that Manning would refute Newman on High Church principles were dashed when Manning wrote in August 1846 to say he could not proceed with the project (Purcell 1.317; Newsome 321). This desertion (an important step on Manning's journey to Rome) prompted Gladstone to take up once again his own work on development.

From mid-September 1846 to August 1847, Gladstone worked occasionally on a manuscript that survives today in the British Library (Add. MSS 44736.264–333). Gladstone began by arguing that Newman's new defense of Roman Catholicism marked "an event of immense and profound importance," a "transition from the tactic of identity to the tactic of development" (265). Newman's main proposition was not that the doctrines of the Roman church "are historically identical with those of the Apostolic Age, that they have been transmitted to her by an unbroken tradition: but that she has received an authority to add what was wanting as well as to bring into view what was unseen" (266). For Gladstone, Newman's fatal flaw was his inability to see that things tend to be purer at their source: "In moral systems, whether they be abstract, or whether they be living and practical as in institutions political or religious, there is the seed of almost certain corruption" (300). While Newman argued that history and nature revealed a trend "generally toward perfection with the lapse of time," Gladstone insisted the opposite was more often true. "Now it will rarely be denied," Gladstone wrote, "that other religions and philosophies, unquestionably involving great ideas, have been purest at and near their source" and that "in the course of time moral darkness commonly thickens over these systems and their adherents" (308). For Gladstone, the general trend toward corruption made it clear that Roman Catholicism, and not Anglicanism, was the church in schism. If it was true, as Gladstone argued, "that traditions entrusted to human keeping, though with the aid of Divine guidance, will be more faithfully kept at first than afterwards; then there is a kindred presumption, that of two Churches differing on certain points that one will be right which assigns the greatest weight to primitive tradition, and which places in relative subordination to it the voice of the living Church" (325).

Gladstone also tried to make it clear that one could still reject Newman's argument from an Anglo-Catholic point of view. Gladstone reaffirmed the fact that the Anglican Church was based on Catholic principles and distanced his critique from the negative critiques of those who identified Anglicanism with Protestantism:

> There are those who consider the papal system as an huge aggregation of falsehoods, containing indeed certain precious truths, but containing them only in order to hide and to stifle them. Such persons may consistently desire to see Romanism assailed by a series of negations and little more. But this is not the view of the Church of England which holds the same foundation of faith with the Church of Rome. Her charge against the latter is that in representing the truth of Christianity she in many respects deforms it. (303–4)

In the end, Gladstone argued that things tend to be purer in the beginning, but he did not answer the essential questions: When did Christian doctrine become corrupt? Which doctrines were revealed from above? Which were invented by humans and given a sanction derived from religion? After a year of reading and writing about development and the competing claims of Rome and Canterbury, Gladstone stood by an odd distinction between "to hide and to stifle" and "deforms." Gladstone realized that this point was nothing to stand the light of day, and he never published his essay.

In the midst of this attempt to answer Newman, Gladstone had begun to read the *Iliad* (GD 1/11/46), an event that developed into an intensive study of Homeric criticism ranging from histories of the ancient Hellenes to works about the history of the Homeric text. For the remainder of his life, Homeric study would be his primary literary avocation, and the fact that Gladstone did not publish on doctrinal development can help explain why he published so much on Homer. Gladstone's focus on Homeric antiquity was in part a turn away from Christian antiquity, but Gladstone also read the Homeric text in terms of contemporary religious controversy. And just as the terms *tradition* and *corruption* had been central to the idiom of what Gladstone considered the church's historic crisis, corruption and tradition were central to his ensuing Homeric work. From his systematic study of the gods in Homer's pantheon in 1846–47, Gladstone concluded that some of them were "Invented deities," and that others were "Tradition deities" (Add. MSS 44736.162). The invented deities were products of the human imagination, but the tradition deities were in part based on corrupt versions of "patriarchal traditions" which reached the ancient Greeks via the Phoenicians (Add. MSS 44684.128). Gladstone's understanding of Homeric religion was in line with an orthodox habit of using the Bible as a major resource for understanding other religions of the ancient world, but his emphasis on tradition also reflected a decade of immersion in a religious debate which centered on the meaning and authority of *traditum* in Christian history. And when Gladstone argued that the ancient Greeks had received extra-scriptural traditions about the true divinity, he was invoking a concept central to Catholic principles and the Anglo-Catholic revival.[16]

Gladstone's religious interests in Hellenic antiquity were parts of a broader tendency that also found expression in George Grote's *History of Greece* (vols. 1–2, 1846), what would become the mid-century's most influential narrative about the ancient Greeks and their early myths.[17] In March 1847, Gladstone had begun to read Grote's *History*, which made it clear that theories about the origin and interpretation of early Greek myths were deeply involved with controversies about Jewish and Christian Scripture. Grote also propounded an influential account of the origin of the Homeric text, arguing, for example, that the *Iliad* was one long poem that had had several shorter poems spliced into it. The theory was proposed as a compromise between the view that a single author had composed the *Iliad* and the other extreme view that the *Iliad* was a collection of vaguely related ballads sung by a multitude of poets and later arranged by a deceptive editor. But if Grote steered a middle course in his theory about the Homeric text, his theory about early Greek myth was radically uncompromising. Grote attacked and rejected the day's most popular approaches to interpreting Greek myth, what he called the semi-historical and allegorical method. Almost all of Grote's predecessors as historians of the Greeks began by extracting historical data from Hellenic myths, the method which Grote called semi-historical. In this mode, the interpreter used myths and ancient genealogies to construct a historical narrative, presuming that the myths had a core of true history. In the allegorical mode, the interpreter assumed that the myths contained a hidden or defaced idea or doctrine that had been cast into a narrative form. Grote insisted that the oldest mythic narratives had no historical value at all, and he portrayed allegorical interpretation as the introduction of new meaning into old stories.

Most important, Grote provided a cultural explanation for the rise of these interpretive modes. He argued that the semi-historical and allegorical methods arose in ancient Greece in 700–500 BC with the development of "the rational conception . . . of a systematic course of nature" (1.480).

This epoch featuring the glories of Periclean Athens was a period of mental progress "when positive science and criticism, and the idea of an invariable sequence of events, came to supplant in the more vigorous intellects the old mythical creed of omnipresent personification." The new historical and scientific view of the world produced a split "between the instructed few and the remaining community," and "the opposition between the scientific and the religious point of view was not slow in manifesting itself" (1.483). Once the critical-minded philosophers of Greece turned back to consider their ancient legends, they began to doubt their miraculous and regret their immoral aspects. They employed semi-historical interpretation as a way to retain the outlines of traditional history while discounting the incredible details. With allegorical interpretations, these reforming philosophers set aside the historical character of some narratives altogether. The "superior men of antiquity" were striving "to save the dignity of legends which constituted the charm of their literature as well as the substance of the popular religion" (1.585). A noble and understandable endeavor, Grote conceded. But these first "modern" interpreters of Greek myth were introducing into the ancient legends meanings that were never intended. The history and the philosophy discovered in them were inventions.

In the closing chapter of volume 1, "The Grecian Mythical Vein Compared with that of Modern Europe," Grote showed how his history of Greece's cultural evolution could be transferred to modern European history, with the Middle Ages being the mythic period and the Reformation beginning the age of science. The popularity of hagiography during the Middle Ages was the best sign that that age, like the age of Homer, was a mythopoeic age. And where Greece had its great intellectual awakening in the fifth and sixth centuries BC, Europe began to emerge from its mythopoeic period in the sixteenth century when "the great religious movement of the Reformation, and the gradual formation of critical and philosophical habits in the modern mind, have caused these legends of the saints—to pass altogether out of credit, without even being regarded among Protestants, as worthy of a formal scrutiny into the evidence" (1.628–29). When he compared medieval Catholicism and the lives of Catholic saints to the fabulous stories of paganism, Grote was mostly flattering his audience at a time when *The Lives of the English Saints* initiated by Newman was being released to a mostly scandalous reception.[18] What Grote refrained from doing, though, was to continue his analogy between the religion of the ancient Greeks and the predominant religion of post-Classical Europe. He did not discuss the rise of the historical criticism of Scripture itself in the seventeenth and eighteenth centuries.

Where Grote left off in volume 1 of his history, his most important source on the interpretation of myth, David Friedrich Strauss had pushed ahead in *Das Leben Jesu* (1st ed., 1835), which had just appeared in an English translation by (the future) George Eliot as *The Life of Jesus Critically Examined* (3 vols., 1846). Strauss's history of the life of Jesus began with a general account of the interpretation of myths in the ancient world that formed the basis of Grote's work. Any time a long period separates a nation or body of believers from its sacred legends, Strauss argued, the critical readers of those narratives will develop moral and historical objections to them—a process that accounts for the semi-historical and allegorical interpretation practiced by Greeks, Jews, and later Christians. These interpretations are attempts to reconcile "the notions of more advanced periods of mental development" with ancient narratives, and the primary intellectual cause of these attempts was the development of a historical and scientific sense which entailed a certain amount of incredulity toward miraculous narratives. "No just notion of the true nature of history is possible," Strauss said, "without a perception of the inviolability of the chain of finite causes, and of the impossibility of miracles" (64). Strauss's boldest move was breaking with the rationalist, semi-historical method that had been pursued by J. G. Eichhorn and H. E. G. Paulus (15–21). These critics minimized the miraculous in their search for a real historical basis for supernatural Christianity; and Strauss declared that this line of interpretation had reached a dead end. The semi-historical interpreters were theoretically compromised between a desire to interpret Scripture with antisupernatural prejudices and a desire to preserve their belief in a supernatural religion. By trying to discover history in the mythic narratives of the Gospels, these Christian interpreters were repeating the hermeneutic folly of the ancient interpreters of Greek myths, those philosophers who discovered primitive history or esoteric doctrines in their native legends. Both Strauss and Grote, in other words, denied the credibility of all miraculous narratives and pressed the point that religious myths are not imperfect histories. And Strauss's conclusion about the historicity of Christianity ("The supernatural birth of Christ, his miracles, his resurrection and ascension, remain eternal truths, whatever doubts may be cast on their reality as historical facts" [xi]) was echoed by Grote's conclusion about the historicity of Greek myths: "And thus the subjective value of the mythes, looking at them purely as elements of Grecian thought and feeling, will appear indisputably great, however little there may be of objective reality either historical or philosophical discoverable under them" (1.609).

Gladstone had been familiar with Strauss's work since at least 1840 when he read Milman's *History of Christianity,* which included a critique of Strauss.

Milman argued that the entire Gospel narrative could not be purely mythic because "no religion is in its origin mythic." Authentic primitive traditions could not be invented because the primitive mind was incapable of writing purposely deceptive history. For this reason authentic ancient traditions did indeed have a kernel of truth: "Mythologists embellish, adapt, modify, idealise, clothe in allegory or symbol, received and acknowledge truths" (1.119). When Milman reviewed Grote's *History* for the *Quarterly Review*, he made the same objection to Grote's wholesale dismissal of the historicity of Greek myths. "We pretend to no key by which we can extract the history from the legend," Milman wrote, "no test by which we can detect the base of fact which may remain after we have decomposed away all the much larger constituent parts of fancy. But while we have unlimited credence in the transmuting power of religious or heroic legend, we do not believe it to be creative" (119). The early Greek legends could not be pure fiction in their inception.

Gladstone began reading Strauss's *Streitschriften zur Verteidigung meiner Schrift uber das Leben Jesu* (1838) on 24 March 1847, five days after first opening his Grote. On 24 April, he read James Martineau's review of Eliot's translation of Strauss in the *Westminster Review* where he had the shared assumptions of Strauss and Grote pointed out: it was not necessary to explain Strauss's mythic theory "at length," Martineau said, because it had been discussed in the January 1847 review of Grote's *History*. From that review, which was written by Eliot's future companion, George Henry Lewes, readers could "derive, and transfer to our present point of view, a sufficient knowledge of the properties of the myth, and its characteristic mode of operation" (149). Lewes's review in turn insisted that Grote's new reading of early Greek myth had been adapted from new biblical hermeneutics (390).

Gladstone put off reading the *Das Leben Jesu* itself until the next year, when he dutifully began to read through the two-volume edition of 1837 in the original German (GD 15/2/48). In November, he noted he had "finished Strauss, a painful book but wh[ich] has its uses as well as its dangers" (GD 3/11/48). As often, the intimate details of Gladstone's life spoke to his ambitious habits of study. The day following his completion of the century's most learned denial of the central Christian miracle, Gladstone found himself advising his father to compose a family testament to refute his sister Helen's account of being cured of cataleptic lockjaw with a holy relic, the knuckle bone of a female saint wielded by Nicholas Wiseman, soon to be made a cardinal and archbishop of Westminster (Shannon 1.210; see also Feuchtwanger 60 and Jenkins 97). With his sister memorializing the miracle in her correspondence, Gladstone urged the necessity of setting the written record strait. He advised his father "to answer [Helen's letter] without disputing but particularly without recognizing the reality of her impressions—& to have the written evidence put together which shows that they are in short fanatical. It is dismal that true miracle should be brought into discredit by these notions[,] sheer products of a heated imagination. But the thing is important; & some day, which God grant, she may be in a condition to consider the evidence" (GD 4/11/48). Helen Gladstone's remarkable quest for salvation and independence—which would include provocative acts such as using the works of Protestant divines as lavatory paper (GD 24/11/48)—exasperated Gladstone. But her behavior only tended to reconfirm his allegiance to the Church of England, an attachment he maintained in the face of counterarguments by both "rationalizing" and "romanizing" extremes. Even the dual conversion of Manning and Hope to the Church of Rome in 1851, though an immense personal blow, was an event, so Gladstone would claim to himself, that had no theological import. By that time, too, Gladstone had come to read Strauss at length, and he had published the first of his many Homeric works, "Lachmann's *Essays on Homer,*" in the *Quarterly Review.* The essay was a detailed quarrel with the methods and conclusions of Karl Lachmann, a German scholar who is now known as the father of the genealogical approach to textual criticism (Tanselle 18–21). More important, the essay and its making shows how Gladstone had discovered in the Homeric Question a field of controversy that offered the chance to dissent from both the Straussian denials of Grote and the new doctrinal affirmations of Newman.

Presenting a review of works by Lachmann that had been published in the 1830s and early '40s, Gladstone's article from September 1847 was strategically conceived. Lachmann was the more inaccessible source for the separatist case (as it was often called) being put forth in the far more popular *History of Greece* by Grote; and he had also been an important authority in Connop Thirlwall's discussion of the Homeric Question in his earlier *History of Greece* (1835–47).[19] Lachmann, in other words, was at the root of two distinct, philo-Germanic strains of classical historiography that included the liberal Anglicanism represented by Thirlwall and the philosophical radicalism represented by Grote. And by choosing to enter the Homeric debates with a critique of Lachmann, Gladstone was challenging the separatist case just as it seemed most promising by way of its positive reception in the works of Thirlwall and Grote.

"The proposition," as Gladstone put it, "which Mr. Lachmann seeks to sustain is, that each of the Homeric Poems consists of many separate and unconnected lays, in some cases perhaps productions of the same author, in others certainly of different authors" (383). For separatists like Lachmann and Grote, the primary labor of a critic was the process of identifying and separating out the constituent parts of the *Iliad* (and, to a lesser extent, the *Odyssey*). To Gladstone, this practice was the tautological fulfillment of the assumption that the *Iliad* could not be the creation of an individual artist. Lachmann and like-minded critics were "slovenly in their modes of induction" (414), and this error led to a series of disturbing conclusions at odds with Gladstone's decidedly deductive mind. Lachmann "would lead us in substance to the conclusion," Gladstone wrote,

> that of the *Iliad* and *Odyssey,* and even the *Iliad,* there was in point of fact no author; that there were many authors of portions of them; that these more ancient portions were put together with scanty care and indifferent success at a particular epoch, that of Pisistratus, by a number of compilers, namely the persons whom he employed; that the great genius whom we venerate under the name of Homer, never existed under that or any other name; that the crude materials of the work never passed through the glowing crucible of one assimilating, informing, and transfusing mind; that it is not a moral and intellectual unity, but a congeries of parts accidentally related by their having the same theme; a motley patchwork, an inorganic form, of which the highest merit would have been skillful imposture on the part of those who could give to such elements the appearance and the effect of creative combination. For it is in the combination of the parts and in the conception of the whole, not in the parts themselves generally speaking, that the master effort and the master triumph lies; and therefore those who can prove what Mr. Lachmann has undertaken, will not only destroy the personality of Homer, but will leave for ever blank that elevated niche in the temple of Fame which hitherto he has occupied. (384)

As this opening makes clear, Gladstone's Homeric interests were confirmed by his understanding that almost everything was at stake in the Homeric Question. In this language there are signs of important aesthetic controversies as well as hints that the movement to deny the *Iliad* and *Odyssey* a single, personal creator was part of a crusade to deny the universe, Earth, and humankind a single, personal Creator. Gladstone understood how evolutionary theories of the origin of the Homeric text were related to an evolutionary theory of Creation that had recently been described by Robert Chambers in his anonymously published *Vestiges of the Natural History of Creation*. And three days before correcting the proof-sheets of his 1847 Homeric article, Gladstone began reading the *Vestiges,* which argued that "organic creation was thus progressive through a long space of time" (153).[20] For Gladstone and many others as well, defending the received text of Homer was a way to defend the authority of the texts attributed to Moses and other biblical authors. When the High Church leader E. B. Pusey addressed a committee on university reform (a process he opposed) in 1853, he approvingly quoted Gladstone's article on Lachmann, insisting that "speculations on Homer were the parents of that manifold brood, the speculations on the composition of Holy Scripture. The skepticism as to Homer ushered in the skepticism on the Old Testament" (1853: 24; 1854: 62).

Gladstone chides Lachmann's "scornful allusions" to religious questions, traces his Homeric skepticism to a more general religious skepticism, and compares his assaults on the integrity of the Homeric text to attacks on the integrity of Holy Scripture (417, 381, 390). But like many controversialists of the day, he more often hides what was a fundamental theological disagreement behind an array of practical matters. The bulk of Gladstone's argument in 1847 was directed at what he considered to be separatist (or analytical) criticism's greatest evidential liability. In analytical criticism, the critic had to dissect the Homeric text and then defend the integrity of the smaller poems. Any separatist argument would be compromised as soon as one was able to show that the shorter poems could be dissected as well. An expert logician such as Gladstone made the most of this opportunity, and in his first Homeric article he argues that analytical criticism was based upon a series of presumptions that were in their sum greater than the simpler presumption that the *Iliad* had been composed by one author. He insists that the ancient idea of one author and two main poems was quantitatively more plausible than any new theory about any number of authors and any number of smaller poems.

The essential presumptions of all of Gladstone's ensuing Homeric work took shape in response to theological and mythographic debates dominated by the voices of Newman, Strauss, and Grote, who had all raised and answered, in different ways, questions about the relationship between literature and revelation, mythology and theology. Independently both Newman and Strauss had become convinced that Protestant hermeneutics were reaching an unavoidable conclusion: Christianity was, like many other religions, a historically important and influential mythology. Newman's reaction to this realization was to desert Protestantism. Strauss gave up supernatural Christianity. Gladstone, like most others of his day, did neither. But his Homeric scholarship was a complicated response to the refusal of both Newman and Strauss to compromise. Gladstone's turn to Homer and Olympian theology was a form of recovery from his failure to distinguish Roman Catholic corruptions from legitimate transformations in Christian theology. If Gladstone could not theoretically distinguish the legitimate from the corrupt in one area, he found comfort in the related but safer exercise of describing legitimate revelations in corrupt forms. And just as he argued that the religion depicted by Homer could not simply be dismissed as a collection of meaningless fables, Gladstone would also argue that Homer's text could not be dismissed as a collection of ballads with no historical relevance. By maintaining the unity of the poems, Gladstone was allowing himself to maintain their antiquity and their value as historical documents of some kind, a value that Grote had dismissed.

Like most English readers of Homer in the 1840s, Gladstone believed that he was reading a semi-historical text that had been composed not long after the fall of Troy, an event that chronologists dated to circa 1200 BC, or roughly correspondent with the establishment of Solomon's Temple (Clinton 1.123–40). Reading his Homer as an author of the eleventh century BC, Gladstone pondered a Homeric age that was relatively isolated from collateral evidence, and, as Gladstone was fond of repeating for years to come, the best evidence for the study of Homer was the text itself. In this respect, Homeric antiquity was very different from Christian antiquity, the age of the fathers who had inspired Newman's apostasy and so much debate among Anglicans. Religious controversialists debating the meaning of Catholic principles were bogged down in the morass of evidence from the fourth and fifth centuries, and the volume and variety of this evidence provided a chance for the production of a multitude of plausible interpretations about the nature of the early church.[21] Gladstone's turn to the eastern Mediterranean during the age of Homer was a way to investigate a less perilous field of antiquity. In contrast to Christian antiquity and patristic theology, Homeric antiquity and Olympian theology offered a field of inquiry in which he could confirm his own beliefs rather than run the risk of making any discoveries that could upset his allegiance to the church. Gladstone's Homeric studies thus had a therapeutic function at odds with ideals of scholarly disinterestedness, but he became a partisan reader of Homer at a time when the individual's spiritual culture and the nation's body politic were increasingly diagnosed and treated in terms of reading. And his willingness to find versions of stability in such programmatic reading was always balanced by his recognition of the ways in which reading was for him also a uniquely dangerous activity.

In the late 1840s Gladstone would become politically unfettered by giving up his attempt to make his theological principles and his theory of statecraft one and the same thing. The clearest public sign of this was his speech on the Jewish Disabilities Bill, delivered on 12 December 1847. It was his first major speech following his election as MP for the predominantly clerical constituency of Oxford, and it ended almost two and a half years of parliamentary silence. Some were surprised by Gladstone's support of the admission of Jews to Parliament (something that did not take place until 1858), but his reasoning at its core echoed his earlier speech on the Dissenters Chapels Bill. This Gladstone made explicit in his preface to the independently published version of the speech, in which he described how the cumulative passage of legislation over the past three and a half decades had brought about a situation where the legislature remained a Christian body only by virtue of a "preponderance" of non-uniform Christian self-identification, not "because its members profess a known and definite body of truth constituting the Christian faith" (*Substance* 7). Gladstone's understanding of Christian orthodoxy remained creedal, but recent history compelled him to acknowledge how the state and its representative bodies no longer had any doctrinal essence. Rather than water down the terms of his own faith, he preferred to respond positively to timely petitions to widen the terms of a deliberately restricted system of political representation. In an earnest revision of a stock argument that we have seen Macaulay make in the previous decade, Gladstone insisted that a Parliament that admitted Unitarians, even while it claimed a nominal Christian character, was in no position to deny the entrance of Jews. In Gladstone's at times labyrinthine route to the endorsement of expanded religious toleration, the admission of Jews to Parliament was a way to affirm the fact that, in his mind, the Unitarian "recognition of our Lord [i.e., Jesus] as an inspired teacher" did not itself qualify as authentic Christianity (*Substance* 10).

Such positioning struck some as overly refined, but even with his detractors, Gladstone was universally recognized as a bright star on the nation's political horizon. Yet his interior life in the late '40s and early '50s was often deeply disturbed. Characteristically, this emotional storm, as it was recorded in his diaries, arose from a volatile combination of religion, desire, and an equivocal passion for books. In January 1847 Gladstone noted how even his attempts to fill his spare time with classical studies could become an excuse to peruse lewd authors such as Petronius. While he read Petronius on this occasion "with some reference to my studies in Homer and Hesiod," he confessed he was falling into the "snares of sin" while pursuing the "acquisition of knowledge" (*GD* 15/1/47). And even though this reading sin was committed while attempting to keep himself occupied, he described the incident as "fresh evidence of the use and necessity to me of filling up my time." In May 1848, Gladstone found himself unable to avoid the bawdy poems in *Fabliaux et contes des poètes françois des XI–XVe siècles* (1808), and he recorded three poignant confessions in Italian about his pattern of self-deception, sin, and guilt. The first, translated by Colin Matthew, is worth quoting in full: "I bought this book because it had within it the name of Mr. Grenville, to whom it had belonged: and I began to read it, and found in some parts of it impure passages, concealed beneath the veil of a quite foreign idiom: so I drank the poison, sinfully, because understanding was thus hidden by a cloud—I have stained my memory and my soul—which it may please God to cleanse for me, as I have need. Have set down a black mark against this day" (GD 13/5/48). There is no better exhibit of Gladstone's ambivalent relationship to books than the following conclusion, in English, to this statement of contrition: "Worked on my books." For Gladstone, books were agents of both evil and good, and on this day he both sinned with a book and turned to the bibliographic regulation of his library as a refuge from that sin (GD 13/5/48).

Gladstone composed his longest memoranda on his sinful reading habits in July 1848 after a visit to a bookshop where he looked into the verse of Lord Rochester. The previous Sunday, while attending communion, he had asked himself if there "was not yet one source of evil, which had not been stopped up by any rule or distinct resolution or conviction." The source of evil impervious to rules, resolutions, and convictions was, he discovered, to be found in books, particularly books that gave no hint of their sinful contents. His rules and resolutions could help him to avoid "books known to have that [sinful] character." But, as he continued,

> there are books whose titles do not tell the corruption that is in them, or which are licentious while weak and which contaminate without powerfully moving, or again the eye may range over books which do not contain polluted matter, with an expectation that of itself pollutes: and then a true Christian instinct detects and repels before an evil is done: and seeing this subject before me I then made a Resolution, with a consciousness that I must be either the better or the worse for it, to avoid the gratuitous perusal or even glance of all books of which the title suggested that they might probably offer food to depraved appetite. (GD 19/7/48)

In 1849 Gladstone added yet another rule to help him control his reading. He resorted to self-flagellation, a ritual recorded alongside his catalogue of sinful reading, and a ritual that was complicated by the fact that these readings, as Colin Matthew has pointed out, included erotic flagellation (GD 22/4/49).

Gladstone, in his most intimate writings, associated his worst sins with books and despaired at their power to defy his regimes of self-denial. At the same time, Gladstone the man of letters and public politician was an eloquent spokesman for the civilizing effect of books and the sponsor of legislation that was designed to make books cheaper and more accessible. In 1851, before his first term as chancellor of the exchequer, he became involved in the effort to break a publishers' monopoly that elevated the price of books by prohibiting retailers from discounting their stock below a certain level. Writing to John Murray, the publisher of many of his works, Gladstone combined a pragmatic materialism, recognizing books were commodities, with a traditional idealism about the power of knowledge. Murray had tried to convince Gladstone of the financial necessity of the agreements between publishers and retailers, but Gladstone insisted on the benefits of a freer trade in knowledge. "It is with unfeigned regret that I can differ from you," he wrote,

> while giving way to the strong impressions I have received from my own pursuits & experience in regard to the principles of trade and their application to the production of books considered as a material article: and while I look with great anxiety to the interests of civilisation which are so concerned in the health & vigour of our book trade I also venture to hope that the more extended & the more economical it becomes . . . the better will be the condition of the generality of those who follow it. (qtd. in Barnes 78)

Linking the campaign against this price protection to the larger issue of free trade, Gladstone spoke in the Commons in May 1852 against the monopoly and called for the complete repeal of the paper duty. Declaring that the "enormously high price of Books" in England was a "monstrous evil" that denied the educated classes "mental food," he denounced the entire system of literary production, from paper making to retailing of the final product, as "a disgrace to our present state of civilisation" (*H* 121.595–96). With Gladstone's help, the retailers triumphed over the publishers in 1852, but it was not until 1861 that Gladstone, serving his second term as chancellor of the exchequer, was able to abolish the paper duty, the last remaining of the "taxes on knowledge" (Matthew 113–14, 135; Shannon 1.406, 414–16).

In between Gladstone's first call for the abolition of the paper duty and its actual repeal, his constantly growing library made what turned out to be its final migration to his wife's family estate, Hawarden Castle in North Wales. Between October 1854 and January 1855, Gladstone was often at work on moving his most important material possessions from his home in London to the Castle, which was owned by his brother-in-law, Sir Stephen Glynne. Most of the books arrived from London by Christmas, and the day after found Gladstone hard at work installing books with his sons Willy and Stephen. The last batch arrived on 30 December 1854, and by 3 January 1855, Gladstone triumphantly recorded: "Worked on my books—finished the whole affair: & found them (Theology & Literature) 5185 Vols" (*GD* 3/1/55). Not only was the installation of Gladstone's books in his wife's ancestral home a typical feat of holiday industry; it was the best outward sign of Gladstone's assumption of the de facto proprietorship of Hawarden Castle in the mid-fifties. Soon after Willy helped translate his father's books to the Glynne home, Willy effectively became Sir Stephen's heir (*GD* 27/6/55). Gladstone's books were resources in "Divinity & Literature" (*GD* 3/10/54). And late in life he was the nation's most famous spokesman for an unabashedly spiritual bibliophilia, calling books "a main instrument of communication with the vast procession of the other world. They are the allies of the thought of man. They are in a certain sense at enmity with the world" ("On Books" 386). But in 1855, Gladstone's 5,185 books were also the collectively imposing physical tokens of his ultimate social arrival, his acquisition (through his firstborn son) of an ancient estate.

In the summer of 1855, Gladstone recommenced his Homeric studies in his library at Hawarden Castle, and these would lead eventually to the publication in 1858 of his three-volume *Studies on Homer and the Homeric Age*. That work described at length Gladstone's position on the unity of the Homeric text and the historical value of its narrative (1.1–92) as well as the ways in which the "Theo-mythology" depicted in the poems had a mixture of sources ranging from sheer human invention to remnants of ancient revelation (2.1–172). Distancing himself from "the far fetched and very extravagant supposition" that Homer himself had been influenced by some kind of access to the "Law of Moses" (2.3), Gladstone's position rested on a flexible claim similar to the ones made by figures such as Coleridge and Newman as well as orthodox members of the Anglican hierarchy such as E. Harold Browne. The latter's authoritative *Exposition of the Thirty-Nine Articles, Historical and Doctrinal* (6th ed., 1864), for instance, would summarize a consensus about three "distinct intimations" of the Trinity found "(1) in the Jewish writings, (2) in the mythology of most ancient nations, [and] (3) in the works of Plato and other philosophers" (15).[22] For Gladstone likewise, it was possible, and also probable, "to recognise in the Homeric poems the vestiges of a real traditional knowledge, derived from an epoch when the covenant of God with man, and the promise of a Messiah, had not yet fallen within the contracted forms of Judaism for shelter" (2.3). Most reviews were positive, particularly on his defense of the unity of the poems and their historical significance; several gushed in a way that gave the author heroic status. In the *Guardian,* for example, Gladstone's Homeric labors were seen as a vindication of the nation's unreformed educational system. "Something at least may be said for that old system," the reviewer remarked, "which can send forth a man qualified both to lead the oratory and direct the finances of the House of Commons, and to write a commentary which will henceforth be as necessary to every student of Homer as Niebuhr is to Livy, or Grote and Thirlwall to Herodotus and Thucydides" (12 May 1858: 391). The *Gentleman's Magazine* linked Gladstone's book to an earlier case against Grote's purely mythic Homeric age and the separatist position in general, William Mure's *Critical History of the Language and Literature of Ancient Greece* (1st ed., 1850). The two together had finally "overthrown these pestilent literary heresies" (May 1858: 496).[23] But a few singled out Gladstone's arguments about Homeric religion as amateurish or backward. E. A. Freeman, for example, said that Gladstone was "acting like a philologer of the last century who derived some Greek word from the Hebrew, without thinking of asking whether the root was found in German or Sanscrit" (69). This notion that Gladstone was applying an outdated, eighteenth-century method was the point of Mark Pattison in an 1863 review of a new biography of William Warburton. In considering Warburton's *Divine Legation of Moses,* Pattison was "forcibly reminded of the *Homeric Studies* of Mr. Gladstone," and he outlined their similar modes of authorship:

> A comprehensive general reading; an heroic industry in marshalling the particulars of the proof; a dialectical force of arm which would twist a bar of iron to its purposes; and all brought to bear to prove a perverse and preposterous proposition. The mischief done by such powerful efforts of human reason is not in the diffusion of erroneous opinion on the subjects of which they treat, but in setting brilliant examples of a false method. A visionary projector carries his own refutation with him; but when a first-rate calculator devotes his powers to squaring the circle, there is so much method to his madness, that his example is sure to be influential on similarly constituted minds. (*Essays* 2.166)

Both Freeman and Pattison claimed that Gladstone was uninformed by a modern philology that was for the second half of the nineteenth century associated with Friedrich Max Müller, who had published in 1856 his "Comparative Mythology," the most important mythographic work to appear since the first two volumes of Grote's *History of Greece*. Müller's long domination of British mythography also marked a larger cultural transition. In the 1850s many British scholars, historians, and theologians were beginning to turn away from describing ancient mythology as corrupted revelation. The trope of corruption was still being used to explain the origin of non-Christian theologies, but now the most promising source for speculation was the corruption of language itself.[24] Müller began "Comparative Mythology" by dismissing both the arch-rationalist position represented by Grote and the older tradition endorsed by Gladstone. For Müller, the ancient myths were not empty of all historical value, as Grote had argued. Nor were they based on corrupt revelation (2.13). Ancient myths were based on the corruption of language; mythology was "the disease of language," as he would famously put it (qtd. in Dowling 72). The new philology found a ready advocate in Benjamin Jowett, who like Pattison was also a contributor to *Essays and Reviews* (1860). In his essay for that volume, "On the Interpretation of Scripture," Jowett called upon the new understanding of the nature of language to justify historical criticism and antidogmatic Christianity. For Jowett, the meaning of the Gospel was inseparable from the degenerate form of the language by which it was spread. "At the time our Saviour came into the world," Jowett wrote, "the Greek language itself was in a state of degeneracy and decay. . . . That degeneracy was a preparation for the Gospel—the decaying soil in which the new elements of life were to come forth—the beginning of another state of man, in which language and mythology and philosophy were no longer to exert the same constraining power as in the ancient world. . . . A religion which was to be universal required the divisions of languages, as of nations, to be in some degree broken down" (511). Or, as he put it later, "The degeneracy of language itself is not a mere principle of desolation, but creative also," and "the decay of an ancient language is the beginning of the construction of a modern one" (514).

Jowett's ideas about the liberating mission of degenerate linguistic forms were ironically close to some of the ideas expressed by Newman in 1845 in his book of conversion. Then, Newman had defined corruption as "a breaking up of the subject in which it takes place": "It is the turning-point or transition-state in that continuous process by which the birth of a living thing is mysteriously connected with its death" (120–21). Jowett agreed that corruption, birth, and death were part of one process. But he dedicated the trope of corruption to an identification of Christianity as a worldwide revelation of the antidogmatic principle. Words, which meant everything to the religion of Newman, must not mean too much in Jowett's version of revelation. "There is a worse fault than ignorance of Greek in the interpretation of the New Testament," Jowett said, "that is, ignorance of any language" (512). The new life promised by Jowett's Gospel was the life that kept emerging from the perpetual decay of language, a decay that convinced Jowett "that Christian truth is not dependent on the fixedness of modes of thought" (519). Using the new philology to refurbish the Pauline message that the letter killeth, the very meaning of the Gospels, in Jowett's eyes, was substantially phrased by linguistic degeneracy.

Brilliant clerical dons who dominated theologically liberal Oxford in the 1860s and after, both Jowett and Pattison impressed an influential generation of undergraduates with the foolishness of Gladstone's Homeric studies, particularly as his version of theological conservatism was accompanied by his increasingly populist political agendas.[25] But Gladstone's Homeric passion was one of many similar ventures, and his long-term interest in "theo-mythology" resembled the competing projects of some of his most influential critics, including Müller himself. In the sixth edition of Müller's *Lectures on the Science of Language* (1871), the enterprising professor printed, with Gladstone's permission, a letter expressing the prime minister's "opinions on the relation of the Homeric Mythology to the sacred traditions of the Jewish race" (2.440–44). Müller claimed that Gladstone's occasional error was the discovery of "Christian ideas—ideas peculiar to Christianity—in the primitive faith of mankind," but he added that "we may boldly look for those fundamental religious conceptions on which Christianity itself is built up." Müller had made a career out of popularizing the notion that "search[ing] through the sacred ruins of the ancient world, we shall be surprised to find how much more of true religion there is in what is called Heathen Mythology than we expected," and he insisted "we ought to learn to treat the ancient religions with some of the same reverence and awe with which we approach the study of the Jewish and our own" (2.466–67).

Some aspects of Gladstone's Homeric work did excite "learned mockery" (Shannon 2.70), but the reception of that work in the popular press was generally positive. And with the much-publicized discoveries made by Heinrich Schliemann in the mid-1870s and after, some version of Gladstone's position—not Grote's—on the historical value of the Homeric poems became the common one.[26] Mostly appearing after the unfettered expansion of the cheap press following his abolition of the final paper duty in 1861, Gladstone's Homerica was often greeted in terms that celebrated the irrepressible energies and passions of the author. While the ability to read ancient Greek was still the threshold to the most prestigious English universities, Gladstone's evolving populist political aura also provided an alternative invocation of classical authority, one that emphasized a manly scholastic ideal at a time when the High Victorian Reform Acts (1867 and 1884) would make it apparent that exclusion from voting rights was now, for most adults, a factor of gender. In 1872, when Gladstone's reported daily reading of Homer had become a topic of debate in the metropolitan press, the admiring *Daily Telegraph* asserted that

> Mr. Gladstone, in every speech he makes, and in every letter he writes, betrays a mind saturated with the spirit of the blind bard of ancient Hellas. Yet the most wonderful part of the matter, surely, is that a statesman upon whose hands devolves the charge of this Empire, should, in the midst of toils and labours under which most men would utterly break down, find time not only to combine the studies of his youth, but to prosecute them with a vigour and an energy which the keenest Heidelberg professor might envy. (5/12/72, 5)[27]

Such public worship of the Liberal leader—"nauseous fawning," the *Saturday Review* called it (21/12/72, 781)—offended some, particularly political opponents, but the celebration of Gladstone's energetic studiousness was a central aspect of Gladstonian Liberalism and its agendas. As he became famous as an inspired orator addressing huge, extra-parliamentary audiences, his political celebrity even assumed a complementary bardic character; he would become the living voice of the nation (or a version of it), an irrepressible oral presence commanding the constant attention of England's first modern press corps, one armed with the reach of the telegraph and the speed of steam and the broad forum of cheap, untaxed paper (Meisel 241–74). Speaking at the opening of St. Martin's Free Public Library in London in 1891, the Grand Old Man, as he became known in the 1880s, characteristically called libraries instruments in a "war against ignorance, a war against brutality, a war against idleness"; they were "in competition with the public-houses of the country" for the spirit of the working classes (qtd. in "Opening" 113). This workingman's choice between books and beer was overtly paternalistic, but Gladstone's didactic habits had always been accompanied by a willingness to lecture up as well as down. In 1872, for instance, at roughly the same time when his devoted reading of Homer was being publicly discussed, the prime minister privately expressed the wish that the queen would encourage the Prince of Wales, then at the tender age of thirty-one, to do some reading. "It would without doubt be a great object gained," Gladstone wrote to Victoria, "if . . . the Prince of Wales could, through your Majesty's influence or otherwise be induced to adopt the habit of reading. . . . Though the Prince's turn appears to move towards the kind of training which is acquired by oral intercourse and by active life, the serious difficulties which are encountered in this direction might weigh in favor of a partial application to the study of books" (Guedalla 1.383–84).

Gladstone's devoted study of Homer was ahistorical in the sense that he could not follow the Lowthian dictum to read his Hellenic classics as an ancient Hellene would. But Gladstone is a good historical witness to how readers and writers expressed religious commitments in new ways and in new contexts because of the state's eroding religious identity. In his Homeric work we see a meeting of two affiliated but jealous categories, the literary and the religious. And the liberal Victorian cultural context is just such a meeting place. Gladstone's Homeric work highlights an uncertain distinction between literature and revelation that defines the religiously plural polity that was more or less in place by the end of his career. These uncertainties existed both before and after Gladstone's age. But it was during his long moment of political relevance, from the 1840s to the 1880s in particular, that the state increasingly declined to resolve these questions. In the end, the lasting tradition of Gladstone's theological eccentricity is mostly a legacy of the ideological shift of the 1840s, when the British state went from tolerating certain forms of religious heterodoxy to being functionally indifferent to Christian theology. This change, more than any other, made the forties a period, as Frank Turner puts it, of "cultural apostasy" (1993: 44).

Gladstone's reading of Homer was somewhat obscurely rooted in his need to reconstruct his aborted ecclesiastical vocation in the context of an increasingly liberal political life. In my final chapter, I propose a new understanding of the pseudo-ecclesiastical career of George Eliot, and I show how her fictional hero in *Daniel Deronda* (1876) lives out Gladstone's real vocational trial in reverse. A talented young man plagued by indecision about his future profession, he will "set himself against authorship" and reject a career in English politics (*Deronda* 185, 383) to become, by adoption, an alien priest.

6

Clerical Fictions
Eliot's Scribal Authority

MARY ANN EVANS, TO be better known as George Eliot, became a published author in January 1840, when the *Christian Observer* printed her poem "Knowing That Shortly I Must Put Off This Tabernacle." With a heart set on saying farewell to all earthly things, the poem's speaker confronts the fact that salvation's threshold will include a valediction to those things that have been her most cherished companions:

> Books, that have been to me as chests of gold,
> Which, miser-like, I secretly have told,
> And for you love, health, friendship, peace, have sold—
> *Farewell!*

And yet there is one book, the Bible, she imagines bringing with her:

> Blest tome, to thee, whose truth-writ page once known,
> Fades not before heaven's sunshine or hell's moan,
> I say not of God's earthly gifts alone,
> *Farewell!*

This was earnest bibliolatry. But as the editor of the *Christian Observer* pointed out, devotion to the Word had culminated in a heterodox position. In "the New Jerusalem," the Reverend Samuel Wilks reminded readers, there will be no "need of a Bible; for we shall not then see through a glass darkly,—through the veil of Sacraments or the written word—but face to face. The Bible is God's gift, but not for heaven's use" (38).

Within the next two years, Eliot's status as a Bible reader was transformed even as books and reading remained central to her own self-fashioning. By waging her "Holy War," she would deliberately reject the "Divine authority of the books comprising the Jewish and Christian Scriptures" and come to "regard these writings," as she explained to her father in February 1842, "as histories consisting of mingled truth and fiction, and while I admire and cherish much of what I believe to have been the moral teaching of Jesus himself, I consider the system of doctrines built upon the facts of his life and drawn as to its materials from Jewish notions to be most dishonorable to God and most pernicious in its influence on individual and social happiness" (*GEL* 1.128). In her departure from the religion of her youth, Eliot bid farewell to the idea that the Bible was a supernaturally blest tome, becoming instead a reader of "the scriptures of the physical and of the moral world," as they were described by Charles Hennell in *An Inquiry Concerning the Origins of Christianity* (2nd ed., 1841): "Here the page is open, and the language intelligible to all men; no transcribers have been able to interpolate or erase its texts; it stands before us in the same genuineness as when first written." And against this reverence for the genuine "book of the universe" (Hennell 488), Eliot honed a critical disdain for Scripture insofar as it embodied a mode of authorship whose hallmark was an ahistorical will to chronicle events in a self-serving fashion, "to flatter national vanity, or to aggrandize a priesthood," as she would put it in 1856 (*Essays* 258).

Privately, Eliot could be blunter in equating an oppressive, hieratic textuality with a contemptible Hebraism. "I bow to the supremacy of Hebrew poetry," she wrote in 1848 after reading Benjamin Disraeli's *Tancred; or, The New Crusade* (1847), "but much of their early mythology and almost all their history is utterly revolting." And in response to Disraeli's philo-Semitic racial theories, Eliot expressed a low opinion of the proverbial people of the book. The Jews had "produced a Moses and a Jesus, but Moses was impregnated with Egyptian philosophy and Jesus is venerated and adored by us only for that wherein he transcended or resisted Judaism. The very exultation of their idea of a national deity into a spiritual monotheism seems to have been borrowed from the other oriental tribes. Everything specifically Jewish is of a low grade" (*GEL* 1.247). By this time, Eliot had embraced the belief that the historical Jesus was a demotic, provincial reformer who had become the victim of the metropolitan priests and scribes whose authority he had challenged in Jerusalem. Indebted to anti-Judaic critiques of Scripture in the tradition of Voltaire and others (Sutcliffe 231–46), Eliot's intellectual revolution in the 1840s more generally turned on a critique of priestcraft in all ages, one that had been essential in both the making of the Bible in antiquity and in its present day misinterpretation by the clergy.

One wonders, then, how it came to be that her career culminates with a work, *Daniel Deronda* (1876), in which the hero becomes the spiritual heir of one Ezra Mordecai Cohen, a man descended from the hereditary

Jewish priesthood and bearing the name of Jewish history's most influential priestly scribe, the Ezra featured in the biblical books of Ezra and Nehemiah. The hero himself of *Daniel Deronda,* of course, has the name of a biblical prophet, but the novel, I argue in this final chapter, has an essential interest in priestly functions; and rather than endorsing the Romantic preference for prophets over priests in any simple way, *Deronda* is an extraordinary clerical fiction, one that comments upon the era's appetite for the representation of clerical life.[1] A portion of this fiction recalls the post-Enlightenment anticlericalism that was an aspect of Eliot's own break with supernatural Christianity; and thus the novel is an acidic portrait of a class fond of the established church as an institution that could put a gentleman in every parish. Just as the character Daniel Deronda will reject the privilege of being an English gentleman, the novel rejects this gentlemanly clerical ideal. But neither the character nor the novel is about dispensing with the "clerical function" (*Deronda* 31). To the contrary, Deronda's character develops as he becomes associated with, first, the sacrificing and absolving priesthood of Roman Catholicism and, later, with the pre-Christian priesthood of the Jews. For Deronda, these encounters are mostly a matter of fulfillment: his quest for his family roots and his search for a public career ultimately coalesce in an idealized Judaism that allows him to make a profession of his own recovered domesticity, to make a home in what he takes to be his homeland, as Monica Cohen has argued (151–85). At the same time, the novel's central female character, Gwendolen Harleth, is subjected to the painful discipline of rods, scourges, and what emerges as the most formidable hierophantic device, the lying pen of the scribe. By making gender essential to the ability of main characters to respond productively to priestly roles, Eliot acknowledged realities that had mostly prevented women from assuming the priestly office. But by flirting with a reunion between the modern novelist and the priestly scribe, she also showed how a form of hierophantic textuality—including her own body of writings—could evade these historical prohibitions. Some thirty-six years after being chided by the Reverend Wilks for imagining a New Jerusalem where the elect inhabitants had brought their Bibles with them, Eliot became the author of her own hieratic and patriarchal fiction, one in which a young man sets forth on a journey to Palestine only after he reclaims the word of his fathers.

To put it more succinctly, I am underscoring how "Daniel Deronda," like "George Eliot," is a professional pseudonym. Not only is the titular hero's family name, Deronda, a purposely deceptive alias but his prophetic first name is a cover for a priestly role he must assume. But before excavating the priestly narrative in *Daniel Deronda,* I want to reevaluate Eliot's initial clerical masquerade as a writer of fictions, relate this masquerade to her critique of priestcraft, and describe the creative consequences of the masquerade's cessation.

Eliot's early anticlericalism has relatively exotic foundations in her experiences as the translator of Strauss, Ludwig Feuerbach, and Baruch Spinoza, the last a writer inspired by the conviction that "the institution of priesthood," as George Henry Lewes wrote in 1843, was "injurious to the general welfare."[2] And on the eve of commencing her career as a writer of fiction, she turned her contempt for the injurious institution into devastating portraits of two clerical authors closer to home, the popular eighteenth-century poet Edward Young and Eliot's contemporary John Cumming. In both cases, in two long articles that appeared in the *Westminster Review,* she insisted it was the man as revealed in his writings, not theology, that was her topic. As she put it in the essay on Cumming, "no theory" and "no opinions, religious or irreligious" made "it a gratification to us to detect him in delinquencies"; her mission was to judge him as a man "founded solely on the manner in which he has written himself down on his pages" (*Essays* 189). And in this setting, the venal cleric emerges as a particular kind of writer. "In Young," as Eliot concluded the second essay, "we have the type of that deficient human sympathy, that impiety towards the present and the visible, which flies for its motives, its sanctities, and its religion, to the remote, the vague, and the unknown" (*Essays* 385). Eliot's understanding of a career committed to the creed of realism was animated by a powerful scorn for the "clerical flesh" embodied in the writings of Young and Cumming (*Essays* 161). And yet, even as Eliot made the rebuke of clerical authors the threshold of her fiction-writing career, her new authorial identity was destined to be ecclesiastical. It was while writing about Young's self-serving "metamorphosis into the clerical form" (*Essays* 337) that Evans, with the help of Lewes, did something of the same. For George Eliot was not only the fictional biographer of Amos Barton, Maynard Gilfil, and Edgar Tryan, the clerical protagonists in *Scenes of Clerical Life* (1857). Many also assumed the author was himself a clergyman. This was the case with Eliot's first reader (other than Lewes), the publisher John Blackwood. After Lewes had called the as yet unnamed author his "clerical friend," Blackwood had a representative reply, writing, "I am glad to hear that your friend is as I supposed a Clergyman. Such a subject is best in clerical hands and some of the pleasantest and least prejudiced correspondents I have ever had are English Clergymen" (2.275).[3]

Eliot's "teaching had been dubbed clerical," as Richard Simpson put it in 1863 (Carroll 225). And her journals from the days surrounding the achievement of her initial fame reveal her fascination with the widespread perception of her clerical status (*Journals* 289–302). The detailed and sympathetic portrayal of Aldolphus Irwine, the clergyman in *Adam Bede* (1859), confirmed this impression for many readers, and that text's bibliographic threshold spoke in a cunning clerical code with each of the three main creative units on the title page—title, author's identification, and epigraph—linked to clerical life. The family name of the book's titular hero invokes England's patriarch of clerical authorship as well as a contemporary heir, Cuthbert Bede, whose *Adventures of Mr. Verdant Green: an Oxford Freshman* (3 pts., 1853–57) was on its way to becoming the mid-century's most popular look into the clerically dominated universities. This latter-day Bede, the clergyman Edward Bradley, provided the kind of details that would allow Eliot to portray convincingly products of the universities long before she had visited them.[4] Moving from the title, a reader then sees "George Eliot" glossed as the "Author of 'Scenes of Clerical Life'" followed by an epigraph identified as coming from Wordsworth. Even for those unfamiliar with the precise source, the moral weight of the language makes it clear that the speaker is no literal swain:

> And when
> I speak of such among the flock as swerved
> Or fell, those only shall be singled out
> Upon whose lapse, or error, something more
> Than brotherly forgiveness may attend.

Eliot's ideal reader would know that the words came from the central clerical hero of the deceased laureate's work, the pastor featured in *The Excursion*. Following all of these preliminary clerical gestures, the first words to come from Adam Bede's mouth ("Awake, my soul, and with the sun" [5]) are borrowed from the "Morning Hymn" of Thomas Ken (1637–1711), one of the emerging saints within the nineteenth-century cult of the priest.[5] And Bede then gives what one of his fellow workers calls a "sarmunt" (8) as part of a broader discussion about the propriety of that evening's preaching by a dissenting woman. So while *Adam Bede* departed from *Scenes of Clerical Life* by having a lay protagonist, its opening pages made references and allusions to the clergy, clerical writers, and clerical functions of various kinds.

More than a general pseudonymity, Eliot's implicit cultivation of a clerical identity offered insulation from two scandals that were antithetical to clerical propriety: the fact that Mariann Evans had been living with a married man since 1853 and the fact that she had been the translator of Strauss and Feuerbach. A fallen woman and a lost soul by conventional standards, Evans became a clerical gentleman for understandably protective reasons. But the polemic aspect of her clerical subject matter and her implicit clerical status has been hurried over in readiness to adopt enticing claims made by Lewes, Eliot's intermediary for publication. Writing to Blackwood for the first time about what would become *Scenes of Clerical Life,* Lewes described a series "of tales and sketches illustrative of the actual life of our country clergy about a quarter of century ago; but solely in its human and not at all in its theological aspect" (2.269). Lewes also insisted such a project was innovative, "the object being to do what has never yet been done in our Literature, for we have had abundant religious stories, polemical and doctrinal, but since the 'Vicar [of Wakefield]' and Miss Austen, no stories representing the clergy like any other class with the humours, sorrows, and troubles of other men" (2.269). There is no reason, however, to believe that Blackwood assented to the idea that the works of George Eliot were innovative on the level put forward. As the proprietor of a firm that would keep John Galt's *Annals of the Parish* (1st ed., 1821) in print into the 1860s, Blackwood knew that readers were interested in the clerical point of view precisely because the vocation demanded that the conscientious clergyman be involved with all levels of society from baptism to burial.

By writing clerical tales—*Adam Bede* was originally called "The Clerical Tutor"—Eliot initiated her fictional career with what was already a representative narrative form. When Charlotte Brontë opened *Shirley* in 1849 by noting "an abundant shower of curates" that had lately "fallen upon the north of England" (5), she registered a professional expansion that was underwritten by ecclesiastical reform and voluntary institutions such as the Pastoral Aid and Additional Curates societies. But she was also participating in the increasingly common activity of depicting clerical life on the printed page, something that took place in the context of realist fiction as well as biographies and narratives about heroic missionary activity. This trend was similarly marked ten years later in Walter Bagehot's review of an unremarkable clerical novel, *The Dean* (1859) by "Berkeley Aikin," the pseudonym of Fanny Aikin Kortright. Suggesting that England's post-Napoleonic female novelists had thrown over the prior age's fascination with soldiers, Bagehot said "the black coat" had replaced "the red-coat" (2.158). Most famously of all, Anthony Trollope found tremendous success with his Barsetshire series starting in 1855; and, in *The Last Chronicle of Barset* (1867), he would conclude it with a general justification of making the social lives of the clergy his subject because "no men affect more strongly, by their character, the society of those around than do country clergymen" (860). Trollope, Eliot, Margaret Oliphant, and other writers emerged as distinct voices in the 1860s as authors of clerical fictions, but all of these authors inherited rather than invented the form. In Trollope's case he had inherited it directly from his mother, Fanny Trollope, a clergyman's daughter whose novel *The Vicar of Wrexhill* (1837) was among her more popular works.

By saying that his clerical friend was reaching back to the days of Jane Austen and Oliver Goldsmith, Lewes was name-dropping and suggesting that the author (if not a clergyman) had been reared, like Austen and Goldsmith, in a clerical household. Moreover, by insisting to a publisher that there would be an interest in the lives of clergymen for "human" rather than "theological reasons," Lewes and Eliot were making covert cases for the religion of humanity. This program—of replacing the theological with the human—distills both Straussian Christology, which sought to get at the human story behind the theological drama, as well as a larger Feuerbachian reading of religion itself, one that insisted that "the true sense of Theology is Anthropology" (Feuerbach xxxvii). In Feuerbach in particular Eliot came to know a habitual rearrangement of the traditionalist's hierarchy of the human and the theological. Feuerbach's subjects in *The Essence of Christianity* (1854), he said, were "men in whom Christianity was not merely a theory or a dogma, not merely theology, but religion. My principal theme is Christianity, is Religion, as it is the immediate object, the immediate nature of man. Erudition and philosophy are to me only the means by which I bring to light the treasure hid in man" (xlii).

With terms that echo her own translation of Feuerbach, Eliot in *The Mill on the Floss* laments Maggie Tulliver's lack of opportunity to acquire "her inherited share in the hard-won treasures of thought, which generations of painful toil have laid up for the race of men" (288). Given the educational limits women faced, the novel suggests in its final volume that Maggie's best available alternative is the solace and sympathy offered by Dr. Kenn, the rector whose name associates him both with the visual faculty that underwrites realism as well as the author of the hymn sung by Adam Bede. Eliot's Kenn is a member of what the narrator calls a "natural priesthood" (435), and he is able to discern Maggie's essential innocence at a time when all of St. Ogg's has ostracized her as sexually fallen. But Kenn, harboring the disgraced Maggie, finds his professional status compromised. With her continued presence "likely to obstruct his usefulness as a clergyman," he must turn her out—and turn her over, as he proposes, to the keeping of "a clerical friend of his, who might possibly take her into his own family, as governess; and, if not, would probably know of some other available position for a young woman in whose welfare Dr. Kenn felt a strong interest" (512–13). Instead of being received into this refuge,

Maggie, along with her brother Tom, is swept away in a devastating flood, and Eliot thereby makes it clear that there is no "available position" in the world for her most autobiographical heroine.

Part of the novel's terminal pessimism was founded on the dramatic cessation of Eliot's clerical masquerade, an inevitable event that was precipitated by the claims of Joseph Liggins, an "impoverished, ne'er-do-well Nuneaton clergyman" (Bodenheimer 137), to being the hand behind the stories of George Eliot.[6] The true identity of George Eliot thus became the focus of a major review of the author's complete works (*Scenes of Clerical Life, Adam Bede,* and *The Mill on the Floss*) in the October 1860 number of the *Quarterly Review.* The author of the review, James Craigie Robertson, was himself a clergyman and a clerical biographer, having recently authored *Becket, Archbishop of Canterbury: a Biography* (1859), and before then he had reviewed Anderdon's *Life of Thomas Ken* for the *Quarterly* (Sept. 1851: 277–306). Robertson began his 1860 review by noting the moral rehabilitation of "Currer Bell" in Elizabeth Gaskell's *Life of Charlotte Brontë* (1857), a work that, in Robertson's eyes, disclosed how the author of *Jane Eyre* had in fact been "the young and irreproachable maiden daughter of a clergyman" (669). "We now know how it was," Robertson writes, "that a clergyman's daughter, herself innocent, and honourably devoted to the discharge of many a painful duty, could have written such a book as 'Jane Eyre'" (470). In contrast, the public was now informed that George Eliot, thought by many to be "'a gentleman of high-church tendencies,'" was in fact a "lady ∴ who had given a remarkable proof of mastery over both the German language and her own, but had certainly not established a reputation for orthodoxy, by a translation of Strauss's 'Life of Jesus'" (471). Robertson went on to insist that Eliot had rather been more recognizable from the start as a member of the "Broad-Church party," but his key point was the obvious answer to his "disturbing question":

> But what is to be thought of the fact that the authoress of these tales is also the translator of Strauss's notorious book? Is the Gospel which she has represented in so many attractive lights nothing better to her, after all, than 'fabula ista de Christo?' ... Has she been carrying out in these novels the precepts of that chapter in which Dr. Strauss teaches his disciples how, while believing the New Testament narrative to be merely mythical, they may yet discharge the functions of the Christian preacher without exposing themselves by their language to any imputation of unsoundness? (497–98)

Composing a narrative that featured the unavailing results of Kenn's "natural priesthood" in *The Mill on the Floss* was thus a more honest acknowledgment by an author who endorsed the day's version of eighteenth-century "natural" religion. With the ruse about Lewes's "clerical friend" fully exposed, it was beside the point to have Maggie Tulliver find happiness under the care of Kenn's "clerical friend." And in Eliot's remaining four novels, she would struggle to realign her earlier positioning of literary culture and ecclesiastical vocations without the resource of an assumed professional respectability. No longer able to compose her fictions, in a covert Feuerbachian key—one that formulaically replaced the theological with the human—Eliot's hard-won faith in Hennell's "book of the universe" would be transformed in a way that allowed the supernaturally blest tome of her young adulthood to have a second life of sorts. In the process, her novels became vehicles for her increasingly complicated views on the culture of letters in general. Eliot would thus repeatedly represent versions of problematic textual devotion that culminate in her final hero's ability to balance submission and self-assertion in his most important decisions as a reader.

Eliot said that she began *Romola* (1862–63) as a young woman and finished it as an old one, and in the stresses of creating that work she opened up a new direction for her remaining fictions *Felix Holt* (1867), *Middlemarch* (1872–73), and *Daniel Deronda* (1876). The nature of this turning point was, perhaps unintentionally, brought out by Leslie Stephen's remark that *Romola* was "a magnificent piece of cram" (Carroll 479). Stephen was expressing his conviction that Eliot's historical novel about fifteenth-century Florence marked an unfortunate departure from the rural world the author knew so well, and he insisted that, even after returning to her homeland in *Middlemarch*, Eliot's heroine, Dorothea Brooke, remained enamored of cramming. "Her faith in her husband receives its death blow," says Stephen, not because she finds out "that he is a wretched pedant, but that he is a pedant of the wrong kind" (Carroll 480). The result is a book that looks like what Stephen knows it cannot be: "a cutting satire upon the aspirations of young ladies, who wish to learn Latin and Greek, when they ought to be nursing babies and supporting hospitals" (Carroll 481). Whatever prompted Stephen's unease with *Romola* and *Middlemarch*, his linking of them was astute, and his lively remark about *Middlemarch* applies just as well to the earlier work: surely *Romola* cannot be an admonition to intellectually ambitious women of the 1860s that they ought to stick to nursing babies in the time-honored maternal mode or take to tending the newly professionalized sickbed? Here too, though, we are in part whistling in the dark. *Romola* does express grave skepticism about the culture of letters while it preserves an abiding faith in that milk of human kindness most likely to flow, so the theory goes, from a self-sacrificing woman.

The force that bars Romola and Dorothea from any culturally exceptional intellectual achievement is a plot—one that also applies to Felix Holt—about inheritance, a repeated story about an attempted act of intellectual transmission from a father or father figure to a younger generation. In *Romola, Felix Holt, Middlemarch,* and *Daniel Deronda,* the inheritable is materialized into an archival entity—Bardo's library, Holt's medicinal formulas, Casaubon's notes and papers, and Daniel Charisi's "precious chest" (746)—and this archive is not only a thing that passes between individuals and states of death and life; it is the repository of the identity of its possessor, so that the reception of the gift comes at the price of assuming the identity contained in it.[7] In the first three versions of this tale, the transfer of the father's archive is either a burden or an imposture that the two heroines—Romola and Dorothea—and one hero—Felix—must reject as part of a process in which an autonomous identity is achieved. In the last of her novels, the transmission of the archive is likewise initially denied, and this failure is again tied to a daughter's success in winning autonomy, one represented by Alcharisi's career as an independent artist. But ultimately in *Daniel Deronda* the archive is passed on in the name of the father. What permits the transmission of the archive, as we shall see, is a betrayal of the liberal cult of letters, something that includes transforming her hero into a traditionally benighted reader and assigning to him a subliterary, scribal vocation.

When Deronda first meets his mother, now the Princess Leonora Halm-Eberstein, on the shores of the Adriatic, she recounts how she had sent him away when not yet two years old to be raised as an "English gentleman." At that time, she was the famed lyric actress Alcharisi, and, recently widowed of her first husband, she had determined to free herself from all ties that bound her up as a "mere daughter and mother" and as a Jew (664). Before then, taking to the stage had been a rebellion against the will of her deceased father, a devout and domineering man who had forbidden her theatrical career; and sending away his namesake to be raised in ignorance of his Jewish heritage was another way to thwart the man who saw his daughter as "a makeshift link" for producing a male heir (631). As Leonora tells her son: "I was to love the long prayers in the ugly synagogue, and the howling, and the gabbling, and the dreadful fasts, and the tiresome feasts, and my father's endless discoursing about Our People, which was a thunder without meaning in my ears. I was to care for ever about what Israel had been; and I did not care at all. I cared for the wide world, and all that I could represent in it" (630). Now haunted by the memory of the father she has betrayed, she becomes his begrudging handmaid, passing on to Deronda his Jewish heritage as well as the chest of writings she had been charged to deliver to her firstborn son. The bold attempt to cut traditional ties has failed, and the once powerful, independent artist has become the "instrument" (662) of her father's word.

The disclosure of the insufficiency of Alcharisi's artistic career is a representative episode in a novel that mounts an elaborate critique of "disinterested culture" (177), the progressive force cited by Sir Hugo, the Liberal MP who has been Deronda's guardian. As Robert Preyer argued long ago, this critical program made Eliot creatively offend aspects of literary realism by adopting the writing and reading habits of "mystics and visionaries" (34). "We want to know," as Preyer put it, "why an urgent concern with personal and social salvation, with finding and doing one's duty, should lead a great master of reality into myth and fantasy and, ultimately, into the occult" (35). Since then a powerful body of commentary has appeared—much of it focused on the troubled epistemology of the novel (Welsh 280–334; Anderson 119–46; Levine; Loesberg 140–47)—that allows us to appreciate how and why Deronda refuses to be enlisted on the side of liberal culture in favor of a cultivated partiality. What has not been understood, however, is the extent to which Eliot uses stories about the priestly office to express her peculiar form of agnosticism about the century's cult of culture. Involving her central characters with an extensive taxonomy of sacerdotal manifestations, Eliot represents varieties of priestcraft as a form of critical therapy for what she sees to be a morally decadent order. And by turning back the pages of the conventional annals of Protestant historiography, Eliot unfolds Deronda's story in what becomes a book of origins about a priestly function that makes Anglican, Roman Catholic, and Jewish hierophantic traditions belated institutions of a universal, historically persistent type. Written at the peak of public controversies about priestly rituals and in response to a crisis about the nature of redeeming culture, *Daniel Deronda* also records a complex historical moment that turned Eliot's mind toward a concept of rudimentary yet redeeming reading.

All of these priestly narratives are present at the novel's pivotal moments in chapters 35 and 36. Set on the turn of a year, from 1865 to 1866, these chapters open the novel's second half by showing the recently wedded Henleigh and Gwendolen Grandcourt visiting Monks Topping Abbey, where Deronda has been raised. As the Grandcourts tour the grounds, they fancy they are wandering about a future possession, and Gwendolen is comforted to see more evidence that she has not sold herself cheaply. When they enter the abbey's "beautiful choir long ago turned into stables," she utters uncontrollable praise for the picturesque scene. "'Oh, this is glorious!'" she "burst[s] forth, in forgetfulness of everything but the immediate impression" (420). Deronda, in a more somber spirit, takes off his hat. Forced to consider the time when he will be a stranger in his own home, he understands how a refrain of desecration and usurpation echoes in the abbey's former choir. For similar reasons, Gwendolen's uncontrollable praise is something she will soon regret, and during the same visit she experiences a type of religious conversion. As she makes this transformation, she seeks out Deronda's spiritual advice in scenes of confession that lead to her "ideal consecration" of him: "Without the aid of sacred ceremony or costume, her feelings had turned this man, only a few years older than herself, into a priest" (430).

These episodes at the abbey revisit the excursion to Sotherton in Jane Austen's last completed novel, *Mansfield Park,* where a Gwendolenesque Mary Crawford slights the clerical profession during a tour of the unused chapel only to learn that Edmund Bertram is soon to be ordained; and in *Mansfield Park,* Austen was herself returning to the first novel she offered for publication, *Northanger Abbey,* which also features for its hero a second son who has entered the church and a heroine who visits a domesticated abbey with conjugal expectations. Though they differ in tone, both *Northanger Abbey* and *Mansfield Park* are clerical novels that defend the dignity of the hero's calling and dispense matrimonial rewards to the woman willing to assume the role of clergyman's wife. Austen's narration of this clerical romance began in *Northanger Abbey* as a satire of readers of the gothic and evolved into a tale that was graver and more realistic in *Mansfield Park*. First, Catherine Moreland shows she is ready for marriage when she comes to understand that sadistically terrorized wives—their degradations modeled on the abuse of innocent nuns (125)—are incompatible with Englishness and reformed religion at a time when "social and literary intercourse," "roads and newspapers lay every thing open" (172). Later, Fanny Price is rewarded with a marital happiness that will unfold in an unexceptional parsonage, conducted there by a narrator given to acts of clemency. "Let other pens dwell on guilt and misery," Austen begins the final chapter in *Mansfield Park,* "impatient to restore every body, not greatly in fault themselves, to tolerable comfort" (312).

Eliot's revision of this story, however, dolefully dwells on guilt and misery. Written in a mode of gothic realism that animates ancestral ghosts in concordance with a contemporary monastic and sacerdotal revival, it makes real, at least for Gwendolen, the terrors that Catherine Moreland comes to know as fictions spun out of her novel reading. In an age of telegraphs, steamships, and railways, gothic furies avenge the crime of marrying the heir of leisure, while the vocational heir—Deronda—is made available to prescribe forms of penance that would have been familiar to Austen's "ill-fated nun[s]" of yore (*Northanger Abbey* 125). Thus when Gwendolen and Deronda meet alone at the abbey, they convene in a library that is "as warmly odorous as a private chapel in which the censers have been swinging" (449), and in that setting she is prepared to treasure Deronda's advice to take up the penitential scourge. "One who has committed irremediable errors," Deronda tells her, "may be scourged by that consciousness into a higher course than is common" (450). Later, as a newly born widow, she is shown to have held tight to the figurative scourge pressed upon her, explicitly recalling Deronda's advice that one "might be scourged into something better" (690). Under Deronda's sought after guidance, Gwendolen intermittently embraces a form of religious discipline and enters a "refuge" of "the higher, the religious life" (451), and Grandcourt will surprise his wife and Deronda in a secret meeting, where he sees "Gwendolen's face of anguish framed black like a nun's" (610). Similarly, the absurdly insightful Hans Meyrick describes Gwendolen as a "young duchess" who has been cowered into submission by Deronda's theological discussions (800), and he worries that Deronda might have the same effect on Gwendolen's diminutive double, Mirah Lapidoth, whom he fears "will get as narrow as a nun" (579).

Gwendolen's awakening to a new religious life under Deronda's direction takes the form of a turn toward elements of both a Roman Catholic past in the nation's history and the contemporary Catholic revival that had, among other things, made ritualism into the church's great controversy in the 1860s and '70s. And this turn is invoked both by the narrator (via the ecclesiastical language quoted above) and by observers within the text, such as Sir Hugo, who accuses Deronda of talking to women in a "Jesuitical way" (361). By associating Deronda with Catholicism and referring to confession, penitential kneeling, priestly vestments, scourges, incense, and censures, Eliot at the work's midpoint was tempting her audience to think that the novel might "follow an archetypal plot of anti-confessional rhetoric," in which Deronda will seduce Gwendolen as he plays the role of her spiritual confessor (Blair 2001: 47; see also Bernstein 105–42). In doing so, Eliot played upon common anxieties in mainstream Protestant thought that regularly portrayed the evils of popery by raising the following gendered image of the rite of confession: a man's wife and/or daughters were required to have a secret relationship with an unmarried man, one whose own sexual ambitions had been screwed to the sticking point by an "unnatural" vow of celibacy. Set at a time when Ritualists were controversially reviving the practice, the novel exploited the fact that the rite of confession was no longer something that could be anathematized as a vice peculiar to the "Roman" priesthood. Eliot was also exploiting interest in and anxieties about a general monastic revival that included the establishment of religious houses—Anglican and Roman Catholic—for both men and women. The nineteenth century witnessed a long-term revival of interest in priestly ritual and in the daily habits of individuals living under religious vows, but a particularly contentious era within that larger history was the period corresponding with the historical setting of *Daniel Deronda* (1865–66) up to its composition and publication (1874–76). From the formation of the First Royal Commission on Ritual in 1865 until the passage of the Public Worship Regulation Bill in 1874, printed debate about what a priest could legitimately do reached unprecedented proportions, and this debate about ritualism was often related to one about the rising numbers entering religious communities. Deronda's "Jesuitical" ways unfolded at a time when this order of men was not confined in England to the pages of gothic novels. "The sight of nuns is no longer a strange thing in English streets," wrote J. M. Capes in the *Contemporary Review* of December 1872. "Monks and friars are pitied, and even almost admired, and Jesuits are despised more than they are hated" (33).[8]

Eliot and Lewes had firsthand exposure to the habits of one of three Ritualist incumbents prosecuted in the late 1860s, the Reverend Hooker Wix, who deserves a footnote in literary history as the man who handed the scourge to Eliot that would ultimately lash Gwendolen's erring conscience. Eliot and Lewes spent Christmas in 1870 in Wix's Swanmore parsonage, which their friend Barbara Bodichon had rented for her winter holiday, and Eliot recorded her attendance at a Christmas Day service at the attached "ritualistic Church," where she noted "some excellent intoning by the delicate-faced tenor voiced clergyman Mr. Hooker Wicks [sic]" (*Journals* 141). Most of all, Eliot and Lewes were struck by the fact that there was "a *scourge* hanging up in the priest's study." On Christmas Eve, Lewes arranged to have it brought to the table in a covered dish. After telling Bodichon that he "had taken the liberty of ordering a new dish—one only met with at recherché tables," he dramatically removed the cover to "immense laughter" (*GEL* 5.126–7).

At the time of this holiday mirth-making, Eliot was "100 pages—good printed pages" into a work she was still calling "Miss Brooke" (*GEL* 5.127), and it is a good measure of the timing of the century's sacerdotal revival that Eliot was unable to make much direct use of either ritualism or monasticism in *Middlemarch*'s historical setting of the late 1820s and early '30s. In that novel's "Prelude," Dorothea's lack of vocational opportunity in the era of the First Reform Bill is contrasted with Saint Theresa's chance, long ago, to find "her epos in the reform of a religious order" (3). But by seeking in *Daniel Deronda* to depict life in the late 1860s, Eliot was

Fig. 9. "Two Girls from the Period," Punch, *20 February 1869: 71, by John Tenniel. As a fashionable lady considering vows looks on, a member of an Anglican sisterhood scrubs the floor of a scriptorium.*

given sanction to speak about ecclesiastical ritual, monks, and nuns in ways that simultaneously appealed to the thrilling dark passages in the Protestant imagination as well as the day's most controversial religious subjects. Gwendolen's adoption of a penitential vocation and her fictional transformation into a nun takes place at a time when such opportunities had greatly expanded from the days of Dorothea Brooke. In the 1860s, one did not need to travel to France and convert to Roman Catholicism, as Brontë's Eliza Reed does in *Jane Eyre,* to take the veil (fig. 9). And references to scourges and incense in the 1870s were not, as they might be in any Austen novel, clear cues that the heroine was being prepared for a check by "modern" English realities. In contrast, when Sir Hugo and Grandcourt share snide comments about "wear[ing] out the stones with kneeling" and "fellows wanting to howl litanies" (416), their contempt was aimed at contemporary events. How one chanted the litany had assumed a controversial cultural seriousness. And one of the major clerical discipline trials of the late 1860s, that against A. H. Mackonochie, featured a defendant charged with "excessive kneeling" (Yates 216–17).

Gwendolen's reliance on Deronda is not simply a case of her turning one man into a priest. It is a form of consecration that calls for, and is in part caused by, a turn from other ecclesiastical types. Most directly, this new pastoral relationship transfers Gwendolen's allegiance from the clergy as represented by her uncle, the Reverend Henry Gascoigne, who is the novel's most closely depicted conventional cleric. Gwendolen seeks out the promise of the Catholic scourge, in other words, because of her growing disappointment in wielding a riding whip, the correlative device for what Eliot elsewhere calls "the cultus of horse-flesh" (*Middlemarch* 139).[9] And if the choral stables featured in chapter 35 are the central location where a devotion to equestrian pursuits stands out as a corrupt national religion, Gascoigne is the priest officiating at the service where Gwendolen is put into matrimonial harness.

On the way to the central scene in the stables, Gwendolen first asserts her illusory dominion over her corner of Wessex on the issue of keeping a horse, and her claims are submitted to Gascoigne's judgment. As it was intended to be for Fred Vincy in *Middlemarch*, Gascoigne's entrance into the church was the seal of his status as a gentleman in an act of self-invention that had prompted "Captain Gaskin [to take] orders and a diphthong but shortly before his engagement" to Gwendolen's aunt. Now at the age of fifty-seven—an age he shares with Mirah's "unreverend father" (737)—and duly performing the "clerical function" by virtue of his "fine person" and "native gift for administration," Gascoigne unites in one pleasing physical frame the role of gentleman, father, magistrate, and pastor. He has proven himself adept at producing both female offspring and male heirs, and he helps to contract and solemnize the marriage rites of the gentry. He is someone whose "tone of thinking . . . had become ecclesiastical rather than theological; not the modern Anglican, but what he would have called sound English, free from nonsense: such as became a man who looked at a national religion by day-light, and saw it in its relations to other things" (31). As a connoisseur of bodies and their carriage, Gascoigne cannot deny that the arresting spectacle of his niece deserves to be seen on a horse. The expense cannot be, strictly speaking, afforded, but it can be justified as a bit of wise speculation. And some months after winning the argument about keeping a horse, Gwendolen shows signs of belonging to the riding classes when she triumphs in the hunt led by Lord Brackenshaw. At the same time, her characterization of the less-successful experience of Rex Gascoigne, the rector's son, looks forward to her subsequent ejaculation of praise in the abbey's stables. Mounted on "his father's grey nag . . . of sober years and ecclesiastical habits," Rex is to Gwendolen's mind "a droll picture" and "a capital caricature" (72, 77), but the essential part of the humor that she perceives is the formal incongruity of "a fine lithe youth . . . stuck as if under a wizard's spell on a stiff clerical hackney" (72). Rex himself is not physically unworthy of Gwendolen; he is stuck on an unworthy horse. As such, this fine youth and the clerical nag invert the significance of Sir Hugo's stables, an ecclesiastical edifice suited to maintain fine horses. To perceive the drollness of one image is to understand the glory of the other.

The episode of the hunt causes Rex to confess to his father his love for Gwendolen (74). And Gascoigne draws out the event's lesson to the two young riders. Rex for his part is sternly reminded that he is "not furnished with a horse which enables [him] to play squire to [his] cousin." Gwendolen, on the other hand, *has* been furnished with a horse to enable her to play maiden before the eyes of local squires, and she is told that "if [she] intend[ed] to hunt, [she] must marry a man who can keep horses" (77). When marriage to Grandcourt—the county's most conspicuous keeper of horses—becomes a possibility, Gascoigne reminds his niece that "Grandcourt, the almost certain baronet, the probable peer, was to be ranged with public personages, and was a match to be accepted on broad general grounds national and ecclesiastical" (140). Assuming that way of speaking so effective from the pulpit and at sessions—a "mode of speech" that "always conveyed a thrill of authority"—Gascoigne explains to Gwendolen how marriage to Grandcourt is a "duty" (141). And Eliot later presents an equestrian spectacle as Gwendolen's immediate reward for accepting Grandcourt's proposal. "They could see the two horses being taken slowly round the sweep," Eliot writes, "and the beautiful creatures, in their fine grooming, sent a thrill of exultation through Gwendolen. They were the symbols of command and luxury, in delightful contrast with the ugliness of poverty and humiliation at which she had lately been looking close" (304). Here Eliot ironically refers not to a traditional ideal of humility and poverty but the ecclesiastical indignities Gwendolen and her family have had to contemplate with the collapse of Grapnell and Co. Initially Gwendolen had seemed to benefit from the social status of the priesthood as embodied by Gascoigne: with her uncle as the handsome and popular Rector, she is granted access to the local gentry that gracefully condescends to certain members of the respectable professions. In these circles, Gwendolen's challenge—carried off lightly—was to avoid aligning herself with superfluous curates, the officious sons of archdeacons, or, as in Rex's case, impecunious readers of law. After the financial crash, though, the church becomes a sanctuary of humiliating opportunities. The mother and Gwendolen's bevy of invisible half-sisters "are going to work a table-cloth border for the Ladies' Charity at Wanchester, and a communion cloth that . . . [Gascoigne's] parishioners are to present to Pennicote Church" (232). Gwendolen will play her part by taking a situation as governess to the three daughters of Bishop Mompert (231–34), a fate made available, like the odd jobs at religious ornamentation, by Gascoigne's professional connections.

Gwendolen makes a final bid to escape this situation by seeking Herr Klesmer's advice on starting a career on stage, and Eliot carefully contrasts this vocational alternative with forms of churchgoing in chapter 23. The first chapter in the novel to begin with the direct speech of a character, it abruptly opens with Gwendolen's command, "Pray go to church, mamma." Insisting on seeing Klesmer alone, Gwendolen's socially unconventional plans depend on her mother taking herself and "all [the sisters] to church" (250); and by packing off the household in this way, Gwendolen, so she thinks, is well on her way to staying out of a bishop's residence. The "delicious Sunday morning," however, turns bitter, as Klesmer describes a dauntingly unattainable discipline of culture, one reserved for those with "natures framed to love perfection" (255). And the chapter ends with Gwendolen resigning herself to a version of the path she has just abstained from traveling. "I am going to the bishop's daughters," she says (265). There, as Gwendolen knows, the imperious command that began the chapter will have to give way to another form of praying.

Gwendolen's dread of being "bound to incessantly edify" her charges and her disgust at the prospect that "the Bishop would examine her on serious topics" are elements of a flirtation with readers excited by her self-consciously fashionable impiety. And the depths of her humiliation are plumbed by the uncle's efforts to describe how highly he thinks of the opportunity. The worst that Gascoigne has to say about Dr. Mompert is that he is too "Low Church . . . ; but though privately strict, he is not by any means narrow in public matters." "The Rector's words," as the narrator comments, "were too pregnant with satisfactory meaning to himself for him to imagine the effect they produced on the mind of his niece. 'Continuance of education'—'bishop's views'—'privately strict'—'Bible Society,'—it was if he had introduced a few snakes at large for the instruction of ladies" (269). Initially introduced to readers as a suggestively supernatural serpent (12), Gwendolen is now subject to a terrifying reptilian authority, and the Rector's promise of a good home is, to Gwendolen, an expulsion from the paradise of her "domestic empire" (41). But this impending fall remains mostly comic while readers have good reasons to guess that Gwendolen will escape a situation that is so blatantly incompatible. On the other hand, in ways that are tragic for her, it is the peculiar dread of serving in a pious priestly household that drives Gwendolen into the arms of Grandcourt, an alternative "situation" that will be privately and strictly tortuous as her husband systematically breaks her in.

By describing the virtues of the Mompert situation, Gascoigne has provided a powerful homily on the wisdom of marrying Grandcourt. For Gwendolen "the name of Mompert had become a sort of mumbo-jumbo" (426), as Eliot writes, expertly using the term as it was moving from its original meaning into the more general one of unintelligible speech. In the original sense, as recounted in Mungo Park's *Travels in the Interior Districts of Africa* (1st ed., 1799), Mumbo-Jumbo was "a strange bugbear, common to all the Mandingo towns, and much employed by the Pagan natives in keeping their women in subjection." When a Mandingo man's polygamous household erupted in a quarrel beyond his control, he would don the "masquerade habit" of Mumbo-Jumbo, and "armed with the rod of public authority," he would summon all the town's married women. "As the person in disguise is entirely unknown to them, every married female suspects that the visit may possibly be intended for herself; but they dare not refuse to appear when they are summoned; and the ceremony commences with songs and dances, which continue till midnight, about which time Mumbo fixes on the offender. This unfortunate victim being thereupon immediately seized, is stripped naked, tied to a post, and severely scourged with Mumbo's rod" (92–93).[10] Gascoigne's pastoral counsel—that marriage to Grandcourt was a duty "national and ecclesiastical"—is only effective when combined with his inadvertent mumbo-jumbo. A rod-wielding bugbear, the clerical magistrate leads Gwendolen into what she knows is a functionally polygamous household. And in this sense, he is like Vaiano in *Romola* (148–49), a mock-priest who makes it possible for a man to keep more than one wife.

Gascoigne is ready with no-nonsense advice to himself about why he should encourage the wedding despite rumors about Grandcourt's vicious character: "Of the future husband personally Mr. Gascoigne was disposed to think the best. Gossip is a sort of smoke that comes from the dirty tobacco pipes of those who diffuse it: it proves nothing but the bad taste of the smoker" (140). It would be "bad taste" to consider Grandcourt's past too closely, and Gascoigne's churchmanship scrupulously adheres to terms defined by Emerson: "The Anglican church is marked by the grace and good sense of its forms, by the manly grace of its clergy. The gospel it preaches is, 'By taste are ye saved'" (224). On the day of her wedding,

Gwendolen is "walking amid illusions," but Gascoigne is pleased to do his part making sure this "bridal party was worth seeing" in his church: "An old friend of the Rector's performed the marriage ceremony, the Rector himself acting as father, to the great advantage of the procession" (353). To the many common observers, Gwendolen shows she is "worthy to be a 'lady o' title,'" and by being the church's central ornament that day, Gwendolen saves her mother and sisters from earning scant bread working on ecclesiastical decorations.

At the novel's midpoint, then—while the basic identity of the eponymous hero remains a mystery—Gwendolen's character has been shaped and challenged by manifestations of the age's major clerical parties: Low, Broad, and High. Initially, she is a possession to be tastefully bartered into marriage by Gascoigne. A kind of Broad Churchman, Gascoigne is most pleased to consider his close association with an Anglican gentry that maintains its religion like any other appealing formality. Yet he is also—and wisely so—friendly with the politically ascendant Low Church, and this worldly tolerance draws out the mumbo-jumbo about Bishop Mompert that drives Gwendolen into Grandcourt's arms. From there, Gwendolen sees intermittent hope in her submission to the penitential therapies proposed by the priestly Deronda, ones associated with the High Church and Ritualism. And Gascoigne—"tolerant both of opinions and conduct" (31)—is at the center of this clerical regime. Like Aldolphus Irwine in *Adam Bede,* Gascoigne is a respected and (in some ways) attractive character. But just like Irwine, Gascoigne plays an essential role in what is—in several senses of the phrase—a pastoral tragedy. Uniquely a creature of the 1860s and later, Gascoigne's tolerance has degenerated into a worldliness that mostly benefits himself at a time when many of the statutory burdens felt by Dissenters, Roman Catholics, Jews, and other non-Anglicans had been eased by liberal reform. In contrast, Irwine preached toleration before the major constitutional and ecclesiastical reforms of the century's second and third decades, and that tolerance could lighten the burdens felt by those branded heterodox. Gascoigne's broad-mindedness has no comparable social agenda; it is a means to self-advancement.

In a novel saturated with duplicitous gestures, Eliot presents Gascoigne in a light that she knew many readers would find attractive; and reviewers of the initial serial publication expressed hopes that Rex, the rector's "favorite son, and a young portrait of the father" (73), would be available to rescue Gwendolen from the despondency of her widowhood (Hughes and Lund 159). Eliot indeed was tempting readers with the prospect that Rex would offer the heroine a portion of that English happiness that is always on good visiting terms with the inhabitants of a pleasant country parsonage. But the narrative ultimately discloses how Gascoigne belongs to a broader male profession; his vocation is a professional maleness. And this order of men includes the more obviously repugnant Mr. Lush, who had been christened with great ecclesiastical ambitions, his full name being "Thomas Cranmer Lush" (321). The "son of a vicar who has stinted his wife and daughters of calico in order to send his male offspring to Oxford," Lush is prepared for holy orders through female deprivation; and the fact that he avoids entering the church by becoming Grandcourt's factotum only provides Eliot the chance to suggest that his clerical training was put to good use: "the bachelors' and other arts which soften manners are a time-honoured preparation for sinecures; and Lush's present comfortable provision was as good as a sinecure in not requiring more than the odour of departed learning" (129).

While Gwendolen's fate is determined by her revulsion at serving an evangelical bishop, Deronda's fate is determined by his growing desire to submit to the spiritual guidance of the "fanatical" Mordecai, an impoverished, physically decrepit Jew who boards with a pawnbroker named Ezra Cohen. Mordecai's full name is later revealed to be Ezra Mordecai Cohen (541), and this man—who is not directly related to the pawnbroker—is doubly hierophantic: his family name claims descent from the *cohanim*, the hereditary priesthood identified with the Temple in Jerusalem, and his first name links his authorial ambitions to the fifth-century Ezra, the priest and scribe responsible for "restoring" the Law following the Babylonian captivity.[11] To a "sound English" tone of thinking, Ezra Cohen the pawnshop boarder is the most despised priest at hand. But he is the key to Deronda's recovered birthright. And the best sign of Deronda's true inheritance at the novel's midpoint is the fact that he "found himself after one o'clock in the morning in the rather ludicrous position of sitting up severely holding a Hebrew grammar in his hands (for somehow, in deference to Mordecai, he had begun to study Hebrew)." According to conventional pedagogies, it is not a successful lesson, as Deronda realizes "he had been in that attitude nearly an hour, and had thought of nothing but Gwendolen and her husband" (413). But *Daniel Deronda* is a narrative that understands the "deference" that put the book into Daniel's hands to be more significant than the legibility of its contents.

On his way to this central reading scene at the Abbey in chapter 35, Deronda is considering his own attachment to the form of "taste" identified with Gascoigne's religion when he stumbles upon what appears to be the reality of his fears: Mirah's brother Ezra Cohen is a common pawnbroker. Deronda is led to this (false) conclusion when his "attention" is "caught by some fine old clasps in chased silver" displayed in the window of what turns out to be Cohen's shop: "His first thought was that Lady Mallinger, who had a strictly Protestant taste for such Catholic spoils, might like to have these missal-clasps turned into a bracelet" (382). On the verge of relocating these relics of devoted reading forward through Protestant time, Deronda is instead embarking on his career as a deferential Hebrew reader, one willing to sign his name to what he can hardly read. And this development is represented as a historical journey backwards. In conventional English historiography, the culture of Protestantism succeeds Roman Catholic Christendom, and behind that cultural formulation (which subsumed classical Greco-Roman culture) stood a primitive Christian age that followed upon a narrower period of divine revelation confined to the Jews. Philologically embodied in the sequence of Hebrew Old Testament and Greek New Testament, this sequence is reversed as Deronda first masters Hellenism (177) and then moves on to Hebrew originals.

Thus, when Deronda returns on the errand initiated by his sight of the missal clasps, he has his first encounter with Mordecai in a scene that plays with notions of original and secondary textual reports. It is at a "second-hand book-shop" that Deronda meets Mordecai, and at this stage, Deronda is still pursuing Hebrew secondhand, through German, just as he did in the synagogue in Frankfurt where he had "an open prayer-book pushed towards him" and he followed the liturgy by reading "the German translation of the Hebrew" (367). When a copy of Salomon Maimon's *Lebensgeschichte* catches his eye, Deronda, in his first words spoken to Mordecai, inquires about the book's "price," while Mordecai claims ignorance about "its market-price." Mordecai would rather know if Deronda had read the book, and then it is Deronda's turn to confess another type of second-handedness when he says he has only "read an account of it" (386). Having admitted his interest in Jewish history, Deronda is disturbed by Mordecai's evident desire to equate his reading interests with his identity. "You are perhaps of our race?" Mordecai asks (387). The conversation abruptly breaks off at this point to be continued at Ezra Cohen's shop later that evening. There Mordecai invokes the implicit linguistic sequence from earlier in the day, asking Deronda if he knows German and, after an anxious pause, says, "Perhaps you know Hebrew?" "I'm sorry to say," Deronda replies, "not at all" (399). Initially, Deronda's negative answer confirms his prior denial of his "race," and Mordecai "went through days of a deep discouragement." Eventually, though, Deronda's linguistic ignorance becomes a virtue for discipleship: "By-and-by it seemed that discouragement had turned into a new obstinacy of resistance, and the ever-recurrent vision had the force of an outward call to disregard counterevidence, and keep expectation awake" (479). As one Jewish leader has said to Mordecai earlier, "If you mean to address our learned men, it is not likely you can teach them anything" (499). In truth, Mordecai's writings will be most valued by a nonreader, and Deronda's regret at not knowing Hebrew is more important than the possession of the skill.

When they meet for the third time, some weeks later in January following the holiday episodes at the abbey, Mordecai tells Deronda an elliptical story about the prior reception of a revelation that is recorded in his own writings, what he calls "a bundle of Hebrew manuscript" (499). Mistaking his interlocutor for a needy author, Deronda offers to finance the translation of Mordecai's writings and their "means of publication." But it is Deronda's faith—"believing in my belief"—that Mordecai wants; he is not a writer whose plight can be assuaged through patronage. Mordecai is looking to bequeath an unpublishable archive in an act that will make Deronda the author of an unreadable book. And if Gascoigne occasionally engages in a complacent, "peaceful authorship," penning "ecclesiastical articles" for the approving eyes of patrons (706), Mordecai is a figure, soon revealed to come from priestly stock, whose authorship has a contrasting intensity.

Fittingly, after Deronda makes a "confession" about his unknown parentage, Mordecai confirms their relationship by recognizing Deronda as an unintelligible text. "You have risen within me like a thought not fully spelled," he tells him: "my soul is shaken before the words are all there." He then goes on to say he could but will not try to convince Deronda in a manner that employs clearly written signs: "I know the philosophies of this time and of other times: if I chose I could answer a summons before their tribunals. I could silence the beliefs which are the mother-tongue of my soul and speak with the rote-learned language of a system, that gives you the spelling of all things, sure of its alphabet covering them all" (502). But Mordecai is, as Garrett Stewart puts it, "yearning beyond the confines of texuality" (313), and to spell things out is to silence another discourse spoken in a primal mother-tongue. The relationship between Mordecai and Deronda thus remains doubly unlearned. Deronda is a desirably ignorant pupil, and he understands that Mordecai is not "some honoured professor, some authority in a seat of learning" (512). They both have versions of unlearnedness at the disposal of their dreams, and they, along with Mirah, are able to cherish unintelligible utterances of various kinds in a way that is contrasted with the instinctive dread of paternal mumbo-jumbo shown by both Leonora and Gwendolen. Finding rewarding communication in the unintelligible, Mordecai, Deronda, and Mirah convert what is normally an epistemological imbalance where intentions outweigh experience into an opportunity to create a community of belief, one that becomes the context for future shared experience.[12]

In exile and finding solace in a library of his own making, Mordecai is a Prospero, but one whose unsuspecting heir "had always felt a little with Caliban, who ... could sing a good song," as Deronda says (331). With his praise of Caliban's singing, with his appreciation for the traces of devotional song in the stables, and with other instances, Eliot links Deronda's discipleship to a particular type of musicality. Thus, immediately before he anxiously confirms his ignorance of Hebrew to Mordecai, Deronda comfortably wins the right to hear Mirah sing a "Hebrew hymn she remembers her mother singing over her when she lay in her cot." Here the initial (ultimately misplaced) anxiety of ignorance is Mirah's because she knows that her song will seem "childish" to anyone who knows proper Hebrew. Insisting that "it will be quite good Hebrew to me," Deronda again becomes the ideal (because ignorant) responsive agent. Afterwards, he equates his appreciation of the lullaby to his response to the Hebrew liturgy. "I don't think your hymn would have had more expression for me if I had known the words," he says to Mirah. "I went to the synagogue at Frankfort before I came home, and the service impressed me just as much as if I had followed the words—perhaps more" (374). Mirah's sophisticated unlearnedness reappears as well when Klesmer is called to appraise her voice in chapter 39 in a scene that mirrors Gwendolen's prior consultation of Klesmer. To Gwendolen, Klesmer had implied that she, as an impoverished, moderately talented, and beautiful actress, would be likely to be invited to engage in the highbrow prostitution that Mirah had to avoid by running from her father. Mirah, on the other hand, is pronounced to be a true musician, and she is invited to enter the sanctuary of high culture in an initiation rite that is anterior to otherwise intelligible communication. Culture's Masonic handshake in this case is a couplet from Goethe, which Mirah completes after Klesmer gives the first line (485). Calling Mirah a "learned puss" after Klesmer's departure, Mrs. Meyrick asks Mirah to explain the "German quotation you were so ready with." The reply is characteristic of the novel's naive version of profound knowledge. Mirah denies "learning" had anything to do with it: "'Oh, that was not learning,' said Mirah, her tearful face breaking into an amused smile. 'I said it so many times for a lesson. It means that it is safer to do anything—singing or anything else—before those who know and understand all about it'" (487).

Often indecipherable and infantile (literally meaning before speech) what passes between Deronda, Mordecai, Mirah and Klesmer is a complexly rudimentary version of culture; the four are members of a choir unintelligible, an exclusive community closely related to the "Choir Invisible" of Eliot's famous poem. As several studies of the role of music and musicians in the novel have made clear, Eliot is typical of her place and time in associating a kind of musicality with the Judaic; and it is characteristic of Eliot's powers of representation that she features this cultural habit in both its primitive orientalist guise as well as its modernist occidental double. On the one hand, the novel stays true to the Lowthian admiration for the Hebrew Bible's preservation of primeval song, an admiration that Eliot could share in 1848, as we have seen, even as she called "everything specifically Jewish . . . low grade" (*GEL* 1.247). On the other hand, with the characters of Klesmer and Alcharisi, who are defined by exceptional musical talent, international living habits, and marriages to gentiles, the novel also presents the nonobservant, cosmopolitan Jew as a figure for the modern artist.[13] Eliot's representation of this ethnographic musicality departs from convention by insisting that its most rewarding manifestation is tied to an unconventional form of reading. Deronda's receptiveness to what his mother will call "gibberish," in other words, is related to his status as a reader. Mimicking Deronda's prior entrance into a kinship of the unreadable with Mordecai, the chest of Daniel Charisi, his grandfather, is passed on immediately after Deronda has been reduced to a state of illiteracy. On the eve of meeting his mother, he was "getting into that state of mind to which all subjects become personal; and the few books he had brought to make him a refuge in study were becoming unreadable, because the point of view that life would make for him was in that agitating moment of uncertainty which is close upon decision" (622). The sense here of superabundant but clouded signification is the culmination of several scenes of highly qualified reading, beginning with the young Deronda's reading of Sismondi's *History of the Italian Republics* in the "Gothic cloister" at Monks Topping Abbey. That reading episode stood for some time as the "chief epoch" in Deronda's life because he then, at the age of thirteen, first understood that he might be Sir Hugo's illegitimate son (164). In this act of recognition, traces of the hyperliterate and the illiterate are balanced. It is inspired by reading and allows Deronda to synthesize a variety of reading experiences: "The ardour which he had given to the imaginary world in his books suddenly rushed towards his own history and spent its pictorial energy there, explaining what he knew, representing the unknown." And the effect of this new knowledge is to make him understand how much of his past reading—in "Shakespeare as well as a great deal of history"—had been about his own status as a "natural" son (167). At the same time, though, the episode is literally gothic in its consequences, as

246   *Clerical Fictions*

Deronda in his distraction is no longer reading but damaging the book that inspires his fateful question about "Popes and Cardinals" (164) and their nephews. He is recalled from his troubling reverie by his tutor who points out that he is "sitting on the bent pages" of his book (167).

Later, during the night following his rescue of Mirah, Deronda is again put in a situation that includes books but precludes conventional reading. Deronda himself is textualized as we are told that "this event of finding Mirah was as heart-stirring as anything that befell Orestes or Rinaldo," the latter not coincidentally being the hero of Tasso's crusading epic *Jerusalem Liberated*. And yet again, a basic form of reading has become impossible: "When he took up a book to try and dull this urgency of inward vision, the printed words were no more than a network through which he saw and heard everything as clearly as before—saw not only the actual events of two hours, but possibilities of what had been and what might be which those events were enough to feed with the warm blood of passionate hope and fear" (205). In these scenes and others like them, Deronda is a pupil at a reading lesson that discloses how the most precious book is one that is inherited and contains nothing more (and nothing less) than the identity of its reader. And Deronda embraces his heritage late in the novel not simply because he has by chance developed a sympathy for Judaism. Deronda accepts Daniel Charisi's chest—and assents to the idea that it is a repository of his identity—because he has already done the same in London. Before traveling to Genoa, Deronda has accepted his "office" as the caretaker of Mordecai, who has "claimed him as a spiritual heir" (546). He has acquired his longed for "partiality" (Anderson 121)—a form of thoughtful zeal—in his acceptance of Mordecai's unpublishable writings. Planning a new abode for Mordecai, Deronda imagines him in "a dressing gown very much like a Franciscan's brown frock" living in a modern day scriptorium where his own manuscript works—and later the papers of Daniel Charisi—will be deposited and preserved. Deronda's answer to the abbey where he was raised, this cloistral home is a synthetically ecclesiastical space where Deronda will keep as well his "best old books in vellum, his easiest chair, and the bas-reliefs of Milton and Dante" (546). With images of these two master poets of exile looking on, Eliot creates an ideal place for her modern Ezra Cohen who, like his ancient namesake and priestly forbearer, is convinced it is God's will that racially pure Jews reestablish a polity centered in Jerusalem.

Just as Mordecai's new scriptorium is being established, we learn that Gwendolen is hoping to transform herself with another course of study that she imagines must meet the approval of Deronda. "She wondered what books he would tell her to take up to her own room," Eliot writes and recalled the famous writers that she had either not looked into or had found the most unreadable, with a half-smiling wish that she could mischievously ask Deronda if they were not the books called "medicine for the mind." Then she repented of her sauciness, and when she was safe from observation carried up a miscellaneous selection—Descartes, Bacon, Locke, Butler, Burke, Guizot—knowing, as a clever young lady of education, that these authors were ornaments of mankind, feeling sure that Deronda had read them, and hoping that by dipping into them all in succession, with her rapid understanding she might get a point of view nearer to his level.

Gwendolen's syllabus of redeeming reading is not, however, particularly useful: "It was astonishing how little time she found for these vast mental excursions. Constantly she had to be on the scene as Mrs. Grandcourt" (548). Gwendolen's ineffectual bout of ingesting culture might be explained as a result of a failure to persevere, as when Austen's Emma regularly fails to keep up "any course of steady reading" after composing her lists of books (*Emma* 22). But the full force of Gwendolen's confinement is not to be understood as an inability to imbibe intellectual anodynes; her misfortune is to seek it in the diluted form of conventional enlightenment. The books that Gwendolen consults are not "unreadable" enough, having been rendered so only by a "sauciness" she can repent of. While Deronda is enlarging his mind with lisping, pseudo-Hebraic lullabies and preparing to adopt as his own an unpublishable revelation he can hardly read, Gwendolen turns to legible classics. Where Eliot has Gwendolen ineptly proposing a rigorous course of edifying reading, Deronda—who has already benefited from the contents of such books—is in position to exploit a kind of radical ignorance.

In making Deronda a vehicle and a vessel for a form of culture allied to creative and coercive inheritance, Eliot was exploring culture's ambivalent status as both a devotion to the authority of native traditions and a curiosity about the foreign, a desire at the least to escape any censure of "provincialism."[14] In this way, *Daniel Deronda* is a commentary on the contradictions embedded in the Preface to Matthew Arnold's *Literature and Dogma* (1873), which had reached a fifth edition the same year Eliot's novel began to appear. That work, no less than its better-known prequel, *Culture and Anarchy* (1867), argued by naming, with its title, a binomial conflict. Just as *culture* was the necessary stay to an *anarchy* that could erupt with the erosion of older forms of authority in English society, only a *literary* reading of the Bible could save it from an inevitable marginalization if left to the stewardship of its *dogmatic* interpreters. But *Literature and Dogma* also records Arnold's reliance on a form of authority that resembles the dogmas it was said to have superseded. In a passage that Eliot transcribed into a notebook, Arnold writes, "When we say that culture is, *To know the best that has been thought and said in the world,* we imply that, for culture, a system directly tending to this end is necessary in our reading.... Such a system is hardly even thought of; a man who wants it must make it for himself. And our reading being so without purpose as it is, nothing can be truer than what Butler says, that really, in general, no part of our time is more idly spent than the time spent in reading" (Eliot, *Some Notebooks* 3.21). "Culture is reading," Arnold says, "but reading with a purpose to guide it, and with system." Arnold thus endorses a version of culture that can be acquired through a proper management of time, saying, "give to any man all the time that he now wastes, not only to his vices (when he has them), but on his useless business, wearisome or deteriorating amusements, trivial letter-writing, random reading; and he will have plenty of time for culture." Behind this conventional message, however, there is a more important appeal to a reader's decision to seek perfection. As Arnold explains himself, "Culture becomes unspeakable" (*CPW* 6.162–63), and finding the time to practice culture is less important than knowing its character, a recognition that becomes identical with one's silent but sure possession of it. This version of culture is an authoritative conviction that one must bring to reading. And while the discourse of culture frequently grounded its authority in opposition to dogmas and creeds, that same discourse often found it necessary to make creedal statements while establishing and invoking genealogies of canonized writers.

Partially rebelling against a conventional faith in reading's agency for individual and social improvement, Eliot expresses substantial creative doubts regarding the library of liberal culture. The many conversations that take place in the library at Monks Topping Abbey, for example, are haunted by Deronda's exclusion from the parchment there representing the Mallinger family tree. And we are invited to a misreading of the implicit juxtaposition of such a document, locked away in a cabinet, and a broader intellectual inheritance offered by the "literature" on the library's open shelves. The lesson of the parchment is, after all, hardly edifying; it demonstrates how Grandcourt, a man given to "abstaining from literature" (319), is destined to inherit the abbey. But the novel does not discount family trees as texts; it is about Deronda's discovery of the right one. And at the root of this paternal word is the dogma of dogmas, the one summed up in Daniel Charisi's saying, "Better a false belief than no belief at all." Deronda will eventually get to affirm a more liberal creed: when asked by his grandfather's old companion if he will "profess the faith of [his] fathers," Deronda answers "I shall call myself a Jew . . . But

I will not say that I shall profess to believe exactly as my fathers have believed. Our fathers themselves changed the horizon of their belief" (724). Deronda's liberal profession of faith nevertheless seems to require a ritual of resanctification, one that partially obscures the fact that he, in the end, effectively repeats the Whiggish historicism of Sir Hugo, who at several points rephrases the liberal creed as pronounced by Thomas Babington Macaulay. Speaking on behalf of Reform in 1831, for example, Macaulay had said: "It is now time for us to pay a decent, a rational, a manly reverence to our ancestors, not by superstitiously adhering to what they, in other circumstances, did, but by doing what they, in our circumstances, would have done" (*WLM* 8.17). Standing on the threshold of the Second Reform Bill in *Daniel Deronda,* Sir Hugo makes a similar reference to a convenient concordance between past and present. Assuring Gwendolen that any monks haunting the abbey were likely to be friendly in spirit, he says that "the ghosts must be of all political parties" and that "those fellows who wanted to change things while they lived and couldn't do it must be on our side" (409). And this comforting political faith, one that comes easily to "a Liberal of good lineage" (793), Eliot carefully connects to Sir Hugo's equally enlightened views on his responsibilities as the proprietor of a historical estate. He had been proud to tell the Grandcourts, for example, that the abbey's mixture of the antique and the modern is "more truly historical": "Additions ought to smack of the time when they are made and carry the stamp of their period," he says. "I wouldn't destroy any old bits, but that notion of reproducing the old is a mistake" (416). Sir Hugo is the author of the novel's most memorable anti-Semitic statement ("I hope you are not going to set a dead Jew above a living Christian" [719]), but the final creed pronounced by Deronda is a reader's revision, slight but important, of that very statement: he will practice a faith that allows living Jews to change the horizon of their beliefs, all the while pledged to honor the ancestral word in spirit.

Over thirty years before creating this portrait of Deronda as a particular kind of reader, Eliot had parted with the religion of her youth as a result of systematically seeking to free the historical Jesus from the scriptural traditions that defined his life and afterlife. From her reading of Hennell and her translating of Strauss's *Life of Jesus* (1846), Eliot had then come to believe that the divine Jesus had his origins in the same scriptural traditions that cost the mortal man his life. The humble teacher from Nazareth, for example, would become a king miraculously born in Bethlehem, the city of David, as part of a process in which the events of his life were made to conform to a body of theological writings. In *Daniel Deronda,* Eliot revisits this decisive episode in her intellectual life by composing a story in which another idealistic Jewish reformer accepts his destiny as a child of two separate but related textual archives, one biologically inherited from a dead man, the other adopted under the auspices of humane intentions toward the living. *Daniel Deronda,* in these terms, is not a book "about" Judaism and modern Zionism. It is more acutely understood as a book about reading and readers, some of whom discover their readerly identity in Judaism. The novel's Zionist horizons, at any rate, are far more conventional than many literary scholars acknowledge. While Deronda departs for Palestine in 1866, the year before had seen the foundation of the Palestine Exploration Fund. Patronized by royalty and influential ecclesiastics, the PEF was inspired by what its most recent historian calls "the English Protestant sense of destiny," one manifestly present in the archbishop of York's 1865 statement to fellow Fund supporters that "this country of Palestine belongs to you and me. It is essentially ours. . . . it is the land to which we may look with as true a patriotism as we do to this dear old England, which we love so much" (qtd. in Moscrop 70–71).

With unexceptional designs on Palestine, *Daniel Deronda*'s acknowledgment of how such attachments have bibliographic dimensions, how they are determined by particular kinds of reading, is exceptionally self-aware. Eliot's representations of Judaism and its scriptural legacies are thus essential parts of her commentary on a cosmopolitan liberalism, its philosophical limitations, and its need for renewal despite those limitations. Here, both the implicit politics of *Daniel Deronda* and its central plot about reading are attempts to balance the commitments of past-obsessed scribes and forward-looking prophets. In this capacity, Eliot was directly influenced by contemporary Broad Church pastoral theology, one on representative display in Arthur Stanley's *History of the Jewish Church*. With volumes 1 and 2 appearing in 1862 and 1865, Stanley's history was based on lectures delivered to candidates for Holy Orders at Oxford, and we know that Eliot read them in preparation for writing *Daniel Deronda*. In them, Stanley regularly describes a priestly morbidity and a prophetic vitality, and he insisted as well that

> there is still one calling in the world in which . . . the Prophetic spirit . . . ought at least in part to live on,—and that is, the calling of the Christian clergy. We are not like the Jewish priests. . . , but we have, God be praised, some faint resemblance to the Jewish Prophets. Like them, we are chosen from no single family or caste; like them we are called not to merely ritual acts, but to teach and instruct; like them, we are brought up in great institutions which pride themselves on fostering the spirit of the Church in the persons of its ministers. (1.401)

In a similar vein, in his lecture entitled "The Jewish Priesthood" (2.348–70), Stanley writes, "The Prophetical office . . . reached out of the Old Testament into the New, and has, to a certain extent, been continued to the Christian Church. But, as an institution, the power of the Jewish Priesthood passed away at the close of the Jewish dispensation. The Prophetic office contained in it elements in their own nature universal and eternal. The Jewish Priesthood was essentially Oriental, local, national and temporary" (2.349). A passage from the third volume underscores as well why Eliot had the prophetically named Daniel become the heir of the priestly scribe Ezra Cohen. "Had the Scribes of the Christian Church retained more of the genius of the Hebrew Prophets, Christianity would have been spared what has too often been a return to Judaism, and it was in the perception of the superiority of the Prophet to the Scribe that [Christianity's] original force and unique excellence have consisted" (3.134).

A well-placed, intensely active cleric, Stanley in the 1860s and '70s was the most powerful living voice for the Broad Church. And Eliot agreed with many of his liberal positions, which included a toleration for theological dissent of many kinds. Stanley also worked with a broad range of public figures to revise or abolish Sabbatarian restrictions that prevented the gainfully employed from visiting cultural shrines on their day of rest.[15] But Stanley's unexceptional theology was insufficient for Eliot's purposes, habitually culminating, as it did, in identifying the errors of faith as a pejorative return to Judaic priestcraft. If Eliot had limited her appreciation for Judaism to its officially permissible prophetic dimensions, she would have been trafficking in "sound English" views, the kind calculated to please some younger version of Mr. Lush, a vicar's son, with stinted sisters, dreaming of carrying on the family trade in prejudice and port. Instead Eliot found inspiration in an anthropological concept of the priesthood and of Scripture, one expressed in Abraham Kuenen's *The Religion of Israel*, a work that she read either before or during her composition of the part of *Daniel Deronda* focusing on Judaism. Kuenen—in a passage transcribed by Eliot—contended that today's received text of the Torah, what he calls the Book of Origins, was composed in Babylon in the sixth century and brought back to Jerusalem by Ezra, its primary modern author:

> In him the necessity arose & the power was present to recreate the past, as it were, & to hold up, as he thought a truer picture of the past to his contemporaries. . . . The author of the Book of Origins succeeded in his undertaking: the conception of the past which he advocated gradually became a part of the consciousness of the Jewish nation, & has remained the traditional account down to the present day. . . . Such a success may be of

no value as evidence for the historical truth of the picture which he designed, yet it must avail as proof of the power of his mind. . . . The priesthood who produces such a book is capable of great things. (qtd. in Irwin, 418; compare Kuenen 2.173)

Here, the priest is an author of pious fictions, a writer who has become historically prophetic by reproducing the old, by revising his nation's sacred books. Long after discovering her vocation as a realist writer in a critique of the antinaturalist tendencies of the clerical flesh, Eliot reconceived the vocational opportunities in those same tendencies, particularly as they characterized ways of reading and writing. And Eliot's final fiction claims that writers who rise—or revert—to an author function that is scribal can determine the nation's character.

In *Romola,* Eliot's first novel to be fully conceived and composed with her true identity exposed, scribal authorship has no such productive social agency. The heroine's oppressive father, Bardo, implicitly discloses how his zealous attention to copying texts without change is another name for his blindness, which is literal, literary, and figurative. "What hired amanuensis," he asks "can be equal to the scribe who loves the words that grow under his hand, and to whom an error or indistinctness in the text is more painful than a sudden darkness or obstacle across his path?" (50). By the time of her writing *Daniel Deronda,* Eliot's understanding of the scribal role had become more supple. On the one hand, the creative scribe was positively distinguished from the economically determined author, a figure who was the hired amanuensis of her readers. "Nowadays books are written by the public and read by nobody," as Oscar Wilde would put it some years later (*Selections* 571). The scribal mode suggested by *Daniel Deronda* also allowed the devoted author to both copy and revise narratives that had the potential to become culturally definitive precisely because they thereby linked past, present, and future. Eliot's liberal conservatism (or her conservative liberalism) was thus a version of her own understanding of her relation to literary tradition, her knowledge of having become part of it, and her developing respect for the privileges of creative interpolation. On the open page of the "book of the universe," as described by Charles Hennell in 1841, "no transcribers have been able to interpolate or erase its texts; it stands before us in the same genuineness as when first written" (488). By the close of her career, Eliot was disenchanted by such literalism even as she remained faithful to the theological conclusions initially drawn from it.

By depicting and playing the scribal role, Eliot also intruded upon a precinct that had been almost exclusively reserved for men. Her characteristic ambivalence about the performance of this role is summed up by the onomastic contradictions she embeds in the full name Ezra Mordecai Cohen. In some ways, Mordecai is demonstrated to have been Ezra Cohen's deceptive pseudonym. The biblical Ezra Cohen had directed a forceful campaign to end intermarriage and linguistic assimilation upon his return from Babylon, with priests and their children required to follow further restrictions. The biblical Mordecai, on the other hand, is the foster father of Esther, a woman whose sexual charisma allows her to make a special plea to her non-Jewish husband, the Persian King Ahasuerus. Esther is a courageous and clever character, but she has become queen—risen through the harem's fleshly ranks after following Mordecai's order to keep her Jewishness concealed—because she was fair to behold and willing to perform the essential duty of any polygamist's wife. For some readers of the Protestant Bible, which includes the sequence of Ezra, Nehemiah, and Esther, there was an important distinction between the priestly Judaism depicted in Ezra and Nehemiah—one tied to the Temple in Jerusalem and the edition of the Law kept there—and the cosmopolitan Judaism in Esther, a text that does not once mention the God of Ezra. Theologically, Eliot would seem to share more with the worldly author of Esther's canonical romance. But in her quest for and display of an authority over the written word, Eliot shared much in common with the makers of books such as those known by the names of Ezra and Nehemiah. The role that Mordecai's Esther goes on to play is a role that Gwendolen, Leonora, and even Mirah (in a rigorously chastened fashion) must play out: they all "may rely on the unquestioned power of [their] beauty as a passport" (259). This was a role that Eliot could not and would not play even as she acknowledges the forces that made that avenue to power one of the few open to women of her day. For herself, the woman born Mary Ann Evans preferred the power confided in that instrument of fictional truth, the lying pen of the scribe. Deronda's passport to Jerusalem is thus a synthetic archive, a blest tome including the collected works of Daniel Charisi and Ezra Cohen, a man whose name is a priestly cipher. While the nature of the archive is prophetic in several senses, a fuller reading of the novel must acknowledge its priestly character as well.

Conclusion

Sacred Anthologies in the Age of Paper

DESPITE HER OWN UNAMBIGUOUS departure from supernatural Christianity, the Eliot who emerges here helps to illustrate how the period between the Second and Third Reform Bills was an intensely clerical age.[1] With the established church's legal privileges waning as the liberal religious agenda was nearing its political climax, Anglican clergymen were in some senses being displaced from their traditional role in the nation's structure of authority. But this same process inspired voluminous and consequential debates about the nature of a broader clerical profession that tended to define itself either in opposition to a nefarious priestcraft or in an open embrace of a revived sacerdotalism.[2] Critics in the twentieth century noted the development of a literary clerisy as one answer to these vocational debates. But too often it was assumed that this clerisy was born in a season of religious drought. This study makes it clear that such a genealogy—even while figures such as Eliot remain central—no longer needs to be taken on faith as a broadly accurate social history. Recognizing that the nineteenth century was, more than any other literary event, characterized by an expansion of readers theologically uninstructed by the state, we can see a more complicated and representative history take shape. In this view of the past, the politics of secularization are attended by a resilient agency of priestly or clerical figures in a variety of creative and institutional modes, particularly ones with affiliations to markets for printed matter. In this setting too the history of the printing press's social triumph, as marked by the creation of a reading nation, was widely perceived to be a religious event, or an event with consequences that were mostly religious.

In Eliot's case, she would come to preside over her own literary cult centered at The Priory, the aptly named home she shared with Lewes. And this comfortable abode was made possible by the exceptional fee she earned for *Romola,* a book conceived as a historical romance about the theocracy established by the Florentine priest Savonarola. To some observers, such as W. H. Mallock, Eliot was nevertheless "the first great godless writer of fiction that has appeared in England," an unusually dangerous artist precisely because she could depict "the Christian religion sympathetically from the inside" even as she exposed the mythical nature of its supernatural claims (Carroll 453). To others, however, there was a real sacredness to her life's work. Henry James would say that "people who had the honor of penetrating into the sequestered precinct of the Priory . . . remember well a kind of sanctity in the place, an atmosphere of stillness and concentration, something that suggested a literary temple." What became known as the "Sunday services" at the Priory, James suggested, were not a mockery, for "religious in a manner, [Eliot] remained to the end of her life" (Carroll 501–2, 492). And for Alexander Main, authorized editor of *Wise, Witty, and Tender Sayings in Prose and Verse Selected from the Works of George Eliot* (1st ed., 1872), there was no hint of irony in the declaration "that what Shakespeare did for the Drama, George Eliot has been, and still is, doing for the Novel. By those who know her works really well, this branch of literature can never again be regarded as mere story-telling, and the reading of it as only a pastime. George Eliot has magnified her office and made it honourable; she has for ever sanctified the Novel by making it the vehicle of the grandest and most uncompromising moral truth" (ix).

Given the contradictory testimony about her, we might rephrase *Daniel Deronda*'s famous opening query and ask the question of Eliot, "Was she religious or was she not religious?" But we should do so knowing in advance that the answer inevitably reflects a willingness to define true and false religions. If we decline to circumscribe the sacred and the profane in any comprehensive manner, we might fall back on less presumptuous tasks. We can, for instance, record the fact that Eliot made annual subscriptions to the "Sacerdotal Fund" starting in 1864 for the support of Richard Congreve, an Anglican clergyman who would transform himself into the minister of the Positivist congregation that attended the Church of Humanity at Chapel Street. And starting sometime in the late 1870s, Eliot's poem "The Choir Invisible" was incorporated into the liturgy of the services held there (Wright 174–76, 73–84). What is certain is that Eliot matured as a London literary celebrity at a time when there was an expansion of celebrity religious leaders or those aspiring to such roles.

A robust print culture and a new, almost overwhelming abundance of clerical types in the 1870s, for instance, was the inspiration for the work of Charles Maurice Davies, whose *Broad Church: A Novel* (3 vols., 1875) can be read with profit alongside Eliot's more innovative clerical novel of the following year. *Broad Church* is not aesthetically ambitious in ways comparable to *Daniel Deronda,* but Davies's novel is interesting for its close relation to an extensive body of reporting on metropolitan religious services that he collected in *Orthodox London* (2 vols., 1873–74), *Unorthodox London* (1874), *Heterodox London* (2 vols., 1874), and *Mystical London* (1874).[3] An Anglican clergyman whose first novel had appeared in 1858, Davies would resign his orders in 1882, and in this guise he is an all too familiar figure: yet another inquiring mind is smitten with authorship and therefore must leave the church behind. Looked at more closely, however, Davies provides a good chance to describe the 1870s as a time when a notably abundant form of modern-day priestcraft—versions both derided and revered—was intimately tied to print as a culturally defining technology. Before appearing in his well-received collections, most of Davies's reports initially ran in the *Daily Telegraph,* which was then the nation's most widely circulated paper thanks to its price (one penny) and its telegraphically charged coverage of topics such as violent crime, divorce, sports, natural disasters, and imperial adventures. And while the pages of the *Daily Telegraph* often conveyed excitement about bringing news rapidly from afar, Davies's special beat was a local exoticism made possible by liberalism's endorsement of religious freedom, one that had created a highly competitive market for religious services in the imperial metropolis. "At no period of history, probably, since the schools of religion and philosophy jostled one another in the streets of Alexandria," as Davies wrote, "have the forms of religious life been more exuberant and diversified than in London at the present time" (260). This variety of formalized religious expression allowed Davies to become a tourist in his own hometown with his chief instruments of exploration being an active daily and weekly press and an efficient postal service. His journeys are often initiated when chance gives him some freedom from his own clerical duties, and by perusing advertisements for services, he was able to plan attendance at what he took to be particularly interesting events. In this way, Davies's articles were advertisements for advertisements: his readers were reminded how the spectacle of London's religious life had its only reliable guide in the dailies, while prospective advertisers could see in the same reports proof of the efficacy of marketing their services, many of them free and open to the public, others requiring or entreating donations.

Driven by the press, Davies's explorations often identify how the market for religious services also engendered specific bibliographic events, as happens on his initial journeys in *Unorthodox London* to the Unitarian congregations at South Place and Little Portland Street. Describing his visit to

Moncure Conway's congregation at South Place as a voyage "to the very *Ultima Thule* of religious London" (2), Davies notes how the liturgy there included readings from "the 'Ancient Chaldee Oracles'" and "an extract on 'Excellences,' from the writings of Buddha" as well as more familiar selections from the Old and New Testaments (5, 23). And in his visit to James Martineau's congregation at Little Portland Street, Davies similarly emphasizes a cultural eclecticism and notes that both the liturgy and the hymnal were "compiled by the preacher," who "may parody a well-worn adage, and say, 'La chapelle, c'est moi'" (33–34). Just as for Davies himself, for both Conway and Martineau being a minister meant becoming the author of collective texts, in Martineau's case the maker of *Hymns of Praise and Prayer* (1876) and in Conway's case the maker of *The Sacred Anthology* (1st ed., 1874), a book that is recognizable within the confines of this study as a belated heir of Thomas Percy's *Specimens of the Ancient Poetry of Different Nations.* Beside offering selections from "the Hebrew and Christian scriptures" (xiv), Conway's anthology included texts originally composed in Chinese, Persian, Sanskrit, and Arabic; and a broader interest in such a collection was manifest by a demand that called for a fifth edition by 1876. As a commodity offered to a reading public (price twelve shillings), Conway's selection had the virtue of "separat[ing] the more universal and enduring treasures contained in ancient scriptures, from the rust of superstition and the dross of ritual" (xiii). But the act of compiling these selections was a task Conway found himself doing by virtue of his duty to officiate at his weekly services. *The Sacred Anthology* was a product of a particular kind of working minister, one who was ready to compose, like Eliot's Ezra Cohen, his own scripture at a time when past definitions of it were being expanded or challenged.

Both Davies and Conway are, one might argue, peripheral to mainstream literary or cultural history, puny figures on whose shoulders we would be foolish to stand as we seek to see things from a critical perspective. In fact, they are useful for understanding specific bibliographic relations between writers, readers, and religion in the 1870s, relations that represented a culmination of the projects of anthologization and collection that distinguished the late eighteenth century, as discussed in chapters 1 and 2 of this study. *The Sacred Anthology* in particular deserves to be recognized as a manifestation of a more general kind of bookmaking practiced by figures closer to the conventional center of cultural authority. One kindred text by such a figure is *Isaiah XL–LXVI with the Shorter Prophecies Allied to It, Arranged and Edited with Notes by Matthew Arnold,* which was published in December 1875. Like Conway's, Arnold's book offered to readers discriminating selection and arrangement based on his ability to discern the best that had been thought and said in the world; it was an attempt, as he said, to present to the general reader "a literary work of the highest order. And the Book of Isaiah, as it stands in our Bibles, is this in a double way. By virtue of the original it is a monument of the Hebrew genius at its best, and by virtue of the translation it is a monument of the English language at its best" (*CPW* 7.58). Despite the statement about Isaiah "as it stands," Arnold's work—like Robert Lowth's translation of 1778—was also a critique of the received Hebrew text and a conservative revision of the Authorized Version. To Arnold's eye, the canonical Isaiah was a flawed poetic collection that mixed an independent sequence composed in the grand style—chapters 40 to 66—with the inferior work of less gifted poets. While Arnold could improve on the selection and arrangement made in antiquity, he also claimed a form of superiority over "purely scientific" translators of the Bible in his own day (*CPW* 7.58), scholars such as those working on what would soon be published as the Revised Version (NT 1881; OT 1885). For Arnold, a sense of literary taste, for instance, preserves "the established expression *The Lord*" in Isaiah even as the scientific critic knew that the text often calls for "Jehovah." Acknowledging that *"Jehovah"* to the English ear "has even, which is fatal, a mythological sound" (*CPW* 7.59), Arnold's commitment to the grand style made it easy to choose the article and the fine-sounding noun over the proper name of the tribal deity.

Arnold's cultivation of a reader able to distinguish between scientific, literary, and religious epistemologies in *Isaiah XL–LXVI* was linked to his major theological writings in the 1870s, *Literature and Dogma* (1873) and *God and the Bible* (1875). And these efforts to rescue the Bible from Philistine readers were related to his descriptions of the debased tastes of the increasingly common reader (and owner) of books. Arnold the biblical critic was thus inseparable from a more general critic who also saw the late 1870s as a time when it was important to check the enduring popularity of the writings of Thomas Babington Macaulay, whose career was celebrated in G. O. Trevelyan's best-selling biography, *The Life and Letters of Lord Macaulay* (2 vols., 1st ed., 1876).[4] In an anonymous essay that ran in the *Quarterly Review* of January 1877, Arnold appropriated Macaulay's most famous flourish—his image of the New Zealander sketching the ruins of St. Paul's—and turned it against him by leading discerning readers into the distant huts of antipodal settlers: "It is said that the traveler in Australia, visiting one settler's hut after another, finds again and again that the settler's third book, after the Bible and Shakespeare, is some work by Macaulay. Nothing can be more natural. The Bible and Shakespeare may be said to be imposed upon an Englishman as objects of his admiration;

but as soon as the common Englishman, desiring culture, begins to choose for himself, he chooses Macaulay." Attributing to Macaulay a special status in the minds of those who are only "beginning to feel enjoyment in the things of the mind," Arnold used that status to distinguish the habits of "the multitude of readers" and an idealized "serious reader" (*CPW* 8.169–70, 167). And yet, even as Arnold made much of his own capacity to discern the best in the face of all that was merely common, he exploited what he understood to be a popular demand for "the best."[5] Any critical edition of Arnold's 1875 *Isaiah* would graphically disclose how Arnold's mission for culture encompassed a rudimentary reader at a time when the Inspector of Schools was acutely concerned with the consequences of the nation's final dash to normative literacy. *Isaiah XL–LXVI* descends directly from *A Bible-Reading for Schools: The Great Prophecy of Israel's Restoration (Isaiah, Chapters 40–66) Arranged and Edited for Young Learners* (1872), a work intended—as Arnold admitted in his 1875 recension of it—"for the benefit of schoolchildren," "for the young and for the unlearned" (*CPW* 7.52), particularly those unable to attend the expensive public schools where instruction in Greek and Latin (rather than scriptural study) still dominated. What stands out from examining both books is how easily Arnold could excise all but one reference to these young learners and their limited prospects in the 1875 work, have the type and paper enlarged, and thereby convert a one-shilling duodecimo primer of 98 pages into an octavo encounter with literary glory commanding 196 pages and costing five shillings.

These select editions of ancient Hebrew poetry were part of a larger publishing enterprise in which the marketing of cultural prestige to a nationally conceived readership conveniently coincided—as was the case with Arnold's influential editions of Wordsworth (1879) and Byron (1881)—with the textual artifacts themselves being unprotected by copyright. More specifically, Arnold's sacred anthologies appeared at a time awash with texts that exploited, in different ways, coordinate forms of bibliographic and biblical devotion. The year 1876, for instance, saw the publication of the first volume of John Ruskin's *Bibliotheca Pastorum,* or what he described as "a series of classic books which I hope to make the chief domestic treasures of British peasants" (7). With the *Bibliotheca Pastorum,* not only was Ruskin producing a national library of sorts; he was attempting to educate readers to be devoutly responsive to a wider canon of sacred writings, what he pronounced "classical scriptures" (8). Critical of the "egotism of Judaic Christianity," or "the habit of fancying that we ourselves only know the true God, or possess the true faith" (18), the *Bibliotheca Pastorum* was Ruskin's tribute to the central claim in Conway's *Sacred Anthology* that "each nation has its full scriptures" (vi). "Every nation which has produced highly trained Magi, or wise men," as the sage of Brantwood said, "has discerned, at the time when it most flourished, some part of the great system of universal truth, which it was then, and only then, in the condition to discern completely; and the books in which it recorded that part of truth remain established for ever; and cannot be superceded: so that the knowledge of mankind, though continually increasing, is built, pinnacle after pinnacle, on the foundation of these adamant stones of ancient soul" (7–8).

This attraction to perdurable textual foundations was also at the heart of the reading nation's interest in another sacred anthology of sorts, George Smith's *Chaldean Account of Genesis* (1876).[6] A banknote engraver of working-class roots, Smith had in his spare time become one of the day's best readers of cuneiform texts at a time when only a handful of competent readers existed. And in December 1872, he had created a stir with a paper read before the Biblical Archaeological Society. It was his translation of ancient Assyrian copies of an older Babylonian account of the survival of a chosen remnant in a great ship that had provided refuge from a flood sent to destroy a world of otherwise sinful creatures. Based on his partial reconstruction of clay tablets that had earlier been deposited in the British Museum, Smith's findings generated a great deal of scholarly and popular interest, including calls for a return to "Assyria" to recover missing portions of the narrative, all of which the *Daily Telegraph*—the same vehicle for Davies's reports—was wise to exploit. In return for periodical updates from the field, the paper pledged one thousand guineas for what became on its own headlined pages the "'Daily Telegraph' Expedition," the "Daily Telegraph Mission to Assyria," and "'The Daily Telegraph' Assyrian Expedition" (9/1/73, 5; 26/3/73, 3; 14/5/73, 3). And on 21 May 1873, readers were notified via a communication from Mosul of a great discovery made in the ancient site of Nineveh: Smith had recovered "a broken tablet containing the very portion of the text which was missing from the Deluge tablet" (7). What was so striking to most readers about these and subsequent events as they were widely reported in the press and in Smith's own books was the idea that it was now possible to have physical contact with documents that might be considered either sources for early portions of the Bible or "independent" confirmation of its historical accuracy. The deluge of ink produced by Smith's otherwise arcane labors was largely prompted by a sense that he might have stumbled upon something akin to the ancient library where past writers had borrowed essential reference works and sat down to compose portions of the Bible. The books from this library, in the form of mostly shattered bricklike tablets, had remained sealed for some 2,500 years, but they were now available for the perusal of any English reader. At least this was the breathless reception encouraged by the *Daily Telegraph* in a series of commissioned articles by Smith and several pieces about him at work in the British Museum that ran before his departure. In an article entitled "In the Beginning," for instance, readers got a glimpse of Smith as the "Mage" laboring in his "Temple of Antiquity" (his office in the Museum) where he edited "the oldest known books in the world's circulating library." Before publicly announcing the sponsorship of Smith's expedition, the *Daily Telegraph* was building up interest in it, telling readers how Smith had "finished" all the books "we have borrowed from the Mudie of Mesopotamia" and how he was eager to take out, or dig up, more: "He can put his hand on the place where Noah's story is told in full, with that of the Creation, the building of Babel, and the rise of diverse tongues—nay, all the great legends of the Bible may find here their fountain text; and he may even hit upon the real *editio prima,* the actual clay or stone from which all these were copied" (9/12/72, 5).

Smith's work culminated with his *Chaldean Account of Genesis,* published in December 1875 (although dated "1876") as the author departed for his third trip to the East where he would die in August of the following year. A heavily illustrated work containing, as its full title asserted, *The Description of the Creation, the Fall of Man, the Deluge, the Tower of Babel, the Times of the Patriarchs, and Nimrod,* the book was presented as nothing less than a reconstructed Babylonian version of the beginning of the Bible. For most scholars today, Smith's work "set the stage for the contemporary understanding of Genesis 1–11 as a polemical, monotheistic rewriting of the older Babylonian epics" (Damrosch 65); and much of the material that Smith led the way in recovering is now valued on its own terms as the *Epic of Gilgamesh*. At the time of their initial publication, however, Smith's texts set the stage for a revived debate about how the Bible was itself an ancient anthology. That notion, as we have seen, was nothing new, but for the first time this debate had to acknowledge physical texts from ancient biblical times. The *Athenaeum* was quick to assimilate the new evidence to the traditional view that Genesis was written by Moses, an author whose working habits and motivations could now be better understood: "Moses, having before him the traditions of the nations around him, selected and arranged those portions we now read, under the name of 'Genesis,' which most clearly served his purpose, as showing that the universe was the creation of an Intelligent Being, and not the result of the chance evolution of any number of material atoms" (18/12/75, 826). The *Spectator,* however, was critical of Smith for "giving so sensational a title to what is, for the most part, a scanty and unsatisfactory collection of fragments" and predicted that the book would be misused by those "who see in the Chaldean legends confirmation of their confident assertion that the materials of the Hebrew book of Genesis were obtained in Babylon during the captivity" (15/1/76, 80–81). According to some commentators and observers, this borrowing, selecting, and arranging of sources was a process of cultural recension at odds with orthodox concepts of revelation. But others were stressing how this form of authorship was typical of the makers of scripture in general. In his article entitled "Bible," for the ninth edition of the *Encyclopaedia Britannica* (also first published in December 1875), William Robertson Smith reminded readers that the Hebrew Bible had been produced at a time featuring a "lack of all notion of anything like copyright" (638).

As a final example of works related to Conway's *Sacred Anthology*, I want to take notice of *The Sacred Books of the East,* edited by Friedrich Max Müller, who was, like Arnold, unusually successful in translating his Oxford posts into a wider social relevance in the 1870s. The first public hint of what would eventually turn into a fifty-volume series came in Müller's glowing review of Conway's *Sacred Anthology* for the *Academy* in October 1874. There Müller gives the editor "our hearty thanks for the trouble he has taken in collecting these gems, and stringing them together for the use of those who have no access to the originals, and we trust that his book will arouse a more general interest in a long-neglected and even despised branch of literature, the Sacred Books of the East" (477). By October 1876 Müller had secured a contract with Oxford University Press for the series by that title, a project that would earn him £2,400 for the first installment of twenty-four volumes published from 1879 to 1884.[7] Müller was happy to use the popularity of Conway's comparatively miniscule anthology to prepare the way for his gargantuan series, but Müller also defined his project in contrast to Conway's collective form. The engendering principle of *The Sacred Books of the East* was completeness. As Müller would put it in his series' general preface, "We must have before all things complete and thoroughly faithful translations of [these] sacred books. Extracts will no longer suffice." Insisting that scholarly responsibility made selection indefensible, Müller went out of his way to admit that he was prepared to publish "much that is not only unmeaning, artificial, and silly, but even hideous and repellent" (xi–xii).

Müller was nevertheless engaging in one of history's most sweeping acts of textual selection, an attempt to canonize humanity's canonical religions. *The Sacred Books of the East* illustrated Müller's argument, first drawn out in his *Introduction to the Science of Religion* (1873), that the world has only eight "book-religions": Judaism, Christianity, Hinduism, Buddhism, Zoroastrianism, Confucianism, Taoism, and Islam. "How few are the religions which possess a sacred canon, how small is the aristocracy of real book-religions in the history of the world," he would exclaim (103). In this canon of canons there is what we might be tempted to consider a refreshing absence of Eurocentrism. Müller said bluntly, "Neither Greeks, nor Romans, nor Germans, nor Celts, nor Slaves [sic] have left us anything that deserves the name of Sacred books" ("Preface" xl). But even while he claimed to be able to oversee this project of complete publication, Müller eventually met the fate of any anthologist: it became clear that he was making personal and pragmatic decisions as well as decisions bound by his own historical horizons. In particular, the decision to turn his series so clearly in the direction of the rising sun, the Far East, was tied to Müller's commitment to a solar key to the interpretation of the world's ancient mythologies; and the project also supported the comforting idea that the English, as a Teutonic race, had in conquering India merely returned to their Aryan homeland. Müller did mention how "important fragments of what may be called a Sacred Literature" of Babylon and Assyria had "lately come to light," but he explained their absence in his canon, along with the absence of any hieroglyphic texts from ancient Egypt, in awkward terms (xli).[8] With the limited durability of its claim to completeness, what stands out about *The Sacred Books of the East* is its representative devotion to the idea of the book, particularly the printed book, its pride in placing all these inaccessible writings "on the shelves of every great library in Europe," as Müller would brag in his essay "Forgotten Bibles" (250). The series was the imperial extension of the mythical fruits of print culture—permanence and enlightened impartiality—to all premodern religious writings worthy of preservation. "The most important works illustrating the ancient religions of the East," Müller said, "have been permanently rescued from oblivion and rendered accessible to every man who understands English" (250). An implicit reply to Macaulay's famous statement from 1835 that "a single shelf of a good European library was worth the whole native literature of India and Arabia" ("Minute" 241), Müller's countercolonization of European "shelves" drew upon the authority of the modern press as well as a new willingness to approach and value texts on scriptural terms.

As a simultaneous tribute to print and the decade's scriptural obsessions, the conception of *The Sacred Books of the East* shares much with an event that William Ewart Gladstone would describe as "the climax and consummation of the art of printing" at the opening of London's Caxton Exhibition of 1877, a celebration of printing's four hundredth anniversary in England. While the university press at Oxford was preparing to make available Müller's canon of canons, that same press participated in a unique ritual in the age's religion of the book on 30 June 1877. On that afternoon, presiding over the opening of the exhibition, Gladstone presented to the watching world a copy of what was called "The Caxton Memorial Bible," one of one hundred Bibles that had been, on that very same day, printed at Oxford University Press. "The materials of this book," as Gladstone put it, "sixteen hours ago did not exist. This book was not bound, it was not folded, it was not printed. Since the clock struck twelve last night at the University Press in Oxford the people there have printed and sent us this book to be distributed here in the midst of your festival" (qtd. in Stevens 144). Gladstone had a special reverence for the contents of the book in his hand, but from today's perspective the Caxton Bible appears as a monument to the medium, a range of interconnected, mechanized technologies that produced the following kinetic events as described by the scheme's originator, Henry Stevens: "The Printers commenced to make their preparations soon after midnight, and the printing actually commenced at two A.M.; the sheets were artificially dried, forwarded to London by the nine o'clock express train to the Oxford University Press Binding establishment, Barbican, where they were folded, rolled, collated, sewn, subjected to hydraulic pressure, gilded, bound and taken to South Kensington before two P.M." (143).

The history of the printed Bible, from 1450 to (precisely) 30 June 1877, commanded a great deal of attention in the exhibition. Out of a total of over 4,000 separately catalogued items divided into fourteen sections, the one devoted to the printing of the Holy Scriptures, with almost 850 items, made up the exhibition's single largest section (Bullen 77–192); and these and other items were legible signs of a traditional veneration for Scripture, one that had been transformed and reconfirmed for English readers by figures such as Robert Lowth one hundred years before. But the exhibition also indicated the ways in which reading as an activity focused on consuming print had been given a sacred status, one that depended on recognizing the printing press as an advanced technology in the nineteenth century no less than in the period of its invention in the fifteenth century. An explicitly religious ideology of The Book was in many ways at the root of the broader cult of print being celebrated in 1877; but we can also detect a veneration for reproductive capacity, a discovery of manifest destiny in the mechanical ability to multiply. And the cyclical exchange between these related versions of the sacred, the one residing in the unique message of the Bible, the other residing in the capacity to disseminate any message with what seemed like a miraculous mechanical power, is captured by Stevens when he writes, "The secular history of the HOLY SCRIPTURES is the sacred history of PRINTING" (25).

Attracting close to 25,000 visitors, the Caxton Exhibition was a great success, and the organizers, participants, and spectators collectively expressed unprecedented levels of cultural devotion to what was represented as a specifically English history of printing. The exhibition is also the decade's most striking confirmation of the way in which the printing press was no longer simply a vehicle for the dissemination of knowledge: it had become a discipline in its own right. One hundred years before, there had been no tercentenary celebration, and that paragon of the Enlightenment Edward Gibbon had lamented how Caxton had been "reduced to comply with the vicious taste of his readers; to gratify the Nobles with treatises on Heraldry, Hawking, and the game of Chess, and to amuse the popular credulity with romances of fabulous Knights, and legends of more fabulous saints" (*English Essays* 537). Having insisted that Caxton had not published learned works, Gibbon's ghost in the 1870s would have been struck by how much learning was dedicated to England's first printer. We can gauge this development in the reception history of Daniel Maclise's painting *Caxton's Printing Office,* which had been pronounced a star of the Royal Academy Exhibition coinciding with the Great Exhibition of 1851. A prominent icon of the mid-century celebration of printing, Maclise's painting was praised for its technical realism. "It is impossible," wrote the *Art Journal,* "to eulogise too highly its faultlessly accurate manner. The drawing and painting of the material are fastidiously careful; as of the types, the press, the work and tools of the artists, we are almost led to consider these before the qualities of the figures, because they are so exquisitely realised" (June 1851: 154). Later, in noticing the publication of an engraving of the painting (fig. 10), the *Art Journal* quoted Bulwer Lytton's tribute to how the famous "precision" of the drawing was matched by its power as historical commentary. Drawing eyes to the extreme left of the image, Lytton had written that in "that monk, with his scowl towards the printer and his back on the Bible, over which his form casts a shadow—the whole transition between the medieval Christianity of cell and cloister, and the modern Christianity that rejoices in the daylight, is depicted, in the shadow that obscures the Book—in the scowl that is fixed on the Book-diffuser" (Aug. 1860: 255). In 1877, however, the official *Guide* to the Caxton Exhibition called attention to the same engraving in order to emphasize Maclise's historical errors:

> The wonderfully true rendering by the artist of the wood, the iron, the glass, the flesh tints, &c, has met with unlimited praise; while Art-critics never tire in their admiration of the composition and balance of the picture. Yet no one seems to have noticed that the scene being laid in 1474 the

> wood could not have been *pine,* the chase could not have been *cast* iron, the bottles could not have had *ground glass stoppers,* the compositors could not have used *steel* composing sticks, the first edition of the Chess-book being at press could not have had the woodcuts of 1482 any more than the Handbill of 1480 could have been issued in 1474, or found itself in juxtaposition with sheets from the press of Wynken de Worde. (*Guide* 4–5)

Formerly known for its exacting verisimilitude, the image is here testily placed back into the shadowy region of romance and legend.

This study has often sought to address two forms of forgetfulness that have influenced much literary criticism and literary history about the eighteenth and nineteenth centuries. One is a tendency to forget how the history of the reading nation that came of age during this period was something that unfolded while ecclesiastical and religious history remained not only significant but also culturally central. In the other, there is a blindness to how print remained a transformative technology long after the earlier "print revolutions," the ones that occurred in the fifteenth and eighteenth centuries and would be considered the material agents for the key conceptual events of occidental modernity: Reformation, Enlightenment, and Revolution.[9] While I have no intention of belittling those earlier histories and their historians, I do have an open gripe with a propensity to see print as a transparent medium in the nineteenth century; and the presumption of that transparency is often connected to a belief that serious creative endeavor took place in a cultural context where benighted religion was marginalized. Indeed, the potency of culture—in its Arnoldian sense—has often been defined in terms of religion's obsolescence.

Given my desire to close this story in 1880 (for the reasons described in chapter 1), it is appropriate, then, that we can look to 1877 and 1878 and see early signs of both of these forms of forgetfulness. The *Saturday Review* alluded to one by noting in the summer of 1877, with apparent relief, that "Parliamentary conflicts no longer rage over the precise relation between theology and the three R's" (22/7/77, 764). Denominational differences, in other words, no longer interfered on a scale that could prevent the institution of a reading nation, and that development was importantly sponsored by the state's evolving refusal to have any precise theological identity. As time passed, one can imagine how some subsequent historians were tempted to believe that this development was synonymous with a broader apathy about or antagonism to religion. But the hundred years preceding this statement by the *Saturday Review* were, as we have seen, saturated with attempts to relate religion and reading in practical and theoretical ways.

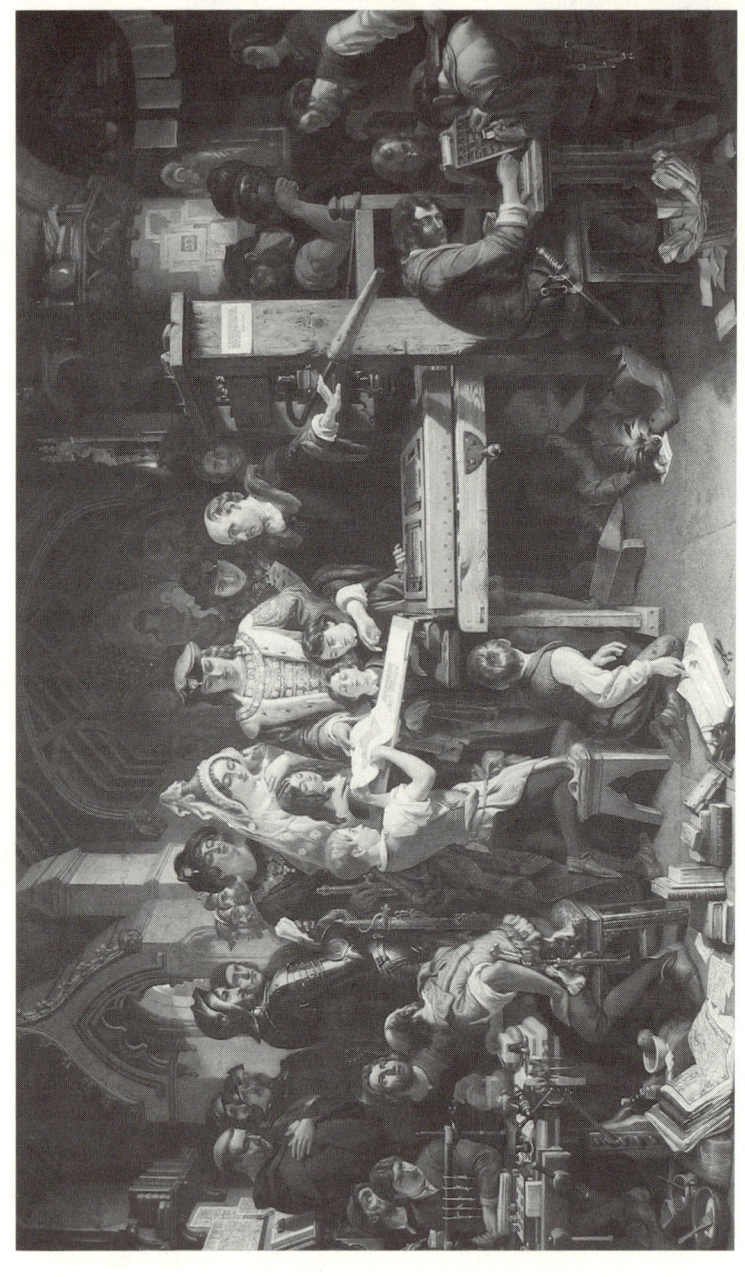

Fig. 10. "Caxton Showing the First Specimen of His Printing to King Edward the Fourth," 1858, engraved by Frederick Bromley (after Daniel Maclise).

Fig. 11. "A Wolf in Sheep's Clothing," Punch, *30 June 1877: 295, by John Tenniel. John Bull tells Britannia, "Whenever you see any of these sneaking scoundrels about, Ma'am, just send for me. I'll deal with 'em, never fear!!"*

The second form of forgetfulness was prophesied in one of *Punch*'s responses to the Caxton Exhibition's shadow scandal in the summer of 1877. This was the furor over *The Priest in Absolution,* a manual for the use of confessors being privately circulated by a society of Ritualist clergy (Yates 244–45). In June 1877 Lord Redesdale read extracts in the House of Lords, many of which focused on how a priest should address wives and minors on the topic of carnal transgressions. The book was widely pronounced obscene, and the practice of confession was reaffirmed as being "injurious to the moral independence and virility of the nation" (*H* 234.1752). Striking at anxieties about a resurgent priestcraft within the church, the scandal also presented a chance to identify manly Protestantism with a chaste and public textuality, and set this ideal against a perfidious order of men who circulated secret texts on how to interrogate others about private matters. *Punch* during the summer of 1877 was filled with references to Ritualism in general, *The Priest in Absolution,* and the Society of the Holy Cross, the clerical confederation that owned the book's copyright (fig. 11). One piece rose above a fairly low standard of creative derision, however, by acknowledging a possible affiliation between the sacerdotal revival and the newest modes of communication. Responding to another publication which pointed out that E. B. Pusey had long been receiving confessions—"not only *vivâ voce,* but by letter"—*Punch* pronounced the High Church leader

> to be considerably in advance of the genuine Roman Catholic Priest, as he allows a Confessional to be made of the letter-box and pillar-post. Perhaps he will go—if he has not gone already—still farther ahead, and receive confessions by electric telegraph, wiring absolution back. Or, what will be a still greater improvement on the Roman practice, he might, when the Telephone is brought sufficiently to bear, have them addressed to him orally through that instrument, and then the confession, from whatever distance transmitted, would have the advantage of being strictly auricular. (28/7/77, 29)

This derisive telephonic priestcraft, only just imaginable in the summer of 1877, would be balanced by a more admired phonographic version enacted the following summer. Max Müller, close to releasing the first volumes of his *Sacred Books of the East,* was then asked to "speak into" Thomas Edison's new phonograph; and he chose to record what he claimed was the oldest hymn in the world, the first in the Vedas, which according to one auditor (our anthologist Conway) sounded like "Agnim ile poruhitam yagnasm yadevam ritvigam hotaram ratnadhatamam." It was the song of an ancient priest that Müller translated as "Agni I worship—the chief priest of the sacrifice—the divine priest—the invoker—conferring the greatest wealth" (qtd. in Conway, *Autobiography* 2.309–10).

Müller's sacerdotal song acknowledges a reverent fascination toward an ancient human role, and a growing conviction that the priest, as Walter Pater would say in 1888, "is still, and will, we think, remain, one of the necessary types of humanity" (158). And the phonograph, which along with the telephone was the communication wonder of the season, was the perfect instrument to show how this sacred function was vital in modernity no less than antiquity. If we credit Edison as the ceremony's master, we might interpret the episode as an unintended fulfillment of Francis Galton's wish, expressed in 1874, to "see the establishment of a sort of scientific priesthood" (qtd. in D. Knight 147). Here the polymath inventor unites the primal fire worshipper and the modern philologist in one Promethean ritual. But as the scandal over *The Priest in Absolution* also made clear, there was still a powerful identification of normative national life gauged by an intolerance for a version of priestcraft said to have been overthrown at the time of the Reformation. *The Priest in Absolution* was a product of the purported engine of the Reformation, the printing press. But because it was privately circulated by a "secret" society of men, it exhibited the vitality of John Milton's portrayal of press censorship as the subjugation of public writers to the imprimatur of "glutton Friers" (503).

In all of these episodes, we can see further evidence for the ways in which reading and religion were so often importantly related, and we can also see here how a powerful social agency—for good and ill—was still attributed to those with religious professions. But perhaps more important, we can see in these gleanings from the late 1870s today's telecommunication miracles well predicted by the technologies of the telegraph, the telephone, and the phonograph.[10] With the benefit of hindsight, we see the beginnings of the displacement of the printing press as society's primary technology for communication and creative linguistic acts seeking large audiences. By the end of the 1870s, in other words, the stage was set for the passing of the Age of Paper. In 1837, in the midst of the period covered by this study, Thomas Carlyle had grasped at the flimsy flammability of France's ancien regime with a similar phrase, "The Paper Age," as he called one "book" of *The French Revolution* (CE 1.27–60). That we can now discern an Age of Paper, one imagined in terms of a material permanence in contrast to the electric impulses animating post-Gutenberg video screens, is fitting tribute to what is truly a paradigm shift. Moveable type, printed books, and reading of course remained important for a long time after 1880, and I hope, dear reader, this book has real weight in your hands. But considering the fact that the idea of a reading nation became prominent only in the late eighteenth century, and considering the fact that it was only in the closing decades of the nineteenth century that the reality of that reading nation was achieved, it is striking how we can justly claim that the relatively short period here described, 1774 to 1880, comprises Britain's great age of the printing press.[11] After 1880, books and reading were increasingly taken for granted. In our times, as the computing revolution continues to unfold, books and their readers have become objects of scholarly curiosity.

Notes

Introduction

1. The "all pervasive, deliberate, and rather self-conscious concern with the relationship between religious and aesthetic experience" has been called "the hallmark of the Victorian age" (Fraser 2). For an account of Arnold's vocation as a "priest of culture," see Sterner. DeLaura in "Carlyle and Arnold" and "The Future of Poetry" documents the public conception of this literary priesthood from the 1820s to the 1890s. Broader accounts of the cultural formulation of culture include Brantlinger (1977), DeLaura (1988), and Herbert 1–28.
2. On the tercentenary, see Foulkes 96–107. The Clerical Subscription Act allowed men entering Anglican orders to express a general assent to the formularies (Moore 223–25).
3. See "The Broad Church" and "Religion as a Fine Art," which appeared (after initial periodical runs) in Stephen's *Essays on Freethinking and Plainspeaking* (1st ed., 1873, 1–81).
4. Here quoted from Super's edition of Arnold's prose (10.467), which provides useful commentary on both Huxley's address and Arnold's reply, "Literature and Science" (10.462–70).
5. St. Clair's work is now the starting point for a consideration of reading in nineteenth-century Britain, while Secord has produced the most extensive case study "of a history reading in the age of the machine" (4). Altick's classic study was recently brought somewhat up-to-date, including a foreword by Rose (Altick 1998), whose account of working-class readers (2001) is often set in but not limited to the nineteenth century. For other influential instances of calling attention to the practice and representation of reading in Britain, see Raven, Small, and Tadmor (both their general introduction and the case studies that follow) and Flint.
6. My point is critical of a past tendency to use *Essays and Reviews* as an excuse to simplify cultural history into periods of innocence and experience. I am not downplaying the significance of the volume itself. That is documented in the Shea and Whitla edition, a work that rivals Secord's book as a heroic piece of scholarship.
7. At least two journals—*Victorian Literature and Culture* (31.3, 2003) and *Nineteenth Century Studies* (17, 2003)—have recently devoted special issues to what might be called the religious context for interpreting the nineteenth century. The Northeast Victorian Studies Association held its 2004 conference on "The Sacred and the Profane," having asked participants to consider why the study of "the workings of religion in culture and society" has come "back into fashion"; http://www.stonehill.edu/nvsa/2004call.html.

ONE Orthodox Narratives of Literary Sacralization

1. Prickett provided the exemplary, late-twentieth-century constructionist account in his related books of 1976 and 1996. I should acknowledge here too debts to a scholar of similar importance, Shaffer. For reasons different from mine, her 1975 study also covers the period 1770 to 1880.
2. See R. Ashton (1988, 1989) and Goetzman. The latter reprints nineteen reviews from March 1849 to September 1850.
3. Earlier, P. Scott came to similar conclusions. On the "religious press" in general during the long nineteenth century, see Altholz. Howsam's book is the essential study of the industrialized distribution of Scripture.
4. See Meisel 107–66 for an account of how the nation's passion for oratory in the 1860s and after inspired an unprecedented market for preaching in print.
5. See Anger 1994 for a good treatment of the topic from a hermeneutic perspective fixed on a conventional Victorian period.
6. For surveys of the clergy as a profession, see Barrie-Curien, Corfield, Gibson, F. Knight, O'Day, and Russell. The collection edited by Aston and Cragoe documents reactions to the profession. There are also helpful accounts of the Victorian clergy by Colloms, Dewey, Haig, Hammond, and Heeney. In these sepia portraits we often see the numerically astounding literary labors of figures such as Sabine Baring-Gould. For an earlier period, E. S. Turner's anecdotal book provides ample evidence for eighteenth-century clerical writing lives. Studies by Collins, Thormählen (173–220), Lovesey, and Jedrzejewski (170–210) have developed the clerical-literary nexus in a promising way as they show how their subjects—Jane Austen, the Brontë sisters, George Eliot, and Thomas Hardy—developed in relation to clerical culture and, in turn, developed the figure of the clergyman in their fiction.
7. In the contest of 1857, Arnold polled 363 votes (56.6 percent), while Bode polled 278 for 43.4 percent of the vote (*Spectator,* 9 May 1857: 489). For a summary of the changing connection between the Church of England and the universities in general from 1850s onward, see Bebbington 1992. To begin further study of these changes and controversies, see Searby, Brooke, L. Sutherland, and Brock.
8. My study foregrounds the activities of religious professionals in the established churches. Ministers leading the Dissenting academies are, however, another important source for the rise of English studies. For the latest account emphasizing this contribution, see T. Miller. Following the important work of Roe, White's dissertation recovers the culture of letters identified with figures such as Joseph Priestley, Anna Barbauld, William Godwin, and Coleridge in the 1790s.
9. Prosopographical studies of the professional origins and destinations of Oxford graduates suggest the same topsy-turvy pattern, one that cautions against professionally institutionalizing a mid-Victorian crisis of faith—even as it asks us to prepare for a story of clerical decline following the 1870s. See Curthoys and Howarth.
10. Besides Miller's book already mentioned, Jay provides an exemplary contribution to this genre. Brett's more recent entry takes in nineteenth- and twentieth-century writers, but it is based on foundations laid by Willey's influential narrative of faith and doubt.
11. See Besserman on the topic of literary periodization in general. R. Griffin and McGann in that collection are of direct concern to the question of a Romantic period. As the following section of my argument should make clear, McGann's exploitation of "the critical possibilities of the anthology-form" (1996: 168) is another rendezvous with the significance of books as things.
12. McGann (2001), Rzepka, and Wolfson have told this story in three different ways. It's important to note, as Hewitt has, that the Victorian period has its detractors as well. Richard

Price has made the most aggressive case against the historical utility of the conventional Victorian period.
13. See Raven 2001 and St. Clair (esp. 111–21). For a pan-European overview of debates about this revolution's foundation in fact, see Wittmann.
14. Crawford (2001: 70–112) provides the best general introduction to the rise of the historical literary anthology. Other important discussions include Benedict (182–228), Bonnell, Ezell (123–39), L. Price (with an excellent bibliographical survey of the topic [171-2]), T. Ross, Terry (216–50), and Wright. For a collection of essays on anthologies of British poetry from the Early Modern period up to the twentieth century, see Korte. Terry makes the best case for viewing the historical anthology boom as the end of a process he inaugurates with William Winstanley's *The Lives of the Most Famous English Poets* (1687). At times, his account might appear an affront to those, the present writer included, who see the massive *Poets* of the 1770s as the birth of a "new literary institution" (Crawford 2001: 85). But all of these studies either emphasize or concede that the significance and nature of literary anthologies changed in the late eighteenth century thanks to the 1774 ruling.
15. See "Forums."
16. Essential studies of this general reading audience include Feather and Raven 1992.
17. See Smart 29, 30, 39. Arnold's second series of *Essays in Criticism* (1888) thus had a substantially different history from the first series of 1865. None of the work in the first series originated as introductions to collections aimed at popular audiences. In the second series, five of the nine essays did. And while many essays collected in both series shared the experience of initial publication in periodicals, there was an important difference in the cycle from periodical to book. The two most influential of Arnold's late "periodical" essays—"Wordsworth" and "Byron"—were run in *Macmillan's Magazine* to promote the forthcoming collections that they introduced. They were a form of virtual journalism.
18. Estimates of clerical incomes in 1760 break down the 11,000 livings in this way: 2,000 were worth from £80 to £199, 9,000 in the range of £50 to £79 (Langford 62–65). The financial rewards for England's established priesthood would grow dramatically from 1700 to 1840, when most benefices increased in value at least 400 percent. O'Day says that even taking inflation and higher taxation into account, there was probably a 200 percent rise in the real incomes of clergy between 1700 and 1830 (199).
19. For a sense of the scale of Dibdin's career, see the bibliography by Windle and Pippin. Most recently Connell and Lynch (2004) have discussed Dibdin's role in a story about the nation's attachment to books.
20. For a less mythic account of Johnson's earnings as a writer, see Fleeman. D. Griffin (1993) makes some productive historical challenges to a variety of related print mythologies.
21. In addition to Howsam's book (mentioned above, n. 3), see Carpenter's account (2003) of the proliferation of illustrated family Bibles, a form that could simultaneously satisfy ornamental and spiritual desires. Hodson's history features excerpts from sermons on the glory of print from Stanley, Bishop Claughton, and Canon Farrar (138–44).
22. See O'Gorman and Turner on this "Victorian repudiation of the eighteenth century" (2).
23. F. Turner (1993: 3–37) has composed the best general critique of the tendency to frame post-Enlightenment history with "the emergence of a secular world view replacing a religious world view" (4). More recent work (C. Brown, S. J. D. Green, and McLeod) indicates that "secularisation theory" is "a narrative in crisis" (C. Brown 2001: 30). In Brown's view, the theory was an influential "field of discourse" between 1800 and 1950, even as religiosity remained high. But the long slow decline of religion—one chiefly coordinated with urbanization—is in his eyes a great myth. He argues instead for a rapid period of secularization from the 1950s onward. C. Smith makes a somewhat similar argument with reference to the American experience (1–96), which, nevertheless, deserves to

be treated separately. For well-documented overviews of past and current historiography on the topic, see McLeod (1–30) and S. J. D. Green (5–16). For a sharply divided version of the debate about the secularization thesis (as conducted by sociologists), see the works of Bruce and Stark. For brief comments about the fluctuating conceptual value of secularization in Victorian Studies, see Kent 110–12.

24. Burns has provided a sweeping account of the way in which "the political and social significance of the rise of Dissent and irreligion" did not change "the fact that during the first half of the nineteenth century the Church of England retained an institutional presence in England and Wales rivalled only by that of secular organs of government" (1999: 1). This attention to the vitality of the church also leads him "to play down the epochal significance so often attached to the post-1832 period" in favor of a gradualist approach commencing in the 1790s (1999: 266). More recently, Burns has highlighted a process of internal church reform commencing in the 1780s (2003: 144). Rosman (2003: 207–32) has described the "vigour of Victorian Christianity" both in the church and in chapel.

25. Canuel's study (2002) is the best book about literature and religious politics within a conventional Romantic period since Ryan's earlier work. I share Canuel's earlier view (1996: 268–72) that there is good reason to think of these topics in ways that disregard the traditional Romantic-Victorian frontier.

26. A version of this irony is at work in Halevy's thesis that "the miracle of modern England" could be explained only by understanding that even its "secular opinion" had religious roots (qtd. in Morris 109). R. Davis (37–52) some time ago described the Repeal of 1828 as the fulfillment of Dissenting petitions from the 1770s, which were in part coordinated with liberalizing tendencies from within the church.

27. For an account of the Subscription controversies, see Young (45–80), whose work draws upon Ditchfield (1988). Ditchfield's other work provides details on the topic of religious toleration in general with respect to Parliament and its petitioners in the late eighteenth century. Gascoigne similarly coordinates theological and political movements across establishment-dissenting borders.

28. Before Parry, Machin's study of late-nineteenth-century politics and the church similarly stressed how the politics of religious liberalism moved from the center to the periphery in the 1880s and after. He mentions a possible growth of religious indifference, but more persuasively recalls how Dissenting political zeal subsided with the erosion of Dissenting penalties (1987: 323). Both Ellens and Larsen, though they don't agree on all details and focus on different periods, also highlight religious routes to the voluntary system.

29. See Heathron and Galbraith on the reading habits of elementary students in 1870 and after.

30. See Altick (1998: 141–87) for an account of elementary and secondary schooling throughout the century. Any broad history of the acquisition of basic reading skills for the period must emphasize two primary sources of popular education before its development into a responsibility of the state: Sunday schooling (by a variety of denominations) and working-class autodidacticism. For the frequent synthesis of both forces, see Laqueur and Rose.

31. For more details on the role of religious politics in obstructing and producing national education, see Machin (1987: 31–40) and Parry (295–332, 376–81). The essential account from the perspective of Protestant Dissent is to be found in Watts (2.535–58). For a complementary account lamenting the church's eclipse as the primary source of elementary enlightenment, see Burgess.

32. This is not to say that in 1880 denominational strife ceased to influence the politics of state-administered education. The issues here described stayed alive for some time, and the Education Bill of 1902, in particular, revived debates from the 1870s and earlier. Nevertheless, it is useful to recognize the 1880s as a time when one political paradigm gave way to a new one. From the 1770s to the 1880s, we can speak of Whig-Liberals and Conservatives superintending a small-scale, noninterventionist state, courting constituencies

primarily with religious issues. From the 1880s to the 1950s, Conservatives, "new" Liberals, and Labour preside over an increasingly interventionist, large-scale state and court support on issues of empire and welfare.

33. Regarding literacy rates in 1837, it is important to note that they were much higher in some (mostly urban) areas and lower in many other areas. But they average out by most accounts to the figures cited. Vincent gives a useful, comparative account of the rise of mass literacy in Europe.

34. For a rewarding discussion of theories of contextualization, historicism (as a principle of literary criticism), and literary history, see Hume.

TWO Zealous Protestants in Literature

1. For this error, see *Companion* 330, 332, 337, 747.
2. See M. Butler xviii and Gamer 49. The latter even has Ritson compose *Observations on the First Three Volumes of The History of English Literature.*
3. Engell 1998 has also described Hurd's influence on German writers. The essential historical source for the study of Hurd during the period of his greatest influence—the 1770s and '80s—is Eddy's bibliography.
4. Nichol's edition of book-trade correspondence is the best guide to Warburton's status in the republic of letters both as the combative custodian of literary authorities (including Moses, Shakespeare, and Pope) and as an author in his own right. Ryley's is the most important general update to A. W. Evans, while Young (1998) sets the stage for seeing this polemic divine as a literary force.
5. Engell's 1999 chapter provides an excellent bibliography concerning Lowth's reception (188–90).
6. Balfour gives a balanced account of Lowth's status as an innovator on this issue (55–56).
7. When Lowth prepared a second edition of the *Lectures* in 1763, he included notes by Kennicott and references to his 1759 dissertation on the Hebrew text (*Lectures* 1.xx–xxi). McCane remains the best introduction to Kennicott's project.
8. See Hepworth's shrewd reading of this juncture in Lowth's career (38) and, more generally, on Lowth's relations with Hoadly and Whig aristocrats from the Cavendish clan (31–38).
9. Lowth's *Grammar* was never published in an authorized form with the author identified, but he never did anything to hide his authorship.
10. In these terms, his *Grammar* has been allied with those notorious instances where eighteenth-century editors produced "accurate" editions of Shakespeare and Milton by "correcting" their solecisms. But there is no evidence that Lowth was an advocate of grammatically bowdlerized editions of the English classics, and, as Freimarck has noted, Lowth used the occasion of the *Grammar* to reject "a number of Richard Bentley's emendations of *Paradise Lost*" (xxx). As Carol Percy has shown with careful attention to the evolution of Lowth's text from edition to edition, he became increasingly open-handed in his acknowledgment of irregularities that had poetic or stylistic virtues.
11. In addition to Young's study, I am here mostly indebted to Lamb's work (1996) on the eighteenth century's reading of Job. Thanks to his deconstructive approach, one that presumes a leveling of all discourse as text, Lamb moves deftly between "religious polemic" and literary debate. Other responses to the Warburton-Lowth feud pretend that literary and religious discourses can be easily or properly separated, as when David Reibel, editor of the facsimile *Major Works of Robert Lowth,* explains the exclusion of the *Letter* from the *Major Works* (ix). As Young has argued more persuasively, "Any ready distinction between theological and non-theological literature" from the time is often made by the force of recent habit (2001: 84).
12. The prophetic text, in large type and in stanzaic forms, takes up 174 pages; Lowth's dissertation and notes, in smaller type, total 357 pages.

13. See D. Norton 2.94–135, Daniell 604–20, and D. Katz 178–211.
14. This particular essay was added sometime after the first edition of the *Essays*, which reached a seventeenth edition in 1815 (Uphaus 346). L. Price (66–77) has discussed Knox's impact and his status as a maker of books addressing the century's new reader.
15. When More died in 1833, she left behind an estate valued at £27,500 (Stott 331), a legacy that made her the most commercially successful woman writer in England's history. See Elliott 56–57 for an overview of criticism that acknowledges More's influence in a variety of ways.
16. In addition to the works just cited, I am most indebted to Fairer's exemplary edition of Warton's correspondence and his extensive historical introductions to recent editions of Warton's major works, the *History* and the *Observations* (1998 and 2001).
17. It was this paradigm in which T. Warton had initially consolidated his poetic reputation, with *The Triumph of Isis* (1750), a reply to Mason's anti-Oxford poem *Isis* (1749). The poems, however, trade in a discourse of invective that became somewhat obsolete by the 1760s.
18. Warton managed to cultivate productive relationships with both Lowth and Warburton. Warburton recognized that Warton was primarily a literary protégé of Lowth (*CTW* 293), but Warburton was also an active champion of Warton's pursuit of the Regius Professorship of History at Oxford in the late 1760s (*CTW* 666–68).
19. Critics have cited these essays as further signs of Warton's digressiveness. Lipking offered them a vindication by reading them in terms of eighteenth-century aesthetic dilemmas: "The dissertations taken together pose just that dialectic of romance and learning, illusion and reason, which Warton balanced throughout his career" (374).
20. The two dissertations in volume 1 are not paginated. I cite the gatherings as printed on the bottom of the page.
21. Coleridge, for example, would testify to this line of influence when he described his early obsession with the sonnets of Warton's disciple, the Reverend William Lisle Bowles (*CW* 7:1.12–17; see also Fairer 1996).
22. Fairer notes that the *Monasticon*, Tanner's *Notitia Monastica*, and Wharton's *Anglia Sacra* are three of the most frequently quoted texts in the *History* (1998: 30).
23. See the *Observations* (1.119–20) for evidence of how Warton had long thought about orthography, its wayward history, and the idea of rhyming for both the eye and ear.
24. In this view Macpherson was a highlander writing back to the imperial centers of Edinburgh or London; Percy was hawking from the press in London songs that had been floating on the wind in the north country; and Chatterton's forgeries were provincial products that he hoped to have published in the metropolis.
25. On the cultural context for all three, see Groom 2002 and Ruthven (5–23), who gives the best brief introduction to the topic.
26. The translation was dedicated to the Duke, the poem to the Duchess of Northumberland. Both were published anonymously, but Percy's authorship was clear.
27. Besides having access to the complete Latin edition published in 1753, Percy, Macpherson, and Blair in 1760 might have known the portion translated at the opening of Joseph Warton's *Essay* on Pope (1.15–18), yet another Dodsley book. Percy borrowed a copy of Lowth's *Praelectiones* from Richard Farmer sometime before June 1762 (*PL* 2.3); he eventually became the owner of the second Oxford edition (1762). An inscription in Percy's hand says: "A present from Mr. Jas. Dodsley to T. Percy. March 21, 1765" (*Library of Thomas Percy*, item 318).
28. Percy's later description of his *Specimens* to Evans (*PL* 5.98) indicates how he considered it to be a project fundamentally different from the *Reliques*, which was all but complete at the time. Blair, in a letter that similarly confirms the distinction, asked Percy in 1772 about the fate of "your early Poetry of all Nations" (qtd. in Schmitz 88).

29. Michaelis was on his way to denying that the Song of Solomon was Scripture. He, like Percy, read it in its literal and historical sense. But reading the text as ancient poetry led to the conclusion that it was simply that—and nothing more: when volume 7 of Michaelis's German translation of the Bible appeared in 1788, the Song was omitted from the canon (R. Clark 1097).
30. The surviving correspondence exchanged between Percy and Michaelis, and Michaelis and Lowth (see Hecht), makes it clear that they were happy to disagree on such topics in service to the idea that religious enlightenment depended on a learned order of men searching out Scripture's meaning.
31. Percy's copies of the last two are bound together at Queen's Library in Belfast (*Library of Thomas Percy*, item 400–400A).
32. The contracts with Dodsley for the Runic poetry and the Song of Solomon had stipulations for both their separate and combined publication (M. Ross 1, 15).
33. The latest surviving pieces of authentic minstrelsy that Percy had been able to discover ("The Rising in the North" and "Northumberland Betrayed by Douglas" [1.248–69]) dated from the late sixteenth century.
34. The new apparatus was published independently—for owners of the first edition—as *Four Essays, as Improved and Enlarged in the Second Edition of the Reliques of Ancient English Poetry* (1767).
35. At turns such as this one, it became clearer that the *Reliques* was becoming closely coordinated with Percy's translation of Henry Mallet's work, which appeared in 1770 as *Northern Antiquities* and included as Percy's major addition an essay emphasizing the distinction between Germanic and Celtic cultures.
36. For a description of the publication of Blair's influential essay, see Rizza, esp. 131. The 1765 visit to Edinburgh is best described in Schmitz 88–90.
37. Blair wrote the preface, but it was based on conversations with Macpherson.
38. See Haugen on Macpherson's relation to other creative and polemic exploitations of druidism. Mee (89–120) gives the best guide to the antagonistic duality of the druids in the conventional historical imagination: they could stand for hieratic priestcraft or sublime and prophetic bardism. Macpherson resolved this tension completely in favor of the former.
39. See Groom's "Celts" for a different comparative discussion of Macpherson's and Percy's approach to written and unwritten literary sources.
40. In the next generation, for instance, John Jamieson (1759–1838) was a prominent clerical philologist, who published, among other works, *An Historical Account of the Ancient Culdees of Iona, and of Their Settlements in Scotland, England, and Ireland* (1811).
41. For a summary of the rearrangement, see Gaskill's edition (413).
42. For a subtle overview of Macpherson's politics, see Kidd 219–35, 270–71.
43. This encounter—both the journey itself and its representation—has a distinguished body of commentary, including K. Temple (73–120), Trumpener (67–127), and Lynch 1990. All of these studies need to be supplemented with Reddick's account (141–69) of Johnson's only significant revision of the *Dictionary* (4th ed., 1773), a task that reunited the nation's lexicographer and its orthodox divines on the eve of Johnson's arrival in the Highlands.

THREE **Entertaining Salvation**

1. Scott figures prominently in Chandler's study of what he calls "the representative practices of Romantic historicism" (307). For more on Eliot's reading of Scott, see Baker 1993.
2. To emphasize how Scott initiated his career with a series of interrelated projects that united collection, preservation, and invention, I cite and quote from the *Works* (5 vols., 1806) whenever possible. The *Works* (Todd 260Aa) is a nonce edition that collects together

the third, 1806 edition of *The Minstrelsy of the Scottish Border* (vols. 1–3) and the second, 1806 edition of *Sir Tristrem* (vol. 4). Volume 5, *The Lay of the Last Minstrel with Ballads and Lyrical Pieces,* contains the fourth, 1806 edition of the *Lay* and "The Fire King," "Frederick and Alice," "The Wild Huntsmen" (*sic*), "The Erl-King," "The Norman Horse-Shoe," "The Dying Bard," "The Maid of Toro," and "Hellvellyn." Scott did not republish "William and Helen" in the *Works,* and in my discussion of that poem I cite the text in the *Poetical Works* (12 vols., 1833–34).

3. Murphy's book, for example, has a chapter that situates the *Lay* in a literary history that commences with the ballad revival of the 1760s (136–81), but his commentary on the poem primarily rephrases Scott's disingenuous "Introduction" of 1830 (*PW* 6.5–31). Similarly, a portion of Gamer's study (163–86) is said to be about Scott's early poetic career, but it is more often a reading of later works that refer to that career. This distance from the early books themselves has sponsored significant errors. Gamer thinks that Scott's most important early poems—"Glenfinlas" and "The Eve of St. John"—appeared in the second edition of the *Minstrelsy* only after the first edition had turned him into "a respectable scholar" (175). Murphy identifies Cranstoun as an "English lord" (146).

4. For the history of the *Lay*'s initial production as part of Scott's larger project, see Millgate's definitive series of studies (1984: 10–18; 1998; 2000; and 2002). Cronin is also useful in considering the *Lay*'s relationship to the *Minstrelsy*.

5. For a recent reading of the Percy-Scott relationship, see L. Davis 144–67. Even though they were separated by over forty years in age, their careers publicly overlapped: the fourth edition of the *Reliques,* for instance, was reviewed in the March 1796 *British Critic* ("Percy's *Reliques*") to be followed in September by a review of four different translations of Bürger's "Leonore" ("Translations").

6. See Groom 2002 (with bibliographical essays on Macpherson, Chatterton, and Ireland on 316–25) and S. Stewart 102–31 on the forces and personalities that closely positioned literary veneration and literary deceit in the late eighteenth century. Groom's 1999 collection includes several articles (esp. 121–252) that underscore the 1780s and '90s as the time when a broader controversy about literary forgery became a discursive institution.

7. Scott's autobiography was first published in Lockhart's *Memoirs* (1.1–47), but before then the passage saw life in a revised form in 1830 in the "Essay on Imitations of the Ancient Ballad" (*PW* 4.53).

8. This same plot is slightly revised in "Frederick and Alice" (*W* 5.344–48), one of Scott's adaptations from Goethe.

9. See Boerner, Jolles, and Lawson-Peebles. McGann acknowledges this moment in his 1993 anthology (organized on chronological principles) by including William Taylor's version of the ballad and two related ballads by Lewis (*Romantic Period Verse* 121–32).

10. On the eager reading of Percy by Germans, see Boyd. For a history of the German Enlightenment's particular interest in Scottish writers and their works, see Oz-Salzberger, especially 57–76. Scott owned Herder's *Volkslieder* (2 vols., 1778–79; see Cochrane 172) and admired his version of "Sir Patrick Spens" in particular. But Scott also suggested the derivative character of Herder's work when he "regretted that the actual popular songs of the Germans form so trifling a proportion" of the collection (*W* 1.6).

11. In "The Friar of Orders Gray," another influential ballad from the *Reliques* composed by Percy (1.225–30), youth and fair lovers are poetically involved with corpses and deception. But the off-stage corpse is a narrative device to test the lady's fidelity. In Percy's ballad, a disguised lover temporarily lies about being dead; in Bürger's ballads, corpses lie about being living lovers.

12. For the importance of Thomas to Scott's authorial identity, see Matthews 54–70. His book provides a new look at its topic thanks to the commitment to "treat the printed tradition

of Middle English as a fruitful area of study" (xxi). Earlier, from a different perspective, Goslee made a convincing case for the centrality of Thomas (1988: 1–15).
13. For Gamer, these different bibliographic settings illustrate how the antiquarian apparatus of the *Minstrelsy* was used to transform Scott's poetic avocation into something respectable after the growing scandal of Lewis's career (174–76).
14. Langan calls the *Lay* "the great unread poem of the romantic period" (55), by which she means, among other things, that good criticism on it is sparse. Her essay makes the convincing case that the poem is a commentary on its own aesthetic context. Manning offers some prudent qualifications. Goslee (1988: 19–40), in a rare close reading, is particularly useful regarding gender and the topic of literacy.
15. These terms were first expressed publicly by Scott's friend Francis Jeffrey ("Scott's *Lay*" 6, 18–19). As Scott often did, he made a point of embracing the criticism. With the poem selling 12,500 copies in its first two years, there was little point to a project of exoneration.
16. In his discussion of romance and Scott's domination of the genre (128–40), Curran gives good reasons to reject the "simple-minded Scott of his own projection and of subsequent critical history" (140).
17. Besides the discussion in the general introduction, such creatures were the subject of Scott's introductory essay to the "Tale of Tamlin" (*W* 2.109–79). The *Lay* refashions characters and subject matter—Michael Scott, magic books, exhumation, and reinterment, and mischievous service by fairy pages—that appeared in the *Minstrelsy* in the linked ballads "Lord Soulis" and "The Cout of Keeldar" (*W* 3.245–302). The *Lay,* which frequently asked readers to turn to the *Minstrelsy* (*W* 5.218, 262, 277, 284, 288), also had its historical subject matter explicated in detail by the *Minstrelsy*. The Kerr and Scott clans are prominent in the "sketch of border history" (*W* 1.liii) included in the *Minstrelsy*'s general introduction. See esp. 1.xiii–liii. An appendix to that introduction ("Bond of Alliance or Feud Staunching, betwixt the clans of Scott and Ker" [*W* 1.cliv–clvii]) describes how pilgrimages were undertaken to end a feud initiated by the Battle of Melrose in 1526 (1.xvii). The *Lay* is about the outbreak of this same feud.
18. The minstrel describes the lady inheriting her skills from one paternal figure, but Scott's note provides historical details that allow the modern reader to imagine the Minstrel (in good faith) conflating no less than "three learned and dignified prelates [who] flourished about the date of the romance" (*W* 5.221).
19. To Deloraine and the Monk, Michael Scott seems to be sleeping serenely, "As if he had not been dead a day" (2.29; *W* 5.56). Following his encounter with Cranstoun, Deloraine is also in a "doubtful state" (3.7; *W* 5.77), appearing to be a "living corse" (3.11; *W* 5.80). Deloraine, who will remain "ghastly" (5.24; *W* 5.157) even when "wakened from his deathlike trance" (5.28; *W* 5.161), is thus the perfect witness of the Wizard's similarly ambiguous bodily presence in canto 6 (27; *W* 5.195–96).
20. All of these ruptures are dramatically compelling, but not very convincing before the bar of history. For the essential challenge to the myth about Scott's "invention" of historical fiction, see Trumpener. Ian Duncan has given a brief but potent account of the ways in which *Waverley* represents an extension of themes, subjects, and narrative techniques found in the *Lay,* which was, in turn, an adaptation of a Scottish gothic tradition (70–76). Duncan says that the ensuing fictions show "a continuous process of creative variation and transformation of the Gothic, national and historical themes in *Waverley*" (75).
21. Both Cottom (102, n. 6) and Maxwell (421) have noted a distinguished list of nineteenth-century readers—including Marx and Nietzsche—who took up their Scott on their sickbeds.
22. Scott's "Hymn for the Dead" became a staple in many other hymnals including *Hymns Ancient and Modern* (1st ed., 1861). Julian notes that it was common for editors to "improve"

the penultimate line ("Be THOU the trembling sinner's stay") by including "Christ" or "Jesus" (297). This tradition of pious interpolation underscores the fact that neither Jesus Christ nor God is explicitly mentioned in the minstrel's song.

FOUR Common Things Hallowed

1. Newman's original letters to the *Times,* signed "Catholicus," are reproduced with useful information, including a report of Peel's original speech, in *LD* 8:525–61.
2. For the best recent work on Brougham's status within a politicized print culture, see Christie (1999 and 2002: 230–33). Secord (46–51) also situates Brougham's early efforts (1825–32) in a context of popular publishing ventures. For more details about Brougham's involvement with the three key institutions cited here, see Ford 1995 and R. Stewart 1986. Brougham makes frequent appearances throughout Altick 1998.
3. The local parish vestry was responsible for collecting funds for the school, and the schoolmaster had to be a member of the established church. The local clergyman had the right to examine the proposed master and the power to veto his candidacy (*H* 2.72–77).
4. A representative article in the April 1825 *British Critic* gave a satirical plan for an "Education Company" (with "the boys to be washed and whipped by steam") as it reviewed the ninth edition of *Practical Observations* along with the *New Monthly Magazine*'s kite for London University ("Brougham and Campbell" 337).
5. The second chapter of Crowther's study (40–65), entitled "The Threat from Germany," is a useful introduction to the Anglican reception of German scholarship in the 1840s and after. But its conclusion, that "many of the clergy" were first introduced to German scholarship in the 1860s (64), is no longer convincing.
6. Taking stock of Pusey's early career is a key step to overcoming the myth that Anglican theology during the 1820s and '30s was innocent of the methods and presumptions of higher criticism. On Pusey in particular, see the classic Victorian account of his brush with theological liberalism in Liddon (1.70–114, 146–77), and the more recent work by Matthew 1981, Frappell, and Forrester (211–231).
7. Thirlwall's success at impressing his undergraduates with Niebuhr's importance gets no better tribute than Alfred Tennyson's comment in the 1860s that "the true origin of modern Biblical Criticism was to be ascribed not to Strauss, but to Niebuhr, who lived a generation earlier" (*Memoir* 2.463). See Stray 2004 for many details regarding the personalities, politics, and religious implications of disseminating innovative German criticism in the 1820s and '30s.
8. For the transatlantic dimensions of the event, see Channing.
9. See Goodwin for a critique of the habit, within this body of work, of casually equating Tractarian aesthetics and literary Romanticism; he also stresses important disagreement between Keble and Newman on aesthetic issues.
10. Skinner's new study (*Tractarians*) has recovered the ways in which the Tractarian program, despite its hallmark identification with reserve and antiquity, was deeply involved with contemporary social issues as well as the period's key paradigm for convivial and controversial sociability: an expanding print culture.
11. See *The Christian Year:* 188 (Tues. in Whitsun-Week); 158 (2nd Sun. after Easter); 345, 346 (St. Matthew); 197 (1st Sun. after Trinity); and 211 (4th Sun. after Trinity). I quote from a copy formerly owned by Keble's godchild, Matthew Arnold, who, like Keble before him, would hold the Oxford Chair in Poetry. This twenty-first edition from 1841 also recalls the pivotal year in the Anglo-Catholic revival. There is no scholarly edition of *The Christian Year,* which was first published in June 1827 and had an important history of revisions, including an infamous one in the first posthumous edition of 1866. The six poems added in 1828 (3rd ed.), to make it more closely mirror the liturgy, were "Forms of Prayer to be

used at Sea," "Gunpowder Treason," "King Charles the Martyr," "The Restoration of the Royal Family," "The Accession," and "Ordination."

12. In addition to K. Blair's essay (2003), several contributors to a recent volume—see Francis, Mason, and Kline—have revived the case for Keble's influence over a wide range of poetic practice. For an earlier but still essential account of that influence, see also G. B. Tennyson 197–211.
13. For an account of Keble's book in a broader tradition of English hymnody, see Watson (326–34) and his definitive study of that topic.
14. Wade insisted that the "Established Clergy" is "by far the most iniquitous" of all "the different classes opposed to the welfare of the community." Besides providing a welter of hard figures and naming hundreds of sinecures, that work reminded its readers that "men in holy orders"—the Reverends Hay and Ethelstone—had recently "directed the barbarous outrage" of the Peterloo massacre (330). See in particular the section "Expense of the Established Clergy" (272–331). As Burns and Innes have pointed out (3, n. 4), Wade was more interested (by measure of scale) in documenting the topic of clerical incomes than the issue of parliamentary representation.
15. Keble was also wary of giving religious convictions a merely sentimental footing. R. H. Froude from the start had objected to some of the poems on these terms. They "did not do enough to sober down into practical piety those whose feelings were acute, and who were inclined to indulge in a dreamy, visionary existence" (qtd. in Lock 54).
16. Homer is the primary subject in lectures 6–16. In lecture 9, Keble refers to Walter Scott's death (21 Sept. 1832) "two years ago" (1.148), indicating that the lectures on the *Odyssey* (11–15) should have been delivered after September 1834, well after Keble had preached "National Apostasy" on 14 July 1833.
17. Tennyson owned the seventh (1831) edition of *The Christian Year,* and its influence on *In Memoriam* has been described by P. Scott (1989) and M. Shaw.
18. See Linley for a discussion of the booming publication of annuals in the 1830s.
19. The evangelical *Record* as early as 1833 was describing the young Macaulay as a prodigal son (Rosman 1984: 41, n. 48). When the first two volumes of his *History of England* were published in 1848, several Christian periodicals, including the *Christian Observer,* censured Macaulay for his religious indifference (Lang 73).
20. One poem singled out for praise was the historical poem on Sennacherib, which is very similar in tone to Macaulay's Paraphrase of Nahum. Macaulay might have been inspired to write the Hebrew Eclogue in part by a reperusal of the review. Surviving correspondence shows that Byron was a frequent family topic; see, for example, *LM* 1.73–74.
21. Macaulay indexed the very volume in which the review of Byron had run (*LM* 1.49n, 56, 321).
22. By virtue of its complicated eroticism coupled with a sacred context, the "Hebrew Eclogue" might also be affiliated with Macaulay's unpublished poem "To Woman," dated July 1822 (qtd. in Clive 39).
23. See C. Knight (1.280–334) for a more candid version.
24. Macaulay's cavalier, for instance, dreams of a "sweet Precisian," while his amorous radical imagines "wooing fair Poissardes."
25. Phillips has made the interesting point that Coleridge and Macaulay can seem to share much in these terms (121). For two more recent discussions of Macaulay's historicism—and its complexities—see Ghosh and Tucker.
26. The probable source for one of Lockhart's turns is another reminder of the age's habit of confusing discussions of classical and biblical philology: in the same journal in 1831, Milman had described how recent German critics had "resolved" the *Iliad* and the *Odyssey* into "the minstrelsy of the Grecian border modelled into a continuous story" (124).

27. Mill's appreciation ([Feb. 1843]: 105–13; *Collected Works* 1.525–32) was strong enough to overcome any resentment at Macaulay's vigorous send-up of utilitarian pieties in the late 1820s (W. Thomas 84–85). See Gray and McKelvy 2000 for the initial reception of the *Lays* and the subsequent decline of the volume's poetic merit in the eyes of some critics.
28. Milman's positive review appeared in March 1843 (453–77). John Wilson Croker was furious at having lost a chance to avenge Macaulay's savage treatment of his 1830 edition of Boswell's *Life* (W. Thomas 116, 159–60).

FIVE Primitive Traditions and Modern Readers

1. Disraeli served his first, brief premiership in 1868, to be replaced by Gladstone from 1868 to 1874. Disraeli was back in power from 1874 to 1880. Following the defeat of the Conservatives in the 1880 general election, Disraeli retired from active political life in order to devote himself to literary pursuits. He died in 1881, while Gladstone followed with three more ministries.
2. The eighth edition was published on 1 November 1870 in a one-volume format containing a General Preface to Longman's forthcoming Collected Edition (10 vols., 1870–71). "Disraeli earned at least £10,600 between 1870 and 1877 from the sales of his novels—and this figure was all, directly or indirectly, due to *Lothair*" (Braun 79). For the reception of *Lothair*, see Weintraub 490–95.
3. For the most complete bibliographies of Gladstone's Homerica, its reception, and the Homeric Question in Britain (1830–93), see McKelvy 1998: 285–94.
4. Morley set the stage when he said that Gladstone's Homeric works were chiefly valuable for the light they shed on Gladstone (3.543). Almost everyone else since has agreed. Ramm, for example, says, "The interest of it all is in what it shows us of Gladstone's mind" (18). For remarks about Gladstone and Homer by the main line of biographers, in chronological order, see Morley (3.543–46), Magnus (122–5, 220, 232–3), Feuchtwanger (99–100), Shannon (1.316–17, 349–51), Matthew (152–54), and Jenkins (14–15, 181–83).
5. Much of what I have to say is indebted to Turner 1981, esp. 159–70. In two ways, though, my account of Gladstone's Homeric work is different. My focus on the 1830s and '40s contrasts with Turner's focus on the 1850s and Gladstone's concerns about the parliamentary reform of Oxford; and while Turner emphasizes a distant patristic source for the idea of primitive tradition, I focus on a broader class of Trinitarian apologetic and standard texts used in the training and indoctrination of Anglican clergy and active laity. In addition to Turner's study, one should consult Jenkyns to understand Gladstone's work in the larger context of nineteenth-century Hellenism. Gladstone's Hellenism has long been understood in contrast to the vision of Greece propagated by George Grote, and that clash remains central in what follows. For a different version of Gladstone's encounter with Grote's work, see Bebbington's 1998 essay "Gladstone and Grote": he explicates the reading of Grote in the context of "Gladstone's early thought" (157) without mention of Strauss, Newman, and debates about tradition and theological corruption. Since then, Bebbington has published an improved account of Gladstone's turn to Homer (2004, see esp. 142–77), one that now more closely resembles mine as it first appeared (1998: 1–23, 245–79). For a critique of Bebbington's general approach to Gladstone, see Shannon 2004.
6. Gladstone began the first volume of Tomline on 31/12/26 and finished the second on 1/7/27 (GD). Tomline quoted at length from Thomas Maurice's *A Dissertation on the Oriental Trinities* (1800), which Gladstone also read (GD 21–25, 28–30/12/36). The *Dissertation* was "abstracted" from Maurice's *Indian Antiquities* (7 vols., 1793–1800), which is at Hawarden.
7. See McKelvy 1997 for a fuller discussion, with a relevant bibliography, of Gladstone as a bibliophile and founder of St. Deiniol's Library. Jagger contains additional information about that foundation.

8. See Skinner's "'The Duty of the State'" for a detailed reading of Keble's review.
9. Between December 1838 and November 1841, Gladstone's books inspired reviews in the *Times,* the *British Magazine,* the *Christian Observer,* the *British Critic,* the *Edinburgh,* the *Quarterly,* the *Foreign Quarterly,* the *Westminster,* the *Eclectic,* and the *Churchman's Monthly* reviews. In addition to Keble and Macaulay, Gladstone's notable readers included Thomas Arnold, Sara Coleridge, F. D. Maurice, William Wordsworth, and John Sterling—to name a few. Carlyle wrote to Emerson in America to tell him how the author had "contrived to insert a piece of you (first Orat[io]n it must be) in a work of his on 'Church and State,' which makes some figure at present!" (*Letters* 11.25–26). Ellens has summarized Gladstone's position, contrasted it with others common to the 1830s, and collected together most of the important scholarship about Gladstone's first book (1994: 4–6). For the reception of the church-and-state books, see Robbins (312–39) and P. Butler (77–92), who provides the best study of Gladstone's early ideas and their theopolitical context. For further analysis, see Helmstadter, Hilton, and Schreuder.
10. Gladstone cited Manning's *Tract 78* in *The State in its Relations* (1841: 2.101, 135). In addition to Keble's famous sermon (*GD* 5/3/37, 11/2/38), *Tract 78,* Manning's *Appendix to "Sermon on the Rule of Faith"* (1838, *GD* 29/3/39), H. A. Woodgate's *The Authoritative Teaching of the Church Shown to be in Conformity with Scripture* (1839, *GD* 29/9/39), and other Anglo-Catholic works on tradition, Gladstone also read many replies, such as Francis Close's *Sermons for the Times: The Authority and Integrity of God's Word, Maintained against Tradition* (1837, *GD* 20/3/38), Philip Nicholas Shuttleworth's *Not Tradition but Revelation* (1838, *GD* 9/9/38), Renn Dickson Hampden's *Lecture on Tradition* (1839, *GD* 2/6/39), and Christopher Benson's *Discourses upon Tradition and Episcopacy* (1839, *GD* 15/9/39).
11. For a study that is openly revisionary in its sympathy for Manning's character and intellect, see Pereiro, who registers as well the mutual importance of the bond between Gladstone and Manning. The closest treatment of the Manning-Gladstone relationship (featured below) will be found in Erb's forthcoming edition of their correspondence. See also McClelland.
12. It is a melancholy fact that "Maynooth and Popery" (not famine) was the major Irish issue for most English readers in the 1840s. On the controversy excited by Maynooth before and after the 1840s, see Cahill, Norman (23–51, 144–58), Lyons, Machin 1967, and Wallis 1987.
13. The historiography of anti-Catholicism achieves its fullest resonance only when sounded in relation to the historiography of the broader Catholic revival and Ritualism in particular. Essential studies of anti-Catholicism—a force that anathematized both Roman Catholicism and the purported Catholicism of the established church—include Arnstein, Paz, Wallis 1993, and Wolffe.
14. In addition to Milman's review, Gladstone read the following works on Newman's argument (listed in the order in which WEG first read them): the *English Review* (Dec. 1845): 501, *GD* 4/1/46; William Josiah Irons's *The Theory of Development Examined* (1846), *GD* 22/2/46; Andrew Irvine's *Romanism, as Represented by the Rev. J. H. Newman, Briefly Considered* (1846), *GD* 3/4/46; W. B. Barter's *Postscript to the English Church Not in Schism . . . A Few Words on Mr. Newman's Essay on Development* (1846), *GD* 19/4/46; M. O'Sullivan's *Theory of Developments on Christian Doctrine* (1846), *GD* 10/5/46; Thomas Williams Allies's *The Church of England cleared from the Charge of Schism* (1846), *GD* 21/6/46; William Palmer's *The Doctrine of Development* (1846), *GD* 3/1/47; the *English Review* on Pius IX's attitude to Development (Dec. 1846): 489, *GD* 29/1/47; and J. B. Mozley's *The Theory of Development* (1847), *GD* 12/8/47. For a discussion of Anglican replies to Newman, see Nicholls.
15. When he accepted his cabinet position in December 1845, he automatically lost his seat in the Commons and was required to stand for reelection. But because of his support for

Peel's new antiprotection policy, he was no longer welcome in Newcastle, and he thus served out his term as colonial secretary without a seat in the House.

16. Gladstone's notes from his Homeric studies in the 1840s are in Add. MSS 44684.40–151 and 44736.42–197. They confirm that Gladstone's Homerica published from 1858 to 1890 was an elaboration of conclusions and critical principles assumed by 1847. In addition to the works discussed with reference to Grote, Gladstone was influenced in the 1840s by his reading of Archdeacon Williams's *Homerus,* which also invoked the controversial theological concept of tradition. Having seen proof-sheets of that work (GD 1/12/40), Gladstone and Williams corresponded about it upon its publication; see Williams's letter to Gladstone (3/3/42, Add. MSS 44359.75) and *GD* 5/3/42 noting the reply. Williams's work was attacked in the *Edinburgh Review* (77 [Feb. 1843]: 44–71), which was habitually hostile to such High Church appropriations of classical ground. Williams replied with a work (*Primitive Tradition: A Letter to the Editor of the Edinburgh Review* [1843]) that defended the habit of using "tradition" in the context in question. Gladstone cited both of Williams's works in his 1858 *Homer* (2.3). The suggested identification of "Homerus" by the editors (*GD* 1/12/40) is almost surely incorrect.
17. See Turner 1981: 85–104 for the best evocation of Grote's stature.
18. Macaulay would note attending a breakfast where Henry Hallam lightened the mood by reading "wondrous extracts from the Lives of the Saints" (Trevelyan 2.196–97). In J. C. Crosthwaite's *Modern Hagiology* (2 vols., 1846), which Gladstone read before his first reading of Grote (GD 25/1/46-15/3/46), the revival of this form of biography was denounced in a more earnest manner. For a sense of how Protestant critics of Newman paid special attention to this project long after its completion, see the *Apologia* 190–92, 280–95, which includes Kingsley's pamphlet "What Then Does Dr. Newman Mean?" (366–72) and Newman's "Answer in Detail" (423–29).
19. See 1.150–248 on Homeric society and the Homeric Question.
20. For Gladstone's reading of *Vestiges,* see GD 12/7/47. Gladstone finished the book on 17/7/47 and began to write about it on 23/7/47. His 1847 writings on evolution are untraced. Charles Darwin's *Structure and Distribution of Coral Reefs* was reviewed in the same number (468–500) that included Gladstone's denial of the evolutionary creation of Homeric epic.
21. As Baden Powell claimed in 1846, entry into the world of the Fathers was a dangerous business that seemed to produce rationalists or romanists, skeptics or mystics (195–96).
22. Browne (*Dictionary of National Biography:* 1811–91) became bishop of Ely in 1864 and of Winchester in 1873. In 1882, when Tait died, he was considered as a possible successor to the see of Canterbury. By the time of Browne's death, his *Exposition* had reached a thirteenth edition.
23. For the earlier, enthusiastic reception of Mure in a conservative setting, see Lockhart's "Homeric Controversy."
24. On eighteenth- and nineteenth-century mythography and its trends, see the introduction to the collection edited by Buller, Burstein, Dorson, Feldman and Richardson, and Kissane. Shaffer 1975 is the classic study of mythological criticism as a hermeneutic and literary concern.
25. One of those students was Lionel Tollemache, whose *Conversations* (1898) has been useful for those in a hurry to pass over Gladstone's Homeric work. Tollemache said that Gladstone "Catholicised Hellenism and almost canonised Homer." The whole endeavor was "the sorry refuge of a theologian at bay" (12, 13). In 1954 Magnus wrote that Gladstone's "attempt to catholicize Hellenism and to canonize Homer was a gesture of defiance on the part of a theologian at bay" (124). Jenkins then used Magnus's words in his 1995 biography (183), apparently unaware that they had been borrowed.
26. See Vaio and Allen (179–81) for the latest additions to this story.

27. In addition to the figure from *Punch* (14/12/72, 247) see the *Spectator* (7/12/72, 1549–50; 14/12/72, 1586), the *Saturday Review* (21/12/72, 781–82) and *Punch* (28/12/72, 267).

SIX   Clerical Fictions

1. The commentary on *Deronda* is legion, and it's almost necessary to fall back on metacritical surveys, as in Henry. By stressing the priestly in contrast to the prophetic, I am not trying to chart a sudden break with the prophetic in Eliot's work; and my work is indebted to Eliot scholars who have focused, in various ways, on prophecy. These include Shaffer (225–91), Carpenter (1984 and 2003: 127–48), Krueger (234–306), and LaPorte. But this sibylline tradition, in my view, does get complicated by a hieratic tendency that was historically coordinated with the century's clerical revival.
2. The phrase comes from his "Spinoza's Life and Works." Providing an intellectual genealogy for the three main writers Eliot translated in the 1840s and '50s, Lewes closes by crediting Spinoza with anticipating "the Hegelian Christology" of Strauss and Feuerbach (216).
3. Lewes replied coyly, saying that "when I referred to 'my clerical friend' I meant to designate the writer of clerical stories, not that he was clericus. I am not at liberty to remove the veil of anonymity—even as regards social position" (*GEL* 2.277).
4. Eliot was successful at passing for a clerical gentleman reared at either Oxford or Cambridge because the age's thirst for clerical fictions and clerical biographies provided so many reliable textual models. In 1849 she had reviewed J. A. Froude's *The Nemesis of Faith*, which, like her own first fictions, confused the genres of novel and biography. In 1851 she reviewed Carlyle's *Life of John Sterling*, which was itself a reply to J. C. Hare's earlier memoir of a real-life doubting clergyman. Other clerical biographies that were read by Eliot before she came to write fictional clerical lives include *The Life of Blanco White* (1845) and A. P. Stanley's *Life of Thomas Arnold* (1845).
5. After being published in a single volume in 1851, John Lavicount Anderdon's *The Life of Thomas Ken* appeared in a second, enlarged edition in 1854. Before then the influential clerical author William Lisle Bowles had inaugurated the modern era of veneration with *The Life of Thomas Ken* (2 vols., 1831). This was followed in 1838 by James Thomas Round's edition of *The Prose Works of the Right Rev. Father in God, Thomas Ken*.
6. Having enjoyed the mostly uncompromised privileges of concealed authorship from January 1857 on, Eliot's identity began to be disclosed in the summer of 1859. The first traces of what would become *The Mill on the Floss* appeared in January 1859, before publication of *Adam Bede* (1 February 1859). In mid-June she gave the first 110 pages to Blackwood, and by 16 October the first volume was complete.
7. As both gifts and curses, these archives are sacred—or marked—in the emergent anthropological sense. On these linguistic chests, see Zimmerman. As P. Milton has argued, Eliot's great theme becomes inheritance in the 1860s and 1870s. What distinguishes Eliot's fascination with inheritance was her commitment to its concurrent literary and biological dimensions.
8. For mainstream periodical commentary on Jesuits in the 1870s, see, in addition to Capes, Cartwright. For a revisionist study of the rise of Anglican sisterhoods from the 1840s on, see Mumm, whose work contains a bibliography on the monastic revival and the many forms it took. The earlier article by Casteras deserves credit for directing much attention to the portrayal of those entering or living among sisterhoods. Adams's book, focusing on a line of literary appropriations of the monastic, contains the best account of the appeal of communities of isolation (or isolated communities) to writers anxious about the status of intellectual labor.
9. See Karlin on *Middlemarch*'s "fine collection of whips" (30).
10. Park's *Travels* were widely read throughout the century (see Marsters and N. Ashton), and we know that Eliot was creatively interested in him: in *Middlemarch*, she invokes his legacy

when Mr. Brooke, in his vocational speculations on Ladislaw's behalf, says, "He may turn out a Bruce or a Mungo Park" (75).
11. See Irwin for Eliot's relevant notes on cohanim (403, 413) and on Ezra (79, 81, 121, 123, 418). Eliot's study of Judaism, ancient and modern, has also been well documented in works such as Baker 1975, Shaffer 1975: 230–38, Carpenter 1984, and Temple. From her adolescence onward, Eliot had been exposed both to Christian studies of biblical Judaism and to a rationalistic or freethinker's history of the Jews.
12. For an elegant discussion of the complicated relations among intentions and outward acts in *Deronda,* see Rodensky 158–69.
13. See Freedman for the best general discussion of this dual vocation in Eliot's day and ours.
14. In part supplying a broad explanation for this duality, Herbert's book generally complicates the tradition that makes the ethnographic sense of culture foreign to its Arnoldian counterpart. See also Pecora 364–65.
15. Along with secularists such as G. W. Foote and Thomas Huxley, Stanley was a founding member of the Sunday Society for Opening Museums, Art Galleries, Libraries and Gardens. Its first public annual meeting was held on 27/5/76 (Marsh 353, n. 13).

Conclusion

1. As evidence for the clerical tone during this period, we can consider the contemporary invention of a new genre, the clerical miscellany, which gave entertaining portraits of the profession in forms distinguished from (but sometimes including) conventional prose fiction. The son of a clergyman's daughter noted in her day for a wide range of commercially successful writing, Anthony Trollope, might be said to have inaugurated the genre with his *Clergymen of the Church of England* (1866). Related works include Doran, Jeffreason (1872), and Larwood (1881). In terms of the increased ability of clerical taxonomies to function as broad social history, Conybeare (1853) was a sign of much that followed. The work of Davies coincided with the full flowering and culmination of these trends. Chapman reveals "the book of the clergy" to be alive (if not culturally central). With material from the long nineteenth century dominating, it supports the notion that that period was rich both with clerical authors and with authors writing about the clergy.
2. For an example of the former, see E. Mellor's standard illustration, published the same year as *Daniel Deronda,* of the argument that the New Testament abolished the exclusive priesthood in favor of a priesthood of all believers. Mellor was a Congregationalist minister. For contemporary bibliographic relics of the sacerdotal revival within the church, see F. Lee (1875)—partially derived from his earlier work—and Littledale (5th ed., 1876). The last was noted with disapprobation in the Lords' discussion of *The Priest in Absolution* in 1877 (H 234.1744).
3. Wolff, who selected three of Davies's fictions for the series "Victorian Fiction: Novels of Faith and Doubt," provides a brief sketch of the author's life (316–18). Davies also appears as a curious observer in Owen (59–60, 123–25).
4. In the reception of Trevelyan's work, Macaulay received the near unanimous designation as *the* Philistine laureate (Jann 100–102). For a more detailed discussion of that moment in the history of policing middle- and highbrow versions of culture, see McKelvy 2000: 302–4.
5. This same stance—what amounted to a highly marketable elitism—often defined Arnold's posthumous publication history. Describing the publication of Arnold's poetry and prose (both in and out of copyright) in the years following his death in 1888, Bell has noted the "ironic . . . frequency with which, in the prefaces of *popular* reprints, Arnold was being promoted as an 'unpopular' writer" (2000: 161–62).
6. See Damrosch (39–77) for the essential account of Smith's short career; a revised and expanded version of that story is forthcoming in *The Buried Book* (Henry Holt).

7. For this financial figure, see Girardot (646, n. 55) and 246–66 more generally on the series.
8. T. W. Rhys David's review of the completed twenty-eight volumes admitted that it was only a lack of "accuracy and certainty" in dealing with hieroglyphic and cuneiform texts thus far that had kept "the Sacred Books of Egypt and of the Euphrates Valley" out of the present series (181).
9. For two important challenges to the radical breaks in the sixteenth century, see Johns and McKitterick.
10. My understanding of the late 1870s in relation to these three technologies—two of them fresh out of the inventor's laboratory—is indebted to Picker's exemplary study (100–45).
11. This is not to say that literary creativity and typographical awareness ceased to interact in the 1880s. As McGann (2003 and *Black Riders,* 3–114), Frankel, and others have shown, aesthetic doctrines and artisanal traditions convened in the late nineteenth century and beyond. From a related book-history perspective, McDonald has also shown how fictions published from 1880 to 1914 spoke in ways determined by, or cognizant of, the medium.

Works Cited

Abrams, M. H. *Natural Supernaturalism: Tradition and Revolution in Romantic Literature*. New York: Norton, 1971.
Adams, James Eli. *Dandies and Desert Saints: Styles of Victorian Masculinity*. Ithaca: Cornell UP, 1995.
Alexander, J. H., and David Hewitt, eds. *Scott in Carnival*. Aberdeen: Assn. for Scottish Literary Studies, 1993.
Allen, Susan Heuck. *Finding the Walls of Troy: Frank Calvert and Heinrich Schliemann at Hisarlik*. Berkeley: U of California P, 1999.
Altholz, Josef L. *The Religious Press in Britain, 1760–1900*. New York: Greenwood, 1989.
Altick, Richard D. *The English Common Reader: A Social History of the Mass Reading Public, 1800–1900*. 2nd ed. Columbus: Ohio State UP, 1998.
———. "The Sociology of Authorship: The Social Origins, Education, and Occupations of 1,100 British Writers, 1800–1935." *Writers, Readers, and Occasions*. Columbus: Ohio State UP, 1989. 95–109.
Anderson, Amanda. *The Powers of Distance: Cosmopolitanism and the Cultivation of Detachment*. Princeton: Princeton UP, 2001.
Anger, Suzy, ed. *Knowing the Past: Victorian Literature and Culture*. Ithaca: Cornell UP, 2001.
———. "Victorian Hermeneutics and Literary Interpretation." Diss. U of Washington, 1994.
apRoberts, Ruth. *The Biblical Web*. Ann Arbor: U of Michigan P, 1994.
Armstrong, Isobel. *Victorian Poetry: Poetry, Poetics and Politics*. London: Routledge, 1993.
Arnold, Matthew. *The Complete Prose Works of Matthew Arnold*. Ed. R. H. Super. 11 vols. Ann Arbor: U of Michigan P, 1960–77.
Arnold, Thomas. "Early Roman History." *Quarterly Review* 32 (June 1825): 67–92.
Arnstein, Walter L. *Protestant versus Catholic in Mid-Victorian England: Mr. Newdegate and the Nuns*. Columbia: U of Missouri P, 1982.
Ashton, Nichols. "Mumbo-Jumbo: Mungo Park and the Rhetoric of Romantic Africa." *Romanticism, Race, and Imperial Culture, 1780–1834*. Ed. Alan Richardson and Sonia Hofkosh. Bloomington: Indiana UP, 1996. 93–113.
Ashton, Rosemary. "Doubting Clerics: From James Anthony Froude to Robert Elsmere via George Eliot." *The Critical Spirit and the Will to Believe: Essays in Nineteenth-Century Literature and Religion*. Ed. David Jasper and T. R. Wright. New York: St. Martin's, 1989. 69–87.
———. "Introduction." *The Nemesis of Faith*. London: Libris, 1988.
Aston, Nigel, and Matthew Cragoe, eds. *Anticlericalism in Britain, c. 1500–1914*. Stroud: Sutton, 2000.

Works Cited

Austen, Jane. *Emma*. Ed. Stephen M. Parrish. New York: Norton, 2000.
———. *Mansfield Park*. Ed. Claudia Johnson. New York: Norton, 1998.
———. *Northanger Abbey*. Ed. Marilyn Butler. Penguin: London, 1995.
Bagehot, Walter. *The Collected Works of Walter Bagehot*. Ed. Norman St. John-Stevas. 15 vols. Cambridge: Harvard UP, 1965–86.
Baker, William. *The Early History of the London Library*. Lewiston: Edwin Mellen, 1992.
———. *George Eliot and Judaism*. Salzburg: Universität Salzburg, 1975.
———. "'Her Longest-Venerated and Best-Loved Romancist': George Eliot and Sir Walter Scott." In Alexander and Hewitt 1993. 523–29.
Balfour, Ian. *The Rhetoric of Romantic Prophecy*. Stanford: Stanford UP, 2002.
Barnes, James J. *Free Trade in Books: A Study of the London Book Trade since 1800*. Oxford: Clarendon, 1964.
Barrie-Curien, Viviane. "Clerical Recruitment and Career Patterns in the Church of England during the Eighteenth Century." *Crown and Mitre: Religion and Society in Northern Europe since the Reformation*. Ed. W. M. Jacob and Nigel Yates. Woodbridge: Boydell, 1993. 93–104.
Barrow, John. "Dr. Granville's Travels." *Quarterly Review* 39 (Jan. 1829): 1–41.
Bebbington, David. "Gladstone and Grote." In Jagger 1998. 157–76.
———. *The Mind of Gladstone: Religion, Homer, and Politics*. Oxford: Oxford UP, 2004.
———. "The Secularization of British Universities since the Mid-Nineteenth Century." *The Secularization of the Academy*. Ed. George Marsden and Bradley J. Longfield. New York: Oxford UP, 1992.
Bell, Bill. "Beyond the Death of the Author: Matthew Arnold's Two Audiences, 1888–1930." *Book History* 3 (2000): 155–65.
———. "From Parnassus to Grub Street: Matthew Arnold and the House of Macmillan." *Macmillan: A Publishing Tradition*. Ed. Elizabeth James. New York: Palgrave, 2002. 52–69.
Benedict, Barbara M. *Making the Modern Reader: Cultural Mediation in Early Modern Literary Anthologies*. Princeton: Princeton UP, 1996.
Bernstein, Susan David. *Confessional Subjects: Revelations of Gender and Power in Victorian Literature and Culture*. Chapel Hill: U of North Carolina P, 1997.
Besserman, Lawrence, ed. *The Challenge of Periodization: Old Paradigms and New Perspectives*. New York: Garland, 1996.
Biller, Peter, and Anne Hudson, eds. *Heresy and Literacy, 1000–1530*. New York: Cambridge UP, 1994.
Blair, Kirstie. "John Keble and the Rhythm of Faith." *Essays in Criticism* 53.2 (April 2003): 129–50.
———, ed. *John Keble in Context*. London: Anthem, 2004.
———. "'Priest and Nun'? *Daniel Deronda*, Anti-Catholicism and the Confessional." *George Eliot Review* 32 (2001): 45–50.
Bodenheimer, Rosemarie. *The Real Life of Mary Ann Evans: George Eliot, Her Letters and Fiction*. Ithaca: Cornell UP, 1994.
Boerner, Peter. "Bürger's Ballad 'Lenore' in Germany, France and England." *Sensus Communis: Contemporary Trends in Comparative Literature*. Ed. János Riesz, Peter Boerner, and Bernhard Scholz. Narr: Tübingen, 1986. 305–11.
Bonnell, Thomas F. "Bookselling and Canon-Making: The Trade Rivalry over the English Poets, 1776–1783." *Studies in Eighteenth-Century Culture* 19 (1989): 53–69.
———. "John Bell's *Poets of Great Britain:* The 'Little Trifling Edition' Revisited." *Modern Philology* 85.2 (Nov. 1987): 128–52.
Boyd, E. I. M. "The Influence of Percy's *Reliques of Ancient English Poetry* on German Literature." *Modern Language Quarterly* 7 (Oct. 1904): 80–99.

Brantlinger, Patrick. "Disraeli and Orientalism." *The Self-Fashioning of Disraeli, 1818–1851.* Ed. Charles Richmond and Paul Smith. Cambridge: Cambridge UP, 1998. 90–106.
———. "1867 and the Idea of Culture." *The Spirit of Reform: British Literature and Politics, 1832–1867.* Cambridge: Harvard UP, 1977.
———. *The Reading Lesson: The Threat of Mass Literacy in Nineteenth Century British Fiction.* Bloomington: Indiana UP, 1998.
Braun, Thom. "Thomas Longman and *Lothair.*" *Publishing History* 6 (1979): 79–83.
Brent, Richard. *Liberal Anglican Politics: Whiggery, Religion, and Reform, 1830–1841.* New York: Oxford UP, 1987.
Brett, R. L. *Faith and Doubt: Religion and Secularization in Literature from Wordsworth to Larkin.* Macon: Mercer UP, 1997.
Brock, M. G., and M. C. Curthoys, eds. *Nineteenth-Century Oxford.* Oxford: Clarendon, 1997–2000. Vols. 6–7 of *The History of the University of Oxford.* 8 vols. 1984–2000.
Brontë, Charlotte. *Shirley.* Ed. Herbert Rosengarten and Margaret Smith. Oxford: Oxford UP, 1998.
Brooke, Christopher. *A History of the University of Cambridge, 1870–1990.* New York: Cambridge UP, 1997.
Brougham, Henry. "Diffusion of Knowledge." *Edinburgh Review* 45 (Dec. 1826): 189–99.
———. "High Church Opinions on Popular Education." *Edinburgh Review* 42 (April 1825): 206–23.
"Brougham and Campbell on Education." *British Critic* 23 (April 1825): 337–60.
Brown, Callum G. *The Death of Christian Britain: Understanding Secularisation, 1800–2000.* London: Routledge, 2001.
———. "The Mechanism of Religious Growth in Urban Societies: British Cities since the Eighteenth Century." *European Religion in the Age of Great Cities, 1830–1930.* Ed. Hugh McLeod. London: Routledge, 1995. 239–262.
Brown, Stewart J. *The National Churches of England, Ireland, and Scotland, 1801–1846.* New York: Oxford UP, 2001.
Browne, E. Harold. *An Exposition of the Thirty-Nine Articles, Historical and Doctrinal.* 6th ed. London: Longman, 1864.
Bruce, Steve. *Choice and Religion: A Critique of Rational Choice Theory.* New York: Oxford UP, 1999.
———, ed. *Religion and Modernization: Sociologists and Historians Debate the Secularization Thesis.* New York: Oxford UP, 1992.
———. "The Truth about Religion in Britain." *Journal for the Scientific Study of Religion* 34.4 (Dec. 1995): 417–30.
Bryce, James. "William Ewart Gladstone." *Studies in Contemporary Biography.* London: Macmillan, 1903.
Bullen, George. *Caxton Celebration, 1877: Catalogue of the Loan Collection of Antiquities, Curiosities, and Appliances Connected with the Art of Printing.* London: Trubner, 1877.
Buller, J. B., ed. *The Sun Is God: Painting, Literature, and Mythology in the Nineteenth Century.* New York: Oxford UP, 1989.
Burgess, Henry James. *Enterprise in Education: The Story of the Work of the Established Church in the Education of the People prior to 1870.* London: SPCK, 1958.
Burns, Arthur. *The Diocesan Revival in the Church of England, c. 1800–1870.* New York: Oxford UP, 1999.
———. "English 'Church Reform' Revisited." In Burns and Innes 2003. 136–62.
Burns, Arthur, and Joanna Innes. Introduction. *Rethinking the Age of Reform: Britain, 1780–1850.* Cambridge: Cambridge UP, 2003. 1–70.
Burrow, J. W. *A Liberal Descent: Victorian Historians and the English Past.* New York: Cambridge UP, 1981.

Burstein, Janet. "Victorian Mythography and the Progress of the Intellect." *Victorian Studies* 18 (1975): 309–24.

Butler, Marilyn. Introduction. *Northanger Abbey*. By Jane Austen. Penguin: London, 1995. xi–xlvii.

Butler, Perry. *Gladstone: Church, State, and Tractarianism*. Oxford: Clarendon, 1982.

Byron, George Gordon. *The Major Works*. Ed. Jerome McGann. Oxford: Oxford UP, 2000.

"Byron's *Hebrew Melodies*." *Christian Observer* 14 (Aug. 1815): 542–49.

Cahill, Gilbert. "The Protestant Association and the Anti-Maynooth Agitation of 1845." *Catholic Historical Review* 43 (1957): 273–308.

Canuel, Mark E. *Religion, Toleration, and British Writing, 1790–1830*. Cambridge: Cambridge UP, 2002.

———. "Romantic Emancipation: Religion and the Nation in British Letters, 1790–1830." Diss. Johns Hopkins U, 1996.

Capes, J. M. "The Jesuits in England." *Contemporary Review* 21 (Dec. 1872): 27–44.

Carlyle, Thomas. *The Collected Letters of Thomas and Jane Welsh Carlyle*. Gen. ed. Charles Richard Sanders. Vol. 11. Durham: Duke UP, 1985.

———. *The Works of Thomas Carlyle*. Ed. H. D. Traill. Centenary ed. 30 vols. New York: AMS, 1969.

Carpenter, Mary Wilson. "The Apocalypse of the Old Testament: Daniel Deronda and the Interpretation of Interpretation." *PMLA* 99.1 (Jan. 1984): 56–71.

———. *Imperial Bibles, Domestic Bodies: Women, Sexuality, and Religion in the Victorian Market*. Athens: Ohio UP, 2003.

Carroll, David. *George Eliot: The Critical Heritage*. New York: Barnes and Noble, 1971.

Cartwright, W. C. "The Doctrines of the Jesuits." *Quarterly Review* 138 (Jan. 1875): 57–106.

———. "The Jesuits." *Quarterly Review* 137 (Oct. 1874): 283–313.

Casteras, S. P. "Virgin Vows: The Early Portrayal of Nuns and Novices." *Religion in the Lives of English Women, 1760–1930*. Ed. Gail Malmgreen. Bloomington: Indiana UP, 1986. 129–60.

Chadwick, Owen. *The Secularization of the European Mind in the Nineteenth Century*. New York: Cambridge UP, 1975.

———. *The Victorian Church*. 2 vols. New York: Oxford UP, 1966–70.

Chambers, Robert. *Vestiges of the Natural History of Creation*. 1844. Ed. James A. Secord. Chicago: U of Chicago P, 1994.

Chandler, James. *England in 1819*. Chicago: U of Chicago P, 1998.

Channing, William Ellery. *Remarks on the Character and Writings of John Milton Occasioned by the Publication of His Lately Discovered "Treatise on Christian Doctrine."* 3rd ed. 1828. New York: AMS, 1975.

Chapman, Raymond, ed. *Godly and Righteous, Peevish and Perverse: Clergy and Religious in Literature and Letters: An Anthology*. Grand Rapids: Eerdmans, 2002.

Chartier, Roger. *The Order of Books: Readers, Authors, and Libraries in Europe between the Fourteenth and Eighteenth Centuries*. Trans. Lydia G. Cochrane. Stanford: Stanford UP, 1994.

Chatterton, Thomas. *The Complete Works of Thomas Chatterton*. Ed. Donald S. Taylor. 2 vols. Oxford: Clarendon, 1971.

———. *The Execution of Sir Charles Bawdin*. London: Goldsmith, 1772.

———. *The Poetical Works of Thomas Chatterton, with an Essay on the Rowley Poems by the Rev. Walter W. Skeat*. 2 vols. London: Bell, 1871.

Chaucer, Geoffrey. *The Works of Our Ancient, Learned, & Excellent English Poet, Jeffrey Chaucer*. London, 1687.

Christie, William. "Going Public: Print Lords Byron and Brougham." *Studies in Romanticism* 38.3 (1999): 443–75.

———. "State Patronage and the Romantic Writer: Henry Taylor's Modest Proposal." *Authorship, Commerce, and the Public: Scenes of Writing, 1750–1850*. Ed. E. J. Clery, Caroline Franklin, and Peter Garside. New York: Palgrave, 2002.

Claeys, Gregory. "Political Economy and Popular Education: Thomas Hodgskin and the London Mechanics' Institute, 1823–8." In M. Davis 1999. 157–75.

Clark, J. C. D. *English Society, 1688–1832*. 2nd ed. New York: Cambridge UP, 2000.

Clark, Robert T. "Herder, Percy, and the 'Song of Songs.'" *PMLA* 61 (1946): 1087–1100.

Clive, John. *Macaulay: The Shaping of the Historian*. Cambridge: Harvard UP, 1973.

Cochrane, J. G. *Catalogue of the Library at Abbotsford*. 1838. New York: AMS, 1971.

Cohen, Monica F. *Professional Domesticity in the Victorian Novel: Women, Work and Home*. Cambridge: Cambridge UP, 1998.

Coleridge, J. T. *A Memoir of the Rev. John Keble, M.A., Late Vicar of Hursley*. 2nd ed. 2 vols. Oxford: Parker, 1869.

Coleridge, Samuel Taylor. *The Collected Works of Samuel Taylor Coleridge*. 16 vols. (in 23 pts.). Bollingen Ser. 75. Princeton: Princeton UP, 1970–2002.

———. *The Literary Remains of Samuel Taylor Coleridge*. Ed. Henry Nelson Coleridge. 2 vols. London: Pickering, 1836.

Colley, Linda. *Britons: Forging the Nation, 1707–1837*. New Haven: Yale UP, 1992.

Collingridge, William Hill. *Comprehensive Guide to Printing and Publishing*. London: City, 1869.

Collins, Irene. *Jane Austen and the Clergy*. London: Hambledon, 1993.

Colloms, Brenda. *Victorian Country Parsons*. London: Constable, 1977.

Combe, William. *The Tour of Doctor Syntax in Search of the Picturesque*. 3rd ed. London: Ackermann's Repository of Arts, 1813.

Connell, Philip. "Bibliomania: Book Collecting, Cultural Politics, and the Rise of Literary Heritage in Romantic Britain." *Representations* 71 (2000): 24–47.

Conway, Moncure. *Autobiography, Memoirs, and Experiences of Moncure Daniel Conway*. 2 vols. Boston: Houghton, Mifflin, 1904.

———, ed. *The Sacred Anthology: A Book of Ethnical Scriptures*. 5th ed. London: Trubner, 1876.

Conybeare, William John. "Church Parties." *Edinburgh Review* 98.200 (Oct. 1853): 273–342.

Corfield, Penelope J. "Clerics." *Power and the Professions in Britain, 1700–1850*. New York: Routledge, 1995. 102–36.

Cottom, Daniel. "The Waverley Novels: Superstition and the Enchanted Reader." *ELH* 47.1 (Spring 1980): 80–102.

Court, Franklin E. *Institutionalizing English Literature: The Culture and Politics of Literary Study, 1750–1900*. Stanford: Stanford UP, 1992.

———. "The Social and Historical Significance of the First English Literature Professorship in England." *PMLA* 103.5 (1988): 796–807.

Crawford, Robert. *Devolving English Literature*. 2nd ed. Edinburgh: Edinburgh UP, 2000.

———. *The Modern Poet: Poetry, Academia, and Knowledge since the 1750s*. New York: Oxford UP, 2001.

———, ed. *The Scottish Invention of English Literature*. New York: Cambridge UP, 1998.

Cronin, Richard. "Walter Scott and Anti-Gallican Minstrelsy." *ELH* 66.4 (Winter 1999): 863–83.

Crosby, Travis. *The Two Mr. Gladstones*. New Haven: Yale UP, 1997.

Cross, J. W. *George Eliot's Life as Related in her Letters and Journals, arranged and edited by her husband*. 2 vols. New York: Thomas Y. Crowell, 1893.

Crowther, M. A. *Church Embattled: Religious Controversy in Mid-Victorian England*. Hamden: Archon, 1970.

Culler, Dwight. *The Victorian Mirror of History*. New Haven: Yale UP, 1985.

Curran, Stuart. *Poetic Form and British Romanticism*. New York: Oxford UP, 1986.

Curthoys, M. C., and Janet Howarth. "Origins and Destinations: The Social Mobility of Oxford Men and Women." In Brock and Curthoys 1997–2000. 7.571–95.

Daiches, David. Foreword (preliminary to all volumes). The Edinburgh Edition of the Waverley Novels. 30 vols. Edinburgh: Edinburgh UP, 1993–2006.

Dale, Thomas. *A Sermon Preached in the Parish Church of St. Bride, Fleet Street, on Sunday, February 17, 1828 . . . for the Benefit of the Printers' Pension Society*. London: John Taylor, 1828.

Damrosch, David. *What Is World Literature?* Princeton: Princeton UP, 2003.

Daniell, David. *The Bible in English: Its History and Influence*. New Haven: Yale UP, 2003.

Davies, Charles Maurice. *Unorthodox London: or, Phases of Religious Life in the Metropolis*. 3rd ed. London: Tinsley Brothers, 1875.

Davis, Bertram H. *Thomas Percy: A Scholar-Cleric in the Age of Johnson*. Philadelphia: U of Pennsylvania P, 1989.

Davis, Leith. *Acts of Union: Scotland and the Literary Negotiation of the British Nation, 1707–1830*. Stanford: Stanford UP, 1998.

Davis, Michael T., ed. *Radicalism and Revolution in Britain, 1775–1848: Essays in Honour of Malcolm Thomis*. New York: St. Martin's, 1999.

Davis, Richard W. *Dissent in Politics, 1780–1830: The Political Life of William Smith, M.P.* London: Epworth, 1971.

DeLaura, D. J. "Carlyle and Arnold: The Religious Issue." *Carlyle Past and Present*. Ed. K. J. Fielding and Rodger Tarr. London: Vision, 1976. 127–154.

———. "The Future of Poetry: A Context for Carlyle and Arnold." *Carlyle and His Contemporaries*. Ed. John Clubbe. Durham: Duke UP, 1976. 148–180.

———. "Matthew Arnold and Culture: The History and the Prehistory." *Matthew Arnold in His Time and Ours*. Ed. Clinton Machann and Forrest Burt. Charlottesville: U of Virginia P, 1988. 1–16.

Dewey, Clive. *The Passing of Barchester*. London: Hambledon, 1991.

Disraeli, Benjamin. *Lothair*. Ed. Vernon Bogdanor. London: Oxford UP, 1975.

Ditchfield, G. M. "Anti-Trinitarianism and Toleration in Late Eighteenth Century British Politics: The Unitarian Petition of 1792." *Journal of Ecclesiastical History* 42.1 (1991): 39–67.

———. "Dissent and Toleration: Lord Stanhope's Bill of 1789." *Journal of Ecclesiastical History* 29.1 (1978): 51–73.

———. "Ecclesiastical Legislation during the Ministry of the Younger Pitt, 1783–1801." *Parliamentary History* 19.1 (2000): 64–80.

———. "The Parliamentary Struggle over the Repeal of the Test and Corporation Acts, 1787–1790." *English Historical Review* 89.352 (1974): 551–77.

———. "The Subscription Issue in British Parliamentary Politics, 1772–79." *Parliamentary History* 7.1 (1988): 45–80.

Dorson, Richard. "The Eclipse of Solar Mythology." *Myth: A Symposium*. Ed. Thomas A. Sebeok. Bloomington: Indiana UP, 1958.

Dowling, Linda. *Language and Decadence in the Victorian Fin de Siècle*. Princeton: Princeton UP, 1986.

Duncan, Ian. "Walter Scott, James Hogg, and Scottish Gothic." *A Companion to the Gothic*. Ed. David Punter. Malden: Blackwell, 2000. 70–80.

Dyson, A. O. "Theological Legacies of the Enlightenment: England and Germany." In Sykes 1962. 45–62.

Eagleton, Terry. *Literary Theory: An Introduction*. 2nd ed. Minneapolis: U of Minnesota P, 1996.

Eddy, Donald D. *A Bibliography of Richard Hurd*. New Castle: Oak Knoll, 1999.

Edwards, Owen Dudley. *Macaulay*. New York: St. Martin's, 1988.

Eisenstein, Elizabeth L. "Gods, Devils, and Gutenberg: The Eighteenth Century Confronts the Printing Press." *Studies in Eighteenth-Century Culture* 27 (1998): 1–24.

Eliot, George. *Adam Bede*. Ed. Valentine Cunningham. Oxford: Oxford UP, 1996.
———. *Daniel Deronda*. Ed. Terence Cave. New York: Penguin, 1995.
———. *Essays of George Eliot*. Ed. Thomas Pinney. New York: Columbia UP, 1963.
———. *The George Eliot Letters*. Ed. Gordon S. Haight. 9 vols. New Haven: Yale UP, 1954–78.
———. *The Journals of George Eliot*. Ed. Margaret Harris and Judith Johnston. Cambridge: Cambridge UP, 1998.
———. "Knowing That Shortly I Must Put Off This Tabernacle." *Christian Observer* (Jan. 1840): 38.
———. *Middlemarch*. Ed. David Carroll. Oxford: Oxford UP, 1998.
———. *Mill on the Floss*. Ed. Gordon Haight. Oxford: Oxford UP, 1996.
———. *Romola*. Ed. Dorothea Barrett. London: Penguin, 1996.
———. *Selected Critical Writings*. Ed. Rosemary Ashton. Oxford: Oxford UP, 1992.
———. *Some George Eliot Notebooks*. Ed. William Baker. 3 vols. Salzburg: Universität Salzburg, 1976.
Eliot, Simon. "Patterns and Trends and the NSTC: Some Initial Observations, I–II." *Publishing History* 42 (1997): 79–104; 43 (1998): 71–112.
———. *Some Patterns and Trends in British Publishing, 1800–1919*. London: Bibliog. Soc., 1994.
———. "Some Trends in British Book Production, 1800–1919." *Literature in the Marketplace: Nineteenth-Century British Publishing and Reading Practices*. Ed. John O. Jordan and Robert L. Patten. New York: Cambridge UP, 1995. 19–43.
Ellens, Jacob P. *Religious Routes to Gladstonian Liberalism*. University Park: Pennsylvania State UP, 1994.
———. "Which Freedom for Early Victorian Britain?" *Freedom and Religion in the Nineteenth Century*. Ed. Richard Helmstadter. Stanford: Stanford UP, 1997. 87–119.
Eller, Ruth. "Themes of Time and Art in *The Lay of the Last Minstrel*." *Studies in Scottish Literature* 13 (1978): 43–56.
Elliott, Dorice Williams. *The Angel out of the House: Philanthropy and Gender in Nineteenth-Century England*. Charlottesville: U of Virginia P, 2002.
Emerson, R. W. *English Traits*. Boston: Phillips, Sampson, 1857.
Engell, James. "Robert Lowth, Unacknowledged Legislator." *The Committed Word: Literature and Public Values*. University Park: Pennsylvania State UP, 1999. 119–40.
———. "Romantische Poesie: Richard Hurd and Friedrich Schlegel." *Cultural Interactions in the Romantic Age*. Ed. Gregory Maertz. Albany: State U of New York P, 1998. 13–28.
Erickson, Lee. *The Economy of Literary Form: English Literature and the Industrialization of Publishing, 1800–1850*. Baltimore: Johns Hopkins UP, 1996.
Evans, A. W. *Warburton and the Warburtonians: A Study in Some Eighteenth-Century Controversies*. London: Oxford UP, 1932.
Evans, Thomas. *Old Ballads, Historical and Narrative*. 2nd ed. 4 vols. London: T. Evans, 1784.
Ezell, Margaret J. M. *Social Authorship and the Advent of Print*. Baltimore: Johns Hopkins UP, 1999. 123–39.
Fairer, David. "Creating a National Poetry: The Tradition of Spenser and Milton." *Cambridge Companion to Eighteenth-Century Poetry*. Ed. John Sitter. Cambridge: Cambridge UP, 2001. 177–202.
———. "Historical Criticism and the English Canon: A Spenserian Dispute in the 1750s." *Eighteenth-Century Life* 24 (Spring 2000): 43–64.
———. Introduction. *Thomas Warton's History of English Poetry*. Vol 1. New York: Routledge, 1998. 1–71.
———. Introduction. *Thomas Warton, Observations on the Faerie Queene (1762) and Richard Hurd, Letters on Chivalry and Romance (1762). A Facsimile Edition*. Vol. 1. New York: Routledge, 2001. v–lvii.

———. "The Poems of Thomas Warton the Elder?" *RES* 26 (1975): 287–300, 395–406.
———. "The Poems of Thomas Warton the Elder? A Postscript." *RES* 29 (1978): 61–65.
———. "'Sweet native stream!': Wordsworth and the School of Warton." In Ribeiro and Basker 1996. 314–38.
Feather, John. *The Provincial Book Trade in Eighteenth-Century England*. Cambridge: Cambridge UP, 1985.
Feldman, Burton, and Robert D. Richardson. *The Rise of Modern Mythology, 1680–1860*. Bloomington: Indiana UP, 1972.
Feuchtwanger, E. J. *Gladstone*. 2nd ed. Basingstoke: Macmillan, 1989.
Feuerbach, Ludwig. *The Essence of Christianity*. Trans. George Eliot. New York: Harper, 1957.
Fielding, Penny. *Writing and Orality: Nationality, Culture, and Nineteenth-Century Scottish Fiction*. Oxford: Oxford UP, 1996.
Fleeman, J. D. "The Revenue of a Writer: Samuel Johnson's Literary Earnings." *Studies in the Book Trade in Honour of Graham Pollard*. Ed. R. W. Hunt, I. G. Philip, and R. J. Roberts. Oxford: Oxford Bibliog. Soc., 1975. 211–30.
Flint, Kate. *The Woman Reader, 1837–1914*. Oxford: Clarendon, 1993.
Forbes, Duncan. *The Liberal Anglican Idea of History*. Cambridge: Cambridge UP, 1952.
Ford, Trowbridge. *Henry Brougham and His World: A Biography*. Chichester: B. Rose, 1995.
Forrester, David. *Young Doctor Pusey: A Study in Development*. Oxford: Mowbray, 1989.
"Forums." *Eighteenth-Century Life* 21.1 (Feb. 1997): 80–107 and 21.3 (Nov. 1997): 79–99.
Foulkes, Richard. *Church and Stage in Victorian England*. Cambridge: Cambridge UP, 1997.
Francis, Emma. "'Healing relief . . . without detriment to modest reserve . . . ': Keble, Women's Poetry and Victorian Cultural Theory." In Blair 2004. 115–24.
Frankel, Nicholas. *Oscar Wilde's Decorated Books*. Ann Arbor: U of Michigan P, 2000.
Frappell, Leighton. "'Science' in the Service of Orthodoxy: The Early Intellectual Development of E. B. Pusey." *Pusey Rediscovered*. Ed. Perry Butler. Oxford: SPCK, 1983.
Fraser, Hilary. *Beauty and Belief: Aesthetics and Religion in Victorian Literature*. Cambridge: Cambridge UP, 1986.
Frazer, James George. *The Golden Bough: A Study in Comparative Religion*. 2 vols. London: Macmillan, 1890.
Freedman, Jonathan. *The Temple of Culture: Assimilation and Anti-Semitism in Literary Anglo-America*. Oxford: Oxford UP, 2000.
Freimarck, Vincent. Introduction. *Lectures on the Sacred Poetry of the Hebrews*. Vol. 1. New York: Garland, 1971. vii–xxxvi.
Froude, James Anthony. *The Nemesis of Faith*. 1849. 2nd ed. London: Libris, 1988.
Froude, Richard Hurrell. *Remains of the Late Reverend Richard Hurrell Froude*. Pt. 1. 2 vols. London: Rivington, 1838.
Frye, Lowell. "Romancing the Past: Walter Scott and Thomas Carlyle." *Carlyle Studies Annual* 16 (1996): 37–49.
Frye, Northrop. *The Great Code: The Bible and Literature*. New York: Harcourt Brace Jovanovich, 1982.
Fyfe, Aileen. *Science and Salvation: Evangelical Popular Science Publishing in Victorian Britain*. Chicago: U of Chicago P, 2004.
Galbraith, Gretchen R. *Reading Lives: Reconstructing Childhood, Books, and Schools in Britain, 1870–1920*. New York: St. Martin's, 1997.
Gamer, Michael. *Romanticism and the Gothic: Genre, Reception, and Canon Formation*. Cambridge: Cambridge UP, 2000.
Garnett, Jane, and Colin Matthew, eds. *Revival and Religion since 1700*. London: Hambledon, 1993.

Gascoigne, John. "Anglican Latitudinarianism, Rational Dissent and Political Radicalism in the Late Eighteenth Century." *Enlightenment and Religion: Rational Dissent in Eighteenth-Century Britain.* Ed. Knud Haakonssen. Cambridge: Cambridge UP, 1996. 219–40.
Gaskill, Howard, ed. *Ossian Revisited.* Edinburgh: Edinburgh UP, 1991.
Ghosh, Peter R. "Macaulay and the Heritage of Enlightenment." *English Historical Review* 112 (1997): 358–95.
Gibbon, Edward. *The English Essays of Edward Gibbon.* Ed. Patricia Craddock. Oxford: Clarendon, 1972.
———. *Memoirs of My Life.* Ed. Betty Radice. New York: Penguin, 1990.
Gibson, William. "The Professionalisation of the Ministry." *The Achievement of the Anglican Church, 1689–1800: The Confessional State in Eighteenth Century England.* Lewiston: Mellen, 1995. 91–126.
———. "The Professionalization of an Elite: The Nineteenth Century Episcopate." *Albion* 23 (1991): 459–82.
Gilfillan, George. *Bards of the Bible.* New York: Appleton, 1851.
Gill, Stephen Charles. *Wordsworth and the Victorians.* Oxford: Clarendon, 1998.
Girardot, N. J. *The Victorian Translation of China: James Legge's Oriental Pilgrimage.* Berkeley: U of California P, 2002.
Gladstone, William Ewart. *Correspondence on Church and Religion of William Ewart Gladstone.* Ed. D. C. Lathbury. 2 vols. New York: Macmillan, 1910.
———. *The Gladstone Diaries.* Ed. M. R. D. Foot and H. C. G. Matthew. 14 vols. Oxford: Clarendon, 1968–94.
———. The Gladstone Papers: Additional Manuscripts 44086–44835. British Library, London.
———. *Juventus Mundi: The Gods and Men of the Heroic Age.* London: Macmillan, 1869.
———. "Lachmann's Essays on Homer." *Quarterly Review* 81 (Sept. 1847): 381–417.
———. "On Books and the Housing of Them." *Nineteenth Century* 27 (Mar. 1890): 384–96.
———. *The Prime Ministers' Papers: W. E. Gladstone.* Ed. J. Brooke and M. Sorensen. 4 vols. London: H. M. Stationery Office, 1971–81.
———. *The State in its Relations with the Church.* 4th ed. 2 vols. London: Murray, 1841.
———. *Studies on Homer and the Homeric Age.* 3 vols. Oxford: Oxford UP, 1858.
———. *Substance of a Speech on the Motion of Lord John Russell for a Committee of the Whole House with a View to the Removal of the Remaining Jewish Disabilities.* London: Murray, 1848.
"Gladstone on *Church Principles.*" *Eclectic Review* 9 (April 1841): 369–96.
Goetzman, Robert A. "*The Nemesis of Faith:* A Critical Edition." Diss. U of Iowa, 1971.
Goodwin, Gregory H. "Keble and Newman: Tractarian Aesthetics and the Romantic Tradition." *Victorian Studies* 30.4 (Summer 1987): 475–94.
Goslee, Nancy Moore. *Scott the Rhymer.* Lexington: UP of Kentucky, 1988.
———. "'Some Hidden Movement': Signs of Embarrassment in Scott's Poetic Language." In Alexander and Hewitt 1993. 72–88.
Grafton, Anthony, Glenn W. Most, and James E. G. Zetzel. Introduction. *Prolegomena ad Homerum.* Princeton: Princeton UP, 1985. 3–35.
Gray, Donald J. "Macaulay's *Lays of Ancient Rome* and the Publication of Nineteenth-Century Poetry." *Victorian Literature and Society.* Ed. James R. Kincaid and Albert J. Kuhn. Columbus: Ohio State UP, 1984. 74–93.
Green, S. J. D. *Religion in the Age of Decline: Organisation and Experience in Industrial Yorkshire, 1870–1920.* Cambridge: Cambridge UP, 1996.
Griffin, Dustin H. "Fictions of Eighteenth-Century Authorship." *Essays in Criticism* 43 (July 1993): 181–94.
———. *Literary Patronage in England, 1650–1800.* New York: Cambridge UP, 1996.

Griffin, John R. *John Keble: Saint of Anglicanism*. Macon: Mercer UP, 1987.
Griffin, Robert J. "A Critique of Romantic Periodization." In Besserman 1996. 133–46.
———. "The Eighteenth-Century Construction of Romanticism: Thomas Warton and the Pleasures of Melancholy." *ELH* 59.4 (Winter 1992): 799–815.
Grimes, Kyle. "Spreading the (Radical) Word: William Hone's Liturgical Parodies of 1817." In M. Davis 1999. 143–56.
Groom, Nick. "Celts, Goths, and the Nature of the Literary Source." In Ribeiro and Basker 1996. 275–96.
———. *The Forger's Shadow*. London: Picador, 2002.
———. *The Making of Percy's Reliques*. Oxford: Oxford UP, 1999.
———, ed. *Thomas Chatterton and Romantic Culture*. Houndmills: Macmillan, 1999.
Guedalla, Philip, ed. *The Queen and Mr. Gladstone: A Selection from Their Correspondence*. 2 vols. London: Hodder and Stoughton, 1933.
Haig, Alan. *The Victorian Clergy*. London: Croom Helm, 1984.
Hall, Peter. "Introductory Memoir." In Lowth *Sermons* [1995]. 1–42.
Hammond, Peter C. *The Parson and the Victorian Parish*. London: Hodder and Stoughton, 1977.
Harrison, Frederic. "Neo-Christianity." *Westminster Review* 146 (Oct. 1860): 293–332.
Haugen, Kristine Louise. "Ossian and the Invention of Textual History." *Journal of the History of Ideas* 59.2 (Apr. 1998): 309–27.
Hazlitt, William. *The Complete Works of William Hazlitt*. Ed. P. P. Howe. 21 vols. London: Dent, 1930–34.
Heathorn, Stephen J. *For Home, Country, and Race: Constructing Gender, Class, and Englishness in the Elementary School, 1880–1914*. Toronto: U of Toronto P, 2000.
Hecht, Hans. *T. Percy, R. Wood und J. D. Michaelis; ein beitrag zur literaturgeschichte der geniepériode*. Stuttgart: Kohlhammer, 1933.
Heeney, Brian. *A Different Kind of Gentleman: Parish Clergy as Professional Men in Early and Mid-Victorian England*. Hamden: Archon, 1976.
Helmstadter, Richard. "Conscience and Politics: Gladstone's First Book." *The Gladstonian Turn of Mind*. Ed. Bruce Kinzer. Toronto: U of Toronto P, 1985. 3–42.
Hennell, Charles. *An Inquiry Concerning the Origin of Christianity*. 2nd ed. London: Allman, 1841.
Henry, Nancy. "George Eliot: Critical Responses to *Daniel Deronda*." *A Companion to the Victorian Novel*. Ed. William Baker and Kenneth Womack. Westport: Greenwood, 2002. 283–92.
Hepworth, Brian. *Robert Lowth*. Boston: Twayne, 1978.
Herbert, Christopher. *Culture and Anomie: Ethnographic Imagination in the Nineteenth Century*. Chicago: U of Chicago P, 1991.
Hetherington, Henry. *Cheap Salvation; or, An Antidote to Priestcraft*. London: Printed and pub. by the author, 1832.
Hewitt, Martin. "Victorian Studies: Problems and Prospects." *Journal of Victorian Culture* 6.1 (Spring 2001): 137–61.
Heyck, T. W. *The Transformation of Intellectual Life in Victorian England*. Chicago: Lyceum, 1982.
Hilton, Boyd. "Gladstone's Theological Politics." *High and Low Politics in Modern Britain*. Ed. Michael Bentley and John Stevenson. Oxford: Clarendon, 1983.
Hitchin, Neil. "The Politics of English Bible Translation in Georgian Britain." *Transactions of the Royal Historical Society* (6th ser.) 9 (1999): 67–92.
Hodson, James Shirley. *A History of the Printing Trade Charities*. London: Allen, 1883.
Hole, Robert. *Pulpits, Politics, and Public Order in England, 1760–1832*. New York: Cambridge UP, 1989.
Howsam, Leslie. *Cheap Bibles: Nineteenth-Century Publishing and the British and Foreign Bible Society*. Cambridge: Cambridge UP, 1991.

Hughes, Linda K., and Michael Lund. *The Victorian Serial*. Charlottesville: U of Virginia P, 1991.
Hume, David. *Letters of David Hume*. Ed. J. Y. T. Greig. 2 vols. Oxford: Clarendon, 1932.
Hume, Robert D. *Reconstructing Contexts: The Aims and Principles of Archaeo-Historicism*. New York: Oxford UP, 1999.
Ireland, William Henry. *Confessions of William Henry Ireland*. 1805. New York: Franklin, 1969.
Irwin, Jane, ed. *George Eliot's "Daniel Deronda" Notebooks*. New York: Cambridge UP, 1996.
Jagger, Peter J., ed. *Gladstone*. London: Hambledon, 1998.
———. "Gladstone and His Library." In Jagger 1998. 235–53.
Jann, Rosemary. *The Art and Science of Victorian History*. Columbus: Ohio State UP, 1985.
Jasper, David. *The Sacred and Secular Canon in Romanticism*. New York: St. Martin's, 1999.
Jay, Elisabeth. *Faith and Doubt in Victorian Britain*. Houndmills: Humanities, 1986.
Jeaffreson, John Cordy. *A Book about the Clergy*. 2 vols. London: Hurst and Blackett, 1870.
"Jebb's Sacred Literature." *Christian Observer* (Dec. 1820): 762–72.
Jedrzejewski, Jan. *Thomas Hardy and the Church*. New York: St. Martin's, 1996.
Jeffrey, Francis. "Campbell's *British Poetry*." *Edinburgh Review* 31 (Mar. 1819): 462–97.
———. "Education of the People." *Edinburgh Review* 41 (Jan. 1825): 508–10.
———. "Scott's *Lay of the Last Minstrel*." *Edinburgh Review* 6 (April 1805): 1–20.
Jenkins, Roy. *Gladstone*. London: Macmillan, 1995.
Jenkyns, Richard. *The Victorians and Ancient Greece*. Cambridge: Harvard UP, 1980.
Johns, Adrian. *The Nature of the Book: Print and Knowledge in the Making*. Chicago: U of Chicago P, 1998.
Jolles, Evelyn B. *G. A. Bürgers Ballade Leonore in England*. Regensburg: Carl, 1974.
Jordan, Ellen, Charlotte Mitchell, and Helen Schinske. "'A Handmaid to the Church': How John Keble Shaped the Career of Charlotte Yonge, the 'Novelist of the Oxford Movement.'" In Blair 2004. 175–91.
Joyce, James. *Finnegans Wake*. London: Faber and Faber, 1939.
———. *Ulysses*. Paris: Shakespeare, 1925.
Julian, John, ed. *A Dictionary of Hymnology*. London: Murray, 1908.
Karlin, Daniel. "Having the Whip-Hand in *Middlemarch*." *Rereading Victorian Fiction*. Ed. Alice Jenkins and Juliet John. New York: Palgrave, 2002. 29–43.
Katz, David S. *God's Last Words: Reading the English Bible from the Reformation to Fundamentalism*. New Haven: Yale UP, 2004.
Keble, John. *The Christian Year: Thoughts in Verse for the Sundays and Holydays throughout the Year*. 21st ed. Oxford: Parker, 1841.
———. "Danger of Sympathising with Rebellion." 1831. *Sermons, Academical and Occasional*. Oxford: Parker, 1847. 105–26.
———. "Gladstone—The State in its Relations with the Church." *British Critic* 26 (Oct. 1839): 355–97.
———. *Keble's Lectures on Poetry, 1832–41*. Trans. Edward Kershaw Francis. 2 vols. Oxford: Clarendon, 1912.
———. *Occasional Papers and Reviews*. Oxford: Parker, 1877.
———. "On the Mysticism Attributed to the Early Fathers of the Church." *Tracts for the Times*, no. 89. London: Rivington, 1841.
Kelley, Maurice. Introduction. Vol. 6 of *Complete Prose Works of John Milton*. New Haven: Yale UP, 1973. 3–116.
Kelley, Theresa M. *Reinventing Allegory*. Cambridge: Cambridge UP, 1997.
Kent, John. "Victorian Religion and the Decline of Britain." *Victorian Studies* 41 (Autumn 1997): 107–17.
Ker, Ian. *John Henry Newman: A Biography*. Oxford: Oxford UP, 1988.

Kidd, Colin. *Subverting Scotland's Past: Scottish Whig Historians and the Creation of an Anglo-British Identity, 1689–c. 1830*. Cambridge: Cambridge UP, 1993.
Kissane, James. "Victorian Mythography." *Victorian Studies* 6 (1962): 5–28.
Klancher, Jon P. *The Making of English Reading Audiences, 1790–1832*. Madison: U of Wisconsin P, 1987.
Kline, Daniel. "'For rigorous teachers seized my youth': Thomas Arnold, John Keble and the Juvenilia of Arthur Hugh Clough and Matthew Arnold." In Blair 2004. 143–58.
Knight, Charles. *Passages of a Working Life during Half a Century: With a Prelude of Early Reminiscences*. 3 vols. 1864–65. Shannon: Irish UP, 1971.
Knight, David M. *Science and Spirituality: The Volatile Connection*. New York: Routledge, 2004.
Knight, Frances. "Clerical Life." *The Nineteenth-Century Church and English Society*. Cambridge: Cambridge UP, 1995. 106–52.
Knights, Ben. *The Idea of the Clerisy in the Nineteenth Century*. Cambridge: Cambridge UP, 1978.
Knox, Vicesimus. *Essays, Moral and Literary*. 8th ed. 2 vols. London: C. Dilly, 1786.
Korte, Barbara, Ralf Schneider, and Stefani Lethbridge, eds. *Anthologies of British Poetry: Critical Perspectives from Literary and Cultural Studies*. Amsterdam: Rodopi, 2000.
Krueger, Christine L. *The Reader's Repentance: Women Preachers, Women Writers, and Nineteenth-Century Social Discourse*. Chicago: U of Chicago P, 1992.
Kuenen, Abraham. *The Religion of Israel to the Fall of the Jewish State*. Trans. Alfred Heath May. 3 vols. London: Williams and Norgate, 1874–75.
Kugel, James L., ed. *Poetry and Prophecy: The Beginnings of a Literary Tradition*. Ithaca: Cornell UP, 1990.
Lamb, Jonathan. "The Job Controversy, Sterne, and the Question of Allegory." *Eighteenth-Century Studies* 24.1 (Fall 1990): 1–19.
———. *The Rhetoric of Suffering: Reading the Book of Job in the Eighteenth Century*. Oxford: Clarendon, 1996.
Lang, Timothy. *The Victorians and the Stuart Heritage: Interpretation of a Discordant Past*. Cambridge: Cambridge UP, 1995.
Langan, Celeste. "Understanding Media in 1805: Audiovisual Hallucination in *The Lay of the Last Minstrel*." *Studies in Romanticism* 40.1 (Spring 2001): 49–70.
Langford, Paul. *A Polite and Commercial People: England, 1727–1783*. New York: Oxford UP, 1989.
LaPorte, Charles. "George Eliot, the Poetess as Prophet." *Victorian Literature and Culture* 31.1 (March 2003): 159–79.
Larsen, Timothy. *Friends of Religious Equality: Nonconformist Politics in Mid-Victorian England*. Rochester: Boydell, 1999.
Larwood, Jacob. *The Book of Clerical Anecdotes*. London: Chatto and Windus, 1881.
Lawson-Peebles, Robert. "Translation in Uncertain Times: The Case of Bürger's 'Lenore.'" *Revolutions and Watersheds: Transatlantic Dialogues, 1775–1815*. Ed. W. M. Verhoeven and Beth Dolan Kautz. Rodopi: Amsterdam, 1999. 7–25.
Lee, Frederick George. *The Directorium Anglicanum*. 3rd ed. London: Bosworth, 1866.
———. *The Manuale Clericorum*. London: Hogg, 1875.
Lee, G. "The History of the Jews." *Monthly Repository* 41 (May 1830): 376–83.
Levine, George. "*Daniel Deronda*: A New Epistemology." In Anger 2001. 52–73.
Lewes, George Henry. "Grote's *History of Greece*: The Homeric Poems." *Westminster Review* 46 (Jan. 1847): 381–415.
———. "Spinoza's Life and Works." *Westminster Review* (May 1843): 198–217.
Lewis, Matthew. *Tales of Wonder*. 2 vols. London: Bell, 1800.
Liddon, Henry Parry. *Life of Edward Bouverie Pusey*. 4th ed. 4 vols. London: Longmans, Green, 1894–98.

Linley, Margaret. "A Centre That Would Not Hold: Annuals and Cultural Democracy." *Nineteenth-Century Media and the Construction of Identities*. Ed. Laurel Brake, Bill Bell, and David Finkelstein. New York: Palgrave, 2000. 57–74.
Lipking, Lawrence. *The Ordering of the Arts in Eighteenth-Century England*. Princeton: Princeton UP, 1970.
Littledale, Richard Frederick. *The Priest's Prayer Book: With a Brief Pontifical*. 5th ed. London: Masters, 1876.
Lloyd-Jones, Hugh. "Gladstone and Homer." 1975. *Blood for the Ghosts: Classical Influences in the Nineteenth and Twentieth Centuries*. London: Duckworth, 1982.
Lockhart, John Gibson. "Heine on Germany." *Quarterly Review* 55 (Dec. 1835): 1–34.
———. "Homeric Controversy." *Quarterly Review* 87 (1850): 434–68.
———. *Memoirs of Sir Walter Scott*. Ed. A. W. Pollard. 5 vols. London: Macmillan, 1900.
Loesberg, Jonathan. "Aesthetics, Ethics, and Unreadable Acts in George Eliot." In Anger 2001. 121–47.
Lootens, Tricia. *Lost Saints: Silence, Gender, and Victorian Literary Canonization*. Charlottesville: U of Virginia P, 1996.
Lovesey, Oliver. *The Clerical Character in George Eliot's Fiction*. Victoria, BC: English Literary Studies, 1991.
Lowth, Robert. *Isaiah: A New Translation*. 1778. London: Routledge/Thoemmes, 1995.
———. *Lectures on the Sacred Poetry of the Hebrews*. 1787. 2 vols. London: Routledge/Thoemmes, 1995.
———. *A Letter to the Right Reverend Author of The Divine Legation of Moses Demonstrated*. 4th ed. London: Millar and Dodsley, 1766.
———. *The Life of William of Wykeham, Bishop of Winchester*. 2nd ed. 1759. London: Routledge/Thoemmes, 1995.
———. *Sermons and Other Remains of Robert Lowth*. 1834. London: Routledge/Thoemmes, 1995.
———. *A Short Introduction to English Grammar*. 2nd ed. 1763. London: Routledge/Thoemmes, 1995.
Lukács, Georg. *The Historical Novel*. Trans. Hannah and Stanley Mitchell. London: Merlin, 1962.
Lynch, Deidre. "'Beating the Track of the Alphabet': Samuel Johnson, Tourism, and the ABC's of Modern Authority." *ELH* 57 (1990): 357–405.
———. "'Wedded to Books': Bibliomania and the Romantic Essayists." *Romantic Libraries*. Ed. Ina Ferris. Romantic Circles Praxis Series. Feb. 2004. <www.rc.umd.edu/praxis/libraries>.
Lyons, Mary Ann. "Maynooth: A Select Bibliography of Printed Sources." *Irish Historical Studies* 29.116 (Nov. 1995): 441–74.
Macaulay, Thomas Babington. "The Lamentation of the Virgins of Israel for the Daughter of Jephthah: A Hebrew Eclogue." *Christian Observer* 19 (Sept. 1820): 587–89.
———. *The Letters of Thomas Babington Macaulay*. Ed. Thomas Pinney. 6 vols. Cambridge: Cambridge UP, 1974–81.
———. "Minute on Indian Education." *Thomas Babington Macaulay: Selected Writings*. Ed. John Clive and Thomas Pinney. Chicago: U of Chicago P, 1972. 237–51.
———. "Oh Rosamond!" [and] "By Thy Love, Fair Girl of France." *Knight's Quarterly Magazine* 1 (June 1823): 219–20.
———. "Scenes from 'Athenian Revels.'" *Knight's Quarterly Magazine* 2 (Jan. 1824): 17–33.
———. "Songs of the Civil War." *Knight's Quarterly Magazine* 2 (April 1824): 321–25.
———. "Songs of the Huguenots." *Knight's Quarterly Magazine* 2 (Jan. 1824): 33–35.
———. *The Works of Lord Macaulay, Complete*. Edited by his sister, Lady Trevelyn. 8 vols. London: Longmans, Green, 1866.

Machin, G. I. T. "The Maynooth Grant, the Dissenters, and Disestablishment, 1845-1847." *English Historical Review* 82 (1967): 61–85.

———. *Politics and the Churches in Great Britain, 1832–1868.* New York: Clarendon, 1977.

———. *Politics and the Churches in Great Britain, 1869 to 1921.* New York: Oxford UP, 1987.

Macpherson, James. *The Poems of Ossian and Related Works.* Ed. Howard Gaskill. Intro. Fiona Stafford. Edinburgh: Edinburgh UP, 1996.

Magnus, Philip. *Gladstone.* 1954. London: Murray, 1968.

Main, Alexander. Preface. *Wise, Witty, and Tender Sayings in Prose and Verse Selected from the Works of George Eliot.* London: Blackwood, 1872. ix–xii.

Malden, Henry. *History of Rome.* London: Baldwin and Cradock, 1830.

Mandelbrote, Scott. "The English Bible and Its Readers in the Eighteenth Century." In Rivers 2001. 35–78.

Mandler, Peter. *Aristocratic Government in the Age of Reform: Whigs and Liberals, 1830–1852.* Oxford: Clarendon, 1990.

Manning, Peter. "'The Birthday of Typography': A Response to Celeste Langan." *Studies in Romanticism* 40.1 (Spring 2001): 71–83.

Manning, Susan. "Walter Scott, Antiquarianism, and the Political Discourse of the *Edinburgh Review*, 1802–11." *British Romanticism and the Edinburgh Review: Bicentenary Essays.* Ed. Massimiliano Demata and Duncan Wu. Basingstoke: Palgrave, 2002. 102–23.

Mansell, Darrel. "Arnold's 'The Study of Poetry' in Its Original Context." *Modern Philology* 83.3 (Feb. 1986): 279–85.

Marsh, Joss. *Word Crimes: Blasphemy, Culture, and Literature in Nineteenth-Century England.* Chicago: U of Chicago P, 1998.

Marsters, Kate F. Introduction. In Park 2000. 1–28.

Martineau, Harriet. *Miscellanies.* 2 vols. Boston: Hilliard, Gray, 1836.

Martineau, James. "Parker and Strauss." *Westminster Review* 46 (April 1847): 136–74.

Mason, Emma. "'Her Silence Speaks': Keble's Female Heirs." In Blair 2004. 125–42.

Matthew, H. C. G. "Edward Bouverie Pusey: From Scholar to Tractarian." *Journal of Theological Studies* 32 (1981): 101–24.

———. *Gladstone, 1809–1898.* Oxford: Clarendon, 1997.

———. "Gladstone, Evangelicalism, and 'The Engagement.'" In Garnett and Matthew 1993. 111–26.

Matthews, David. *The Making of Middle English, 1765–1910.* Minneapolis: U of Minnesota P, 1999.

Maxwell, Richard. "Inundations of Time: A Definition of Scott's Originality." *ELH* 68.2 (Summer 2001): 419–68.

McCalman, Iain, ed. *Oxford Companion to the Romantic Age: British Culture, 1776–1832.* Oxford: Oxford UP, 1999.

McCane, W. "Benjamin Kennicott: An Eighteenth-Century Researcher." *Journal of Theological Studies* 28.2 (Oct. 1977): 445–64.

McClelland, V. Alan. "Gladstone and Manning." *Gladstone, Politics, and Religion: A Collection of Founder's Day Lectures Delivered at St. Deiniol's Library, Hawarden, 1967–83.* Ed. Peter J. Jagger. New York: St. Martin's, 1985. 148–70.

McDonald, Peter D. *British Literary Culture and Publishing Practice, 1880–1914.* New York: Cambridge UP, 1997.

McGann, Jerome. *Black Riders: The Visible Language of Modernism.* Princeton: Princeton UP, 1993.

———. "Herbert Horne's *Diversi Colores* (1891): Incarnating the Religion of Beauty." *New Literary History* 34.3 (Summer 2003): 535–52.

———. "The Infatuated Worlds of Thomas Chatterton." *Early Romantics: Perspectives in British Poetry from Pope to Wordsworth*. Ed. Thomas M. Woodman. New York: St. Martin's, 1998. 233–41.

———. Introduction. *The New Oxford Book of Romantic Period Verse*. Oxford: Oxford UP, 1993. xix–xxvi.

———. "Rethinking Romanticism." In Besserman 1996. 161–78.

———. "Who's Carving Up the Nineteenth Century?" *PMLA* 116.5 (Oct. 2001): 1415–21.

McKelvy, William. "Gladstone's Homeric Passion: Sacralizing National Literature and Secularizing the State, 1760–1860." Diss. U of Virginia, 1998.

———. "Primitive Ballads, Modern Criticism, Ancient Skepticism: Macaulay's *Lays of Ancient Rome*." *Victorian Literature and Culture* 28.2 (Sept. 2000): 287–309.

———. "William Ewart Gladstone." *Nineteenth-Century British Book-Collectors and Bibliographers*. Ed. William Baker and Kenneth Womack. Detroit: Gale, 1997. 161–72.

McKitterick, David. *Print, Manuscript, and the Search for Order, 1450–1830*. New York: Cambridge UP, 2003.

Mee, Jon. *Dangerous Enthusiasm: William Blake and the Culture of Radicalism in the 1790s*. Oxford: Clarendon, 1992.

Meisel, Joseph S. *Public Speech and the Culture of Public Life in the Age of Gladstone*. New York: Columbia UP, 2001.

Mellor, Enoch. *Priesthood in the Light of the New Testament*. 2nd ed. London: Hodder and Stoughton, 1876.

Mill, John Stuart. *The Collected Works of John Stuart Mill*. 33 vols. Toronto: U of Toronto P, 1963–91.

Miller, J. Hillis. *The Disappearance of God: Five Nineteenth-Century Writers*. Cambridge: Harvard UP, 1963.

Miller, Thomas P. *The Formation of College English: Rhetoric and Belles Lettres in the British Cultural Provinces*. Pittsburgh: U of Pittsburgh P, 1997.

Milles, Jeremiah, ed. *Poems, Supposed to have been Written at Bristol, in the Fifteenth Century, By Thomas Rowley, Priest, &c*. London: Payne, 1782.

Millgate, Jane. "The Early Publication History of Scott's *Minstrelsy of the Scottish Border*." *Papers of the Bibliographical Society of America* 94.4 (Dec. 2000): 551–64.

———. "For Lucre or for Fame: Lockhart's Versions of the Reception of *Marmion*." *RES* 44 (May 1993): 187–203.

———. "From Kelso to Edinburgh: The Origins of the Scott-Ballantyne Partnership." *Papers of the Bibliographical Society of America* 92.1 (Mar. 1998): 33–51.

———. *Macaulay*. London: Routledge and Kegan Paul, 1973.

———. "Scott the Cunning Tailor: Refurbishing the *Poetical Works*." *The Library: The Transactions of the Bibliographical Society* 11.4 (Dec. 1989): 336–51.

———. "Scott's *Lay of the Last Minstrel*: The History of a Book." *European Romantic Review* 13.3 (Sept. 2002): 225–38.

———. *Walter Scott: The Making of the Novelist*. Toronto: U of Toronto P, 1984.

Milman, H. H. "Grote's *History of Greece*." *Quarterly Review* 78 (June 1846): 113–44.

———. *History of Christianity*. 3 vols. London: Murray, 1840.

———. "Milton on Christian Doctrine." *Quarterly Review* 32 (Oct. 1825): 442–57.

———. "Origin of the Homeric Poems." *Quarterly Review* 44 (1831): 121–68.

Milton, John. *Areopagitica*. Vol. 2 of *Complete Prose Works of John Milton*. New Haven: Yale UP, 1959.

———. *Complete Poems and Major Prose*. Ed. Merritt Y. Hughes. New York: Macmillan, 1957.

———. *A Treatise on Christian Doctrine: Compiled from the Holy Scriptures Alone*. 2 vols. Boston: Cummings, Hillard, 1825.

Milton, Paul. "Inheritance as the Key to All Mythologies: George Eliot and Legal Practice." *Mosaic* 28.1 (Mar. 1995): 49–68.

Mineka, Francis Edward. "The Critical Reception of Milton's *De Doctrina Christiana*." *Texas Studies in English* 23 (1943): 115–47.

———. *The Dissidence of Dissent: The Monthly Repository, 1806–1838*. Chapel Hill: U of North Carolina P, 1944.

Moor, John Frewen. *The Birth-Place, Home, Churches, and Other Places Connected with the Author of "The Christian Year."* 2nd ed. London: Parker, 1867.

Moore, James R. "The Crisis of Faith: Reformation versus Revolution." In Parsons 1988–97. 2.220–37.

More, Hannah. *Bible Rhymes*. 1821. *The Complete Works of Hannah More*. 2 vols. New York: Harper, 1835.

———. *Sacred Dramas, chiefly intended for young persons: The subjects taken from the Bible. To which is added, Sensibility, a poem*. 2nd ed. London: Cadell, 1782.

Morley, John. *Life of William Ewart Gladstone*. 3 vols. London: Macmillan, 1903.

Morris, Marilyn. *The British Monarchy and the French Revolution*. New Haven: Yale UP, 1998.

Moscrop, John James. *Measuring Jerusalem: The Palestine Exploration Fund and British Interests in the Holy Land*. New York: Leicester UP, 2000.

Müller, Friedrich Max. "Comparative Mythology." 1856. *Chips from a German Workshop*. 2 vols. London: Longmans, Green, 1867. 2.1–143.

———. "Forgotten Bibles." 1884. *The Essential Max Müller: On Language, Mythology, and Religion*. Ed. Jon R. Stone. New York: Palgrave, 2002. 249–64.

———. *Introduction to the Science of Religion*. London: Longman, 1873.

———. Preface. Vol. 1 of *The Sacred Books of the East*. Oxford: Oxford UP, 1879. ix–lv.

Mumm, Susan. *Stolen Daughters, Virgin Mothers: Anglican Sisterhoods in Victorian Britain*. London: Leicester UP, 1999.

Murphy, Peter T. *Poetry as an Occupation and an Art in Britain, 1760–1830*. New York: Cambridge UP, 1993.

New, Melvyn. "Sterne, Warburton, and the Burden of Exuberant Wit." *Eighteenth-Century Studies* 15.3 (Spring 1982): 245–74.

Newlyn, Lucy. *Reading, Writing, and Romanticism: The Anxiety of Reception*. New York: Oxford UP, 2000.

Newman, John Henry. *Apologia Pro Vita Sua*. Ed. Martin J. Svaglic. Oxford: Clarendon, 1990.

———. *Arians of the Fourth Century*. London: Longmans, 1919.

———. *Correspondence of John Henry Newman with John Keble and Others, 1839–1845*. New York: Longmans, 1917.

———. *Discussions and Arguments on Various Subjects*. London: Longmans, 1924.

———. *Essay on the Development of Christian Doctrine*. Ed. J. M. Cameron. Harmondsworth: Penguin, 1974.

———. *Essays Critical and Historical*. 2 vols. London: Longmans, 1919.

———. *The Letters and Diaries of John Henry Newman*. Ed. Ian Ker, Thomas Gornall, and Gerard Tracey. Vols. 1–8. Oxford: Clarendon, 1978–99.

———. "Remarks on Certain Passages in the Thirty-Nine Articles." *Tracts for the Times*, no. 90. 4th ed. London: Rivington, 1842.

Newsome, David. *The Wilberforces and Henry Manning: The Parting of Friends*. Cambridge: Belknap, 1966.

Nicholls, David. "Gladstone and the Anglican Critics of Newman." *Newman and Gladstone: Centennial Essays*. Ed. James D. Bastable. Dublin: Veritas, 1978. 121–44.

"Niebuhr's History of Rome." *British Critic* 4 (Oct. 1828): 360–403.

Nockles, Peter. "'Lost causes and . . . impossible loyalties': The Oxford Movement and the University." In Brock and Curthoys 1997–2000. 6.195–267.

Norman, E. R. *Anti-Catholicism in Victorian England*. London: Allen and Unwin, 1968.
Norton, David. *A History of the Bible as Literature*. 2 vols. Cambridge: Cambridge UP, 1993.
O'Day, Rosemary. "The Anatomy of a Profession: The Clergy of the Church of England." *The Professions in Early Modern England*. Ed. Wilfrid Prest. New York: Croom Helm, 1987. 25–63.
———. "The Clerical Renaissance in Victorian England and Wales." In Parsons 1988–97. 1. 184–212.
O'Gorman, Francis, and Katherine Turner. Introduction. *The Victorians and the Eighteenth Century: Reassessing the Tradition*. Aldershot: Ashgate, 2004. 1–13.
O'Halloran, Clare. "Irish Recreations of the Gaelic Past: The Challenge of Macpherson's Ossian." *Past and Present* 124 (1989): 67–95.
"Opening of the St. Martin's Free Public Library." *Library* 3 (March 1891): 109–15.
Owen, Alex. *The Darkened Room: Women, Power, and Spiritualism in Late Victorian England*. Philadelphia: U of Pennsylvania P, 1990.
Oz-Salzberger, Fania. *Translating the Enlightenment: Scottish Civic Discourse in Eighteenth-Century Germany*. Oxford: Clarendon, 1995.
Park, Mungo. *Travels in the Interior Districts of Africa*. 1799. Ed. Kate F. Marsters. Durham: Duke UP, 2000.
Parry, Jonathan. *Democracy and Religion: Gladstone and the Liberal Party, 1867–1875*. New York: Cambridge UP, 1986.
Parsons, Gerald, ed. *Religion in Victorian Britain*. 5 vols. Manchester: Manchester UP, 1988–97.
Pater, Walter. *Essays on Literature and Art*. Ed. Jennifer Uglow. London: Dent, 1990.
Pattison, Mark. *Essays*. 2 vols. Oxford: Clarendon, 1889.
Paz, D. G. *Popular Anti-Catholicism in Mid-Victorian England*. Stanford: Stanford UP, 1992.
Pecora, Vincent P. "Arnoldian Ethnology." *Victorian Studies* 41.3 (Spring 1998): 355–79.
Percy, Carol. "Paradigms Lost: Bishop Lowth and the 'Poetic Dialect' in His English Grammar." *Neophilologus* 87 (1997): 129–44.
Percy, Thomas. *Five Pieces of Runic Poetry: Translated from the Islandic Language*. 1763. *The Old Norse Poetic Translations of Thomas Percy*. Ed. Margaret Clunies Ross. Turnhout, Belgium: Brepols, 2001.
———. "Fragments of Chinese Poetry: With a Dissertation." *Hau Kiou Choaan; or, The Pleasing History*. 4 vols. London: Dodsley, 1761. 4.197–256.
———. *A Key to the New Testament*. London: Davis and Reymers, 1766.
———. *The Percy Letters*. Gen. eds. David Nichol Smith and Cleanth Brooks (1944–61) and Cleanth Brooks and A.F. Falconer (1977–88). 9 vols. Baton Rouge: Louisiana State UP, 1944–57; New Haven: YUP, 1961–88.
———. *Reliques of Ancient English Poetry*. 1765. 3 vols. Intro. Nick Groom. London: Thoemmes, 1996.
———. *Reliques of Ancient English Poetry*. 2nd ed. 3 vols. London: Dodsley, 1767.
———. *The Song of Solomon, newly translated from the Original Hebrew*. London: Dodsley, 1764.
"Percy's *Reliques,* fourth edition." *British Critic* 7 (Mar. 1796): 301–12.
Pereiro, James. *Cardinal Manning: An Intellectual Biography*. New York: Oxford UP, 1998.
Phillips, Mark. "Macaulay, Scott, and the Literary Challenge to Historiography." *Journal of the History of Ideas* 50.1 (Jan.–Mar. 1989): 117–33.
Picker, John M. *Victorian Soundscapes*. New York: Oxford UP, 2003.
Pocock, J. G. A. *Barbarism and Religion*. 3 vols. New York: Cambridge UP, 1999–2003.
Powell, Baden. "Mysticism and Scepticism." *Edinburgh Review* 84 (July 1846): 195–223.
Presland, John. *The Divine Mission of the Printing Press*. London: Allen, 1884.
Preyer, Robert. "Beyond the Liberal Imagination: Vision and Unreality in *Daniel Deronda*." *Victorian Studies* 4 (Sept. 1960): 33–54.

Price, Lawrence Marsden. *The Reception of English Literature in Germany*. Berkeley: U of California P, 1932.

Price, Leah. *The Anthology and the Rise of the Novel: From Richardson to George Eliot*. Cambridge: Cambridge UP, 2000.

Price, Richard. *British Society, 1680–1880: Dynamism, Containment and Change*. New York: Cambridge UP, 1999.

Prickett, Stephen. *Origins of Narrative: The Romantic Appropriation of the Bible*. Cambridge: Cambridge UP, 1996.

———. *Romanticism and Religion: The Tradition of Coleridge and Wordsworth in the Victorian Church*. Cambridge: Cambridge UP, 1976.

Priestman, Martin. *Romantic Atheism: Poetry and Freethought, 1780–1830*. Cambridge: Cambridge UP, 1999.

"Publications on the Oxford Tracts." *Christian Observer* (Aug. 1842): 498–511.

Purcell, Edmund Sheridan. *Life of Cardinal Manning*. Vol. 1. New York: Macmillan, 1896.

Pusey, Edward Bouverie. *Collegiate and Professorial Teaching and Discipline in Answer to Professor Vaughan's Strictures: Chiefly as to the Charges against the Colleges of Germany and France*. Oxford: Parker, 1854.

———. "Evidence." *Report and Evidence Upon the Recommendations of Her Majesty's Commissioners for Inquiring into the State of the University of Oxford*. Oxford: Oxford UP, 1853. 1–173.

Quaritch, Bernard. "William Ewart Gladstone." *Contributions towards a Dictionary of English Book-Collectors*. London: Quaritch, 1896.

Ragussis, Michael. *Figures of Conversion: "The Jewish Question" and English National Identity*. Durham: Duke UP, 1995.

Ramm, Agatha. "Gladstone as Man of Letters." *Nineteenth Century Prose* 17 (Winter 1989/90): 1–29.

Raven, James. "The Book Trades." In Rivers 2001. 1–34.

———. *Judging New Wealth: Popular Publishing and Responses to Commerce in England, 1750–1800*. Oxford: Clarendon, 1992.

Raven, James, Helen Small, and Naomi Tadmor, eds. *The Practice and Representation of Reading in England*. New York: Cambridge UP, 1996.

Reddick, Allen Hilliard. *The Making of Johnson's Dictionary, 1746–1773*. Cambridge: Cambridge UP, 1996.

Reibel, David. Introduction. *Sermons and Other Remains of Robert Lowth*. London: Routledge/Thoemmes, 1995. v–xix.

Reid, Hugh. "Jenny: The Fourth Warton." *Notes and Queries* 231 (1986): 84–92.

———. "'Those beck'ning ghost(s)': The Subscribers to Thomas Warton's *Poems* (1748)." *English Studies in Canada* 25 (1999): 277–94.

Rhys David, T. W. "The Sacred Books of the East." *Quarterly Review* 163 (July 1886): 180–203.

Ribeiro, Alvaro, and James G. Basker, eds. *Tradition in Transition: Women Writers, Marginal Texts, and the Eighteenth-Century Canon*. New York: Oxford UP, 1996.

Riede, David G. *Oracles and Hierophants: Constructions of Romantic Authority*. Ithaca: Cornell UP, 1991.

Rivers, Isabel, ed. *Books and Their Readers in Eighteenth-Century England: New Essays*. London: Leicester UP, 2001.

Rizza, Steve. "A Bulky and Foolish Treatise? Hugh Blair's 'Critical Dissertation' Reconsidered." In Gaskill 1991. 129–46.

Robbins, Alfred. *The Early Public Life of William Ewart Gladstone*. London: Metheun, 1894.

Roberts, W. "Bookworms of Yesterday and To-Day: The Right Hon. W. E. Gladstone, M.P." *Bookworm* 30 (May 1890): 161–65.

Roberts, William. *Memoirs of the Life and Correspondence of Mrs. Hannah More*. 2 vols. New York: Harper, 1837.

Robertson, James Craigie. "George Eliot's Novels." *Quarterly Review* 108 (Oct. 1860): 469–99.
Rodensky, Lisa. *The Crime in Mind: Criminal Responsibility and the Victorian Novel*. New York: Oxford UP, 2003.
Roe, Nicholas. *John Keats and the Culture of Dissent*. New York: Clarendon, 1997.
Rorty, Richard. *Contingency, Irony, and Solidarity*. Cambridge: Cambridge UP, 1989.
Rose, Jonathan. Foreword. In Altick 1998. ix–xiii.
———. *The Intellectual Life of the British Working Classes*. New Haven: Yale UP, 2001.
Rosman, Doreen. *Evangelicals and Culture*. London: Croom Helm, 1984.
———. *The Evolution of the English Churches, 1500–2000*. Cambridge: Cambridge UP, 2003.
Ross, Margaret Clunies. Introduction. *The Old Norse Poetic Translations of Thomas Percy*. Turnhout, Belgium: Brepols, 2001. 1–17.
Ross, Trevor. "Copyright and the Invention of Tradition." *Eighteenth-Century Studies* 26 (1992): 1–27.
———. *The Making of the English Literary Canon: From the Middle Ages to the Late Eighteenth Century*. Buffalo: McGill-Queen's UP, 1998.
Ruderman, David B. *Jewish Enlightenment in an English Key*. Princeton: Princeton UP, 2000.
Ruskin, John. "Editor's Preface." *Bibliotheca Pastorum*. Vol. 31 of *The Complete Works of John Ruskin*. Ed. E. T. Cook and Alexander Wedderburn. London: Allen, 1907.
Russell, Anthony. *The Clerical Profession*. London: SPCK, 1980.
Ruthven, K. K. *Faking Literature*. Cambridge: Cambridge UP, 2001.
Ryan, Robert M. *The Romantic Reformation: Religious Politics in English Literature, 1789–1824*. Cambridge: Cambridge UP, 1997.
Ryley, Robert M. *William Warburton*. Boston: Twayne, 1984.
Rzepka, Charles. "The Feel of Not to Feel." *PMLA* 116.5 (Oct. 2001): 1422–31.
Sack, James J. *From Jacobite to Conservative: Reaction and Orthodoxy in Britain, c. 1760–1832*. Cambridge: Cambridge UP, 1993.
Savory, Jerold J. *Thomas Rowlandson's Doctor Syntax Drawings: An Introduction and Guide for Collectors*. London: Cygnus Arts, 1997.
Schiefelbein, Michael E. *The Lure of Babylon: Seven Protestant Novelists and Britain's Roman Catholic Revival*. Macon: Mercer UP, 2001.
Schreuder, Deryck. "Gladstone and the Conscience of the State." *The Conscience of the Victorian State*. Ed. Peter Marsh. Syracuse: Syracuse UP, 1979.
Scott, Patrick. "The Business of Belief: The Emergence of Victorian Religious Publishing." *Sanctity and Secularity: The Church and the World*. Ed. Derek Baker. Oxford: Blackwell, 1973. 213–24.
———. "Rewriting the Book of Nature: Tennyson, Keble, and the *Christian Year*." *Victorians Institute Journal* 17 (1989): 141–55.
Scott, Walter. "Chatterton's Works by Southey and Cottle." *Edinburgh Review* 4 (April 1804): 214–30.
———. "Ellis's *Specimens of the Early English Poets*." *Edinburgh Review* 7 (April 1804): 151–63.
———. "Ellis's *Specimens of English Romance* [and] Ritson's *Metrical Romances*." *Edinburgh Review* 7 (Jan. 1806): 387–413.
———. "Herbert's *Miscellaneous Poetry*." *Edinburgh Review* 9 (Oct. 1806): 211–23.
———. *The Letters of Sir Walter Scott*. Ed. H. J. C. Grierson. 12 vols. London: Constable, 1932-37.
———. *The Poetical Works of Sir Walter Scott*. Ed. J. G. Lockhart. 12 vols. Edinburgh: Cadell, 1833–34.
———. *The Prefaces to the Waverley Novels*. Ed. Mark A. Weinstein. Lincoln: U of Nebraska P, 1978.
———. *Scott on Himself: A Selection of the Autobiographical Writings of Sir Walter Scott*. Ed. David Hewitt. Edinburgh: Scottish Academic, 1981.
———. *Waverley: or, 'Tis Sixty Years Since*. Ed. Claire Lamont. Oxford: Oxford UP, 1986.

———. *The Works of Walter Scott, Esq*. 5 vols. London: Longman, Hurst, Rees, and Orme; Edinburgh: Constable, 1806.

Searby, Peter. *A History of the University of Cambridge, 1750–1870*. New York: Cambridge UP, 1993.

Secord, James A. *Victorian Sensation: The Extraordinary Publication, Reception, and Secret Authorship of Vestiges of the Natural History of Creation*. Chicago: U of Chicago P, 2000.

Shaffer, E. S. *"Kubla Khan" and The Fall of Jerusalem: The Mythological School in Biblical Criticism and Secular Literature, 1770–1880*. Cambridge: Cambridge UP, 1975.

———. "Religion and Literature." *Romanticism: The Cambridge History of Literary Criticism*. Ed. Marshall Brown. Vol. 5. New York: Cambridge UP, 2000.

Shannon, Richard. *Gladstone*. 2 vols. Chapel Hill: U of North Carolina P, 1984–99.

———. "Too Busy Reading." *TLS* 5 Nov. 2004: 11.

Shaw, Harry E. *Narrating Reality: Austen, Scott, Eliot*. Ithaca: Cornell UP, 1999.

Shaw, Marion. "*In Memoriam* and *The Christian Year*." In Blair 2004. 159–74.

Shaw, W. David. *The Lucid Veil: Poetic Truth in the Victorian Age*. London: Athlone, 1987.

Shea, Victor, and William Whitla. *Essays and Reviews: The 1860 Text and Its Reading*. Charlottesville: U of Virginia P, 2000.

Sher, Richard B. *Church and University in the Scottish Enlightenment: The Moderate Literati of Edinburgh*. Princeton: Princeton UP, 1985.

———. "Percy, Shaw, and the Ferguson 'Cheat': National Prejudice in the Ossian Wars." In Gaskill 1991. 207–45.

Shock, Peter A. *Romantic Satanism: Myth and the Historical Moment in Blake, Shelley and Byron*. New York: Palgrave, 2003.

Siegel, Jonah. "Among the English Poets: Keats, Arnold, and the Placement of Fragments." *Victorian Poetry* 37.2 (Summer 1999): 215–32.

Skinner, S. A. "'The Duty of the State': Keble, the Tractarians and the Establishment." In Blair 2004. 33–46.

———. *Tractarians and the "Condition of England": The Social and Political Thought of the Oxford Movement*. Oxford: Clarendon, 2004.

Smart, Thomas Burnett. *The Bibliography of Matthew Arnold*. 1892. New York: Franklin, 1968.

Smith, Christian S. *The Secular Revolution: Power, Interests, and Conflict in the Secularization of American Public Life*. Berkeley: U of California P, 2003.

Smith, Margaret M. "Prepublication Circulation of Literary Texts: The Case of James Macpherson's Ossianic Verses." *Yale University Library Gazette* (April 1990): 132–57.

Smith, William Robertson. "Bible." *Encyclopaedia Britannica*. 9th ed. Vol. 3. Edinburgh: Black, 1875.

Sousa Correa, Delia da. *George Eliot, Music and Victorian Culture*. New York: Palgrave, 2003.

Spalding, William. *The History of English Literature*. Edinburgh: Oliver and Boyd, 1853.

Stanley, Arthur Penrhyn. *Lectures on the History of the Jewish Church*. New ed. 3 vols. London: Murray, 1887.

Stark, Rodney, and Roger Finke. *Acts of Faith: Explaining the Human Side of Religion*. Berkeley: U of California P, 2000.

Stark, Rodney, and Laurence R. Iannaccone. "Truth? A Reply to Bruce." *Journal for the Scientific Study of Religion* 34.4 (Dec. 1995): 516–19.

St. Clair, William. *The Reading Nation in the Romantic Period*. Cambridge: Cambridge UP, 2004.

Stephen, Leslie. *Essays on Freethinking and Plainspeaking*. New York: Putnam's, 1905.

Sterne, Laurence. *Tristram Shandy*. Ed. Howard Anderson. New York: Norton, 1980.

Sterner, Douglas W. *Priests of Culture: A Study of Matthew Arnold and Henry James*. New York: Peter Lang, 1999.

Stevens, Henry. *The Bibles in the Caxton Exhibition, MDCCCLXXVII*. London: Simpkin Marshall, 1878.

Stewart, Garrett. *Dear Reader: The Conscripted Audience in Nineteenth-Century British Fiction.* Baltimore: Johns Hopkins UP, 1996.
Stewart, Robert Mackenzie. *Henry Brougham, 1778–1868: His Public Career.* London: Bodley Head, 1986.
Stewart, Susan. *Crimes of Writing: Problems in the Containment of Representation.* New York: Oxford UP, 1991.
Stott, Anne. *Hannah More: The First Victorian.* Oxford: Oxford UP, 2003.
Strauss, David Friedrich. *The Life of Jesus Critically Examined.* Trans. George Eliot. 3 vols. London: Chapman, 1846.
Stray, Christopher. *Classics Transformed: Schools, Universities, and Society in England, 1830–1960.* Oxford: Oxford UP, 1998.
———. "From One Museum to Another: *The Museum Criticum* (1813–26) and the *Philological Museum* (1831–33)." *Victorian Periodicals Review* 37.3 (Fall 2004): 289–314.
Sutcliffe, Adam. *Judaism and Enlightenment.* New York: Cambridge UP, 2003.
Sutherland, Gillian. *Policy-making in Elementary Education, 1870–1895.* London: Oxford UP, 1973. 125–45.
Sutherland, John. *The Life of Walter Scott: A Critical Biography.* Cambridge: Blackwell, 1995.
———. "The Victorian Novelists: Who Were They?" *Victorian Fiction: Writers, Publishers, Readers.* New York: St. Martin's, 1995. 151–64.
Sutherland, Kathryn. "The Native Poet: The Influence of Percy's Minstrel from Beattie to Wordsworth." *RES* 33 (1982): 414–33.
Sutherland, L. S., and L. G. Mitchell, eds. *The Eighteenth Century.* Vol. 5 of *The History of the University of Oxford.* Oxford: Clarendon, 1986.
Swinburne, Algernon Charles. *William Blake: A Critical Essay.* 1868. Lincoln: U of Nebraska P, 1970.
Sykes, Norman. *Church and State in England in the XVIIIth Century.* Hamden: Archon, 1962.
Tanselle, G. Thomas. "The Varieties of Scholarly Editing." *Scholarly Editing: A Guide to Research.* Ed. D. C. Greetham. New York: MLA, 1995. 9–32.
Temple, Kathryn. *Scandal Nation: Law and Authorship in Britain, 1750–1832.* Ithaca: Cornell UP, 2003.
Tennyson, G. B. *Victorian Devotional Poetry: The Tractarian Mode.* Cambridge: Harvard UP, 1981.
Tennyson, Hallam. *Alfred Lord Tennyson: A Memoir.* 2 vols. London: Macmillan, 1897.
Terry, Richard. *Poetry and the Making of the English Literary Past, 1660–1781.* New York: Oxford UP, 2001.
Thirlwall, Connop. "Introduction by the Translator." *A Critical Essay on the Gospel of St. Luke,* by Frederick Schleiermacher. 1825. Ed. Terrence N. Tice. Lewiston: Mellen, 1993. v–cliv.
Thomas, William. *The Quarrel of Macaulay and Croker: Politics and History in the Age of Reform.* New York: Oxford UP, 2000.
Thormählen, Marianne. *The Brontës and Religion.* Cambridge: Cambridge UP, 1999.
Tieken-Boon van Ostade, Ingrid. "Robert Dodsley and the Genesis of Lowth's *Short Introduction to English Grammar.*" *Historiographia Linguistica* 27 (2000): 21–36.
Todd, William B., and Ann Bowden. *Sir Walter Scott: A Bibliographical History, 1796–1832.* New Castle: Oak Knoll, 1998.
Tollemache, Lionel A. *Gladstone's Boswell: Late Victorian Conversations.* Ed. Asa Briggs. New York: St. Martin's, 1984.
Tomline, George. *Elements of Christian Theology.* 4th ed. Vol. 2. London: Cadell and Davies, 1803.
"Translations of Bürger's Lenora." *British Critic* 8 (Sept. 1796): 276.
Trevelyan, George Otto. *The Life and Letters of Lord Macaulay.* New ed. 2 vols. London: Longmans, 1880.

Trollope, Anthony. *Clergymen of the Church of England*. London: Chapman and Hall, 1866.
——. *The Last Chronicle of Barset*. Ed. Sophie Gilmartin. London: Penguin, 2002.
Trumpener, Katie. *Bardic Nationalism: The Romantic Novel and the British Empire*. Princeton: Princeton UP, 1997.
Tucker, Herbert F. "Wanted Dead or Alive: Browning's Historicism." *Victorian Studies* 38.1 (Autumn 1994): 25–39.
Turner, E. S. *Unholy Pursuits: The Wayward Parsons of Grub Street*. Lewes: Book Guild, 1998.
Turner, Frank M. *Contesting Cultural Authority: Essays in Victorian Intellectual Life*. Cambridge: Cambridge UP, 1993.
——. *The Greek Heritage in Victorian Britain*. New Haven: Yale UP, 1981.
——. *John Henry Newman: The Challenge to Evangelical Religion*. New Haven: Yale UP, 2002.
Vaio, John. "Gladstone and the Early Reception of Schliemann in England." *Heinrich Schliemann nach hundert Jahren*. Ed. W. M. Calder and J. Cobet. Franfurt: Klostermann, 1990. 415–30.
——. "Schliemann and Gladstone: New Light from Unpublished Documents." *Heinrich Schliemann: Grundlagen und Ergebnisse moderner Archäologie 100 Jahre nach Schliemanns Tod*. Ed. J. Herrmann. Berlin: Akademie Verlag, 1992. 73–76.
Vanden Bossche, Chris. *Carlyle and the Search for Authority*. Columbus: Ohio State UP, 1991.
Vincent, David. "The Progress of Literacy." *Victorian Studies* (Spring 2003): 405–31.
——. *The Rise of Mass Literacy: Reading and Writing in Modern Europe*. Malden: Blackwell, 2000.
Wallis, Frank. *Popular Anti-Catholicism in Mid-Victorian Britain*. Lewiston: Mellen, 1993.
——. "The Revival of the Anti-Maynooth Campaign in Britain, 1850–52." *Albion* 19.4 (Winter 1987): 527–47.
Walsh, Marcus. "Literary Scholarship and the Life of Editing." In Rivers 2001. 191–215.
Walsham, Alexandra. "'Domme Preachers'? Post-Reformation English Catholicism and the Culture of Print." *Past and Present* 168 (2000): 72–123.
Ward, Mary. *A Writer's Recollections*. 2 vols. New York: Harper, 1918.
Ward, Thomas Humphry. Preface. *The English Poets*. Vol. 1. London: Macmillan, 1880. v–vii.
Warner, William. "Licensing Pleasure: Literary History and the Novel in Early Modern Britain." *The Columbia History of the British Novel*. Ed. John Richetti. New York: Columbia UP, 1994. 1–22.
Warton, Joseph. *An Essay on the Genius and Writings of Pope*. 2nd ed. London: Dodsley, 1762.
——. *Odes on Various Subjects*. 1746. Intro. Joan Pittock. Delmar: Scholars' Facs. and Repr., 1977.
Warton, Thomas. *The Correspondence of Thomas Warton*. Ed. David Fairer. Athens: U of Georgia P, 1995.
——. *History of English Poetry*. 1774–81. 4 vols. Intro. and additional vol. ed. David Fairer. New York: Routledge, 1998.
——. *Observations on the Fairie Queen*. 2nd ed. 1762. Intro. David Fairer. New York: Routledge, 2001.
——. *Poems: A New Edition, with Additions*. London: Becket, 1777.
Watson, J. R. *The English Hymn: A Critical and Historical Study*. Oxford: Clarendon, 1997.
Watt, James. *Contesting the Gothic: Fiction, Genre, and Cultural Conflict, 1764–1832*. Cambridge: Cambridge UP, 1999.
Watts, Michael R. *The Dissenters*. 2 vols. Oxford: Clarendon, 1978–95.
Weinbrot, Howard D. *Britannia's Issue: The Rise of British Literature from Dryden to Ossian*. New York: Cambridge UP, 1993.
Weintraub, Stanley. *Disraeli: A Biography*. New York: Truman Talley/Dutton, 1993.
Wellek, René. *The Rise of English Literary History*. Chapel Hill: U of North Carolina P, 1941.
Welsh, Alexander. *George Eliot and Blackmail*. Cambridge: Harvard UP, 1985.

White, Daniel E. "Religious Dissent and Tempered Dissidence: Community and Publication in the Early Romantic Period." Diss. U of Pennsylvania, 1998.

Wiener, Joel H. *The War of the Unstamped: The Movement to Repeal the British Newspaper Tax, 1830–1836*. Ithaca: Cornell UP, 1969.

Wiggins, Deborah. "The Burial Act of 1880, the Liberation Society, and George Osborne Morgan." *Parliamentary History* 15.2 (1996): 173–89.

Wilberforce, Samuel. "Essays and Reviews." *Quarterly Review* 109 (Jan. 1861): 248–305.

Wilde, Oscar. *The Complete Letters of Oscar Wilde*. Ed. Merlin Holland and Rupert Hart-Davis. New York: Henry Holt, 2000.

———. *Oscar Wilde: Selections*. Ed. Isobel Murray. New York: Oxford UP, 1989.

Willey, Basil. *Nineteenth Century Studies: Coleridge to Matthew Arnold*. New York: Columbia UP, 1949.

Williams, Raymond. *Keywords: A Vocabulary of Culture and Society*. Rev. ed. New York: Oxford UP, 1985.

Windle, John, and Karma Pippin. *Thomas Frognall Dibdin, 1776–1847: A Bibliography*. New Castle: Oak Knoll, 1999.

Wittmann, Reinhard. "Was There a Reading Revolution at the End of the Eighteenth Century?" *A History of Reading in the West*. Ed. Guglielmo Cavallo and Roger Chartier. Trans. Lydia G. Cochrane. Amherst: U of Massachusetts P, 1999. 284–312.

Wolf, Friedrich August. *Prolegomena ad Homerum*. 1795. Ed. Anthony Grafton, Glenn W. Most, and James E. G. Zetzel. Princeton: Princeton UP, 1985.

Wolff, Robert Lee. *Gains and Losses: Novels of Faith and Doubt in Victorian England*. New York: Garland, 1977.

Wolffe, John. *The Protestant Crusade in Great Britain, 1829–1860*. Oxford: Clarendon, 1991.

Wolfson, Susan J. "Our Puny Boundaries: Why the Craving for Carving Up the Nineteenth Century?" *PMLA* 116.5 (Oct. 2001): 1432–41.

Womersley, David. *Gibbon and the "Watchmen of the Holy City": The Historian and His Reputation, 1776–1815*. Oxford: Clarendon, 2002.

Wooll, John, ed. *Biographical Memoirs of the Late Revd. Joseph Warton*. London: Cadell and Davies, 1806.

Wordsworth, Jonathan. Introduction. *The Lay of the Last Minstrel: A Poem*. 1805. Oxford: Woodstock, 1992.

Wordsworth, William. *The Prose Works of William Wordsworth*. Ed. W. J. B. Owen and J. W. Smyser. 3 vols. Oxford: Clarendon, 1974.

Wright, Julia M. "'The Order of Time': Nationalism and Literary Anthologies, 1774–1831." *Papers on Language and Literature* 33.4 (Fall 1997): 339–65.

Wu, Duncan. *Wordsworth's Reading, 1800–1815*. Cambridge: Cambridge UP, 1995.

Yates, Nigel. *Anglican Ritualism in Victorian Britain, 1830–1910*. Oxford: Oxford UP, 1999.

Yonge, Charlotte Mary. "Gleanings from Thirty Years' Intercourse with the Late Rev. John Keble." *Musings over the "Christian Year" and "Lyra Innocentium."* 2nd ed. Oxford: Parker, 1872. i–lvi.

Young, B. W. "Knock-Kneed Giants: Victorian Representations of Eighteenth-Century Thought." In Garnett and Matthew 1993. 79–93.

———. *Religion and Enlightenment in Eighteenth-Century England: Theological Debate from Locke to Burke*. New York: Oxford UP, 1998.

———. "Theological Books from *The Naked Gospel* to *The Nemesis of Faith*." In Rivers 2001. 79–104.

Index

Italicized page numbers refer to illustrations

Abrams, M. H., 10
allegory, 60–62, 76, 139–40, 142, 204–5
Altick, Richard, 12, 15
Akenside, Mark, 57
Anderson, Robert, 96–97
Anglo-Catholics, 93–94, 191, 203
annuals, 152–53
anthologies, 6, 17–20, 69, 77, 107, 121–24, 145, 258–64, 275n14
anthologist: Arnold as, 19–20, 258–60; Müller as, 263–64; Percy as, 74–77, 258; Ruskin as, 260–61; Scott as, 121–25; G. Smith as, 261–63
anticlericalism, 24, 26, 136, 144, 223, 224
antiquarianism, 59, 67, 105, 175, 176
Apostolic succession, 190
Arnold, Matthew, 1–2, 6–7, 10–11, 14, 19–20, 142, 181, 247–48, 258–60
Arnold, Thomas, 2, 132–33, 137, 170, 178, 188
Articles of Religion, 1–2, 29, 30, 136, 193, 215. *See also* Subscription (clerical)
Austen, Jane, 11, 15, 226–27, 232–33, 235
authorship: clerical, 12–15, 20–27, 46, 83–84, 88–89, 255–58; editorial labor as version of, 67–71, 77, 83–84, 105, 258–64; histories of, 11; Keble on, 138–39; of liturgies, 127, 143–44; romantic concepts of, 5, 125; scribal, 250–53

Bagehot, Walter, 132, 226
bards, 62, 78–79, 81, 83, 105; biblical, 176–78; Irish, 86–87; Keble on, 150; Macpherson's anti-sacerdotal order, 85–90, 96;
Roman, 171, 174. *See also* druids; Homer; minstrels
Beattie, James, 23
Bell, Alexander, 129
Bell, Bill, 20
Benedict, Barbara, 275n14
Bentham, Jeremy, 94
Bible, the: and allegory, 47, 61, 76, 140, 148, 206; as anthology, 54, 262; Authorized Version of, 45–46, 50, 51–53, 259; authorship and dating of, 47–49, 259, 261–63; corruption of text, 40, 51; editing of, 51; as exceptional book, 221; historical value of, 132; inspiration of, 133; literary character of, 11, 176–78, 247; as literary classic, 53–54; as minstrelsy, 175; as model for literary production, 52–55, 155–57; mystical interpretation of, 76, 142, 149; mythic character of, 132, 175, 204–7, 222, 228; poetic nature of, 40–41, 50, 58, 76, 134, 155–57, 165, *177*, 178, 258–60; priestly production of, 170, 177–78, 222–23; its prophetic character, 170; readers of, 51, 221–22; to be read "like any other book," 139, 140; read without note or comment, 33, 129, 131; as "record of revelation," 177; Revised Version of, 52, 259; and *sola scriptura* principle, 136; translations of, 41–43, 45–46, 50–54, 258–60. *See also* scriptures; tradition (theological concept)
bibliography, 200, 213
bibliomania, 24
bibliophilia, 186, 215, 265, 284n7
Blackwood, John, 224, 226
Blackwood's Magazine, 175

316   Index

Blake, William, 39, 40, 53, 54
Blair, Hugh, 14, 21, 23, 84, 87–89
Blair, Kirstie, 143
blasphemy, 34–35, 100, 103
Bode, John Ernest, 14
Bodichon, Barbara, 234
Bonnell, Thomas, 17, 275n14
book history, 11–12, 36, 266–67, 271
Book of Common Prayer, 46, 143, 145–46, 148, 154, 194. *See also* anthologies; anthologist
books. *See* readers and reading
Boswell, James, 90–91, 175
Bowden, Ann, 94
Bowles, William Lisle, 22
Bradley, Edward (Cuthbert Bede), 225
British and Foreign School Society, 129
British Critic, 93, 134, 187
Broad Church, 14, 184, 228, 240, 250–51
Brontë, Charlotte 11, 15, 226, 228, 235
Brooke, Charlotte, 91
Brougham, Henry, 128–32, 159
Brown, John, 21
Browne, E. Harold, 215
Bryce, James, 179
Bürger, G. A., 95, 98–100
Byron, George Gordon, 110, 125, 140, 144, 150, 157, 158, 164, 260

Carlyle, Alexander, 23
Carlyle, Thomas, 2, 6–7, 9, 11, 25–26, 27–28, 124–25, 132, 145, 192, 200, 271
Campbell, George, 23
Catholic Relief Act (1778), 31
Catholic revival, 70, 93, 139, 153, 189–92, 233, 285n13; as resurgent sacerdotalism, 126, 190, 255
Caxton, William, 59, 266, *268*
Caxton Exhibition (1877), 27, 264–67, 269
Chambers, Robert, 209
Chartism, 32
Chatterton, Thomas, 25, 54, 71, 91, 96
Chaucer, Geoffrey, 19, 62, 68, 78
Christian Observer, 155–58, 221–22
Churchill, Charles, 21
Church of England, relations with state's authority, 3, 28–34, 134, 150, 169, 174, 176, 184–85, 187–94, 211–12, 220, 240, 255, 267. *See also* Anglo-Catholics; Articles of Religion; Book of Common Prayer; Broad Church; High Church; Low Church; Subscription (clerical)
Church of Scotland, 23, 88–89
Clapham Sect, 154
Clarke, Samuel, 43
classics: English, 19–20, 97; Hebrew, 48, 259; Hellenic, 220; reading of, 246–47
clergy: depiction of, in print, 11, 226–27, 287nn4-5, 288n1; as educators, 33–34, 129–31; and Eliot's clerical masquerade, 224–49; and Gladstone's reconfigured clerical career, 186–87, 190–91, 220; as productive agents in print market, 12–15, 20–27, 46, 83–84, 88–89, 255–58; Protestant ideal of, 76, 83, 223. *See also* priesthood
Clerical Subscription Act (1865), 2, 273n1
clerisy, 2, 14, 255
Clive, John, 154
Coleridge, Samuel Taylor, 2, 6–7, 10, 28, 67, 94, 98, 110, 125, 131, 183–84, 188, 215
Collins, William, 57
Conder, Josiah, 138
Congreve, Richard, 256
Conway, Moncure, 258, 260, 263, 270
Conybeare, William John, 288n1
Corn Laws, 201
corruption: linguistic, 45, 217–18; textual, 41–42, 51–52, 86–87; theological, 42, 183–85, 199, 202–4, 210–11, 216
cult of literature, 9–11, 15–16, 26, 30, 34–35, 135
culture: Arnoldian ideal, 1–3, 20, 267; ethnographic concepts of, 19, 288n14; identified with reading, 231, 248; liberal ideal of, 230–31, 248–49, 250; tensions in formulations of, 247–48
Cumming, John, 224
Crabbe, George, 21
Crawford, Robert, 105, 275n14
Cronin, Richard, 107

Dale, Thomas, 14, 131
Daniel (book of), 176
Darwin, Charles, 5, 199
Davies, Charles Maurice, 256–58, 261
Davis, Richard, 276n26
Dibdin, T. F., 24
Disraeli, Benjamin, 180–81, *182,* 222

Dissenters, 30–32, 33–34, 129–30, 137, 169, 185, 196, 212, 240
Dissenters' Burials Bill (1880), 33
Dissenters Chapels Bill (1844), 212
Dissenters Relief Act (1779), 31
Dodsley, James, 72, 278n27
Dodsley, Robert, 46, 72, 73
Donaldson v. Beckett (1774), 17, 20, 77, 97
druids, 87–88, 279n38. *See also* bards; minstrels; priesthood
Dryden, John, 62
Dugdale, William, 68
Duncan, Ian, 281n20
Dyer, John, 21

Eagleton, Terry, 9
Edinburgh Review, 127, 132, 137, 141
education (national). *See* reading nation
Education Act: of 1876, 34; of 1880, 33–34
Education Bill (1820), 130
Eliot, George, 2, 6, 7, 15, 93, 126, 207, 220–56, 258; *Adam Bede,* 225; *Daniel Deronda,* 222–24, 230–53, 257; *Felix Holt,* 229–30; *Middlemarch,* 229–30, 234, 235, 236; *The Mill on the Floss,* 227–29; *Romola,* 229–30, 239, 256; *Scenes of Clerical Life,* 224–25
Eliot, Simon, 12
Engell, James, 39
Emerson, R. W., 239
Enlightenment, the, 9, 19, 27, 50, 66–67, 84, 223, 267
episcopacy, 33, 136
Erickson, Lee, 140
Essays and Reviews, 5, 176–78, 217–18
Evangelicalism, 70, 154, 189
Evans, Evan, 74–75
Evans, Mary Ann. *See* Eliot, George
Evans, Thomas, 105–6
evolutionary theories, 199, 209, 262, 286n20. *See also* Chambers, Robert; Darwin, Charles
Ezell, Margaret, 275n14
Ezra (book of), 47, 223, 241, 246, 251–53

Fairer, David, 55, 57
Farmer, Richard, 21, 78
Faussett, Godfrey, 134, 187
Ferguson, Adam, 23
Feuerbach, Ludwig, 224, 225, 226
Fox, Charles James, 31

Frazer, James, 175
Freeman, E. A., 216
freethinkers, 3, 126, 175
French Revolution, 26–27, 31, 195, 267, 271
Froude, James Anthony, 11, 13
Froude, Richard Hurrell, 138, 192, 194
Frye, Northrop, 10
Fyfe, Aileen, 12

Galt, John, 226
Galton, Francis, 270
Gamer, Michael, 95
Gaskell, Elizabeth, 228
German scholarship (classical and biblical), 132–35, 137, 170, 175, 208, 283n26. *See also* Niebhur, Barthold; Schleiermacher, Friedrich; Strauss, David Friedrich; Wolf, Friedrich August
Gibbon, Edward, 22, 24–25, 266
giftbooks. *See* annuals
Gilfillan, George, 178
Gilgamesh (epic of), 262. *See also* Smith, George
Gill, Stephen, 20
Gladstone, Helen, 194, 207–8
Gladstone, William Ewart, 6, 178–220, *182,* 264–65; bardic character as Grand Old Man, 219; on Catholic character of the Church of England, 194–96, 198–99; on *The Christian Year,* 178; civilizing effects of books, 212–14; and *Diaries* as unique record of reading, 185, 186; on Homer, 203–4, 208–11, 215–16, 217–20; *Juventus Mundi,* 180–81; "Lachmann's *Essays on Homer,*" 208–10; on *The Lays of Ancient Rome,* 179; on Newman's *Essay,* 202–3, 285n14; populist aura of, 218–19; and sinful reading, 212–13; *The State in its Relations with the Church,* 187–92; *Studies on Homer and the Homeric Age,* 180, 215–16
Goldsmith, Oliver, 226–27
Gray, Thomas, 57, 63, 64
Gregory, George, 39–40
Griffin, Dustin, 21
Griffin, Robert, 57
Groom, Nick, 73
Grote, George, 130, 192, 204–8

hagiography, 195, 205
Halevy, Elie, 276n26

318   Index

Hallam, Arthur, 183
Hampden, Renn Dickson, 137
Hare, J. C., 133–34
Harrison, Benjamin, 187, 194
Harrison, Frederic, 177–78
Hazlitt, William, 26–27, 131–32
Hebraism and Hellenism, 181, 242
Hebrew (language), 49, 51, 241–47
Hellenism, 182
Hennell, Charles, 222, 229, 249, 252
Hetherington, Henry, 136
High Church, 126, 145, 192, 201, 202, 210, 240, 270
historical criticism, 50
historicism: dual genealogy of, 175; Keble's critique of, 140, 148–50, 153; Scott's, 176
Hoadly, Benjamin, 43
Home, John, 23
Homer, 48, 77, 135, 179
Homeric Question, 135, 149, 181–83, 203–4, 208–11, 215–16, 217–20, 284n3; and evolutionary theories of textual origins, 209; and minstrelsy, 283n26; relations to Scriptural skepticism, 210
Hone, William, 144
Hope, James (later Hope-Scott), 191, 195, 208
Hume, David, 23, 88–89
Hurd, Richard, 21, 37–38, 62–63
Huxley, T. H., 3

illiteracy: becomes a social pathology, 34–35; representations of, 111, 114, 245–46. *See also* literacy
Ireland, William Henry, 96
Isaiah (book of), 50–52, 54, 58, 165, 258–60

Jacobites and Jacobitism, 49, 63
James, Henry, 256
Jasper, David, 10
Jeffrey, Francis, 18, 128–29
Jesuits, 180, 233, 234, 287n8
Jesus (of Nazareth), 45–46, 111, 136, 190, 206–7, 222, 228, 249
Jewish Disabilities Bill (1847), 211–12
Job (book of), 47–49
Johnson, Samuel, 26, 44, 58–59, 70, 90–91, 136, 175
Jowett, Benjamin, 217–18
Joyce, James, 126
Judaism, 222–23, 241–43, 244–46, 249–52

Kant, Immanuel, 10, 28
Keble, John, 5–6, 7, 15, 93, 126, 127–28, 138–40, 142–54, 169, 178, 192; and *The Christian Year,* 142–48, 150–53; on Homer's unity, 149; *Lectures on Poetry,* 144, 149–50; on minstrels and minstrelsy, 150–52; *Primitive Tradition,* 191; review of Gladstone's *State in its Relations,* 188; and Scott's *Lay,* 151
Ken, Thomas, 225, 228
Kennicott, Benjamin, 41, 50, 55
Knight, Ben, 14
Knight, Charles, 159, 160–61
Knight's Quarterly Magazine, 159–66
Knox, Vicesimus, 21, 53–54
Kuenen, Abraham, 251–52

Lamb, Jonathan, 47
Langan, Celeste, 107
Lewes, George Henry, 207, 224, 226, 227, 234, 255
Lewis, Matthew, 95–96
liberal hemeneutics, 191
liberalism: based on nondogmatic principle, 171; defined as literary religion, 2, 134–35; described as literary scenario, 189; Peelite accommodation of, 201; religiously inspired resistance to, 194. *See also* private judgment
liberal theory of the state, 30–32, 169, 188–89; religious routes to, 185, 212, 255, 276n28
libraries, 192
Liggins, Joseph, 228
Lipking, Lawrence, 55, 59
literacy, 1, 33–34, 260, 277n33
literary history: ecclesiastical context for, 21, 30, 37; and the nineteenth-century caricature of the eighteen century, 27; and periodization, 16–17, 32, 36–37, 274nn11-12; with reading at center of, 56, 58–62; as a replacement for Church history, 9, 26
literature: different meanings of, 3, 17, 19; post-theological authority, 1, 4; relations with religious authority, 210, 220; as rival of religious authority, 28. *See also* cult of literature
Lockhart, John Gibson, 94, 96, 107, 126, 175–76

London University (and University College), 128, 130–31
Lootens, Tricia, 29
Low Church, 238, 240
Lowe, Robert, 33
Lowth, Robert, 4, 6, 7, 21, 37–55, *42*, 56, 58, 63–64, 73–74, 76, 127, 155, 259, 265; *Isaiah: A New Translation*, 50–53, 55; *Lectures on the Sacred Poetry of the Hebrews*, 40–41, 50–52; *Letter* to Warburton, 47–49; *The Life of William of Wykeham*, 43, 64; *A Short Introduction to English Grammar*, 44–47
Lynch, Deidre, 275n19, 279n43
Lytton, Bulwer, 266

Macaulay, Thomas Babington, 5–6, 127–28, 140–42, 154–79, 192, 259–60, 264; "Hebrew Eclogue," 156–59; indexer of *Christian Observer*, 157; *The Lays of Ancient Rome*, 166–79; "Minute on Indian Education," 264; review of Gladstone's *State in its Relations*, 188; "Scenes from 'Athenian Revels,'" 162–64; "Songs of the Civil War," 164–66; "Songs of the Huguenots," 161–62
Macaulay, Zachary, 154, 155, 159–63, 165
Mackonochie, A. H., 236
Maclise, Daniel, 266–67
Macpherson, James, 71, 73–75, 77, 84–91, 96
Main, Alexander, 256
Malden, Henry, 170–71
Mallock, W. W., 256
Malory, Thomas, 77–78
Manning, Henry, 191, 194–95, 199, 201, 202, 208
Manning, Susan, 105
Mansell, Darrel, 19
Marsh, Joss, 10, 15, 34
Martineau, Harriet, 126, 137
Martineau, James, 258
Mason, William, 21, 57, 62–63
Mathias, Thomas James, 22
Matthew, Colin, 179, 182, 188
McCalman, Iain, 15, 36
McGann, Jerome, 25, 124
McGowan, John, 85
mechanics institutes, 128, 130, 131
Michaelis, J. D., 76, 84
Mill, John Stuart, 14, 23, 94, 175, 189–90, 192

Miller, J. Hillis, 12–13
Milles, Jeremiah, 25
Millgate, Jane, 94, 107, 161
Milman, H. H., 134, 137–38, 176, 187, 192, 201, 206–7
Milton, John, 58, 62, 69–70, 135–42, 271
minstrels, 78–83, 97–98, 126, 150–52, 168–69, *177*; and ministers, 81, 96, 150; as religious functionaries, 81–82, 91, 102, 105, 106, 110. *See also* bards; oral tradition
monastic revival, 232–36, 287n8
Monthly Repository, 134, 137
More, Hannah, 54–55, 154–56, 159, 185–86
Moses, 132, 210, 215, 222, 262
Müller, Friedrich Max, 216–18, 263–64, 270
Mure, Wiliam, 216
Murphy, Peter, 106
Murray, John, 140, 214
myths and mythography, 204–8, 216–18, 264, 286n24

National Society, 129
Newman, John Henry, 2, 93, 128, 153–54, 169, 183–84, 190, 192, 193, 194–95, 198–203, 205, 217; on corrupt revelations, 183–84, 215; *Essay* on development, 199–203; rejects theological corruption of Roman Catholic creeds, 199
Newton, Thomas, 70
Niebuhr, Barthold, 132–35, 149, 169–70, 176–78, 282n7

Oliphant, Margaret, 226
oral tradition, 78, 88–89, 119–20, 167, 168, 171; print culture's interest in, 90, 106
Oxford Movement, 5, 139, 142, 187, 192, 194

Palestine Exploration Fund, 250
Park, Mungo, 239
parody: Keble and, 127–28, 144–45; Macaulay and, 127–28, 154–55; Scott and, 101, 116, 125–26
Pater, Walter, 2, 270
patristic authority, 142. *See also* tradition (theological concept)
Pattison, Mark, 216–18
Peel, Robert, 128, 187, 190, 194, 197–98, 201

Pegge, Samuel, 80
Penny Magazine, 130
Percy, Thomas, 4–5, 6, 21, 70–85, *74,* 90–91, 99–100, 105, 110, 127, 167, 169, 175; *Five Pieces of Runic Poetry,* 75; "Fragments of Chinese Poetry," 73; influence on Germans, 100, 279n30, 280n10; *Key to the New Testament,* 83–84; reading of Lowth, 73–74, 278n27; *Reliques of Ancient English Poetry,* 77–83, 84–85; Scott's reading of, 96–98; *Song of Solomon,* 75–76; *Specimens of the Ancient Poetry of Different Nations,* 74–77, 258, 278n28
periodization. *See under* literary history
Peterloo, 157
philology (classical and biblical), 40, 44, 46, 66, 133, 166–67, 216–18, 270, 283n26
Pinney, Thomas, 160
Pocock, J. G. A., 24–25
Pope, Alexander, 38, 57–59, 62
Preyer, Robert, 231
Price, Leah, 275n14, 278n14
Prickett, Stephen, 10
priestcraft, 141, 158, 173, 194, 222, 255, 257, 269–70
priesthood: of all believers, 288n2; ancient Roman, 174; Anglican, 231; Jewish, 222–24, 231, 241, 246, 250–53; literary, 2–3; Roman Catholic, 223, 231. *See also* clergy; druids; Jesuits
Priestman, Martin, 15
primitive poetry, 40, 73–77, 80, 169
printing press, 13, *23,* 26–27, 255, 264–67, *268,* 271
private judgment, 135, 139, 189–90, 196
Prosody, Dr., 23
Protestantism, 193, 196–97, 236–41; defined as bibliocentric, 27, 199, 265
Public Worship Regulation Bill (1874), 234
Pusey, Edward Bouverie, 133–34, 169, 187, 190, 220, 270

Quarterly Review, 128, 132, 133, 137–38, 175, 176

rationalism, 133, 204–5
readers and reading: Arnold on, 247–48, 259–60; Brougham on, 128, 130–32; cost of reading material, 17–18, 20, 129, 132, 137, 214, 219, 242, 257, 258, 260; devotional, 241; Eliot on, 221–22, 230–31, 241–50; for entertainment, 106, 125; forbidden, 111–12; 219; Gladstone on, 199–200, 212–14, 219–20; images of, *22, 23, 42, 112, 182, 268, 269;* intensive, 97–98, 219; Keble on, 139–40, 142, 145–49, 153; Lowth on, 40, 51; necromantic, 97–98, 219; Scott on, 97–98, 108, 110–15, 125–26; for spiritual salvation, 106, 111–12, 125; Thomas Warton on, 58–59, 64–65, 68–70. *See also* illiteracy; literacy
reading nation, 3–4, 18, 20, 30, 37, 127–42, 219, 255, 267, 271, 273n5; and agenda for religious liberty, 32–35; religious obstacles to making of, 129–31, 267, 269. *See also* St. Clair, William
Reformation, the, 19, 41, 61, 66, 105, 131, 189, 192, 195, 205, 267, 271
Reform Bill: of 1832, 31–32, 167–69, 187, 249; of 1867, 32–33, 218, 249, 255; of 1884, 32–33, 218, 255
Reid, Thomas, 23
reserve, doctrine of, 142
Riede, David, 9, 29
Ritualism, 232–36, 269–70
Roberston, James Craigie, 228
Roberston, William, 23
Roman Catholic Emancipation (1829), 186–87
Roman Catholicism, 82, 168, 180, 185, 192, 194, 197, 199, 202–3, 223, 235
Rorty, Richard, 185
Rose, Hugh James, 133–34, 187
Rose, Jonathan, 273n5, 276n30
Ross, Trevor, 17, 19, 275n14
Royal Commission on Ritual (1865), 234
Ruskin, John, 260–61
Ruthven, K. K., 71

Sack, James, 31
"Satanic School," 150
Schleiermacher, Friedrich, 133
Schliemann, Heinrich, 218
Scott, Walter, 5, 7, 25, 90–126, 153–54, 175–76; "Eve of St. John," 100–101; "Glenfinlas," 101–4; *The Lay of the Last Minstrel,* 106–25, 151; *The Minstrelsy of the*

Scottish Border, 95, 167; theme of resurrection (antiquarian and poetic), 101, 103–5, 115–19, 121–25; "Thomas the Rhymer," 104–5; *Waverley,* 125–26
Scottish Enlightenment, the, 23
scriptures: Etruscan, 172, 261–63; expanding notions of, 258, 260–64; origin and transmission of, 170–77; Roman, 171; Ruskin on "classical scriptures," 260–61. *See also* Bible, the
Secker, Thomas, 41
Secord, James, 273n5
secularization, 3–4, 6, 14, 28–35, 220, 255, 275–76n23
Sewell, Elizabeth Missing, 13
Sewell, William, 13
Shaffer, E. S., 27–28
Shakespeare, William, 1–2, 19, 53, 54, 58, 78, 96, 137, 139, 245, 256, 259
Shea, Victor, 13
Shenstone, William, 85
Sher, Richard, 23, 71, 88
Siegel, Jonah, 19
Simpson, Richard, 224
sisterhoods, 234–35, 287n8
Skeat, Walter, 91
Smart, Christopher, 57
Smith, Adam, 23
Smith, George, 261–63
Smith, William Robertson, 263
Society for the Diffusion of Useful Knowledge, 128, 130, 131, 159, 170
Spenser, Edmund, 58–63, 65, 67, 77–78, 139–40, 142, 144–45
Spinoza, Baruch, 224
Stanley, Arthur Penrhyn, 250–51
St. Clair, William, 4, 17
Stephen, Leslie, 3, 229
Sterne, Laurence, 21, 38–39, 54
Stevens, Henry, 265
Stewart, Garrett, 243
Stott, Anne, 55
Strauss, David Friedrich, 126, 206–8, 210, 224, 225, 226, 228
Subscription (clerical), 2, 30, 193, 276n27
Sutherland, John, 15
Sumner, Charles Richard, 135
Swinburne, Algernon Charles, 3
Syntax, Dr., *22*–*24*

taxes on knowledge, 27, 132, 213–14
Temple, Kathryn, 279n43
Tennyson, Alfred, 11, 150, 282n7
Tennyson, G. B., 143
Terry, Richard, 275n14
Test and Corporation Acts, repeal of, 31, 186
Thirlwall, Connop, 133–34, 137, 170, 208, 216
Thirty-nine Articles. *See* Articles of Religion
Tillotson, John, 43
Times (London), 194
Todd, William, 94
Tomline, George, 184
Tractarians, 94, 139, 176, 191, 194
Tracts for the Times, 126, 138, 149, 191, 193, 194, 198
tradition (theological concept), 129, 189–91, 203–4, 285n10, 286n16
Trevelyan, George Otto, 140, 259
Trevor, Richard, 41
Trinity (doctrine of), 43, 136–37, 183–84, 193, 196, 215
Trollope, Anthony, 226–27
Trollope, Fanny, 227
Trumpener, Katie, 279n43, 281n20
Turner, Frank, 182, 220

Unitarians, 136–37, 185, 193, 196, 212, 257–58
Unitarian Toleration Act (1813), 31
Universities Tests Act (1871), 2
Upton, John, 21

Vanden Bossche, Chris, 9–10
Victoria, Queen, 219

Warburton, William, 22, 37–39, 47–49, 62–63, 216
Ward, Thomas Humphry, 20
Warton, Joseph, 21, 56–58, 62–63; *Essay on Pope,* 58; *Odes on Various Subjects,* 58
Warton, Thomas, 4–5, 6, 7, 21, 36–37, 55–70, 77–78, 82, 127; *History of English Poetry,* 55–56, 64–67; *Observations on the Fairie Queen,* 58–62; *Poems,* 67–69
Weinbrot, Howard, 39

Wellek, Rene, 55
Westminster Review, 175, 177
Whately, Richard, 137
Whita, William, 13
Wilberforce, Samuel, 176–78
Wilde, Oscar, 2, 24, 252
Wilkie, William, 23
Williams, Raymond, 17

Williams, Rowland, 176
Wolf, Friedrich August, 135, 149
Womersley, David, 24
Wordsworth, William, 18, 54, 69–70, 225, 260

Yonge, Charlotte, 15
Young, Edward, 21, 224